The American Family Home, 1800-1960

The American Family Home, 1800-1960

Clifford Edward Clark, Jr.

The University of North Carolina Press

Chapel Hill and London

© 1986 The University of North Carolina Press

All rights reserved

Manufactured in the United States of America

paper   05   04   03   02   01   10   9   8   7   6

Library of Congress Cataloging in Publication Data
Clark, Clifford Edward, 1941–
    The American family home, 1800–1960.
    Bibliography: p.
    Includes index.
    1. Dwellings—United States—History—19th century.
2. Dwellings—United States—History—20th century.
3. Architecture and society—United States. I. Title.
NA7205.C58   1986   728.3′7′0973   85-24496
ISBN 0-8078-1675-2
ISBN 0-8078-4151-X (pbk.)

Parts of chapters 1 and 2 appear in somewhat different
form in "Domestic Architecture as an Index to Social
History: The Romantic Revival and the Cult of
Domesticity in America," *Journal of Interdisciplinary History*
7 (1976): 33–56, reprinted by permission of the *Journal of
Interdisciplinary History* and the MIT Press. Copyright
1976 by the Massachusetts Institute of Technology and
the *Journal of Interdisciplinary History*.

Title-page illustration: A late Victorian suburban home.
(Shoppell, *The Builder's Portfolios*)

For Susan, Christopher, and Cynthia

Contents

Acknowledgments

The National Endowment for the Humanities, through a younger humanist grant, helped support some of the early research for this book. Richard Hunt and the Hunt Foundation demonstrated their faith in this project by providing a grant to Carleton College for the purchase of the camera equipment that was used to photograph houses and to provide illustrations from magazines. I am grateful also to the Bush Foundation that, through Carleton College, provided funds for research at the Smithsonian Institution. Librarians at the Smithsonian, at the New York State Historical Society, at the Minnesota Historical Society, at the Carleton College Library, and at the Henry Francis Du Pont Winterthur Museum were particularly helpful in locating trade catalogs and building advertisements. I am especially indebted to Betty and Bill Hulings for their support of the American Studies Program at Carleton College, which has helped me in ways too numerous to mention. The Dean's Fund at Carleton supported the typing costs.

I was fortunate also to have the help of numerous research assistants—Nancy Hoyt, Greg Hague, Laura Tilly, Sarah Holt, and Laura Dameron—who generously helped me track my way through the immense popular magazine literature on domestic housing. Anne Crippen provided useful editorial comments at an early stage. I am also grateful to Gwendolyn Wright, Ken Ames, Cary Carson, Elizabeth Cromley, and Helen Horowitz, who read the entire manuscript with great care and saved me from numerous errors, and to Kirk Jeffrey and Peter Stanley, who made helpful suggestions on the early sections. John La Pan shared with me his extensive knowledge of the construction industry after World War II. I am indebted, as well, to Hendrika Umbanhower, Sarah Crippen, and Jacqueline Walcome for typing my drafts and to Sandra Eisdorfer of the University of North Carolina Press for her helpful editorial comments. To all of these generous persons, I extend my warmest thanks for making tangible the meaning of the scholarly community.

Finally, to my wife and children, thanks for putting up with the endless trips, the constant stopping to photograph houses, and the extra hours spent working in my office.

Introduction

If we would discover the little backstairs door that for any age serves as the secret entranceway to knowledge, we would do well to look for certain unobtrusive words with certain meanings that are permitted to slip off the tongue or the pen without fear and without research; words which, having from constant repetition lost their metaphorical significance, are unconsciously mistaken for objective realities.

——Carl Becker, *Heavenly City of the Eighteenth-Century Philosophers*

Be it ever so humble, there's no place like home.

——John Howard Payne

In his study of American society in the 1830s, Alexis de Tocqueville, the aristocratic French traveler, described the American family home as one of the most powerful forces for stabilizing a democratic society. Having visited much of the new nation and talked to Americans from various walks of life, Tocqueville was confident his observations were accurate. "[W]hen the American retires from the turmoil of public life to the bosom of his family," Tocqueville explained to his French audience, "he finds in it the image of order and peace. . . . While the European endeavors to forget his domestic troubles by agitating society, the American derives from his own home that love of order which he afterwards carries with him into public affairs." Tocqueville's glorification of the American family was not unique. Nor was it unusual that he should use the terms "family" and "home" interchangeably. From the eighteenth century on, American social commentators have associated the family with the house and have viewed the family unit as an instrument for social improvement. Tocqueville was only one of the numerous nineteenth- and twentieth-century writers who proclaimed the virtues of the single-family dwelling. Insecure about the chaotic growth of American society, these writers have constantly held up the twin ideals of family and home as benchmarks against which the progress of the nation might be measured. In sermons and self-help manuals, builders' pattern books and country almanacs, popular magazines and advice books, the importance of the American family home has been constantly extolled. Protecting, strengthening, and reforming the family home has been a national pastime.[1]

It was the power of this idealized vision of the American family home that first attracted my attention. When I began this book my objective was to study the American middle-class family ideal by tracing the influence of certain popular house types—the early and late Victorian styles, turn-of-the-century bungalows, and 1950s and 1960s ranch houses—and examining their relationship to the changing nature of the middle-class family. I wanted to know why middle-class Americans, in suburbs and in small towns, spent so much time and energy fixing and remodeling their homes. Why were these homes, which seemed so similar, treasured as symbols of independence and personal identity? How did the house get so closely associated with the ideal of the family? And most important, was there any connection between the popular ideals of home and family as expressed in advice books, popular prints, magazines, and pattern books, and the actual relationship between individual houses and the families who lived in them?

My concern with these questions was not merely academic. My parents built one house themselves and considerably remodeled two others. With a young family, I remodeled rooms in my own 1917 bungalow home. Bruised thumbs and nicked fingers testified to my personal involvement with the ideal of the American family home.

I was also well aware that the ideal of the independent middle-class family home was never shared by the entire population. From the eighteenth century on, people lived in urban row houses, apartments, slave cabins, boardinghouses, and workers' mill houses—not to mention the radical alternatives offered by Shakers and other utopian socialists. But, as I read through the existing literature, I was struck by the persistent antiurban bias and the glorification of the single-family dwelling that has dominated middle-class consciousness. The pervasiveness and persistence of this ideal, despite the other obvious housing alternatives, captured my attention.

Initially, I focused on questions of definition and typicality. How should I define "middle-class"? Did it make sense to talk about "typical" middle-class houses or families? Were there common patterns in middle-class dwellings

during the nineteenth and twentieth centuries? How could anyone assert that one house style or floor plan was representative? Perhaps most important, Was it possible to speak of a "typical" middle-class family in the 1870s or 1920s, given the diversity of life-styles and individual personalities that always have existed?

My approach to trying to answer these questions has been essentially pragmatic. Clearly the term "middle-class," for example, is somewhat vague when used in popular parlance. Americans tend not to like class distinctions. From the American Revolution on, the upper classes have preferred not to be called wealthy because such labels carry the implicit suggestion of being aristocratic or undemocratic. Neither have the lower classes favored being singled out as poor. Instead, both rich and poor have liked to picture themselves as being members of the middle class. Indeed, housing and family reformers, by associating certain kinds of single-family homes with certain kinds of communities and by suggesting that any American could purchase a home, have helped reinforce the myth that all Americans are or are becoming part of the middle class.

If the popular use of the term "middle class" offers little help, there are also problems with academic definitions that seek to locate people precisely by occupation or income. Certainly a steady income that provides the means to live a reasonably independent and secure life is a part of being "middle class." And occupations, especially middle-management and service positions such as teachers, clerks, accountants, small businessmen, and salesmen in the industrializing late nineteenth century were key to the expansion of the middle class. But what income level should be listed as the cutoff point for entering this class? Should lawyers, for example, be included?

My own preference, following the suggestion of Michael Katz and other scholars, is to view "middle class" in terms of level of income, nature of occupation, and, most important, outlook on life. Given this definition, some lawyers—those living in small towns and having incomes slightly above salesmen and accountants—are in the middle class. Those who belong to major urban legal firms and draw salaries only slightly below the presidents of major companies are clearly in the upper class. The key feature, in either case, is the particular combination of income, occupation, and level of expectation.[2]

Recognizing that there is a degree of circularity in all definitions, I have focused my definition of middle class on home ownership because, in my survey of popular literature and advice books, owning one's own home was evidence both of a certain level of income and of a particular outlook on life. The middle class, as I define it, would range from the skilled laborer whose income, when combined with that of his children, enabled him to buy a house to the middle-managerial ranks of clerks, shopkeepers, and professionals such as engineers and accountants—those people, in other words, who owned the majority of single-family dwellings during the past century.

My search for answers to the questions of what constituted "typical" houses or "typical" families followed a similar pragmatic approach. To get at the most common attitudes toward the home and the family I read through much of the popular periodical literature published in the last century, including house plan books, advice manuals, magazines, and reform pamphlets. I also traveled extensively—down the Mississippi, across the lower South, up the East Coast to New England, back to the Midwest, and eventually out to the Rockies and the California coast. These travels and the research in the surviving literature have convinced me that certain general house styles and plans have been almost universally popular.

Practically every older town or city had its Gothic or Italianate houses at mid-century, its Victorian extravaganzas during the Gilded Age, its rustic bungalows in the Progressive period, and its ranch houses in the 1950s and 1960s. In river towns like Galena, Illinois, the shifting fashions in house design were as apparent as the layers in a geological deposit. From Galena to Salt Lake City, from Mobile, Alabama, to Springfield, Massachusetts, the same house

types dominated. Although there has been considerable variation in the layout and exterior details of these houses, certain features were shared by all. Not only was there a general agreement on the kinds of rooms and their functions, but the vast advice and plan-book literature expressed a common philosophy of house use for each of the major styles.

The remarkable agreement about housing standards within the advice literature, and the pervasiveness of common house types and styles convinced me that there was good reason to generalize about typical patterns of middle-class housing. It also made me aware, however, that the end product—the house types that eventually came to dominate—were often the survivors of a hard-fought and vitriolic conflict among competing interests. Architects, housing promoters, builders, trade associations, and family reformers often did not see eye to eye. The house types that became most prominent did so only after caustic debates and bitter struggles.

Despite the relative uniformity of the house types that have become popular, moreover, the unevenly documented history of home construction has made it difficult, on the level of individual communities, to reconstruct the battles among competing housing interests. To overcome this problem, I have illustrated the tensions in the construction of middle-class housing with examples drawn from my own research and from recent studies that have resulted from the current interest in community history and historic preservation. Although these examples initially may appear somewhat random, I am convinced that they reflect a larger process that was typical.

Even more difficult than reconstructing the process by which certain house types became dominant is the attempt to generalize about middle-class families. The problem already identified—the diversity of personalities and individual styles—is evident in the houses themselves.

The more I looked over the evidence, however, the more I became convinced that the great advantage of these mass-produced housing types was that, within a common stylistic vocabulary, they allowed individual families to design and decorate their homes in a distinctive and individual way. Although bungalows, for example, shared common features such as the use of rough materials like stucco or shingles on the exterior, and often had built-in buffets and screened-in front porches, the actual layout of the interior was subject to many variations. The great benefit of these homes, even of the prefabricated houses sold by companies such as Aladdin, Sears, Roebuck, and Montgomery Ward in the 1920s, was that they allowed individuals a range of choices. Each family home, while sharing a common house type, could express a distinctive family outlook.

Eventually I concluded that I could avoid generalizing about the typical middle-class family by addressing primarily those features of everyday life which were shared by most households, recognizing that within these larger patterns there were always a considerable number of individual choices to be made. One way to do this was to focus on the kinds of rooms generally present in a particular house type and style. Victorian houses, for example, almost always had porches and front and back parlors. These common spaces exerted constraints on the families who lived within them. The number of rooms, the opportunity or lack of opportunity to shut off space with doors, and the general location of halls and stairs influenced the pattern of circulation and the nature of intrafamily contact.

This information about the nature and limitations of spaces within the house was particularly helpful when I examined it in light of the recent scholarship on the family. Studies by Tamara Hareven, Howard Chudacoff, and others have made the useful point that families were never static. The composition of households changed continuously over time as children were born, relatives or boarders taken in, or family members died. Hence, the house itself has functioned in different ways as the composition of the family changed. Some floor plans were clearly more flexible than others,

and this flexibility, or lack of it, had an impact on family relationships. By comparing what we know about the demography of the family to the arrangement of spaces within the house, I believed I could document the common features of middle-class family relationships within the home.[3]

But the information on family composition and household space, useful as it is, did not provide a complete picture of middle-class family life. Additional evidence came from another key source—the vast advice literature about housing and the family that projected an image of what the American family home ought to have been like. In reading the extensive promotional literature on the family in the popular magazines, advice manuals, builders' plan books, and commercial advertising, I was struck by the intensity and earnestness of the debate over the ideal middle-class home. Architects, builders, social reformers, feminists, psychologists, and family advocates over the years have continued to lash out at each other, denouncing their opponents and pleading with the public to recognize the validity of their own position. Whereas some have seen the family as an antidote to the instability of contemporary society and as a cure for a wide range of social problems, others have condemned the family as an instrument of oppression and as a source of psychological and social pressure.

Such a literature obviously has to be used cautiously as a guide to actual behavior. Few individuals probably lived up to all the ideals espoused by the reformers. Inevitably, too, radical feminists, professionally trained social scientists, and romantic traditionalists disagreed, sometimes vehemently, about principles and tactics as well as about desired results. Nevertheless, a general reform consensus usually resulted which exerted great power on the public consciousness. It is clear from the plan-book houses actually built and the diaries and letters that survive that many if not most middle-class Americans accepted the reformers' central argument that the home was a personal and symbolic statement for the family that owned it. Indeed, the very power of the debate among family reformers, concerned as it is with fundamental values, testified to the symbolic importance middle-class Americans attached to their homes. For the middle-class suburban public of salesmen, clerks, accountants, business managers, and others who had achieved a degree of independence by virtue of having a fixed salary or steady income, the house has been a symbol for ideal family relationships. The home has not only been a place in which to live, it has been an emblem for family cohesiveness and identity.

The promotional literature thus provides the crucial insight into the expectations about family relationships and the symbolic functions of the family home. Sometimes directing new trends and consumer patterns, other times playing to existing norms or idealistic notions of perfect harmony, the promotional literature has helped to shape the popular self-awareness of family and housing ideals. When used in conjunction with the history of particular families and with recent scholarship on the architecture of cities and suburbs that has been written for the purpose of historic preservation, the advice literature gives us a more complete understanding of the hopes and aspirations of middle-class families. When added to the evidence about family size and household space, such information provides a key to understanding the changes in middle-class family life that have taken place within the last century.

The commitment to the middle-class home, like the commitment to individualism and democracy, has remained constant since the Civil War. But if the terms have stayed the same, their meaning has been modified in subtle but significant ways. What has changed is not only the average number of children per family, the size of the house, and the regularity of changes in the life cycle—the age at which the children leave the home permanently, for example—but also, more important, the expectations about family relationships and what constitutes personal satisfaction. By tracing within the advice literature the changing image of what consti-

tutes a "happy" family life, we can develop a fuller understanding of the expectations about interpersonal relationships within the family itself.

The debate over the middle-class ideal of the American family home, if anything, has become more intense recently as the rising rate of divorce, the increase in single-parent households, the growing number of two-career families, and the escalating costs of single-family dwellings have made the older ideals seem out of date. Indeed, some of the best recent historical scholarship has been written by women who were either eager to prove that significant alternatives to the single-family dwelling did exist in the past century or that the older ideals were themselves highly coercive. What the current scholarship demonstrates is the continuing moral intensity of the older ideals. It is difficult for me or anyone else to be neutral in a discussion of family history. At stake is not only one's self-image and identity, but also one's perception of the strengths and limitations of American society itself. Since the American family is often seen as the bulwark for the larger society, the debate over the changing nature of the American family often becomes a platform for discussing the values and limitations of society itself.[4]

To stand outside the debate, as I try to do in this book, is neither to deny its importance nor to pretend to total neutrality. Its virtue is simply to recognize the power that the image of the ideal American family has had on the general public. Whether they were able to live up to the ideal or not, most families could use it as a reference point, a lens through which they might view their own lives and measure their achievements or failures. The middle-class ideals of family and home have thus been far more influential than most people would be willing to admit. They may not have changed the ways in which people have acted to the extent that reformers would have wished, but they have strongly influenced middle-class self-perceptions, and, if we can judge by the houses themselves, strongly shaped the built environment. No one can deny their importance as a source of influence, inspiration, and, at times, coercion.[5]

A final word about the structure of this book. Once I had sifted through the voluminous evidence about the American family home and had established my position about the context in which the advice literature should be analyzed, the structure of the book fell into place. The first eight chapters in the book are divided conceptually into four sections representing the major shifts in house layout and design and in family ideals that have taken place in the last century and a half. Within each of these sections I begin the initial chapter by setting forth the reformers' vision of the ideal family and home. Then, in a subsequent chapter, I compare those ideals to the houses that were built, and document the experiences of individual families. Although the chapters themselves focus on the Gothic, Queen Anne, bungalow, and ranch houses, my central concern is not so much with the styles themselves as with the ways in which the homes have been perceived. For that reason—and to capture the excitement and intensity of the reformers' and promoters' visions—I have let them speak for themselves as much as possible.

The American Family Home

Chapter 1

Reforming the Foundations of Society

Not even the cholera is so contagious in this country as the style of architecture which we happen to catch.

—Charles Dudley Warner

The Victorian crusade to improve the American family home was similar in many respects to the other waves of reform that swept across the nation in the middle decades of the nineteenth century. Energetic, aggressive, and intensely moral, architects, plan-book writers, journalists, and housing reformers fought to create a new standard for single-family dwellings. As Henry Cleaveland and William Backus, authors of the popular plan book, *Village and Farm Cottages*, proclaimed, "he who improves the dwelling-houses of a people in relation to their comforts, habits, and morals, makes a . . . lasting reform at the very foundation of society." Like the abolitionists who idealized the slave in order to galvanize public opinion, the housing reformers glorified the virtues of the single-family dwelling. The house was praised as "the quiet repository of man's fondest hopes, and the cherished sanctuary of earthly happiness." Like the temperance advocates who condemned those who drank as sinful and morally degenerate, the housing reformers attacked poorly designed houses as "inconceivably ugly," useless, and corrupting. But where the main thrust of the temperance and abolitionist crusades was essentially restorative—to reaffirm the earlier republican virtues of liberty, freedom, and sobriety—the middle-class housing promoters and reformers were more ambitious. They wanted nothing less than the creation of a new national family ideal.[1]

Not content simply to improve the housing standards of the nation, plan-book writers and housing reformers set forth a new vision, an ideal of the American family home which fused their conception of innovative housing designs with their idealization of the family. Indeed, for many Americans, the idea of home was so blended with the association and references to the family that the two became inseparable. As Cleaveland and Backus asserted, "most men are more intimately affected by the character of their homes than by the potions they absorb, whether doctrinal, legal, or medical. It is true 'houses' and 'homes' are not identical, but the relationship is very close and peculiar. In studying for a plan . . . , I confess my inability to draw the line between the material and the spiritual, the economical and the moral, the sanitary and the aesthetic, the useful and the beautiful." By equating the benefits of the material world with moral excellence and by associating the useful and the beautiful together, plan-book writers and housing reformers elevated the single-family dwelling to a new position of importance[2] (Figure 1.1).

The architects and plan-book writers at mid-century were candid about this effort to create a new ideal of the American family home. "We pray that our people may think more and think better of home," wrote one crusader. "We hope too that as our people come to think more of the home feeling, they will also think more of the home structure; and that we shall not only build as though for one generation alone, as though we expected our children quickly to desert the house of their nativity and the place where they have received the principles which are to shape and color all subsequent life." If the children could not be expected to overcome the American penchant for moving west, they could at least make periodic pilgrimages to their homes "as to a shrine more sacred than that of Mecca or Jerusalem." From the architects' and reformers' perspective, the family home was the most important institution in the life of the individual. By tying together housing standards and appropriate family behaviors, they hoped to improve the nature of society itself and to contribute to the world advance toward civilization.[3]

This new vision of the ideal American family home proved to be enormously persuasive. Supported by architects, writers, ministers, and family reformers who filled numerous tracts, books, almanacs, advice manuals, and magazines with glowing accounts of the importance of the home ideal, this perfectionist vision of the family became a powerful national standard. Transmitted by architects and local builders, celebrated by social reformers and plan-book writers, it set forth new architectural and social ideals against which contemporary conduct might be judged. If middle-class Americans did not fully accept the reformers' vision, they nevertheless could not ignore the warnings. For those who joined the cause would continue to remind them, both by word and personal example, of the need to reevaluate their own family life.

In the early stages of the housing crusade, the targets of the reform effort were the traditional house types and implicit assumptions about the family that gradually had come to be generally accepted by the middle class during the eighteenth century. One variant of these styles, the traditional New England house built by British immigrants, had been well adapted to the skills and needs of a primarily rural society. Simple in design and sturdily built with large ten- or twelve-inch-square timbers pegged together with mortise and tenon joints, the traditional rectangular, two-story house could easily be recognized by its three- or five-bay exterior, consisting of one or a pair of windows on either side of a central door. A similar symmetry often characterized the interior. Early dwellings consisted of one room on either side of a central entrance hall. An early example was the Fairbanks house in Dedham, Massachusetts, built in 1636. Later, in the seventeenth and early eighteenth centuries, the traditional plan was enlarged, following English Georgian modes, by adding a room on either side of the hall, making the ground floor two rooms deep. Typical examples of these houses, often with a rear wing added later, can be found throughout New England. Heating was pro-

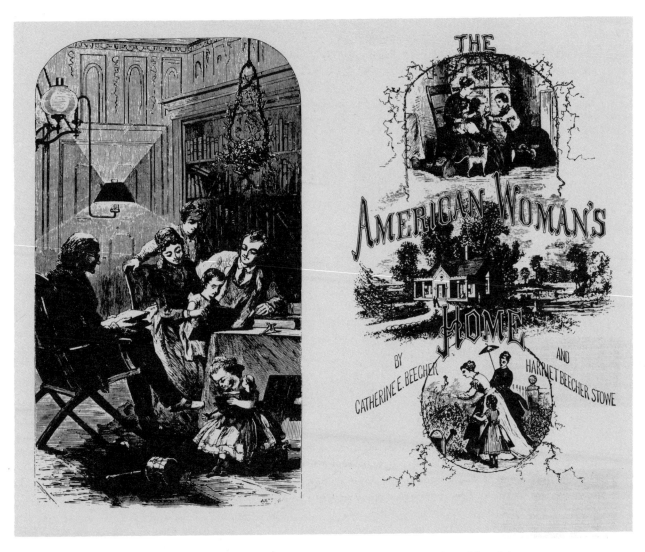

Figure 1.1
According to this
popular advice book,
the middle-class
home was a shel-
tered, secluded ref-
uge run by the
mother. (Beecher
and Stowe, *Ameri-
can Woman's
Home*)

vided either by a central core of fireplaces, by fireplaces on the interior walls between the front and back rooms, or by chimneys at both gable ends of the house (Figures 1.2 and 1.3). After 1800, as settlement moved west, the simple two-storied, rectangular design was sometimes modified by the addition of a one-story wing set off at a right angle from the original structure[4] (Figure 1.4).

In the South, after a period of pole-anchored two-room structures built in the seventeenth century, more permanent one-and-a-half-story frame structures with one or two rooms on each floor became the norm for moderately well-to-do whites. By the middle decades of the eighteenth century, as historian Dell Upton has shown, the traditional Virginian smaller house types had been modified by the addition of a central hall between the two rooms and often by the division of the space to the right of the hall into two rooms, a "dining-room" and a "chamber." Although these houses, with their simple massing, minimal decoration, and occasional exterior symmetry, bore some resemblance to the Georgian house form, variations were common and Virginians often disguised the fact that the houses were two rooms deep. Even wealthy Virginians who knew of the

Figure 1.2
The traditional,
eight-bay Georgian
house had a sim-
plicity and charm all
of its own. This one,
built ca. 1840, is in
Bennington, Ver-
mont. (Photograph
by author)

more fashionable English designs only slowly
adapted them to their own local customs. Not
until the early 1800s did the story-and-a-half
Georgian model, so prevalent in New England,
become more commonplace in the South.[5]

Nevertheless, although significantly different regional vernacular house forms still persisted, by the start of the nineteenth century the
Georgian frame house, modified to meet local
needs, had become increasingly well accepted
by the middle class. Variations on the basic plan
could be seen up and down the Eastern seaboard. Local artisans would learn the standard
building techniques when they apprenticed
with the town carpenter. The simplicity of the
design, the balanced proportions, the accepted
customs for room size and ceiling height—
which could be traced back to the Renaissance

proportions popularized in Andrea Palladio's
Four Books of Architecture (1570)—all dictated
that the houses when built would meet the
traditional middle-class ideals for good house
design and construction.

One indication of the power of this traditional model was the unusual care taken by
Asher Benjamin, an early builder-architect and
builders' guide author, when he described possible modifications to the accepted standards in
his 1806 builders' guide, *The American Builder's
Companion*. Following the lead of Thomas
Jefferson, and echoing the new styles developed in England by Robert Adam, Benjamin
filled his builders' guide with examples of columns, windows, and doors in the fashionable
Greek and Roman revival forms that could
be incorporated into the traditional Georgian

Figure 1.3
An early nineteenth-century Georgian house in Lincoln, Massachusetts, ca. 1830. (Photograph by author)

Figure 1.4
The Greek Revival house with its one-story wing became a popular house form in the rural Northeast and Midwest in the middle of the nineteenth century. (Drawing by Humphrey Costello of an 1835 farmhouse, Meredith, New York)

Figure 1.5
Since the overall
form of the house
was the traditional
eight-bay style, Ben-
jamin offered sepa-
rate designs for
doors and for the
windows that would
be placed above
them. The window
designs were based
on Greek motifs.
(Benjamin, *The
American Builder's
Companion*)

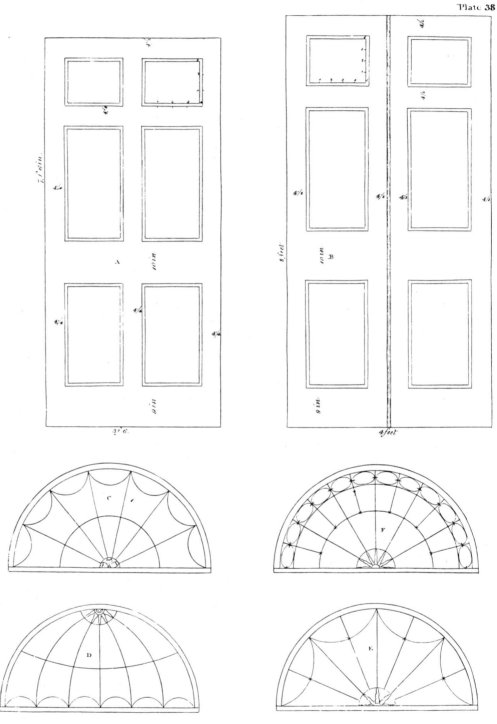

mode (Figure 1.5). He assumed, quite under-standably, that the new architectural details, with their implicit references to the neoclassi-cal virtues of ancient civilization, would be used by the local carpenter to embellish his traditional designs. Indeed, the book's subtitle was "a new system of architecture particularly adapted to the present style of building in the United States of America."

Asher Benjamin hoped, like other leaders in the early republic, to establish fixed principles on which all architecture would be based. He also functioned as a purveyor of upper-class standards to a rising middle class. To be up to date, Benjamin suggested, the local builder had only to add a Greek or a Roman portico to the gable end of the house and face that templelike side to the street. Concerned that the correct proportions be maintained when the classical details were used—a part of his fascination with the adoption of standards—Benjamin be-gan his builders' guide with a course in plane geometry and included information on the ap-propriate setting for the Ionic, Doric, and Co-rinthian styles. "Where elegance, gaiety, and magnificence are required," as for theaters, ballrooms, and hotels, he counseled, Corin-thian detail is most appropriate since its pro-portions are "elegant in the extreme" and "abundantly enriched with a diversity of orna-ment." But for rural homes, the simple and solid Tuscan forms were ample[6] (Figure 1.6).

The American Builder's Companion and the seven other builders' guides published by Asher Benjamin helped reinforce the stately simplicity of traditional house designs and gave them a new image of fashionableness at the turn of the nineteenth century. In the four decades after American independence, they reinforced the American distaste for the more complex European house styles and reaffirmed the commitment to republican simplicity. Reaf-firming the classical ideals on which Greece and Rome had been built, Americans had tried to set themselves apart from European tradi-tions. In upstate New York, on land taken from the Indians and awarded to the Revolutionary soldiers in lieu of pay, the new settlers put up

stately white homes in towns and cities with the appropriate neoclassical associations—Utica, Rome, Troy, and Syracuse (Figure 1.7). Built as soon as the settler could clear the land and set up a water-powered sawmill, these rectangular houses were given an appropriate dignity by the builders' guides of Benjamin and others that set them off from the disorder of the landscape and quickly established the settler's presence on the scene.

Asher Benjamin's builders' guides made few references to the family. Like most of his con-temporaries, he took for granted the family as a functional necessity. Family life in the two cen-turies between 1600 and 1800 had changed dramatically. Because life in the seventeenth century was unpredictable and society was vul-nerable to the ravages of disease, crop failure, and war, the family had functioned in a highly utilitarian way as the basic mechanism for sur-vival. First and foremost, it was an economic unit, harvesting crops that could be sold for profit and producing food, clothes, and medi-cine for its own immediate use. It trained the children, taught them trades, and supplied them with the rudiments of education. In its function as a school, church, charity organi-zation, hospital, orphanage, retirement home, and welfare agency, the seventeenth-century family, as historian John Demos has suggested, resembled an autonomous community, uniting a diverse group of individuals around a collec-tive purpose.

The growing affluence of life in the eigh-teenth century, reflected in the presence of knives and forks, crockery, and tea equipment in even the poorest families, modified without entirely replacing this earlier functional basis for family life. Everyday meals became more sociable occasions, marriages based on ties of affection were now common, and the houses themselves became more spacious and com-fortable places for the family to spend time. Nevertheless, as the diaries and letters of poor and middle-class eighteenth-century New En-gland families attest, the economic survival of the family in a largely agricultural society was often difficult. Sickness in the family, acci-

Figure 1.6
This is a plan for a Tuscan column, suitable for a home, with instructions and measurements for drawing it. Benjamin's guidebook appropriately begins with a course in plane geometry which provided the skills necessary for accurate plans. (Benjamin, *The American Builder's Companion*)

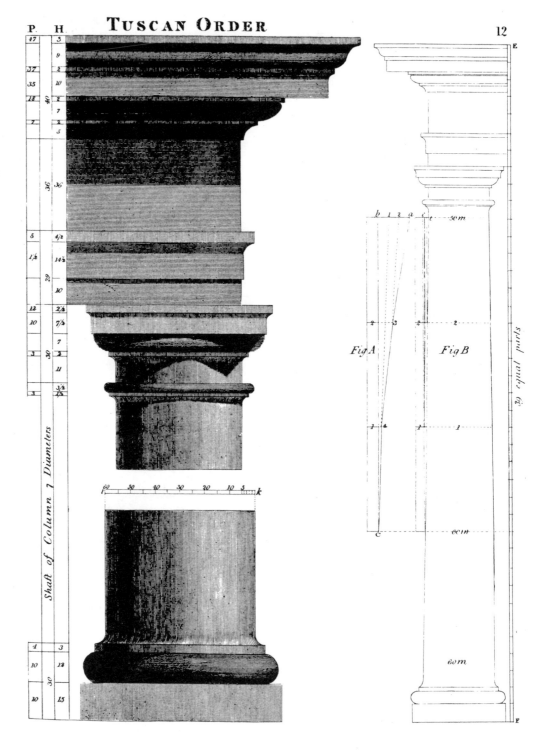

Figure 1.7
This Greek Revival house with Tuscan columns, built in Bennington, Vermont, in 1851, sits on a hill near the center of town. With its wings and side porch, it is a good example of how the Greek Revival style became more complex toward the middle of the nineteenth century. (Photograph by author)

dents, a downturn in the economy, or adverse weather conditions could be devastating.[7]

Given the somewhat unstable economy in the eighteenth century, the family retained some elements of the mutually supportive goals and the close ties that had existed earlier. Although the basic family unit, then as today, consisted primarily of parents and their children, non-kin such as orphans, laborers, apprentices, and other children, "bound out" under conditions of fosterage and designated as "servants," also lived in the house. As late as the early nineteenth century, town officials placed convicts and indigent people in private homes for supervision. Here, care, restraint, and rehabilitation were exchanged for economic services.

The varied membership of the household, together with the close proximity of living and working relations and the continual need for protection against accidents and economic disasters, molded the eighteenth-century family into an affectionate unit. The interdependent nature of individual lives, sharing work, education, worship, and even leisure-time activities such as celebrating holidays or visiting friends and relatives, bound parents and children together in a common enterprise and created a sense of belonging.

This collective and cooperative nature of family life was tested and reaffirmed by the hardships of the American Revolution. When men left home to fight, women were forced to keep the farm in operation or run the family business. The ideal of "Republican Motherhood" that emerged from the revolutionary experience, as Linda Kerber has pointed out, reinforced women's commitment to both civic and family life by asserting that the mother's nurturance of public-spirited male citizens would guarantee the steady infusion of virtue into the Republic. Female support for the family as a cohesive unit was thereby publicly recognized as having a dual function; it strengthened the family and contributed to the civic morality of the new nation.

opposite
Figure 1.8
This symmetrical embroidered sampler done by Sarah Chandler in 1808 reflects the acceptance of a hierarchical view of the family. (Courtesy New England Historic Genealogical Society, Boston, Massachusetts)

Not that differences in outlook or expectation did not occasionally arise within the family. They did. But they were handled according to the functional needs of family life. Turn-of-the-century ministers and other town officials, for example, stressed the importance of "family government" and the "due subordination" of children. Such obedience to the wishes of the elders was demanded in part because the children played an important economic role. Not only did they help with the work on the farm and in the house, but their marriages were also a source of important business and political connections. Especially for the middle and upper classes where trade networks and political appointments were often based on family alliances, the marriage of a daughter into an important family could be a significant factor in social stability. Hence some parental control over the children's social relations as well as their work habits was seen as desirable.[8]

Out of these functional and interdependent relationships, there emerged by the end of the eighteenth century an implicit and often unstated image of family life. The ideal relationship among family members, like the unstated assumptions about Greek Revival architecture, was a balanced combination of mutually dependent parts. Love was balanced off with duty, family responsibilities with public commitments, individual concerns with social welfare, thought with piety. Whereas the Greek Revival homes connected the ancient world to the present, the family was rooted to the community through ties of place, friendship, and responsibility. Yet, within this social and physical world of balanced responsibilities, a clear hierarchy existed. Parents were expected to control and dominate children, husbands were responsible for the family finances, and wives were legally subordinate. If a clear sense of hierarchy persisted, however, the major emphasis remained on the ideal of a balanced and well-ordered family since common purposes, close associations in work, and relatively limited contact with the outside world all reinforced a sense of shared responsibility[9] (Figure 1.8).

Not surprisingly, by the start of the nineteenth century, the uses of the internal spaces of the house had evolved to the extent that the function and layout of the rooms corresponded to the cooperative ideal of family life. Initially, in the seventeenth century, following English practice, the settlers had used the same room for multiple purposes. The variety of uses was reflected in the different names applied to the same space. In Virginia before 1700, until a kitchen was added at the back, the left front room was often labeled in inventories as the *hall, great room, outer room, dwelling room, fireroom,* or even "house." A center of family activity, the hall was used for cooking and dining, household handicrafts, and amusements. In Virginia, the hall was the center of the planter's world, the general-purpose living and working space. The other front room, called the *chamber, parlor,* or *inner room,* was also used for multiple purposes, and often contained beds, benches, tables, chairs, and hoes. To meet the changing needs of family life much of the furniture—in particular the chairs, tripod tables, and benches—was light enough to be moved from place to place. In the winter, the furniture was positioned near the fireplace; in the summer it was moved to cooler locations. English genre paintings from this period show that chairs and tables were generally pushed back against the walls and only moved out into the center of the room to form activity groups when necessary.[10]

By the second quarter of the seventeenth century in Virginia, the room at the right had been divided into a *dining room,* although it still contained chairs, tables, beds, and hoes, and a more private *chamber* in back of it that connected directly to it. By the middle of the eighteenth century, in both Virginia and New England this plan had further evolved into the more easily recognized Georgian forms—the five-bay house, two rooms deep with a central hall (Figures 1.9a and 1.9b). Front rooms remained more important than the rear ones on the first floor, reflecting a growing awareness of the boundaries between public and private space. Upper chambers came to be used more

Figures 1.9a and 1.9b
The Fairbanks house, ca. 1637, in Dedham, Massachusetts. With a left room "hall" and a right room "parlor," it is an early example of a two-room frame house that was expanded before 1668 by the addition of a rear lean-to. (Floor plans by Humphrey Costello)

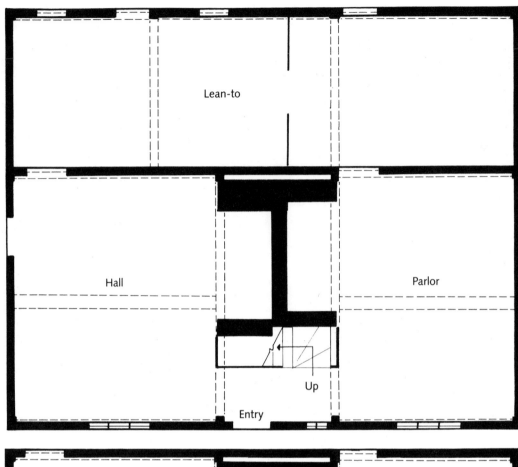

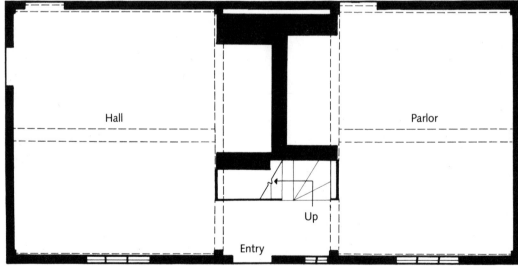

exclusively for sleeping. Although there was considerable regional variation, by 1800 rectangular structures representing vernacular adaptations to Georgian designs could be found up and down the East Coast. Thus, to a considerable degree, the internal physical arrangements of the house had come to correspond with the family ideal. Whereas the family had a hierarchy that ran from the father at the top down to the children below, so, too, did the house with the most important rooms in front and the kitchen and the service areas relegated to the rear.

The great versatility and the simple, informal functionality of middle-class eighteenth-century homes, like the utilitarian understanding of family life, were largely taken for granted. The needs of day-to-day existence seemed, in the phrase so often repeated, to be self-evident. Hence few people developed an explicit rationale for family life; nor did they feel the need, as later generations have, to justify their behavior toward one another. The historian who searches eighteenth-century diaries and letters will look in vain for a publicly expressed ideology that was used to justify either the family or the household. Even Thomas Jefferson, who devoted a significant portion of his life to the construction and remodeling of Monticello and who hoped to create a sense of "high" taste for architecture among his countrymen, is curiously silent about the meaning of his house. Indeed, his famous complaint to James Madison that his fellow countrymen lacked "taste" and understanding of architectural styles was testimony to the paucity of explicit standards in his day for either "high" or "common" house forms.[11]

Jefferson's complaint received little public attention until the 1840s and 1850s. By then an unusual combination of concerned citizens, reform interests, and middle-class activists had coalesced into a broad crusade to replace what they saw as the older eighteenth-century ideal of home and family with a set of new standards for domestic architecture and social behavior. Architects who aspired to a more professional status, ministers with an interest in family counseling, feminists who sought to improve the position of women within the family, promoters of tract and benevolence societies who wished to spread Christianity, and almanac and magazine editors who hoped to capitalize on the popular middle-class fascination with self-help and self-improvement schemes all joined in a massive promotional effort to create a new ideal for the American family home. The most remarkable feature of this reform movement was that it lacked both centralized leadership and systematic organization. What united its membership and motivated its most active participants was the common conviction that the pace of social change at mid-century was too great. The middle-class reformers believed that American democratic society, vulnerable as it was to outside forces that did not share traditional beliefs, was in danger of collapsing. Immediate action had to be taken.

Everywhere the middle-class reformers looked they saw a society without strong controls that was changing in ways that were threatening. The rapid expansion westward, the beginnings of the factory system, the haphazard settlement of new states, and the unchecked competition for railroad franchises and new lands upset the stability that had been the hallmark of small-town life. Even worse was the phenomenal urban growth between 1820 and 1860, the highest in American history, which saw the proportion of persons living in cities skyrocket 797 percent. Cities like Philadelphia, Boston, and New York were flooded by more than 4.3 million German and Irish immigrants. Although land in Boston and other cities was subdivided and settlement spilled over into peripheral communities such as Charlestown and Cambridge, these new sections themselves quickly became congested, mixing the homes of immigrants and native workers with factories. The immigrants, who had little understanding of the American way of life, seemed particularly threatening. Coming from Catholic backgrounds and organized socially around the saloons and fraternal orders, they appeared to be a foreign power that menaced the political stability of the community. As Boston minister Lyman Beecher warned, "Of all influences, none is more pernicious than a corps of men acting systematically and perseveringly for its own ends upon a community unapprised of their doings, and undisciplined to meet and counteract them. A tenth part of the suffrage of the nation, thus condensed and wielded by the Catholic powers of Europe, might decide our elections, perplex our policy, inflame and divide the nation, break the bond of our union, and throw down our free institutions." When riots broke out in Philadelphia, Boston, and New York in the 1840s, the worst fears of Beecher and other reformers seem to have been confirmed.[12]

Most unsettling of all and most difficult for the middle-class plan-book writers and family reformers to understand was the gradual transformation of the economy and its impact on family life. The beginnings of the factory system, the creation of large-scale business enterprises such as railroads, and the growth of public education and the professions changed the nature of production and increasingly separated the place of work from the home. Close ties between family members, which had been reinforced in the earlier agricultural economy by everyday contact, now were more difficult to maintain. As historian Mary P. Ryan has pointed out, the dispersal of family members to places of work outside the household, by providing younger sons and daughters with new sources of income, eroded the traditional ideal of a patriarchal family government and created tension. In the pell-mell scramble for wealth in the middle decades of the nineteenth century, American society appeared to have outgrown the old standards for family life without having developed any new ones. The middle-class reformers set out to rectify this omission.[13]

The crusade to establish a new middle-class ideal for the American family home derived its strength from a variety of sources. Architects and home designers were the most active early converts to the movement. Like lawyers, doctors, and other quasi-professionals, house designers in the early years of the century were in

a vulnerable position. The term "architect," for example, was vague and imprecise. Almost anyone could—and often did—call himself an architect throughout the nineteenth century. In the middle decades of the century, competition for designing homes was particularly intense. Just as doctors were forced to compete with mid-wives, barber-surgeons, and patent-medicine quacks, those who aspired to the status of "architect" were threatened by local carpenters and village mechanics. To improve their own position and undermine the competition, these self-styled architects in the 1840s seized upon the growing social discontent and aggressively asserted that new standards were needed for domestic housing and family life. In the process, they not only helped to codify a new ideal for family relationships, but they also developed a more effective rationale for their own profession. Insistent on higher standards, they asserted that the proper education and training of architects would raise building standards and thereby benefit the masses. In so doing, they hoped to create a professional architectural elite whose value would be recognized both socially and financially.

An early spokesman for architectural reform was a New York landscape designer named Andrew Jackson Downing. Although he borrowed many of his ideas from the English landscape architect, John Claudius Loudon, Downing showed great insight by developing a new form of builders' guide that combined designs for entire houses with an elaborate rationale and theory of taste. In the 1840s Downing crystallized public opinion by publishing his *Treatise on the Theory and Practice of Landscape Gardening . . . With Remarks on Rural Architecture . . .* (1841), *Cottage Residences: or, A Series of Designs for Rural Cottages and Cottage Villas* (1842), and *The Architecture of Country Houses* (1850). These three works, which went through more than twenty editions in the next thirty years, codified the aesthetic theory of the new movement and provided plans and pictures of the most innovative designs. In place of the older, often rectangular Classical Revival designs built with a system of mortised and tenoned twelve-by-twelve-inch posts placed at eight- or ten-foot intervals, Downing's houses used the new balloon frame made out of two-by-fours spaced at eighteen-inch intervals. The new frame was lighter and stronger than the older post-and-beam method of construction. Unlike the earlier houses that required a technical knowledge of joinery, the new structures were simpler to build, used smaller-dimensioned lumber, and allowed the designer to create more complex and flexible house plans (Figures 1.10a and 1.10b).

Stimulated by the success of Downing's early books, other designers turned out "pattern books" by the hundreds. Only twenty editions of builders' guides had been published between 1820 and 1840; in the following two decades the number tripled. Using these plan books as a mechanism for self-promotion, those who had drafting skills and who desired to be called "architects" became the early advocates of a standardized approach to domestic architecture based on accepted principles of design.[14]

Downing and his fellow architects aggressively began their campaign for new housing standards by mounting a savage attack on traditional Greek Revival houses. They scornfully depicted the older structures as boring, monotonous, deceitful, and ugly. It was absurd, cried one critic, to design a house like a Greek temple. It was like draping "the skin of the lion on the body of an ass." Other commentators were equally condescending. "Square boxes set along in rows," fumed Edward Shaw in the *North American Review*, "if they are not positively offensive by some manifest excrescence of deformity, they are usually bald, tame, and expressive of the utter absence of taste in the builder." However useful for public buildings, Greek Revival houses were simply unsuited for private homes. It was absurd, continued Shaw, to design "a Grecian temple in clapboards with its kitchen and cooking apparatus at one end and its prim fluted columns at the other! A temple of Minerva with its sauce-pans and pianos."[15]

More sophisticated critics complained that

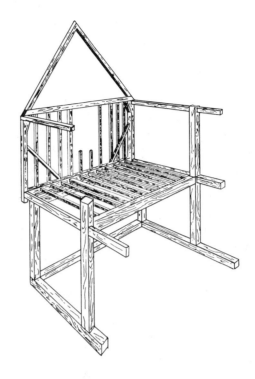

the traditional housing forms were inflexible. Porches or bay windows, appreciated because they allowed the homeowner greater contact with the world of nature, they asserted, could not be added to the temple shape without distorting it. Even the color white, which was customarily used for Greek Revival homes, was disliked because it set the houses off too starkly from the soft green and brown tones of the natural landscape. Russets, browns, and other earth colors, urged the critics, would have a far softer and more relaxing effect.

These caustic critiques of Greek Revival styles, with their complaints about historical inaccuracies and aesthetic bad taste, initially appealed to a generation of middle-class Americans who were unsure of their own social status and eager to cling to more convincing authorities. In the unstable boom-and-bust economy of the early nineteenth century, the argument for creating a more authentic historical style and using it for the appropriate purposes had a logic to it that gave it power. The weakness in the critics' position was that for more than half a century many Americans had

Figure 1.10b
This is a typical popular magazine's illustration of the balloon frame, which replaced the post-and-beam construction at mid-century, giving the architect and carpenter a new freedom in creating more complex house shapes. ("Balloon Frames")

his skill, has developed a principle in construction that has sufficient merit to warrant its use by all who wish to erect in a cheap and substantial manner any class of wooden buildings.

Like all successful improvements, which thrive on their own merits, the Balloon Frame has passed through and survived the theory, ridicule and abuse of all who have seen fit to attack it, and may be reckoned among the prominent inventions of the present generation, an invention neither fostered nor developed by any hope of great rewards, but which plainly and boldly acknowledges its origin in necessity.

The increasing value of lumber and labor, must turn the attention of men of moderate means to those successful plans which have demonstrated economy in both, and at the same time preserved the full qualities of strength and security so generally accorded to the old fogy principles of framing, and which, we presume to say, is inferior in all the true requisites of cheap and substantial building. Light sticks, uninjured by cutting mortices or tenons, a close basket-like manner of construction, short bearings, a continuous support for each piece of timber from foundation to rafter, and embracing and taking advantage of the practical fact, that the tensile and compressible strength of pine lumber is equal to one-fifth of that of wrought iron, constitute improvements introduced with this frame.

If, in erecting a building, we can so use our materials that every strain will come in the direction of the fibre of some portion of the wood work, we can make inch boards answer a better purpose than foot square beams, and this application of materials is one reason of the strength of Balloon Frames.

The Balloon Frame belongs to no one person; nobody claims it as an invention, and yet in the art of construction it is one of the most sensible improvements that has ever been made.

That which has hitherto called out a whole neighborhood, and required a vast expenditure of labor, time, and noise,

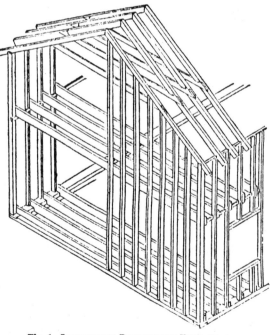

Fig. 1—Isometrical Perspective View of the
Balloon Frame.

been modifying the older designs, adding a wing to the side or an addition to the rear of the house. Although it was historically inappropriate, they would continue to do so despite the sarcastic jibes of the critics.

Perhaps in response to the unpersuasiveness of their arguments because of the general public's preference for function over stylistic purity, the critics in the 1840s and 1850s brought out a more dramatic argument—Greek Revival homes were unpatriotic. The endless repetition of forms taken from antiquity undermined Americans' need for a distinctive national architecture. How could borrowed Greek Revival styles ever be truly American? If the American people, as politicians like Andrew Jackson argued, were unfettered by the aristocratic traditions that shackled Europeans, why didn't they develop their own original architecture?

Of all their arguments to the new middle-class audience of shopkeepers, small businessmen, and farmers, the most damaging was the assertion that the traditional middle-class houses did not supply the proper associations for the American family. The problem with the Greek mode was its peaceful serenity and lack of passion. Trying to imitate the Greeks simply created a lifeless parody that was completely out of step with "the spirit of this locomotive age." The American people needed a domestic architecture, asserted the plan-book writer Calvert Vaux, that would give the family a sense of protection and inspiration, a feeling of closeness and cooperation, and most important, a greater appreciation of art and beauty. For a middle-class audience obsessed with self-improvement and eager to differentiate themselves from the immigrant workers, the latter ideal was particularly appealing.[16]

This aggressive plan-book critique of older architectural designs represented a dramatically innovative and challenging approach to popular housing standards. Instead of considering the house primarily as a shelter and a workplace as earlier generations had done, the plan-book writers, and later the family reformers, insisted that the house be given moral attributes. Henceforth houses would be de-

scribed in *moral* terms as good or bad, honest or dishonest. Even when their own designs were only minor variations on traditional vernacular forms, plan-book writers and architects now had a promotional tool of great potential. By labeling the common single-family dwelling as a moral structure, they now had a new and dramatically effective basis for promoting their own designs.

In place of the older Georgian and Greek Revival designs, the architectural reformers offered a variety of new styles. Of these, three designs in particular became most widely accepted. The first, the "Gothic" revival home, was described by one contemporary as "a building, the character of whose architecture is distinguished by the upward direction of its leading lines, and by such curves as may be introduced meeting, or having a tendency to meet, in a point."[17] In its most popular form as a rural cottage, the Gothic style emphasized verticality by its steep pitched roofs, board-and-batten siding, sharply pointed dormers, and ornamentation on the gables (Figure 1.11). The rural Gothic revival style not only harmonized well with natural surroundings, but because of its origin in a more religious age, it was also thought to symbolize an eminently Christian form of private dwelling. In such a rural home, isolated from the vices of city life, the Christian family could worship God and make the house a religious sanctuary (Figure 1.12). The early Gothic Revival reached its peak as a house style on the East Coast in the 1840s and 1850s, but it remained popular through the 1880s in small towns in the Midwest like Northfield, Minnesota, and mining communities in the West like Blackhawk, Colorado. By that time, the writings of John Ruskin had also sparked a renewed interest in the style as appropriate for college dormitories and civic buildings such as the Jefferson Market Courthouse (1875) in New York City and the Syracuse Savings Bank (1876).[18]

Even more popular than the Gothic Revival was the Italianate style, inspired by the villas of Tuscany and known by its asymmetrical grouping of forms. The Italianate style could most

Figure 1.11
The Gothic house pictured here was built for an upper-class man of wealth. Andrew Jackson Downing urged that such houses be built of stone, following the example of English gentry. (Downing, *The Architecture of Country Houses*)

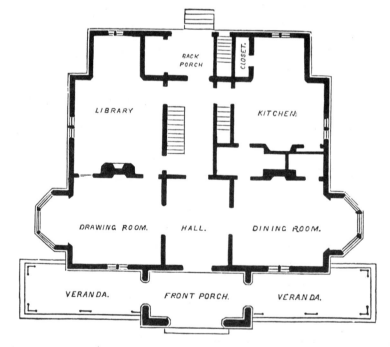

easily be recognized by its flat-roofed tower and broad veranda or porch, which was thought to "convey at once an expression of beauty arising from a superior comfort or refinement of the mode of living" (Figure 1.13). Contemporaries recommended this style for the rectangular suburban lot. As architect Gervase Wheeler wrote, "Its form possesses sufficient regularity to harmonize with the buildings in the city, whilst its character shows it to be a link between town and country."[19]

The third basic style was known as "bracketed" because of the heavy brackets under the projecting eaves (Figure 1.14). Similar in some respects to the Italianate style, it became enormously popular in part because it was a modification of the earlier classical rectangular shape and in part because it appeared to be highly functional. As Andrew Jackson Downing suggested, "the coolness and dryness of the upper story, afforded by the almost veranda-like roof, will render this a delightful feature in all parts of our country where the summers are hot." The ease of construction and picturesqueness achieved by modifying the windows and the porch made the "bracketed" style the most popular building form at mid-century.[20]

To justify these new house styles, architects insisted that the new designs expressed aesthetic ideals that had come into vogue during the romantic movement in the 1830s. Drawing support from the writings of Europeans such as Immanuel Kant and William Wordsworth, the architects provided an extensive aesthetic rationale for their designs. These new justifications for improved designs were considerably different from the implicit standards that had been used for houses in the eighteenth century. Public and private structures designed earlier by architects like Charles Bulfinch and Benjamin Latrobe had rested on the implicit assumptions that forms were beautiful in themselves and that architecture should display the principles of simplicity, harmony, and proportion; the romantics, borrowing from Scottish aesthetic theorists like Archibald Alison, now argued that structural forms were beautiful both in terms of the thoughts that they raised in the

Figure 1.12
The Gothic-style cottage with the cross prominently displayed above the door symbolized the true Christian home. (Beecher and Stowe, *American Woman's Home*)

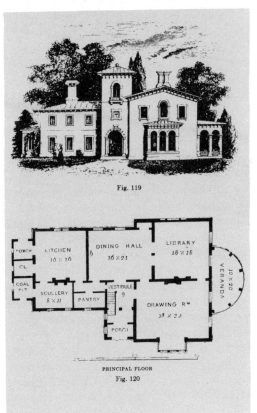

Figure 1.13
Villas in the Italianate style were known for the asymmetrical grouping of forms and the use of a tower to provide a healthy view of the countryside. (Downing, *The Architecture of Country Houses*)

Figure 1.14
This small house, with its board-and-batten siding that stresses verticality, was designed for middle-class families. (Downing, *The Architecture of Country Houses*)

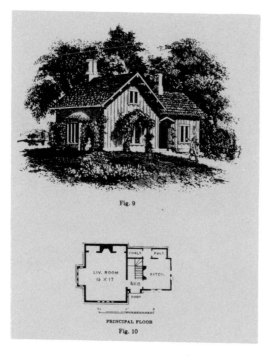

mind of the viewer and in terms of their appropriateness to their surroundings. Using the ideas of Kant and Wordsworth that in a different realm there existed pure types of which the earthly examples were only a copy, they argued that the architect was the only one who understood the real principles of harmony and beauty. Thus Gothic architecture, which was popularized in the works of Byron, Sir Walter Scott, and Augustus W. Pugin, became representative of the ideals of an earlier Christian age. "The sublime, the glorious Gothic," wrote one reformer, was "the architecture of Christianity."[21]

To an aesthetic theory that associated architectural forms and spiritual ideals, American reformers added an ethical dimension. Taste and the perception of beauty were inextricably related to the moral development of the individual. Searching for a proper justification for their position, New York architects Henry Cleaveland and William Backus quoted the words of the Federalist, Timothy Dwight of Yale, who argued that "the first thing powerfully operated on, and, in its turn, proportionally operative, is the taste. The perception of

beauty and deformity, of refinement and grossness, of decency and vulgarity, of propriety and indecorum, is the first thing which influences man to escape from a groveling, brutish character. . . . In most persons, this perception is awakened by what may be called the exterior of society, particularly by the mode of building." It followed from this theory that the environment that surrounded the individual was a crucial force in shaping his personality. The morals, civilization, and refinement of the nation, according to the housing reformers, depended upon the construction of a proper national domestic architecture.[22]

The choice of a quotation from Dwight to justify their position is significant, for it reveals both the continuities with and the differences between the ideals of the reformers and the objectives of the sponsors of the earlier Greek Revival. When earlier neoclassical leaders like Dwight spoke of the importance of "the exterior of society," they meant to emphasize that the exterior of the buildings should mirror a public order of balance and equilibrium. The very placement and arrangement of public buildings—as for example, in the planned layout of Washington, D.C.—was seen as exemplifying in a geographical manner the precise divisions that were embodied in the Constitution in terms of checks and balances. Although the new plan-book writers shared the earlier Federalist interest in creating an environment that would symbolize important ideals, their major concern was not with public buildings but rather with social improvement and private behavior. What architects like Cleaveland and Backus wanted was to take that part of the aesthetic theory that had supported the earlier revival of neoclassical styles and turn it into a justification for creating a new, private, domestic life-style for the middle class. Instead of emphasizing public order and republican virtues, they wanted to stress the importance of private discipline and self-control in an ordered environment. Like the writers of etiquette manuals who insisted that a true gentility could only be seen in the course of perfect physical and emotional self-restraint, they asserted that only an ordered and disciplined household could help the middle class move up further on the ladder of success. Thus the proper house would both improve the town or city in which it was located and also reflect the commitment to order and decorum of its owner.[23]

As a part of their new emphasis on the moral dimension of house design, the architectural reformers stressed that their plans were "honest," "truthful," and "beautiful." Since the exterior of the house was to be a form of self-expression, it had to correspond to the values revealed in the interior rooms. "Without this qualification," wrote plan-book author Daniel Atwood, "it can have neither true value nor real beauty." Downing himself stressed that an understanding of beauty was a prerequisite for improving house design. Beauty was "a worship by the heart, of higher perfection manifested in material forms" which could be perceived in nature. Since nature was a manifestation of the divine spirit, Downing argued that "to see, or rather to feel how, in nature, matter is ennobled by being thus touched by a single thought of beauty, how it is almost deified by being made to shadow forth, even dimly, His attributes, constitutes the profound and thrilling satisfaction which we experience in contemplating the external works of God."[24]

By emphasizing the symbolic role of architecture and by making a direct connection between the material world and the knowledge of God, Downing was utilizing an approach expressed by landscape painters, ministers, and writers in their own work. The perception of the natural world as a reflection of underlying moral laws and as a revelation of divine purposes was directly related to the Protestant, didactic outlook of Victorian Americans. Thus, by stressing the symbolic role of domestic architecture as an emblem of social and domestic virtue, Downing and the other architectural reformers strengthened their authority as arbiters of taste and allied themselves directly with those people most interested in improving family life.

Downing and the other housing reformers were not content to rest their case for new domestic architectural styles on arguments about taste and beauty alone. They were also quick to point out the technological advantages of their designs. Only the architect, they asserted, could combine the most tasteful interiors with the latest plumbing, heating, and construction technologies. As Daniel Atwood bluntly put it, "If there are such intimate relations between aesthetic beauty and moral excellence, why not employ more tact and talent in marrying the useful and beautiful together here?" The house plan books thus placed a strong emphasis on the functionality of the dwelling. "In arranging the apartments," wrote another designer, "special attention should be given to the saving of needless labor." Toward the end of the nineteenth century, the architects who had set themselves up as the arbiters of style and taste now turned their energies to explaining the more complicated household technologies including heating, plumbing, and wiring. From 1880 on, the increasing use of central heating, lighting (with gas), and, after 1900, indoor plumbing, sewers, electricity, and refrigeration, encouraged the architect to establish himself as the specialist in these areas as well.[25]

The architects also justified these new house designs by citing their appropriateness to the social needs of the times. Concerned about the pace of social change and the transient character of many friendships and social relations, they spoke out in favor of a need for more emphasis on continuity and tradition. Their house designs, they asserted, were an effective antidote to the destructive movement of the population westward.

"These frequent changes of residence," wrote J. H. Hammond in *The Farmer's and Mechanic's Practical Architect*, ". . . are destructive of much of that home-feeling which is essential to the education of the affections and moral sentiments." Other plan-book writers complained that "a constant moving from house to house causes one to acquire thriftless habits, and is opposed to the practice of a wise and judicious economy." To counteract the

Figure 1.15
As is evident in this picture, the middle-class woman's sphere within her home was a protected refuge of culture and enlightenment. (Courtesy Smithsonian Institution, Collection of Business Americana)

The irony was that the architects, by setting new standards, both in terms of style and utility, encouraged middle-class Americans to buy a more up-to-date residence, creating the very neighborhood transiency that they supposedly opposed.

Never entirely consistent in their arguments, the architect promoters also encouraged the middle class to move to the newer housing developments on the outskirts of cities. Taking advantage of expansion of the housing market, the increases in population, and the construction of railroads that made it possible to commute to work, the plan-book writers insisted that building their kind of home at the city's edge would combine "urban conveniences" (new forms of heating) with "the substantial advantages of rural conditions of life." These included not only direct access to nature, which was thought of as a source of truth and beauty, but also a defense against the ruinous rents and vices of city life. At the center of the city, with its prevalence of intemperance and open vice, wrote one reformer, there could be "no feeling of privacy, no security from intrusion." The neighborhoods on the city's outskirts, in contrast, were protected retreats where the shared values of the middle-class family would be safe. Parks in particular became the common ground that symbolized the unity of outlook. "[T]he essential qualification of a suburb is domesticity," wrote Frederick Law Olmsted, the landscape architect. "The fact that the families dwelling within a suburb enjoy much in common, and all the more enjoy it because it is in common . . . should be everywhere manifest in the completeness, and choiceness, and the beauty of the means they possess of coming together . . . and especially of recreating and enjoying them together on common ground."[27]

restless movement of population from town to town, these writers urged the public to develop a deeper commitment to a single dwelling place. "Thus," wrote Samuel Sloan in his *City Homes, Country Homes, and Church Architecture,* "the man who has a home, presenting comfort allied to taste, feels a love for it, a thankfulness for its possession, and a proportionate determination to uphold and defend it against all invading influences. Such a man is, of necessity—we might say selfishly, a good citizen; for he has a stake in society." The house at mid-century thus became perceived as an island of stability in an increasingly restless society[26] (Figure 1.15).

Given the rapidity with which most Americans moved during the nineteenth century, such arguments clearly appealed to those who were worried about Americans' lack of roots.

By mid-century, then, domestic architecture promoters and plan-book writers had stimulated public interest in the American family home by stressing how properly designed houses would stabilize society, attest to the moral development of the owners, meet the needs for new housing evident in the expansion of the suburbs, and help improve society at large. But before their ideals could gain a national consensus, they needed further support. This additional backing came from an unexpected source; it was a by-product of the changes taking place in Protestantism and other reform movements of the period.

In the 1840s a major shift began to take place in the outlook of American Protestants. In the previous two decades, the massive revivals that had occurred during the Second Great Awakening had strongly shaped Protestant theology. Led by Charles Grandison Finney, Lyman Beecher, and others, the revivalists had placed an emphasis on individual conversion. Save the individual, Finney urged, and persuade him to dedicate his life to Christ, and that individual would observe the Sabbath, free the slave, and banish alcohol from the world. Although Finney's arguments, known to his contemporaries as "moral suasion," were persuasive at the time, by the 1840s they had become out of date. For the aggressive reformer who hoped to wipe out sin and perfect the individual, moral suasion seemed weak. There were too many professing Christians who continued to go about their sinful ways. The revivals, moreover, had proved to be enormously disruptive to communities. By inspiring people to make their own peace with God, they made individuals distrust the settled churches. As a result, sects and denominations broke apart and the churches began to squabble internally.[28]

By the 1840s a major reaction had developed in the Eastern churches against revivalism. It was led by Horace Bushnell, a Hartford minister, who published his views in 1847 in a book entitled *Christian Nurture*. The true approach to Christianity, Bushnell argued, was that the child should "grow up a Christian, and never know himself as being otherwise." How could this be accomplished? Simply place the child in a Christian home and surround him with Christian parents who would set the proper example. In a sermon entitled "The Organic Unity of the Family," Bushnell argued that the child "breathes the atmosphere of the house.

He sees the world through his parents' eyes. Their objects become his. Their life and spirit mold him."[29]

Housing promoters were quick to take this religious argument and turn it to their own ends. "We are in no little danger of losing sight of the importance which God has attached to the family relation," wrote one architect in 1846. Those who are wise should recognize the importance of the nursery. "There is so intimate a connection between taste and morals, aesthetics and Christianity," wrote plan-book author William Ranlett, "that they in each instance mutually modify each other; hence whatever serves to cultivate the taste of the community ... will give to Christianity increased opportunity and means of charming the heart and governing the life."[30]

Having agreed with Bushnell that the home was a crucially important influence in shaping the religion of the child, the housing reformers set out to design as Christian a home as possible. The result was the conception of the house as a church, an idea that reached its fullest development in the Gothic Revival style. No efforts were spared in providing the house with the proper associations. One of the most heavily used symbols was the cross. The house could be designed on a cross plan, and crosses were often attached to the tops of the gables. Philadelphia architects Thomas U. Walter and John J. Smith, in their book *Two Hundred Designs for Cottages and Villas* (1846), offered twenty different cross designs that might be used. In addition to the crosses, stained glass became popular for providing accents in the windows and some of the guide books suggested that three primary colors be used to symbolize the Trinity. For the front parlor, a pump organ could be purchased upon which the family's favorite hymns could be played. Even stoves and bedroom furniture could be designed following Gothic standards (Figures 1.16a and 1.16b). All in all, the pattern-book writers in the 1840s and 1850s touted the rural Gothic house as the perfect place for Christian nurture.[31]

If the shifting outlook of Protestantism

Figure 1.16a
Since middle-class Americans at mid-century believed that the individual was shaped by his or her environment, they designed their furniture in the Gothic style to reinforce their image of the Christian home. (Downing, *The Architecture of Country Houses*)

opposite
Figure 1.16b
Early houseware and furniture advertisements stressed the quality and integrity of the sellers, which were reflected in this case by their fashionable building rather than by the way in which a typical room might be furnished in the home. (Advertisement, undated. Courtesy Smithsonian Institution, Collection of Business Americana)

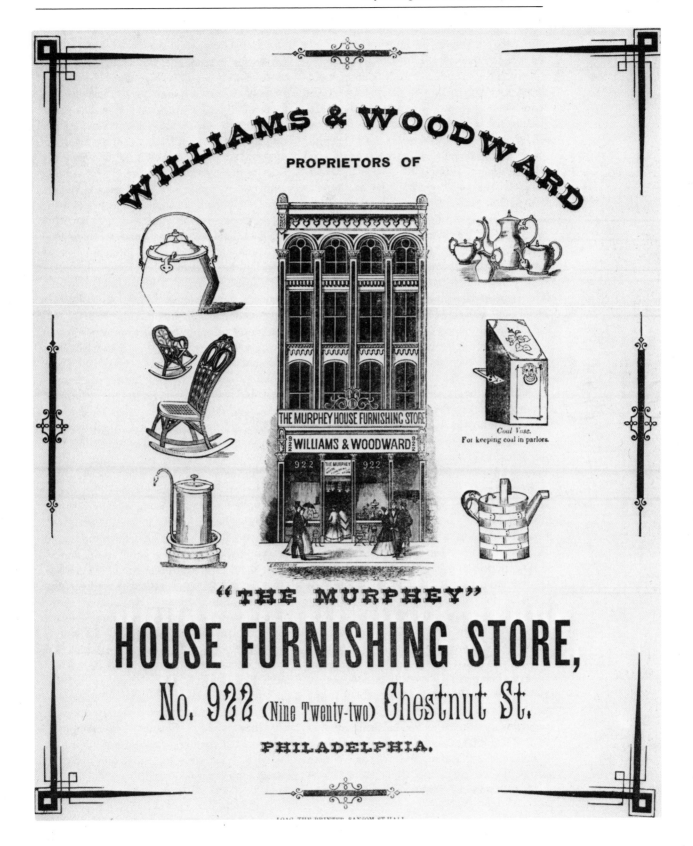

stimulated an interest in housing reform, so, too, did the new approach that was becoming evident in the temperance and abolitionist crusades. Like the revivalists, the antislavery and temperance advocates had first emphasized reforming the individual. By the 1840s they realized that their tactics were not working. Individual commitments had to be strengthened by institutions. Turning away from their earlier belief in moral suasion, the abolitionists both sought support in the political arena and stressed the importance of the family as a new instrument of social reform. As the popular abolitionist Henry Ward Beecher argued, "a few usages maintained, a few rights guaranteed to the slaves, and the system is vitally wounded. The right of chastity in the woman, the unblemished household love, the right of parents in their children—on these three elements stands the whole weight of society." Significantly, too, when Abraham Lincoln tried to explain the Republican party's attitude toward property to the lower classes, he did it by making an analogy to the ownership of a home. "Let not him who is houseless," Lincoln argued, "pull down the house of another; but let him labor diligently and build one for himself, thus by example assuring that his own shall be safe from violence when built." In a similar manner, as the temperance leaders shifted from an emphasis on moral suasion and began to seek legal sanctions, they, too, stressed the harmful influence of alcohol on the family.[32]

The intensive propaganda campaigns waged by the temperance and abolitionist crusaders with their stress on the family served to strengthen the program of the housing promoters and reformers. All these crusaders directed their energies toward persuading the growing middle class—that segment of society that was becoming increasingly more financially secure and hence had heightened fears about losing their material possessions—that their reform programs were essential for the stabilization of society. "Nothing has more to do with the morals, the civilization, and refinement of a nation, than its prevailing Architecture," wrote New York architect, Oliver P. Smith. "Virtue

and Beauty are twin sisters; while Vice and Deformity are in constant association. The moral and refined seek a home where the virtuous influences that are reflected from Beauty and Order, are congenial to their cultivated minds and moral constitutions." Other reformers went even further. Improvements in domestic architecture would not only cure the vices of the individual, they would reform and uplift society itself. As Cleaveland and Backus wrote: "No man, we think, could live just the life in a well-proportioned and truly beautiful dwelling that he would in a mud shanty or rude log cabin. Certain elevating influences would steal into him unawares . . . that would lift his life above its otherwise lower level. It would be made, unconsciously perhaps, more human, more dignified and tasteful. . . . And so, too, this power of the tasteful is seen very often in the influence which a single dwelling will exert upon almost all in its neighborhood." The man who improved the dwelling houses of the people would make a lasting reform in the foundations of society.[33]

Thus, by the 1850s the domestic housing crusade had reached its full power. Allied with abolitionist, temperance, and religious leaders, and drawing support from architects and plan-book writers, the crusade for the ideal American family home had become a central feature of what historians have come to call the American Victorian outlook. The reform movement shared the basic Victorian belief in the importance of reform and the possibility of perfection. Supported by an articulate and forceful segment within the middle class, housing promoters, temperance advocates, family reformers, and plan-book writers argued that society was evolving to a higher level of civilization and the American family home was the key instrument for progress. Their responsibility, like that of the other Victorians, was to teach and enlighten the rest of the nation. By utilizing what they viewed as the moral laws inherent in the world of nature, the housing reformers hoped to eradicate vice, stabilize society, and create a more perfect world.[34]

The new image of the middle-class American family home developed by the architects and social reformers projected a powerful ideal for family life—a cult of domesticity that was shared by a host of other essayists, advice-book writers, and ministers. Having personally experienced the economic changes wrought by the beginnings of the factory system, the growing specialization of work, and the creation of a commercial network of regional and national markets, the architectural reformers and domesticity advocates agreed that the older pattern of family relationships had changed. To gain public support, they dramatized these changes, often stereotyping earlier family relationships as peaceful and idyllic. No longer, they argued, did the family serve as a church, a school, a business, a hospital, an orphanage, and a corrective institution as it had in the eighteenth century. Now these responsibilities were taken over by agencies outside the home. Nor did the middle-class family, protected somewhat from the uncertainties of the economy by salaried working arrangements, have to play as crucial a role as a mechanism for economic survival. Instead the family was free to take on different responsibilities and more specialized functions. According to the reformers, the new, mid-nineteenth-century ideal of the family—the canon of domesticity—would stabilize and strengthen the social order.

The new standards for family life that emerged in the 1830s, 1840s, and 1850s were expressed in numerous books, tracts, and magazine articles. Books such as the Reverend John S. C. Abbott's *The Mother at Home* (1833), the Reverend Heman Humphrey's *Domestic Education* (1840), Lydia Sigourney's *Letters to Young Ladies* (1841), and Lydia Maria Child's *The Mother's Book* (1831) all pictured the family in its newly redefined role as the stabilizer of society.

The central tenet of the new canon of domesticity expressed in these books was the assertion that the household should be a refuge from the outside world, a fortress designed to protect, nurture, and strengthen the individuals within it. "Home is not merely four square

walls adorned with gilded pictures," suggested pattern-book author Sereno E. Todd, "but it is where love sheds its light on all the dear ones who gather round the sweet home fireside, where we can worship God, with none to molest or make us afraid." The very terms used suggested that the home was a place of almost religious importance, a sacred enclave strengthened by feelings of loyalty, reverence, and dedication.[35] Nor was it surprising that this glorified image of the sacred home was strenuously promoted in the literature published by the tract and Bible societies. One religious almanac suggested that "one of the holiest sanctuaries on earth is home. The family altar is more venerable than any altar in the cathedral. The education of the soul for eternity begins by the fireside. The principle of love, which is to be carried through the universe, is first unfolded in the family."[36]

Within this holy sphere, women were pictured by the pattern books and advice manuals as best suited, both biologically and emotionally, to counteract the disruptions caused by the expanding and transient economy in which 50 percent of the population moved once every decade. Sensitive to religious issues and morally superior to men, females alone could provide the proper balance of comfort and guidance to their working husbands. As a writer in the *North American Review* in 1836 suggested, "leave the rude commerce of camps and the soul-hardening struggles of political power to the harsher spirit of man, that he may still look up to her as a purer and brighter being, an emanation of some better world, irradiating like a rainbow of hope, the stormy elements of life."[37]

Since the primary function of the home was supportive and restorative, advocates of the cult of domesticity most often pictured the house in a protected rural or small town setting, nestled in a pleasant grove of trees with children playing unattended out in front. When the New York printers, Currier and Ives, depicted the ideal home environment in their popular lithographs, they invariably chose a peaceful rural setting, a "middle-landscape," neither wild nor

Figure 1.17
For the Victorian farm family, the yard, like the house, became a controlled and protected environment where the children could play. Note the position of the women and children in this picture and in Figure 1.18. (Currier and Ives, *The Farmer's Home —Harvest* [1864]. Courtesy The Harry T. Peters Collection, Museum of the City of New York)

entirely cultivated, where the advantages of urban proximity could be adapted to the benefits of a tamed and harmonious natural environment (Figures 1.17 and 1.18). Whereas cities for middle-class Americans served as symbols of greed, corruption, and temptation, the bucolic countryside, where the excesses of the frontier and wilderness had long been tamed, was emblematic of the healthful and restorative powers of nature. The domestic ideal curbed the excesses of both cities and wilderness while preserving the advantages that each had to offer. As landscape architect Frederick Law Olmsted expressed it, "the outward tendency of town populations is . . . not a sacri-fice of urban conveniences, but their combination with the special charms and substantial advantages of rural conditions of life."[38] Implicit in this image of the homogeneous and protected rural setting was the exclusion of the lower classes. Foreign immigrants of German or Irish descent would be kept out unless, of course, they had dropped their distinctive ethnic behaviors and accepted middle-class standards of speech and deportment. So, too, would be the poor and the transient. The naive hope was that a community of like-minded individuals, in a parklike setting, would somehow automatically exclude violence and crime which were identified with an urban way of life.

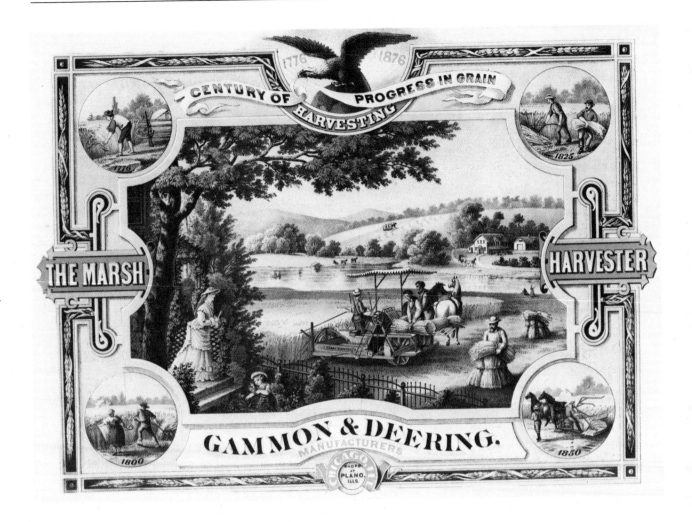

By drawing a rigid distinction between the protective home and the aggressive, materialistic world of work, housing and social reformers created a nostalgic image of the family home as a place of strong feelings and delicate emotions. Writing about "home" in *The Family Circle and Parlor Annual* for 1851, Mrs. C. A. Riley painted the typical sentimental picture of the household when she argued that "there is a magic in this simple word that thrills the heart with unutterable pleasure and vibrates upon the ear like sweet-toned music. With it comes bright memories of happy hours spent with loved ones, endeared by ties of consanguinity and affection, hours of sweet and holy communion in this blest retirement from a cold and calculating world."[39]

By stressing the importance of personal and emotional relationships between family members, Mrs. Riley and other advice-book writers created an image of the family as united by powerful ties of affection even though family members spent most of their time apart from each other. Although the eighteenth-century family had been tied together by common needs and economic necessity, the nineteenth-century family ideally was bound together by feelings of warmth and intimacy. Family relationships were supposed to be based on expectations of love and affection.

Figure 1.18
Most middle-class Americans liked to picture their houses as set in a protective, pastoral environment. (Advertisement, 1876. Courtesy Smithsonian Institution, Collection of Business Americana)

Two further consequences of the rigid distinction between home and work made by the advice-book writers are worth noting. When men's daily work was removed from the house, the home came to be viewed by the middle-class public more as a place of consumption than of production. Leisure activities, meals, and recreation thereby were invested with greater importance. Even the consumption of food was considered more as enjoyment than necessity. Mealtimes, they argued, should encourage the sharing of experiences around the family dining-room table. Home life was thus pictured as pleasant and fun. As a writer in the *American Builder and Journal of Art* declared, "if the family is the foundation of the State, home should be an association of individuals in which each has invested a good deal of existence, for which each must make a good many sacrifices, and from which each should receive large dividends of happiness." The business metaphor, with its emphasis on rewards, demonstrated the extent to which expectations about positive family relationships and personal happiness were central parts of the advice books' mid-century image of domesticity and the family home.[40]

By accentuating the split between the "separate spheres" of "work" and "home" and proposing the latter as a place of salvation and happiness, the domestic ideal, as promoted in almanacs and in the advice manuals of Lydia Maria Child and others, encouraged specialization of individual sex roles. If the male sphere of expertise was the commercial world, the female was expected to dominate at home. Her world was "the domain of the moral affections, the empire of the heart, the co-equal sovereignty of intellect, taste, and social refinement." As Sarah Josepha Hale, editor of the influential *Godey's Lady's Book*, explained, the woman was man's superior when dealing with moral and religious issues and when raising the children. "The province of the man, then," Hale continued, "is to find the means—it is the duty of the woman to use these means in such a manner as will secure the best interests and the purest enjoyments of the household with which

she stands connected." Another commentator was more blunt. "The home is the wife's province," advised the editor of *Hill's Manual of Social and Business Forms*. "It is her natural field of labor. It is her right to govern and direct its interior management."[41]

Although the housing and family reformers expected women to function primarily within the home, they stressed that careful attention to the moral and educational needs of the children would have a profound impact on society at large. As Sarah Josepha Hale explained, "And not only in domestic life is the moral effect of women's character and conduct thus influential, but the prosperity and greatness of the nation are equally dependent upon her." She and the other advice-book writers clearly expected that the moral example set by women would improve the nation by counterbalancing the corruption of politics and the aggressive commercialism of the business world. Women, insisted the reformers, could save and transform society.[42]

For all the emphasis of the family reformers on morals and social improvement, they also expected that women would become better masters of the household. The domestic obligations to bear and rear the children, sew, cook, and clean the house, wash, preserve food, and nurse the children still remained. In one sense, therefore, the family reformer's idealized vision of the cult of true womanhood helped to dramatize the power and influence of women at a time when the burdens of running the household were immense. Mothers could see their role as invested with a new moral purpose even as they did the dishes, took out the garbage, and scolded the kids.

Still, the ideal had considerable appeal for middle-class women because it clearly elevated them in status over those in the working class who had to work outside the home. In comparison to their less wealthy working-class counterparts who labored in the mills and had responsibilities at home as well, the trials of middle-class women were far less burdensome.[43]

Most advice manuals were surprisingly

vague when it came to giving specific advice on how to run the house. Even *Godey's Lady's Book*, like the self-help books written for young men, was preoccupied with warnings against neglect of responsibilities and contained little detailed advice. Some limited suggestions were made about arranging the furniture, but most books and articles held up abstract ideals, stressing the need for women to "hold the reins of family government," to exert "considerable self-sacrifice," and to work for "laws that shall be a wall of defense around the hallowed shrines of home, and a flaming sword that shall guard the paradise of pure affections." Continuous moral exhortations raised expectations and set standards for married women's behavior but left them free to decide how they should run the everyday affairs of the household. Perhaps that is why many of the most strident advocates of the cult of domesticity were women.[44]

By the 1850s women themselves were beginning to fill the gap created by abstract advice books and make specific recommendations about how the household should be managed. Probably the most influential of these writers was Catharine E. Beecher. A close friend of Mary Lyon, the founder of Mt. Holyoke College and an early convert to the need for women's education, Catharine Beecher published in 1841 her *Treatise on Domestic Economy, for the Use of Young Ladies at Home and at School*. Beecher's *Treatise*, which came out in yearly editions and was widely adopted by schools, was succeeded by an even more popular manual, *The American Woman's Home*, written with her sister, Harriet Beecher Stowe, in 1869. In many ways, *The American Woman's Home* was a distillation of conventional wisdom. Like the house plan books, it idealized the family as the "ablest earthly illustration of the heavenly kingdom," praised the wife as the "chief minister" whose mission was to provide an example of service and self-sacrifice, and set forth a vision of family life as the epitome of harmonious social interdependence. But in addition to depicting the idealized family and "Christian House," the Beecher sisters, whose father and seven brothers had all been minis-

ters, provided specific instructions to improve the efficiency, organization, and economy of everyday life. Cleaning, ventilation, heating, storage, laundry, food preparation, and house decoration were all subjected to meticulous attention. Their aim was to make the woman a professional home expert who was able to combine the latest technological innovations for stoves and washtubs with a basic understanding of Christian principles.[45]

The house that they designed was an unusual combination of traditional forms and new technology. As architectural historian David Handlin has pointed out, the basic plan was drawn from the eighteenth-century New England vernacular house with rooms placed on either side of a central fireplace core (Figure 1.19). To this layout was added gothicized details such as pointed windows, gable crosses, and bay windows. The overall design was described as being particularly suitable for a "colony of Christian people." Even the basement was redesigned to minimize the hauling of coal, water, and ice for the icebox. Yet the emphasis on design efficiency was justified as part of "the plainest requisitions of Christianity." Since the Creator was "a Being of perfect system and order," it was the responsibility of the Christian wife to manage her house with as much efficiency as possible. Therefore, the Beecher sisters' desire to blend traditional housing arrangements with the latest technological innovations was symptomatic of an American Victorian outlook that saw no contradiction in fusing the best of the past with the insights of the present.

Historians such as Dolores Hayden, writing from the perspective of contemporary feminism, have viewed Catharine Beecher as one of the central architects of the Victorian woman's entrapment within the home. No one would dispute that in setting up woman as both a spiritual authority and a professional homemaker Beecher set forth persuasive arguments for making woman into the authority at home. From Beecher's other writings, particularly her public letters to abolitionist Angelina Grimké, it is also clear that Beecher preferred women to

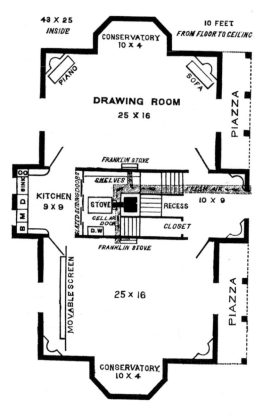

sibility to instill in the children "habits of submission, self-denial, and benevolence." Although Catharine and Harriet Beecher favored rewards more than penalties, they shared the more general belief that children were apt to get into trouble unless they were properly brought up. As another family reformer put it, "Cultivate it [the child] as carefully and as diligently as we may, weeds will spring up; but if we remove them as soon as they appear, they will be prevented from taking deep root, and from injuring those valuable and tender plants which it is our ambition to rear." Thus, the view of the vulnerability of childhood reinforced the emphasis placed by family reformers on the idea of the home as a refuge from the outside world.[47]

Adolescents, in particular, had potential for growth, but they were passing through a dangerous period of life marked by stormy tensions and great temptations. Some reformers feared that children had too much free time and needed even more supervision. Writing in the *Atlantic Monthly*, one author compared French to American families and suggested that "the moral restraints growing out of this haphazard combination of individuals [in America] into a family group are likewise feeble. Parental cares and duties, the material difficulties of living, prevented both father and mother from carefully superintending the education of their offspring." Other reformers like the Beecher sisters acknowledged that in a well-run household the parents would have to lead by example and teach their children through experience. Instilling correct "habits" was seen as particularly useful since such behavior would be carried on in later life when supervision was not possible. One almanac writer argued that these household tasks were the best preparation for adulthood. She glorified the value of her eldest daughter's role. "Now she presides at the table, now directs the kitchen, now amuses the fretting babe, now diverts half a score of little folks in the library. . . . Always ready with a helping hand and a cheerful smile for every emergency, she is an angel of love and a blessing to the home circle. Should she be called out of it to

address political issues indirectly through the family rather than by speaking publicly and agitating for the vote. But what Hayden tends to overlook is that for Beecher's generation of mid-nineteenth-century women the home *was* considered the center of power in society. Insofar as middle-class women in the nineteenth century accepted Beecher's idealization of the power of the family, and there is extensive indication that most did, the ideal functioned in the way in which Catharine Beecher intended—it made mothers respected authority figures and arbitrators of power within the middle-class family.[46]

The Beecher sisters also reserved special comments for the care and training of children. Like other family reformers, they believed that children were symbols of innocence who, nevertheless, were easily corruptible. Since adults were stronger and wiser, it was their respon-

originate a home of her own, would she be any less lovely or self-sacrificing?"[48]

The housing reformers were quick to accept the popular image of adolescent vulnerability and turn it to their own ends. Rural almanacs advised farmers to spend more attention on their farmhouses so that children would not leave home for the lure of the cities. Other reformers, recognizing that domesticity and service might not be all that appealing, expanded the earlier ideal of family togetherness by urging that even within the home circle, members of the family deserved a place to be alone. Thus they stressed the importance, if possible, of giving each family member his or her own special room. As Gervase Wheeler warned, "The young girl that, finding no intrinsic pleasure at home, nor regarding it otherwise than as the sphere for her domestic duties, would seek away from its shelter and with other companions . . . [find] pleasure and excitements neither so wholesome or refining as a fond parent would wish." To keep the children at home and to protect them from outside influences, the housing reformers urged that individuals be given their own special room. "Without it, it is only their father's home, not theirs. . . . But, by giving them their own apartment, they themselves become personally identified with it, and hence love to adorn and perfect all parts." The family home thus needed to have enough bedrooms to provide each member of the family with a degree of privacy and solitude. One reformer was blunt about the provision of separate spaces for children and adults. Children, he asserted, were noisy and disruptive. "I counsel every man who must have a corner to himself to fix his study in the attic," he warned, "for the only way to avoid noise without wasteful complication is to be above it."[49]

By the 1860s, the canon of domesticity for middle-class families that had been widely popularized by a host of writers and social commentators was thoroughly blended into an image of the ideal family home. The family was considered to be a hierarchy ranging from the husband at the top to the children at the bottom. It was a hierarchy in which each person was independent and had individual responsibilities and yet all were united by ties of affection and intimacy. Isolated from the outside world, the family served as a refuge to nurture, restore, and support its members. A utopian retreat from the crude and dangerous elements of society, it taught by example, shaped the character of the children, and exerted a corrective force on national development. Set off as it was from the corrosive activities of commerce and business, the family ideal separated life into distinct public and private spheres and held up somewhat different expectations for each.

This middle-class family ideal, so passionately defended, was ultimately not without problems. When closely examined, it was evident that a tension existed within this image of the ideal family between the encouragement of freedom and the need for social control. Children, for example, were given the opportunity and were encouraged to develop their own talents. But they were to do so within defined limits. Public behaviors were clearly spelled out; children were to be obedient and helpful, courteous and subordinate to the wishes of their elders. Yet they were also given their own rooms and an opportunity for privacy. Even within the private sphere, however, the reading of illicit novels or the touching of certain parts of the body except for purposes of cleanliness were forbidden. In short, the ideal family was designed to serve as a vehicle for enhancing the growth and development of its individual members, but mutual responsibilities and an appropriate sense of hierarchy and subordination were maintained.

The remarkable feature of this early Victorian ideal of the family—a feature that provides an insight into an idiosyncratic dimension in the middle-class outlook—was that the contradiction between freedom and social control was so easily accepted. Victorian Americans were not troubled by their apparently contradictory ideals for family life. Any inherent contradictions were diffused by emphasizing organic growth. Just as Abraham Lincoln could play down potential class conflict by stressing that the inherent abundance of American society would allow the poor who worked hard to rise quickly into the ranks of the middle class, family reformers and pattern-book writers insisted that initial subordination was not inherently unfair. Children might be subordinate now, but later when they grew up, they would achieve independence, freedom, and their own separate existence. Tight control and proper discipline early in life were the necessary prerequisites for the proper exercise of self-governance later in life. Without this initial discipline, freedom could only degenerate into anarchy.

Women, too, were caught between contradictory ideals. Catharine Beecher and other advice-book writers expected them both to be powerful centers of family morality and authority, and yet often pictured them as weak and prone to nervousness and ill-health. They were expected to be sweet, pure, and kind, and yet discipline the children and deal firmly with merchants and salesmen. Advice-book writers reconciled these contradictions by appealing to the authority of the Bible and to the New Testament vision of Jesus Christ. Deeply religious herself, Catharine Beecher expected mothers to imitate the example of Christ, to demonstrate their strength by being patient and self-sacrificing in their service to the family. For the ultimate reward for living this life of sacrifice and service would be salvation in the world to come.

Given the contradictions inherent in these middle-class ideals of women and the family, it is interesting to speculate about why such ideals were so popular among the family advisers and plan-book writers. I can only suggest that the families that had grown up during the recessions and depressions of the early nineteenth century and that had experienced the unsettling dislocations caused by immigration, urbanization, and westward expansion were not willing to pass on the improved economic conditions to their children without trying to protect them, too. In the chaotic world of the mid-nineteenth century, the hope for the future was based on an attempt to create new standards of behavior that would work for a mass society. Just as revivalism was a technique for bringing religion to a mass audience and the transformation of the political process under Democratic, Whig, and Republican parties was a means of organizing a mass electorate, deliberate creation of an ideology that idolized the home, women, and the family was an attempt to stabilize society. Both political parties and family ideology were mechanisms for mobilizing energies and yet keeping them under tight control. The instillation within children, for example, of a basic concern for self-discipline and self-control early in life seemed to them to be the best way to ensure that their children could enjoy the rewards of a progressive society. The idealization of the family and the emphasis on the cult of true womanhood were but attempts to guarantee that men and women would also discipline themselves and extend their energies to controlling society. One plan-book writer aptly summed up these concerns in the dedication of his book when he stated that it was written

To those, who happy homes have always
    known,
To those, who plan and work such homes to
    own;
To all, who building homes would bless
    mankind,
To all, who in their homes a refuge find.
To youth, whom wedded life will soon employ,
To children dear, each day their parents'
    joy;
To all who favor honor, truth, and love,
To all whose virtues promise homes
    above.[50]

Chapter 2

Dreams and Realities

Love, my dear ladies, is self-sacrifice; it is love out of self and in another. . . . Love is giving, not receiving.

—Harriet Beecher Stowe,
Pink and White Tyranny

By the middle decades of the nineteenth century, family reformers, feminists, architects, housing promoters, and plan-book authors had created and aggressively presented to the public a complete image of the ideal middle-class Victorian family. A benevolent hierarchy, united by ties of obedience and responsibility, the ideal family was to be the instrument for the reform of the nation. Within its walls, the individual would learn lessons that would guide him or her for a lifetime. "The experience of mankind has shown that the family is the best school for the development of character," explained the editor of the *Manufacturer and Builder*, a trade journal published in New York. "The child can be better trained at home than abroad; and the man and woman find a discipline in the relationships of home which life outside can never supply. This is indeed the function of the family—to perfect individual character."[1]

The authoritative tone of this comment, the emphasis on discipline and control, the expectation of progress, and the possibility of perfectionism that were endlessly echoed in the popular press testified to the power of the Victorian family ideal. Not surprisingly, expectations about the ideal family were also incorporated by plan-book writers into their most popular house plans. The layout of the rooms and the arrangement of the interior spaces were supposed to enhance the development of a family life that was built on interaction and affection, deep concern for others, and a sentimental vision of cooperation. The houses that were actually built were described in the same dramatic terms that domestic reformers had used to praise the ideal of the family. Like the family ideal, the newly designed homes were most often portrayed as radical innovations that would overcome the defects of older, more traditional Georgian and Greek Revival structures and help perfect society.

A number of questions naturally arise from today's perspective about the middle-class family ideal itself and the so-called innovations in the plan-book houses that were supposed to fulfill these expectations. Was the design and layout of the new Gothic, Italianate, and bracketed houses actually that different from that of the traditional rectangular Georgian and Greek Revival designs? Did these new house styles realistically support the reformers' vision of the family? Did the family itself function in practice the way the reformers envisioned it would?

As one might suspect, both the so-called innovations in design and the one-to-one correspondence between house layout and family ideals were exaggerated. Moreover, given the extraordinary promises made by the promoters and the reformers, actual behavior, as far as we can determine from the available evidence, fell short of the mark. Few house designs were radically new in terms of the interior plans. Few individuals or families could exercise the continuous self-denial and control within the context of the copious affection that was demanded by the middle-class home ideal. But what is most surprising is that the gap between the ideal and the actual behavior initially did little to undermine the ideal. If middle-class Victorian Americans sometimes failed to live up to promised expectations, most were unwilling to admit their faults in public. Although some complained privately that they lacked the patience and persistence to fulfill the ideal, they continued to support enthusiastically the goals advocated by family reformers and plan-book promoters.

Take, for example, the question of the relationship between the assumptions about the ideal family and the houses that were actually built. On the surface there appeared to be a close correspondence between the two ideals. Builders, plan-book writers, and architect promoters argued that the commonplace assumptions about the American family ideal were incorporated directly into their house designs. Like the ideal family, the home was portrayed in popular magazines and plan books as a sheltered retreat, a sanctuary set apart from the storms of commercial life. The illustrations envisioned the house as a protected Christian environment, visually associated with cross plans, stained-glass windows, and Gothic arches. The plan-book houses were almost always pictured in isolated rural settings. No other homes were visible and the surrounding trees and shrubs seemed to provide both a sense of spaciousness and a feeling of privacy. The popularity of towers or cupolas on the houses, which gave a clear view of the surroundings, was further testimony to the desire to dominate the natural landscape. In this ideal environment, the family was literally cut off from the dangers of the outside world (Figure 2.1).

As in the family ideal, where each individual was given a degree of independence and yet was expected to contribute to the good of the whole, the plan-book houses were depicted as containing separate but interdependent spaces. Architect Gervase Wheeler set forth his own theory in an 1855 book with the typical elaborate Victorian title, *Homes for the People in Suburb and Country; the Villa, the Mansion and the Cottage, Adapted to the American Climate and Wants. With Examples Showing How to Alter and Remodel Old Buildings. In a Series of One Hundred Original Designs.* The particular mix of old and new ideals, so typical of the mid-century pattern books, was implicit in Wheeler's title. His plans were especially suited to a natural environment and represented designs that were purported to be distinctively American. But the United States had been primarily rural throughout its first two centuries, so the pastoral setting was hardly original. And Gothic Revival houses were already popular in England.

Even more interesting was Wheeler's suggestion that one could either remodel older structures or could adopt a more original design. What his comment implied was that by 1850 traditional middle-class usage dictated a

Figure 2.1
This Italianate house in a protected, natural setting, like thousands built in the middle decades of the nineteenth century, was described as "a dwelling expressive of an air of modest and refined neatness." (*The Illustrated Register*)

Fig. 57 ITALIAN FARM HOUSE.

This design is intended to exhibit a dwelling expressive of an air of modest and refined neatness, free from any bold or prominent peculiarity of architecture. Its general air is that of the Italian style, presenting the varied outline and freedom from stiffness for which this mode of building is distinguished, but without a rigid adherence to architectural rules. It is intended for an intellectual family in moderate or comfortable circumstances, and either as a farm or suburban residence. Without any attempt at costly ornament, it aims to give a tasteful exterior. A profusion of decoration, or as commonly termed, "gingerbread work," is one of the most common faults in our newer country dwellings, much oftener showing a want of architectural taste than its presence.

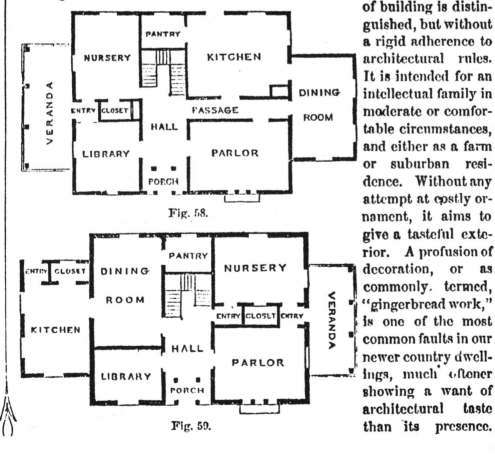

Fig. 58.

Fig. 59.

more or less accepted floor plan. What plan-book writers often praised as "innovations"—front porches, often called "piazzas," entrance halls containing staircases, front parlors used as drawing rooms, a second front room serving as a sitting room or dining room, nonpublic work rooms located at the back of the house and serviced by a secondary stairs, and upstairs rooms given over exclusively to bedrooms, at first segregated by sex, but increasingly assigned to individual members of the household—had become commonplace in middle-class homes by the 1830s and 1840s. So one could remodel a farmhouse, as Wheeler does in his plan book, to bring it up to date stylistically, without dramatically altering the interior spaces (Figure 2.2). Changes in style and ornament were far less expensive than those which involved moving interior walls.

If the so-called innovations in floor plans and room usage were only a codification of what had become standard middle-class practice along much of the East Coast, what was genuinely new was the careful manner in which the plan of the house was presented and justified. Gervase Wheeler's arguments, like those of other popular plan-book writers, were carefully revised to take the new middle-class family ideal into consideration. Using the kind of organic metaphor that was popular at mid-century, Wheeler argued that "a building is, in fact, as it were a human body; its parts are all dependent upon one another, and progressive in degree, and yet they are members of one united whole—imperfect if one be removed or not fully developed." By the phrase "progressive in degree," Wheeler meant that the individual development of each family member was compatible with the larger good of society. Like the laissez-faire economic theory that was coming back into vogue at mid-century and which implied that the individual's pursuit of his own economic self-interest would contribute to the social good, Wheeler and the other plan-book authors pictured their newly designed houses as self-contained entities which reinforced the cohesiveness of the whole family

while also providing for the needs of each individual member[2] (Figure 2.3).

Plan-book writers like Wheeler stressed that each room in the house, like each member of the family, should have a clearly defined role and function. Orson Squire Fowler, known widely for his writings on phrenology—the "science" that explained personality characteristics on the basis of the shape of the skull—supported this emphasis on room specialization in his popular plan book for octagon houses. "Merchants find the classification of their goods indispensable, or separate rooms for different classes of things," he wrote. "And why [is] not this principle equally requisite in a complete house?" Other plan-book writers suggested that the library, usually located near the back in a more quiet part of the house, was for the gentleman who "has either professional occupations, or literary taste." It had its own side entrance so that his comings and goings would not disturb the rest of the family.[3]

Upstairs, in similar fashion, space was reserved for "the lady of the house." It was expected that the wife should spend some time in her bedroom, reading her favorite books or doing needlework. Specialized rooms also existed for the children. A separate room upstairs was often designated as the nursery, indicating both the importance placed on the early years of life and the desire not to be awakened in the night by the crying of children. Although children of the same sex usually shared a bedroom, the ideal in the plan books remained that, if it were possible, each child should have a separate room of his or her own.

Plan books also designated rooms where the family could be together. One of these was the front parlor, which was supposed to be "accessible to visitors" and to display "elegance and the appearance of lady habitancy." Equal in importance to the front parlor was the dining room. As architect Calvert Vaux wrote in 1857, "it is in this apartment that the different members of the family are sure to assemble . . . and it is highly desirable that such a room should fitly and cheerfully express its purpose, . . . so

Figure 2.2
The Georgian house depicted in this best-selling print represents the way in which Gervase Wheeler would "improve" an old design by the construction of new porches or "piazzas." (Currier and Ives, *American Country Life. October Afternoon* [1855]. Courtesy The Harry T. Peters Collection, Museum of the City of New York)

Figure 2.3
Large, rambling, interconnected houses, like the one pictured in this lithograph, were designed to cater to the needs of large families. (Currier and Ives, *A Home in the Country* [undated]. Courtesy The Harry T. Peters Collection, Museum of the City of New York)

Figure 2.4
This early advice book, written in 1833, pictured mother and daughter talking together in an upstairs bedroom. (Abbott, *The Mother at Home*)

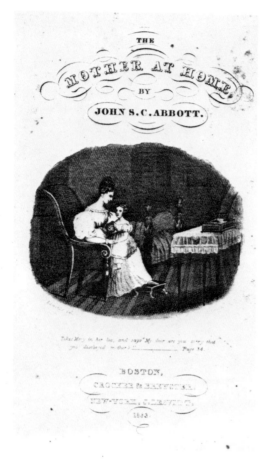

divisions had become an obsession. In the vast magazine and plan-book literature, the house grounds and floor plans were carefully designed to mirror this contemporary social preoccupation. Some spaces were clearly private. It was important, said the new housing promoters, that the service aspects of the house be hidden from the eyes of visitors. Kitchens were usually placed to the rear of the house, sometimes even in the basement. If the family were wealthy enough to hire servants, a back staircase was put in to give them access to the kitchen and keep them out of sight. Upstairs bedrooms, too, were clearly off-limits to the public (Figure 2.4). Although the stairs to the second floor usually occupied a prominent position in the front entrance hall, social conventions dictated that they should be used only by family members (Figure 2.5). As Florence Hartley insisted in her 1860 *Ladies' Book of Etiquette*, the proper lady should stay upstairs until the visitor's card had been brought up. Then it was appropriate to go and talk to that person in the front parlor.

Other spaces were clearly meant to be public. On the first floor the location of the front parlor and the elaborate suggestions for its furnishings implied that the parlor was to be a place for social interaction and display rather than for relaxation. Here the family could converse with friends, and the great transition moments in life—births, baptisms, graduations, weddings, and even funerals—could be celebrated with appropriate dignity. When individuals visited who were not close friends, relationships were defined by elaborate social conventions spelled out in considerable detail in the plan books and etiquette manuals. In her advice book, Florence Hartley, for example, advised the lady in polite society who wished to increase the circle of her acquaintances to go calling at another lady's house between eleven and two in the afternoon, but Hartley also suggested that she only stay between ten and twenty minutes. In a society where immigration, a highly transient population, and the desire to move up the social ladder sometimes strained personal relationships, the front parlor

as to heighten this constant and familiar reunion as much as possible." Vaux and other plan-book writers intended meals to be formal occasions at which the family could interact and enjoy one another. Hence it was important to stress both the functionality and the comforts of the dining room. Its easy access to the pantry or kitchen and the attractiveness of the room were supposed to encourage family members to spend considerable time there.[4]

Nowhere did the ideal middle-class house at mid-century fit more closely with the vision of the family than in the preoccupation with the separation of "public" and "private" spheres. Although the differentiation between public and private spaces in the house had been well underway by the end of the eighteenth century, by the middle of the nineteenth century such

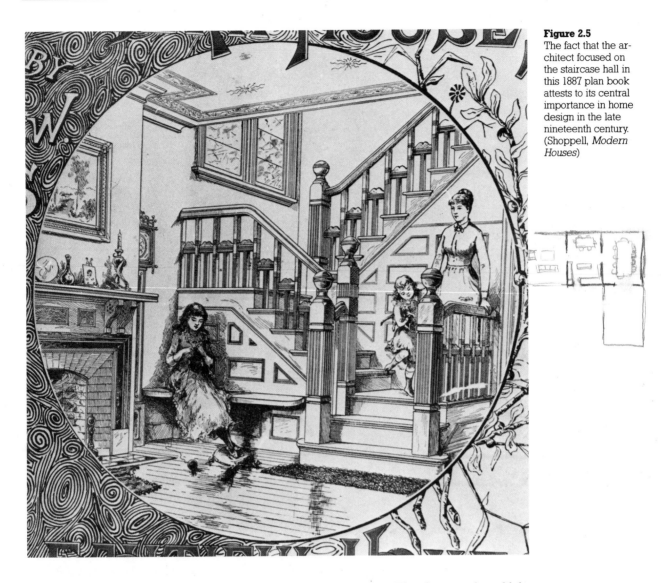

Figure 2.5
The fact that the architect focused on the staircase hall in this 1887 plan book attests to its central importance in home design in the late nineteenth century. (Shoppell, *Modern Houses*)

helped fill the need for a more controlled social environment in which the rules governing social interaction could be formalized.[5]

Plan-book writers also divided the grounds around the house into public and private spaces. By the 1860s and 1870s, a large front lawn had become an important symbol of status for the well-to-do, middle-class family, a means of extending the formal public spaces of a house beyond the front rooms. With its cast-iron furniture, elaborate plantings, and long walkway, the front lawn was clearly designed as a public area that would provide a sense of spacious formality. The front yard could be used as a site for croquet or badminton, or for greeting visitors. In contrast, the service parts of the house, including the barn or stable, were tastefully hidden behind a screen of evergreen trees or other plantings. Servants, who were increasingly necessary for the functioning of the spacious Victorian house, had their own back porches where they could enjoy the outdoors without being seen. And if the grounds were large enough, gazebos and grape arbors provided secluded retreats for family members who wished to be alone. Mid-Victorian Ameri-

cans left little to chance. Even the natural world, so seemingly wild and haphazard, was carefully planted to meet the accepted divisions between public and private (Figure 2.6).

In addition to those spaces that were clearly public and those that were private, a third category of spaces existed to mediate between the other two. The more important of these was the front entrance hall. Most mid-sized houses of three or four bedrooms contained a large public entrance hall filled with special furniture to hold hats, umbrellas, and calling cards (Figure 2.7). The hall served as a mediating space between the front porch and the library, front parlor, and dining room. By providing a separate entry into each room, it preserved the privacy and specialized functions of the other spaces. The front hall also was a formal space where guests could be greeted and visits announced to ladies or young daughters. The elaborate mirrored hallstands, as historian Kenneth Ames has pointed out, set the tone for the house, suggesting the importance of grooming and providing a backdrop for the ritual of card leaving (Figure 2.8).

According to the etiquette books, card leaving was a way of issuing or responding to invitations to young ladies, of sending sentiments of congratulations or condolence, and generally of ritualizing social relations. Card leaving was part of the more general practice of social calling for middle- and upper-class society. If a young man wanted to meet a particular young lady, he could have a female friend leave his card. If the young lady were not interested, she could simply fail to notice the card. Etiquette books described the proper duration of the social call, how to make polite conversation, and how to leave graciously without overstaying one's time.

The hall thus served as a vehicle for managing social relations. It had to be large enough to accommodate several visitors and give them a sense of the quality of the house. But it also was a place where people of different social status might interact on a more formal basis. The hall added ceremony to everyday life and revealed the importance of material possessions as indicators of the quality of life. As Ames has suggested, the hall was "a space which was neither wholly interior nor exterior, but a sheltered testing zone which some passed through with ease and others never went beyond."[6]

In addition to controlling the relations between public and private, the plan-book ideal family home, like the image of the family itself, expressed a clear sense of hierarchy. Not only were some rooms like the front parlor clearly more formal than others like the upstairs bedrooms, but the placement of the spaces signified the different values accorded them. The public rooms were located at the front of the

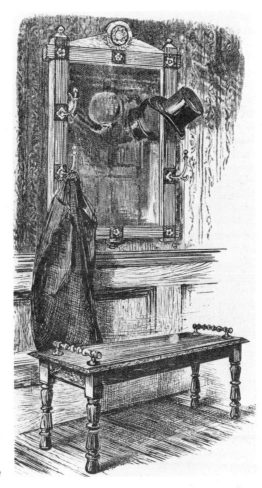

Figure 2.7
Special hall furniture was designed to accentuate the visitor's presence. (Cook, *The House Beautiful.* Courtesy Henry Francis du Pont Winterthur Museum Library, Collection of Printed Books)

house, the private ones to the rear. Each family, through its house, made clear its commitment to display and privacy as well as to its understanding of beauty and good taste.

If plan-book writers deliberately created a hierarchy of spaces within their designs, they were also concerned to balance public commitments with private needs by providing, where possible, individual rooms for each family member. At the same time that family roles were becoming more specialized and the limits of personal behavior in social situations were becoming more codified, there was also an attempt to enlarge the limits of private freedom. By deliberately drawing boundary lines in all segments of family life—by placing cast-iron

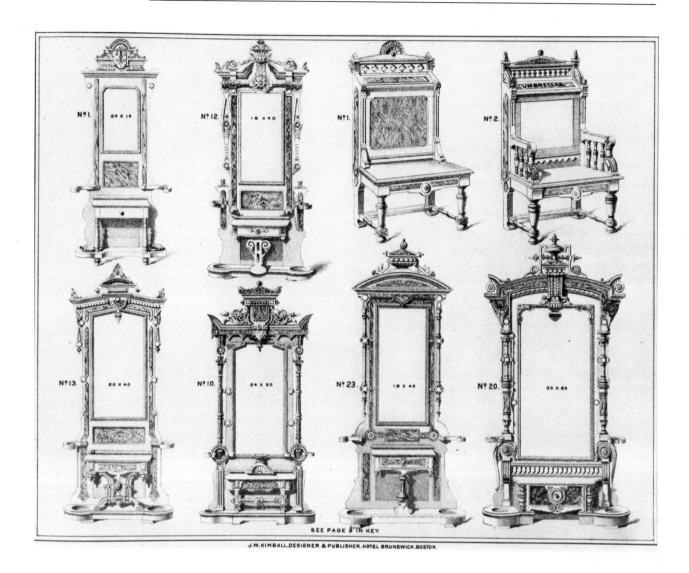

SEE PAGE 9 IN KEY.

J.W.KIMBALL,DESIGNER & PUBLISHER.HOTEL BRUNSWICK.BOSTON.

Figure 2.8
Ornate hallstands in the 1870s were available in a wide variety of sizes and shapes. (Nelson, Matter and Co., *Sales Catalog* [ca. 1878]. Courtesy Ken Ames and the Henry Francis du Pont Winterthur Museum Library, Collection of Printed Books)

fences around the lawns, by separating downstairs spaces within the house from the upstairs, public from private—mid-Victorian advice-book writers and housing promoters sought to encourage a greater degree of individualism, albeit within specifically designated limits. Mrs. E. B. Duffey, in her 1873 advice book *What Women Should Know*, put the matter bluntly when she asserted, "I do not accept the common definition of the word home which, if put into plain, brief language, would read, a prison-house for women. It has to me a broader, sweeter, grander significance. The true home is a world within a world. It is the central point of the universe around which all things revolve. It is the treasure-house of the affections, the one serenely bright spot in all the world, toward which its absent members always look with hope and anticipation" (Figure 2.9). Only within such a protected environment, Mrs. Duffey argued, could the woman develop her talents to the fullest.[7]

Given this vast body of exhortatory literature about the ideal house and family, what can be

A HAPPY FAMILY.

WOMAN

AS A WIFE AND MOTHER.

IN TWO PARTS.

COMPRISING

PART I.

ADVICE TO A WIFE.

PART II.

ADVICE TO A MOTHER.

BY

PYE HENRY CHAVASSE.

Written by one of the world's most celebrated physicians, and commended by the medical talent and most experienced midwives of this country. Every American woman who would retain health should carefully read this work.

PHILADELPHIA:

WILLIAM B. EVANS & CO.

740 SANSOM STREET.

New York, W. D. Myers, 37 John Street. *Boston,* L. P. Crown & Son, 199 Washington Street. *Chicago,* M. A. Parker & Co., 100 Madison Street. *San Francisco,* R. J. Trumbull & Co., 420 Montgomery Street.

said about the relationship between theory and practice? To what extent was the ideal of the middle-class family home carried out in everyday life? Although no precise statistics exist on the number of houses actually built, there can be no doubt about the enormous popularity of the plan-book designs. Practically every community had its Italianate, Gothic, and bracketed houses. Often, in older towns, the wealthier citizens first established a trend by building fashionable homes from plan-book designs that was later taken up by the middle class. But in the expanding cities on the East Coast and in the rapidly growing towns in the Midwest, the new styles were picked up by people of moderate means right from the start.[8]

Although most towns and suburbs eventually displayed a wide range of fashionable, new house designs, the process by which the new homes were accepted varied considerably from place to place. In some towns, particularly in New England, the older Greek Revival designs persisted with little change into the post–Civil War era. In others, there was a curious blend-

Figure 2.9
The image of a mother and her children resting in a peaceful setting near their house implied that women were coming to see the home as their own special place. (Chavasse, *Woman as a Wife and Mother*)

Figure 2.10
The carpenter who built this Gothic house in Bennington, Vermont, added classical columns to the side porch, thus violating the principles established by Andrew Jackson Downing, who urged that historical revival styles be built with utmost fidelity. (Photograph by author)

ing of old and new styles, much to the dismay of those professional architects like Andrew Jackson Downing, who argued for stylistic purity. In Bennington, Vermont, for example, a local carpenter built a plan-book Gothic house, complete with board-and-batten siding, steep-pitched roof, and pointed windows, but used Greek Revival columns to support the side porch (Figure 2.10). In Webster Groves, Missouri, Christopher M. Hawken, a successful businessman, built a home in 1857 with a traditional five-bay Georgian exterior, but the interior was given a more up-to-date cast by the addition of an elaborate entrance hall with a decorated newel post, front and back parlors, and a formal dining room. Yet another variation was evident in an Italianate house in Morristown, New Jersey, built in 1853, ostensibly following plan-book designs (Figure 2.11). Despite the fashionable exterior details, however, a vernacularized Georgian-Federal tradition was implicit in the overall structure, particularly in the steep pitch of the roof and in the symmetry of the three-bay main block with its

central tower (Figure 2.12). These traditional elements were skillfully made more fashionable by attaching a two-bay wing to the side of the main structure and by adding an elaborately detailed front porch, hooded round windows, and numerous brackets. These stylish details gave the house an up-to-date picturesque guise. In the Morristown home and in countless other homes, old and new were blended in a way that made change and innovation manageable and controllable.[9]

The South also had its plan-book adaptations. In Mobile, Alabama, where Italianate styles dominated, the same modification of old designs was evident. When Martin Horst, an early mayor of Mobile, built his two-story Italianate townhouse in 1867, he transformed the traditional five-bay brick house form into an Italianate villa by adding cast-iron window cornices and sills, large terra cotta brackets under the roof cornice, an elaborate cast-iron fence and front porch (shipped from iron works in Philadelphia), and a service wing set off at one side to the rear (Figure 2.13). He gave the

interior his own personal stamp by placing carved bas-relief busts of southern generals Robert E. Lee and Stonewall Jackson on the elaborate arch that separated the front and back parlors. Yet, despite its fashionable design and elaborate interior—complete with carved ceiling medallions and Carrara and Sicilian marble mantels—the house retained the formal symmetry of the traditional Georgian forms.[10]

From these examples it is clear that the earliest response of builders to the flood of new house plan books in the 1840s and 1850s was to graft the newer stylistic elements onto the more traditional forms. A well-documented case is that of Jacob W. Holt, who built more than ninety houses near Boydton, Virginia, and Warrenton, North Carolina, between 1840 and 1880. Clearly influenced by traditional builders' guides and later by plan books, Holt, as historian Catherine Bishir has pointed out, initially built large, boxy, five-bay houses using Asher Benjamin's Greek Revival design motifs. When he turned to the pattern books of Downing, Calvert Vaux, and William Ranlett in the 1850s, Holt often retained the traditional house forms but used details of mantels, win-

Figure 2.11
This 1869 photograph of the Crane family in front of their house, Acorn Hall, in Morristown, New Jersey, was typical of family portraits which identified the family with its home during much of the nineteenth century. (Courtesy Morristown Historical Society, Morristown, New Jersey)

Figure 2.12
Acorn Hall in Morristown, New Jersey, built by a doctor in 1853 probably from a plan book, is composed of Italianate and Georgian-Federal decorations. (Courtesy Morristown Historical Society, Morristown, New Jersey)

dows, brackets, and porches to give the structures a more Italianate look. Despite the pleas of the pattern-book authors that their designs should be adopted in toto, Holt and many other builders simply added new design motifs to make the traditional house forms more up to date.[11]

Another way to analyze the slow and haphazard process by which new designs were accepted is to look at the history of individual communities where the overall pattern of house construction can be seen as a whole. The towns of Westminster, Maryland, Kalamazoo, Michigan, and Galena, Illinois, are a case in point. All three towns experienced a burst of growth in the middle decades of the century caused by the arrival of the railroad and, in the cases of Galena and Kalamazoo, by the expansion of

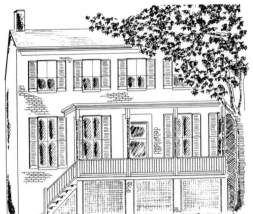

Figure 2.13
This Italianate adaptation of a traditional five-bay house was built by Martin Horst, the mayor of Mobile, Alabama, in about 1867, at a cost of $26,000. Its lavish interior was matched on the exterior by elaborate ironwork railings and fences that were made in Philadelphia. (*Historic Mobile*)

Figure 2.14
The Jacob Utz house, ca. 1800, of Westminster, Maryland, followed Georgian design, except for the rear wing. (Drawing by Humphrey Costello)

manufacturing. Westminster began as a rural hamlet in 1764 and grew slowly as a terminus on the main western Maryland turnpike route. In 1837, with a population of five hundred, the town became the county seat and business began to increase. But not until 1861, when the railroad arrived, did it grow large enough to support a variety of manufacturing and commercial establishments.

In Westminster, the typical house designs established in the eighteenth century continued on into the nineteenth. Thus when Jacob Utz, a German immigrant, built a home on Main Street around 1800, he followed the customary two-story, five-bay, symmetrical, Georgian design, deviating only from local practice by adding a wing to the rear (Figure 2.14). Continuing the eighteenth century's flexible approach to the use of space, Utz kept a small store in one of the front rooms where he and his wife sold candy and provisions. This traditional style continued to dominate house building in Westminster until just before the Civil War.

The first attempt to introduce plan-book designs to Westminster was made by William W. Dallas, a local businessman. Dallas built an Italianate mansion in 1855 using the fashionable brackets and chimney designs that were depicted in the nationally circulated builders' guides and plan books. But this precedent attracted little following because Dallas was driven out of town during the Civil War when

he sided with the Confederacy. Returning in 1869, Dallas built a new home on Main Street in the French Second Empire style, complete with mansard roof and soaring chimneys. Despite the use of plan-book exterior decorations, the most notable feature of the house was its retention of a traditional floor plan consisting of a symmetrical grouping of rooms around a central hall. Tradition was slow to change in Westminster.

The largest and most innovative dwelling in Westminster in the post–Civil War period was John L. Reifsnider's house, which was built in 1873 on a 4.75-acre hilltop site overlooking the city. Son of the local lumberyard owner, Reifsnider joined his father in business, then moved into the wholesale tobacco trade, and eventually became president of the town's largest bank and president of the Westminster Gas Company. In keeping with the Victorian sense of hierarchy, Reifsnider built his suburban villa on a summit overlooking the town, graphically demonstrating his preeminent role in community life (Figure 2.15). Yet like Dallas, Reifsnider failed to set a new trend in Westminster. Traditional styles persisted. When Charles V. Wantz, another prominent businessman, built a new home in the 1870s, he followed a traditional three-bay pattern, adding only superficial exterior details such as brackets, hooded windows, and an allegorical stained-glass fanlight. Despite the urgent pleas of the plan-book writers for total designs that would protect the family and reform the nation, Westminster's builders continued, like Jacob Holt in North Carolina, to stay with the traditional house forms.[12]

The acceptance of plan-book houses proceeded much faster in Kalamazoo than it had in Westminster. The citizens of Kalamazoo were willing to accept new house designs more readily than the people in Westminster probably because the town had grown a good deal more rapidly and the power of tradition was weaker. Founded in 1831, Kalamazoo quickly became a magnet for new settlers. In less than three decades the town grew into a major manufacturing center for the production of paper, cast-iron stoves, sleds, carriages, millwork lumber, and corsets. By the 1860s, the population had surpassed ten thousand.

The dramatic growth of Kalamazoo created a demand for new housing which the local builders quickly met by erecting a wide range of Italianate and bracketed plan-book houses. Unlike Westminster, the middle class took the lead in establishing new precedents. Typical of the smaller residences was the simple Italianate house built in 1859 by furniture dealer Edwin Corder. The modest house was a three-bay structure with low-hipped roof, heavy scroll-sawn brackets, and an ornate portico over the front door. The house sold a few years later for $1,650. Significantly, when Charles Bates, a very wealthy grocer and dry-goods merchant, decided to construct a new home in the 1860s, he chose the same Italianate style as the Corder cottage, borrowed his design from Samuel Sloan's plan book, *Homestead Architecture*, and erected his rambling brick-and-stone villa on an impressive hilltop site overlooking the city. The popularity of small Italianate homes continued into the 1880s. The Nancy Moore house, built in 1883, was typical of the continuing use of simple Italianate lines in a modest L-shaped structure.[13]

House-building practices in Westminster and Kalamazoo, therefore, seemed to support two oft-asserted plan-book arguments. One was that fashionable house designs could be built on a scale suitable for either the rich or the poor. The other was that the Victorian community, through the vehicle of the plan books, could be bound together by the acceptance of a common vocabulary of architectural design. Clearly the first assertion was accurate. Despite the elitism of Andrew Jackson Downing and the other plan-book writers who asserted that the houses of the wealthy should be made of stone while the cottages of the poor should be built from wood, and notwithstanding their continual argument that no person should build a house above his or her social standing, the fact was that they deliberately included designs for the laborer and working man as well as for the middle class and the wealthy. But in arguing that the same design vocabulary could be used for both rich and poor, they were not being as innovative as they insisted. After all, despite some regional variation such as for the Germans in Pennsylvania, for most of the previous century the same practice had been true. In New England, for instance, both rich and poor had built rectangular structures with Greek Revival details.

The use of a common architectural stylistic vocabulary to reinforce a sense of community, which the plan-book promoters also claimed as their great achievement, was in reality only the persistence of local building and design traditions. In Westminster, Maryland, on the East Coast, the traditional rectangular forms, a legacy from the eighteenth century, continued into the nineteenth. In Kalamazoo and other Midwest cities, where the starting point for their tradition was the Italianate styles, those styles became the accepted pattern and persisted into the 1870s and 1880s. In both cases the key to the persistence of design standards was not the plan-book persuasiveness but rather the general design conservatism of the community.

Like Kalamazoo, Galena experienced rapid growth in its early years. Prosperous lead mines and steamboat operations that connected the Galena River to the Mississippi quickly attracted settlers. The early immigrants from New England brought with them the traditional five-bay Greek Revival house with the usual room layout, a style that persisted from the first half of the nineteenth century (Figure 2.16). Even when the Greek Revival exteriors lost their vogue in the 1850s and were replaced with Gothic Revival or Italianate details, new houses continued to include the same form, floor plan, and arrangements of doors, windows, and roofs. The main difference was that after 1860 individual home owners expressed their particular preference for ornamentation by choosing their own elaborate millwork from the fashionable pattern books. As in Kalamazoo, the wealthy simply built enlarged versions of the most popular styles and sited them further up the hillsides that surrounded the town, preserving a literal sense of class hierarchy. Typical was the home of J. Russell Jones, a wholesale grocer and secretary and treasurer of the Galena and Minnesota [steamship] Packet Company. Jones's house was designed by a Chicago architect, but it was clearly recognized at the time as nothing more than an elaborate example of the usual Italianate plan-book design.[14]

The building practices in Westminster, Kalamazoo, and Galena reveal that what appeared as the almost universal acceptance of the new house-pattern designs was deceptive. Beneath the new styles and profusion of architectural detail, strong continuities with earlier vernacular styles persisted. The dramatic pleas of the domestic housing reformers for a radically new vision of the American family home were not fulfilled. Traditional living arrangements persisted. In places like Westminster and Galena, the acceptance of Gothic or Italianate exteriors had little impact on interior layout of the house. In Kalamazoo, in contrast, the new designs were more quickly adopted, but that was largely because the relatively new community had little tradition to build upon.

What made the arguments of the plan-book promoters most effective was that they had sensed the basic conservatism of the middle class and incorporated it into their design theories. Thus they could insist that their new styles were appropriate for both rich and poor, and

Figure 2.15
This house, built by John L. Reifsnider in 1873, had an irregular roofline that gave it a picturesque quality. (Drawing by Humphrey Costello)

Figure 2.16
The Chandler House, built in Galena, Illinois, in 1868 by a local dry goods merchant, had the same floor plan and window arrangement as the earlier symmetrical Greek Revival houses. (Drawing by Humphrey Costello)

could stress that a common building vocabulary would create a sense of visual community because both ideas had already become commonplace in rural and small-town America.

What is most clear is that the pattern books gave the home builder a new range of choices and alternatives in *ornament* and *philosophical justification*. Not only could the exterior details of the home and the overall design be modified or adapted to fit the needs of a particular family, but within the general rubric of "Italianate," a great variety of mass-produced woodwork made it possible to "individualize" a house. A new structure might fit the common aesthetic of a plan-book Italianate house, but it was possible, by choosing particularly detailed trim and accessories, to present the house as unique—the only one with that particular combination of features. Of course, the local carpenter in the eighteenth century who custom-made the molding and the trim for a local homeowner performed the same function. The difference was that with the advent of the plan-

book promoters, "individualization" of homes became easier and more fashionable.

Practicing architects, with their detailed knowledge of historical precedent, furthered this pattern of individuality within a mass style. Some architects simply used the plan book as a substitute for drawing up their own plans, as is indicated by a plan book in the University of Illinois library in which an architect has written in his client's name above particular pictures (Figure 2.17). Others, using the aesthetic standards set forth by Andrew Jackson Downing, Calvert Vaux, Gervase Wheeler, and their followers, designed each structure from scratch in consultation with the client. But even in those instances, family members often wanted to copy features of other homes that they had seen in the town.

The same was true for the small village carpenter. He could use the plan books directly or copy examples from the more prestigious local houses, using windows, doors, and trim that came from the same sash and blind mill. In the small village of Dundas, Minnesota, for example, the most impressive Italianate home was built in 1860 by John Sidney Archibald, founder of the town and owner of the local wheat-grinding mill (Figure 2.18). As the mill prospered in the post–Civil War period and the town expanded, the new residences of the mill workers, although modest in comparison with Archibald's house, adapted features of the mill owner's home. Here the front door would be copied, there the treatment of the windows, and in another house the detailing on the porch. Thus the common architectural vo-

Figure 2.18
The Archibald
family home in
Dundas, Minnesota,
helped set the style
for the small town.
(Photograph by au-
thor)

cabulary made possible by the trim and mill-work available in the town bore witness to the acceptance of a common architectural style.

The sense of shared values and reciprocal responsibilities so central to the Victorian outlook was often evident in the design of factories, workers' housing, and the owner's home. In Bennington, Vermont, for example, a local businessman, Henry E. Bradford, built his home on Main Street in the Italianate design (since modified by the addition of a Greek Revival porch), complete with spacious front lawn and elaborate coach house (Figure 2.19). He sited his knitting mill and the workers' houses on the stream across the street and built both structures in the same Italianate style (Figure 2.20). John Roebling, whose New Jersey wireworks helped build the Brooklyn Bridge, used an etching of his home and factory as the design for the letterhead of his business stationery (Figure 2.21). The unity of factory and house design together with the close proximity of the owner's house and workers' dwellings reflected the paternalistic attitude toward industrialization at mid-century. Workers were expected to identify with the outlook and ideals of the factory owners while the owner, in turn, was supposed to set an example of concern, rectitude, and responsibility. Mill owners used the image of the extended family to encourage cooperation and increase a sense of personal identity and individual security in the uncertain economic atmosphere at mid-century.[15]

If pressures existed within the factory towns and cities to accept similar styles, there was

Figure 2.19
The main house here in Bennington, Vermont, was a remodeled coach house, brought up to date at the turn of the twentieth century by the addition of a neoclassical porch. Both the main house and the newer coach house display the same flat roofline, cupolas, and brackets as the mill across the street. (Photograph by author)

Figure 2.20
The Bradford knitting mill in Bennington, Vermont, built in ca. 1854, burned in 1865 and was rebuilt that year. The bell in the cupola, a common feature of early factories, was used to signal the starting and stopping of work. (Photograph by author)

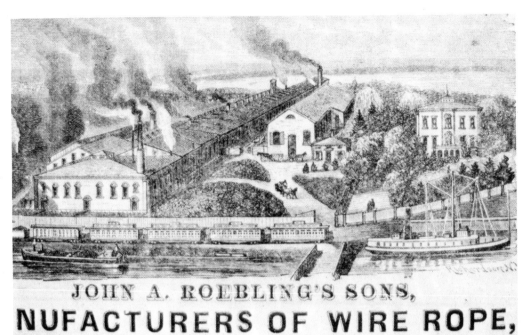

Figure 2.21
The pride that
John A. Roebling
took in his house can
be seen in the way it
is prominently pic-
tured on his letter-
head with his wire
factory. Notice that
both the house and
the factory shared
the hooded windows
of the Italianate
style. (Letterhead of
the Roebling Wire
Works. Courtesy New
York State Historical
Society, Coopers-
town, New York)

also an incentive to individualize structures by choosing slightly different ornamentation for the interior and exterior of the house. What made possible the preservation of individuality within a larger pattern of popular national house styles was the advance in millwork and construction technology. Power-driven shapers and scroll saws enabled Victorian lumber-yards at mid-century to turn out vast quantities of different moldings, brackets, window sash, newel posts, and shingles. These materials were made available to the builder through wholesale catalogs that gave a description and price for each piece of porch gingerbread or roof bargeboard, tin ceiling or wood rug—the inlaid veneer hardwood floor, three-eighths-of-an-inch thick, with walnut or mahogany banding (Figures 2.22, 2.23, 2.24, and 2.25). Until the turn of the century, the little advertis-ing that existed in these catalogs was primarily testimony to the quality of the goods produced, their cheapness in price, and the integrity of the company. Often they contained only a picture of the factory and a pledge to produce the

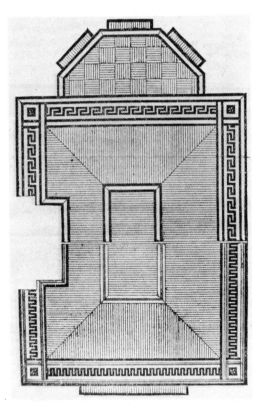

Figure 2.22
A late nineteenth-
century advertise-
ment for veneer
flooring, or "wood
rugs," as they were
called, shows the
various decorative
borders that were
available. This is a
good example of
mass-production
techniques that were
used on Victorian
houses. (Courtesy
New York State His-
torical Society,
Cooperstown, New
York)

Edwards Interlocking Metal Shingles

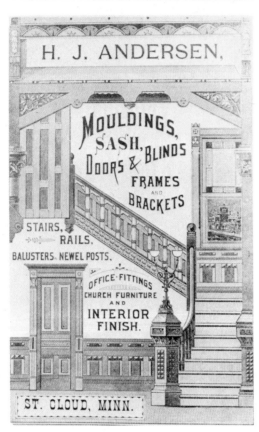

(1850) had no advertising, but later best-
sellers like George E. Woodward's *Woodward's
National Architect* contained more than seven-
teen pages, offering the latest in building materials, furnaces, and paints.[16]

The plan books thus served as an advertising
medium that helped to justify an expanding
housing market. Set forth initially as a means of
codifying aesthetic standards and creating a
demand for the services of architects, the books
succeeded far better than originally might have
been expected, setting new national stylistic
standards. But the success was far from total.
Readers felt free to violate the aesthetic canons
set forth in the plan books and to modify
or distort the plans in any way they wished.
They were encouraged to do so by a split that
gradually emerged among the plan-book writers themselves. Some, like Andrew Jackson
Downing in the 1850s and 1860s, argued for
explicitly following their directions. Others,
like Amos Jackson Bicknell in the 1870s, deliberately gave readers choices and suggested
variant combinations of details. The prevalence
of innumerable moldings and vast quantities of
mass-produced millwork, moreover, enabled
the readers to create their own distinctive
homes. Instead of using the services of trained
architects and following carefully set forth
theories of design, they were free to work with
the local carpenter and to avoid the use of an
architect altogether.

Nevertheless, the vast majority of middle-
class homes built at mid-century did reflect to
some extent the house promoters' and reformers' desire to create a new American domestic
housing ideal. Yet once the ideal was accepted,
the promoters and reformers lost control over
it. Although they could continue to plead for
purity of style and authenticity in historical
associations, the contractors and carpenters
who built the majority of houses adapted and
modified the structures as they wished. The
endless variations and adaptations of Italianate
and bracketed houses are themselves testimony
to the ingenuity and creativity of local builders.
Thus consciously and intentionally, middle-
class Victorian Americans at mid-century ful-

finest goods possible. Even early trade journals such as the *Manufacturer and Builder* concerned themselves primarily with technical details about construction and contained little
aesthetic justification for their choice of products. Since the catalogs contained almost no
advertising, the opportunity for advertising and
supplying a rationale for particular styles was
left open to the plan books. The early editions
of Downing's *The Architecture of Country Houses*

filled one of their own central goals—the preservation of variation within limits.

If the plan books and builders' guides increased personal choice by providing a range of alternative designs, they also helped justify the increased public emphasis on material possessions. The architectural reformers were always careful to stress that the house should fit the income and social standing of the individual. Most cautioned against the danger of building a house that was too expensive to maintain. "A cottage," wrote Samuel Sloan in his 1871 pattern book, *City Homes, Country Homes*, "indicates a disposition in the proprietor to live within his income, and to appropriate his means rather for the convenience and comfort of his family, than for show which he is ill-prepared to sustain." If it were wrong to overspend, however, it was entirely appropriate "to secure as much of display as [the owner] can afford to pay for." The good architect should combine "show" and "comfort" to reflect the individual's appropriate social status.[17]

When individuals did attempt to build an exact duplicate of a plan-book design, they often found that the results were more expensive than they had anticipated. When Henry Boody, a teacher of rhetoric at Bowdoin College in Maine, had a large, twelve-room, Gothic house designed by Gervase Wheeler, for example, he expected the price to be $2,500. Indeed, Andrew Jackson Downing listed a "slightly modified form" of the same house in his book, *The Architecture of Country Houses*, as costing not more than $2,800 (Figure 2.26). But in March of 1850 Boody wrote his mother that the house "actually cost me $5000, independent of the land for which I paid $1000." Still, what is significant is not the cost overrun, which few contemporaries would have known of, but rather the plan-book example that held out the hope that good housing could be built at a modest cost within the reach of any middle-class family. When Boody sold the house in 1870 and moved to New York City, he realized a profit on his investment, a profit that had been widely advertised by the plan-book writers. As they constantly emphasized,

Figure 2.25
Patent metallic weather stripping, like patent furniture, was valued in the nineteenth century as one of the many signs of progress. (Advertisement, undated. Courtesy New York State Historical Society, Cooperstown, New York)

"the man who buys a little cottage when he is first married, and continues to hold it, almost invariably accumulates property" and makes his mark on the world.[18]

The single-family home thus remained, as it had in the eighteenth century, an indicator of social class, but it now became an even more acceptable form of material indulgence. Since the home was promoted by the plan-book writers as a form of art and since the function of art was to uplift and inspire, the expenditure of large sums of money to document social status was now entirely legitimate. As Gervase Wheeler expressed it, "a well-designed and truthful building in a country place is a perpetual lesson, and the wealthy man that erects one does a good to the community that books and teaching cannot equal." In the hierarchical world where social differences were closely noticed, teaching by personal example, even if

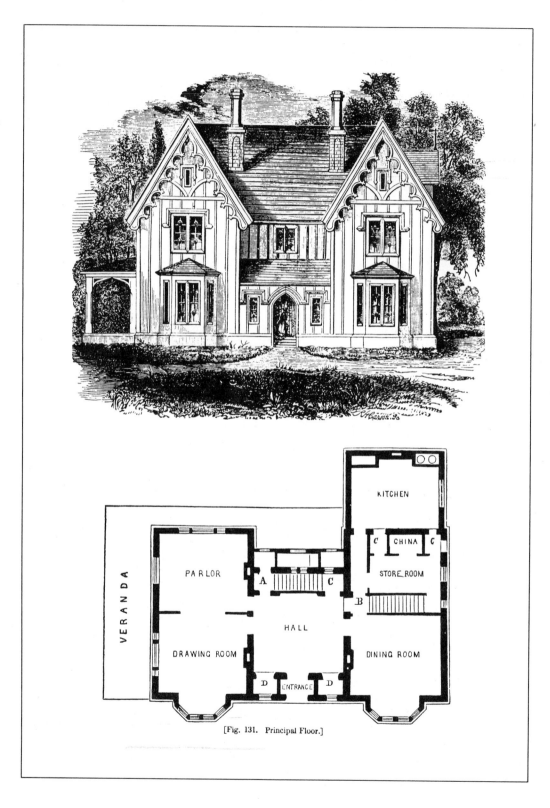

[Fig. 131. Principal Floor.]

it entailed elaborate expenditures, was now encouraged. Like Horatio Alger, who always urged the newsboys and city waifs to improve their personal appearance as the first step in climbing the ladder of success, plan-book writers argued for an appropriate emphasis on improving the material basis of family life.[19]

The limited but pervasive power of plan-book exhortations is most evident when one looks at the pattern of family life in the nineteenth century. All the theory about house designs and family relationships was ultimately influenced not only by individual preferences but also by the shifting composition of the family at mid-century. Using the most recent demographic studies it is clear that the nineteenth-century family was never a static unit; its composition was continually changing. The birth or death of children, their entry into the world of work or retreat from it if they lost their jobs, their marriages and departures from home, the housing of friends, relatives, or boarders, and the need to take care of the elderly all influenced the composition and size of the household. The basic statistics on population in this area are instructive. Life expectancy at birth in Massachusetts in 1860 was 46.4 years for males and 47.3 for females. But if the boy survived to age ten, his total life expectancy would be 63 years. What this meant was not that the average life expectancy was a great deal less than today—it was not—but rather that the high mortality rates among children lowered the average life expectancies for the population at large. If they lived past childhood, most people could expect to live a reasonably long life. The same life expectancies were probably a bit lower for the South and for parts of the Midwest because malaria, most frequent in the river country that was first settled, generally weakened young and old alike and made them more susceptible to other diseases.

The average couple at mid-century married when the man was 26.1 years and the woman 22. The first child usually arrived within a year or so, and children were born at regular intervals every two years thereafter. Although miscarriages and illnesses sometimes disrupted this pattern, women could expect to have between five and nine children over the fifteen or more years of childbearing. In practice this meant that some families had more than ten children while others had only two or three. Childhood deaths, too, were unevenly distributed. Most occurred within the first month of life or as a result of epidemic diseases such as smallpox or "throat distemper" (diphtheria). Even if the family were spared, they usually had close friends or relatives who suffered the loss of a child. Not until after 1900 did the mortality rate for children decline significantly.[20]

Within these families, the timing of the children's departures either to attend school, become an apprentice in the labor market, or leave home permanently varied much more widely than is the case today. Because schooling was somewhat haphazard during the first part of the century, the child might be placed in a public or private school for a few years and, if the family moved, be withdrawn and given most of his or her education at home. The same was true of working in the New England mills. In the 1830s and 1840s before the major influx of immigrants into Lowell and Providence, a teenage girl might secure a job in a mill through a relative and leave her family for a year or more to earn money on her own. Sometimes, if the mill were in her hometown, the girl might continue to live with her own family. If the mill were in a strange town, she would live in one of the carefully supervised boardinghouses. In either case, today's life pattern of entering the job market after high school or college was not common. Two-thirds of the early mill workers did not see millwork as a permanent position, but returned home and were married.

This changing pattern of family life at mid-century had important implications for the nature of house design. The large numbers of children and the extended period of childbearing meant that families had children of widely differing ages in the house. Today's phenomenon of the "empty nest," the household consisting only of parents whose children have left

[handwritten marginal note: Did this power to hinder the affectionate family relation?]

home, was not common. In addition to the continual presence of children, the family in the middle of the nineteenth century often took in aging parents. The limited studies we now have suggest that it was quite common to have married children return to live with parents before the birth of their first child in order to save enough money to buy a house of their own. If the children eventually moved out, the parents might then take in boarders to help with small chores and provide some additional income. But even when families did not often have to take care of elderly parents, they did have to put up, sometimes for months at a time, with visiting relatives, maiden aunts, and friends who were in the process of relocation.[21]

The large Victorian middle-class houses were well adapted to meeting these changing patterns of family life. The sizable number of bedrooms, sometimes including a first-floor room for "sickness and age," gave the home the ability to accommodate the needs of large families with either grandparents, boarders, or newly married children. The provision of rooms that could be closed off, the proliferation of entrances and exits, the construction of front and back staircases, and the placement of outside entrances at the front, sides, and back of the house allowed individuals to come and go with a minimum of disruption. Young married couples or boarders could live in such houses without interrupting the routine of the owners and still have some privacy. The large number of rooms allowed children to be separated from adults and their noise made more tolerable. The Victorian adage that in public "children were to be seen but not heard" tacitly recognized both the need for peace and quiet at certain moments and the tolerance of some degree of noise and confusion when children were at play.

The large number of doors—including large sliding partition doors between the front parlor and the back parlor—served the changing composition of the Victorian family well by allowing for the expansion or contraction of usable space. If a party were in process, a large area for entertainment could be created by opening the doors between the front and back parlors. But if there were few visitors during the cold winter months, certain rooms could be closed off to conserve heat. The house itself, by virtue of its size and the diversity of its enclosed spaces, provided a flexibility that matched the changing needs of the Victorian family.

The other notable feature of these houses was the size of the service areas—kitchen, attic, summer kitchen, and cellar. These areas needed to be quite large to support the large number of people in the household. To feed the family, heat the house, and supply water for washing (and for bathrooms which became more prevalent after the 1870s and 1880s) was a time-consuming and difficult task. The preparation of meals alone, which might require chickens to be killed and plucked, peas to be shucked, bread to be baked, and potatoes to be peeled, might take a significant part of the day. For the larger houses, servant help of some kind, whether live-in or visiting, was a necessity.

The kitchen was the place of activity. It had to be large both to allow preparation of elaborate, many-course meals and to moderate the heat of the stove. Since wood and coal stoves produced considerable quantities of heat when cooking, the Victorian kitchen needed to be ventilated by several doors and windows. Many houses in this period also added a summer kitchen, a room behind the main kitchen that could be used to prevent overheating the house during the summer and could also be used to contain the wood or coal burned in the winter. Since the Victorians bought flour and sugar in large quantities and had to prepare almost everything at home, pantry or cellar areas were needed for food storage.

Perhaps the most difficult chore in the Victorian home was the washing and ironing of clothes, which was often done in the kitchen. Before hot-water heaters became prevalent near the turn of the century, water had to be carried and heated directly on the stove. In the Midwest, where the minerals in well water made washing difficult, soft water had to be carried from cisterns that caught and stored

Figure 2.27
The implication of this trade card was that the "blue Monday" experience of washing could be tolerated more easily if helped by new inventions such as this wringer. (Courtesy Henry Francis du Pont Winterthur Museum, Joseph Downs Manuscript Collection/Mendsen, vol. 36, p. 3)

Figure 2.28
The Irish frequently worked as grooms and servants in the East Coast cities. This card displays the prejudice that they often faced. (Courtesy Henry Francis du Pont Winterthur Museum, Joseph Downs Manuscript Collection/Mendsen, vol. 36, p. 23)

rain. Washing and ironing clothes for the family on "blue Monday" could often take the entire day[22] (Figures 2.27, 2.28, and 2.29).

Running such a house, preparing meals and preserving food, cleaning the rooms, washing and ironing the clothes, caring for the children, and maintaining an array of flowers and plants that inevitably brightened the rooms was hard and time-consuming work. The image of the genteel middle-class woman, extolled by domestic reformers and plan-book writers, constantly collided with the persistent effort needed to run the mid-century Victorian house.

Despite the great flexibility of the Victorian family home, it, too, occasionally failed to meet the owner's needs. If the owner were pressed for space, he might add on to the original structure—an option made easier by the asymmetry and picturesque character of the Victo-

rian house—or he might move to a larger house. The numerous community and city histories attest to the frequent use of both options. In Dubuque, for example, William Ryan, a wealthy meat packer, built a large Italianate villa. When his family changed in size, he simply moved next door into a bigger house. And Currier and Ives, when they depicted the ideal Italianate family home at mid-century, pictured a striking plan-book structure in a setting with a stable that obviously was a holdover from an earlier era[23] (Figure 2.30).

This pattern of house use, while most common among the middle and upper classes, seems also to have been widely prevalent among all but the poorest people in the working class. The available evidence is fragmentary because the lower class left less written evidence, but the studies that exist for Massachusetts suggest that the home functioned in the

Figure 2.29
Trade cards provided a good indication of the time-consuming work necessary to run a house. Mrs. Potts' Cold Handle Iron (front and reverse of the trade card), though advertised as easing the chore of ironing, demonstrated the difficulty of using cast-iron irons. (Courtesy Henry Francis du Pont Winterthur Museum, Joseph Downs Manuscript Collection/Mendsen, vol. 36, p. 7)

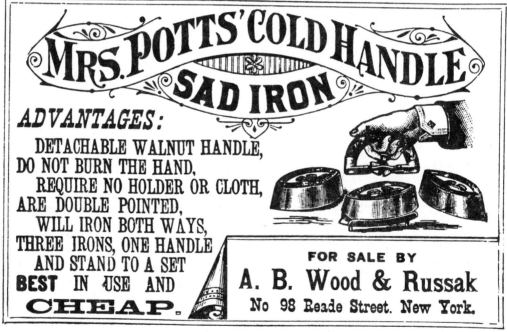

same way for immigrants as it did for the middle class. We know, for example, that the great majority of the adult population in the nineteenth century was literate and that the working class read avidly much of the advice-book literature. We also know that the elderly used the home as a form of economic security, particularly important during downswings in the economy when housing was scarce and taking in boarders could supplement a family's declining income. Where the pervasiveness of the advice literature and its support by the church set the tone for the thinking about domestic life at mid-century, the ownership of a house provided a degree of economic security that acted as a form of insurance against accidents and unforeseen financial difficulties.[24]

The difference between the housing reformers' ideal of the American family home and the actual pattern of everyday life can be seen in the experiences of Harriet Beecher Stowe. Examining the personal writings of a domestic reformer also enables one to discover the source of the reform ideals and to see how they worked in practice. As the historian Paul Boyer has suggested, regardless of their impact on society at large, the reform crusades clearly influenced the lives of the participants. Not only did participation in the reform movements provide a sense of identity and purpose for life, but it also established standards to aspire to and a self-consciousness about behavior that the reformers applied to their own lives.[25]

Harriet Beecher Stowe was born in 1811 into the large, extended family of Lyman Beecher, an intense Presbyterian minister who devoted his life to fostering revivals during the second Great Awakening. Because of her shared interest in religion, Harriet grew up with a sense of mission. She felt herself to be part of a cooperative family effort to improve society and spread the gospel. Accordingly, in the early 1830s when her brothers and sisters moved westward, she joined the family in Cincinnati and lived with her father who had just become the president of the newly formed Lane Theological Seminary. Four years later

she married the Reverend Calvin Stowe, a recently widowed professor at the seminary.

Like the heroines in her later novels, Harriet Stowe wanted to glorify woman's role as a wife and mother and to idealize her relationship to her husband. In her story "My Wife and I," Stowe extolled marriage "as something sacred as religion, indissoluble as the soul, endless as eternity—the symbol chosen by Almighty Love to represent his redeeming eternal union with the soul of man." She expected in her own life to have a harmonious home, where she and her husband would share their responsibilities and cooperate in all things. But her own experience failed to live up to the ideal that she portrayed so well to others.

The gap between the ideal and the real was evident early in Harriet Beecher Stowe's marriage. Her relationship with her husband was beset with continual crises. The arrival of seven children in twelve years and at least two miscarriages created the first strains and wore her down physically. The death of one child from cholera was traumatic, but the daily routine of washing, cooking, and caring for the children, especially when Calvin Stowe was away from home raising money for the seminary, proved even more frustrating. As she wrote to him in these early years,

> My dear Husband,—It is a dark, sloppy, rainy, muddy disagreeable day, and I have been working hard (for me) all day in the kitchen, washing dishes, looking into closets, and seeing a great deal of that dark side of domestic life. . . . I am sick of the smell of sour milk, and sour meat, and sour everything, and then the clothes *will* not dry, and no wet thing does, and everything smells moldy; and altogether I feel as if I never wanted to eat again.

With a daily schedule that began at 5:30 A.M. and included supervising two Irish servant girls, cleaning the house, teaching the children, and planning and cooking the meals, she was only able to keep up her spirits by believing that her work was part of God's plan for testing

Figure 2.30
To the left of this Italianate home is a stable which is obviously a holdover from an earlier period of time. (Currier and Ives, *American Country Life. May Morning* [1855]. Courtesy The Harry T. Peters Collection, Museum of the City of New York)

her strength and commitment to higher purposes.[26]

On her eleventh anniversary, Harriet Beecher Stowe wrote a letter to her husband, reviewing their life together. Most of her feelings were negative. The burdens of motherhood largely overshadowed its joys. "Here came in trail again sickness, pain, perplexity, constant discouragement, wearing, wasting days and nights. Ah how little comfort had I in being a mother," she mused, "and how all that I proposed met and crossed and my way ever hedged up!" The few positive moments in her life came not from being home, but when she left husband and children to visit her brother Henry Ward Beecher in Cincinnati. Only her brother's house provided the "calm, placid

quiet retreat I have been longing for." Indeed, Harriet Stowe's health was so disturbed and her mental stability so shaken by the burdens of raising her family that she retreated for almost a year to a water cure in Brattleboro, Vermont. The physical difficulties of child-rearing and the tensions and apprehensions about her purpose in life soured her marriage. As she wrote in one of her many complaining letters to her husband, "sometimes it [seems] as if anxious thought [has] become a disease with me from which I could not be free."[27]

The difficult years of childbearing convinced Harriet of the need to protect her sexual and emotional autonomy from the desires of her husband. To defend her health, she felt it necessary to limit her sexual contact with him, much to his consternation. Angry and frustrated, he retaliated by complaining bitterly and urged her to take over the burden of home finances.[28]

Despite and perhaps because of her difficulties in managing the home, bringing in additional income through writing, and living with her husband who was moody and demanding, Mrs. Stowe had no doubts about her inner strength and her own power as a woman. To Calvin Stowe's worrying letters about the family debts, she responded that he lacked faith. "My love if you were *dead* this day—and I feeble as I am with five little children I would not doubt nor despond nor expect to starve. . . . Were I a widow standing just as I am I would not have one fear." She was confident that Jesus Christ would take care of them, and she made it clear that she herself felt capable of running all the family's financial matters.[29]

As historian Mary Kelley has suggested, Harriet Beecher Stowe's fictional vision of the self-sacrificing wife was closely tied to her frustrations with her own family. Although she admitted to her husband that "I do not love and never can love with the blind and unwise love with which I married," her pronouncements in *Pink and White Tyranny* that "love, my dear ladies, is self-sacrifice; it is love out of self and in another" and that "love is giving, not receiving" were indicative of the way in which she rationalized her own needs. The ideal of self-sacrifice for a higher good justified her writing to support the family and the denial of her husband and children which that implied. But her commitment to wifehood and motherhood both made her captive to an ideal and allowed her to express freely her own ideas on religious and social subjects. Denied the ministerial role that her father and her brothers held, Mrs. Stowe compensated by controlling her own life, asserting her autonomy within the household, and writing novels and advice books.

The extent of her success could be seen not only in her accomplishments as a writer, particularly after the publication of *Uncle Tom's Cabin* in 1852, but also in the ways in which she managed family affairs and problems. In

the 1860s Calvin Stowe retired from Andover Theological Seminary and the family moved back to Hartford, Connecticut, to be close to Mrs. Stowe's sisters, Mary and Isabella. In 1866 they built their own home, sold it when factories began to encroach, and took up residence on Forest Street, close to the home of Mark Twain. Despite the new surroundings, managing family affairs continued to take much time. The oldest twin daughters, Hattie and Eliza, never married and lived at home. Mrs. Stowe had to support them and also financially help out Charley, who entered the ministry, and Georgiana, who married a minister. The eldest living son, Frederick Stowe, was wounded in the Civil War and became an alcoholic. He was in and out of institutions until he disappeared in San Francisco in 1866. As a writer of some fame, Mrs. Stowe also had to deal with the scores of visitors and well-wishers who came to see her at home.[30]

Mrs. Stowe's new house, built according to the standard plan-book assumptions, aptly met the needs of her family (Figure 2.31). The ground floor consisted of a small front veranda, a large front entrance hall complete with umbrella stand and Gothic side chairs, and the traditional front and back parlors (Figure 2.32). The parlors were spacious enough to entertain visitors and both contained large bay windows, so closely associated in the public mind with graciousness and hospitality (Figure 2.33). Each room was decorated with paintings and a collection of statues.

Like other Victorian Americans, Harriet Beecher Stowe clearly demonstrated her moral, artistic, and religious concerns in the furnishings of her parlors. Her own life demonstrated that she had accepted the implicit belief, widely shared in the 1850s, that the woman of the house should be its major decorator. In the front room she displayed an impressive collection of books, a large picture of her favorite brother, Henry Ward Beecher, the Brooklyn preacher, and a copy of Galadaou's religious painting, *The Madonna of Goldfinch*. In the rear parlor, she placed a tufted sofa and a "square" piano on which she played hymns and

Figure 2.31
Harriet Beecher
Stowe's house in
Hartford, Connecti-
cut, built in 1871,
was similar to the
plan-book houses de-
signed by Calvert
Vaux and Gervase
Wheeler. (Courtesy
Stowe-Day Founda-
tion, Hartford)

Figure 2.32
The floor plan of
Harriet Beecher
Stowe's house has
the traditional dra-
matic entrance hall,
front and back par-
lors, and multiple
porches or verandas.
(Courtesy Stowe-Day
Foundation, Hart-
ford)

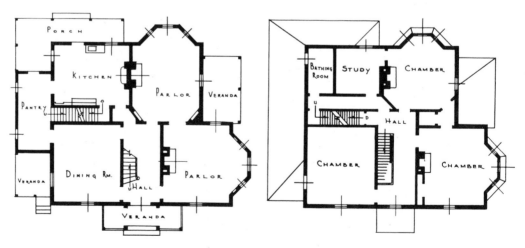

Figure 2.33
This picture of Harriet Beecher Stowe and the front and rear parlors provides an insight into her ideas about pattern and decoration. (Courtesy Stowe-Day Foundation, Hartford)

spirituals. As she and her sister Catharine Beecher had suggested in the *American Woman's Home*, Mrs. Stowe framed the bay windows with plants rather than with heavy drapes, as was the usual custom. Whereas the front parlor served well for entertaining the stream of literary guests and relatives who visited, the back parlor was the family retreat where the Stowes could read, play cards, and sing.

To the left of the entrance hall was a formal dining room which was connected to the kitchen by means of a pantry. Mrs. Stowe kept a large potted orange tree in the front window to remind her of her winter home and her orange grove in Mandarin, Florida. Like the other first floor rooms, the dining room was decorated with print wallpapers and the doorways were framed with heavy moldings. The dining room table could serve eight or ten people and the sideboard had realistic carvings of birds and

fruits on its doors and panels. In one corner stood a "whatnot" table and shelf containing mementos from Mrs. Stowe's travels and some of her china. The overall decor of the room displayed the mixture of patterns in tablecloth, wallpaper, and rugs that Victorians loved because it represented the complexities of the world of nature.

The dining room was separated from the kitchen by means of a pantry which kept out the noise and heat of cooking. An outside entrance allowed the help to come and go unnoticed and enabled delivery people such as the iceman to load the icebox without disrupting the family. A back staircase connected directly to the kitchen.

Upstairs, the arrangement of rooms fit well the needs of the Stowe family. The left front bedroom over the dining room was occupied by the Stowe twins, Hattie and Eliza, who never married. Across the hall was Calvin's bedroom where he pursued his biblical studies. Calvin's bedroom was connected to Harriet's by a curious passageway which doubled as a closet. Given Harriet Stowe's ambivalent attitude toward sexual relationships and the continual existence of grown daughters in the household, the connection between Harriet's and Calvin's bedrooms allowed them to pursue their own separate interests and to keep private any encounters that did take place.[31]

Harriet Stowe's bedroom was also connected to a small sitting room which she used as her study. There she worked on some of her thirty-five books of essays, short stories, and novels. The location of the study in her home allowed her to write and at the same time to minister to the needs of her children and her husband, particularly during his later years. The house thus allowed her to fulfill her image of the ideal Victorian woman, combining as it did the goals of service, sacrifice, independence, and morality. First and foremost, she was devoted to her own family; only secondarily was she a writer. And yet the tensions and ambiguities in this dual role were never far below the surface. She wrote to her husband, "You must not expect very much writing of me for it drinks up all my strength to care for and provide for all this family—to try to cure the faults of all—harmonize all." And she urged him "to try to be considerate and consider how great a burden I stagger under." It was difficult to live up to the mid-century ideal of the American family. But such responsibilities brought their own sense of mission and purpose as their rewards.[32]

Harriet Stowe's experience with her home and family had its unique features—no two families were ever exactly the same—but the strengths and limitations of the mid-century Victorian ideal of the American family home are inherent in her life. Like most Victorian Americans, she had high expectations about her family life. Like most, too, she realized that it never came as close to the ideal as she would have liked. But that neither caused her to lower her expectations nor to stop trying to improve herself and her household. What it did do was to perpetuate a sense of guilt, frustration, and, at times, self-righteousness. Harriet Stowe was always conscious of her burdens and responsibilities, but family ties provided her both with a sense of mission and a degree of mutual support. To look at her letters to her brother before she wrote *Uncle Tom's Cabin* is to see how much encouragement and reinforcement the two gave each other. The constant, candid expression of ideals and frustrations in letters and conversations also acted as a safety valve. If the middle-class Victorian ideal of family life created inevitable frustrations for both husband and wife, the commitment to improvement, the frankness about one's own limitations, and the constant discussion of problems dissipated inherent conflicts. The Victorian commitment to accepting individual differences and to providing "separate spheres" in which individuals might express their emotions and concerns provided a means of living with family frustrations and problems. The strength of the family bonds, the commitment to sacrificing for the children, the intense ties of affection and emotion, and the sense of mission all made the middle-class Victorian family at mid-century a remarkably strong institution. By virtue of the constant reaffirmation of the domestic ideal in plan books, family-advice manuals, and sentimental novels, even those men and women who had doubts about the ideal—and the frenetic quality of the affirmation suggests that many did—were forced to commit untold energies to making their own families function smoothly.

The Victorian house exhibited some of the same tensions that were implicit in the family ideal. Given the eclectic nature of styles and the wide range of choices portrayed in the plan books and in magazine articles, it was technically possible for a middle-class family to choose a house that would fit its particular aspirations. A persuasive theory of aesthetics and mass-produced lumber and millwork made the Victorian house appear to complement the middle-class family ideal. Many houses seemed to provide that combination of decorativeness and show, formality and privacy, freedom and control that Harriet Beecher Stowe and middle-class Victorians wanted. But trying to put theory into practice was always difficult. Financial resources were often limited. Compromises in style and design were almost inevitable. Finding an appropriate house from those that happened to be on the market was often troublesome. Nevertheless, as the proliferation of plan-book houses attest, most middle-class families did modify their homes to satisfy their own tastes and interests. Thus, with the appropriate interior decorations and historical associations, the middle-class plan-book home could become a statement of the personal values of a family.

The advice-manual and plan-book crusade for a new ideal for the middle-class family home was ultimately, like most reform movements, only partially successful. The inflated rhetoric used to describe the homes and the idealization of family life raised expectations in a way that made them difficult to realize in practice. Valued family relationships required more than an appropriate physical setting. What the vast literature of advice manuals and plan books did supply were new stylistic criteria for the middle-class family house that carefully blended older practices with more up-to-date fashions. Along with the advice manuals and religious tracts, the plan books also helped codify a persuasive ideology about the role of women within the home.

The result for women was clearly a mixed blessing. If the cult of domesticity gave women a new identity and a greater power within the home, it also created difficult expectations for behavior and placed significant restrictions on their activities in the community at large. Although the plan-book writers and family reformers had envisioned a perfect home life that would dramatically improve society, the reality remained one in which each individual family had to work out its own compromises. The new styles for single-family homes did not result automatically, as the reformers and promoters implied, in matrimonial harmony. Middle-class Victorian Americans who accepted the family ideal at mid-century had little choice but to try and mediate the problems that inevitably arose and to accept some degree of conflict within the family as a necessary part of the march of progress in which they believed.

Chapter 3

The Suburban Neighborhood Ideal

Put your money where it will be safe and sure to increase, and buy yourself a residence where the pure air will prolong your lives and make your children strong.

—*Chicago Tribune*, August 29, 1880

So it is, that in the present age, all great communities are providing themselves, with individual effort, with country houses, to be enjoyed in common with a city business, and the improvements and conveniences of city life.

—*Descriptive and Pictorial Catalogue of . . .*
    Eden Park Property

The Victorian ideal of family and home had achieved wide public acceptance by mid-century. Praised from the pulpit and popular press, touted by architects and social reformers, it had become part of the popular middle-class litany of Victorian life. The irony was that at the very height of its public acceptance, sweeping social changes were taking place that were to modify the ideal in the 1870s and 1880s in subtle but important ways.

At the root of these changes was a spectacular population growth and a consequent demand for new housing. The massive nature of these changes is sometimes overlooked. In the three decades before the Civil War, the urban population of the nation had expanded over 700 percent, growing from 500,000 to 3.8 million. This feverish growth had been the catalyst for the early housing reformers' view of the city as an emblem of chaos and disorder. The post-war increase was even more astounding. The high birthrate, together with the influx of more than 11 million immigrants, forced urban growth to skyrocket. New York City's population alone in 1900—3.4 million—almost equaled the nation's total urban population in 1850! Up and down the eastern seaboard, in the river cities of Pittsburgh, Cincinnati, and St. Louis as well as in the lake cities of Buffalo, Cleveland, Detroit, Milwaukee, and Chicago, the spectacular pattern of expansion was similar. Changes of this magnitude could not help but create new opportunities for housing developers, architects, and social reformers alike.

Consequently, the last third of the nineteenth century was marked, as architectural historian Gwendolyn Wright has pointed out, by a power struggle between architects, plan-book writers, builders, and social reformers to gain control of this vast new middle-class housing market. At stake were not only millions of new customers and the opportunity to make a fortune but also the ideals of home and family and the chance once again to remake the single-family housing standards for the nation.[1]

If the struggle to improve the ideal of the American family home in the last three decades of the nineteenth century was similar in many respects to the housing reform crusade that had preceded it, there was one crucial difference. The debate over national housing standards in the later period benefited from a transportation revolution that now allowed middle-class families to move to the suburbs and commute to work. Beginning with horse cars (horse-drawn railway cars) and later with steam railroads and electric trolley lines, the expanding transportation facilities helped promote a new vision of suburban neighborhood living that stood in glaring contrast to what the middle class perceived as the evils of urban life and replaced what, a scant thirty years earlier, had been a rural ideal.[2]

The outstanding feature of both the growth of the suburban ideal and the struggle for power among architects, plan-book writers, developers, and social reformers was the internal dynamic of the debates. Positions no sooner emerged on either the question of the ideal house or the most desirable feature of neighborhood life than events forced their modification. When architects criticized plan-book designs for lacking aesthetic coherence or practical layouts, the pattern-book writers shifted their rationales to emphasize the artistic value of the house and stressed the practical arrangements of kitchens and service areas. When reformers stereotyped cities as dangerous and degrading, urban planners and landscape architects redid areas such as Back Bay Boston and the Chicago street system by constructing libraries, museums, and parks to give the city a new sense of monumentality. The spectacular urban growth thus pushed the debate about both landscape design—the city versus the suburban neighborhood—and family and home ideals to the logical extension of earlier positions. Too much was at stake in terms of money, power, and influence for the ideals to remain static.[3]

Plan-book writers were among the first to shift their tactics in the 1870s in an effort to gain greater public approval. The most influential advocates of residential design in the pre–Civil War era, men such as Andrew Jackson Downing, Gervase Wheeler, Calvert Vaux, Samuel Sloan, and Minard Lafever, had all been professional architects. They had written treatises on the theory of aesthetics and the nature of design to improve national housing standards and to promote the need for trained professionals. They hoped thereby to elevate their own status. Not content only to design commercial and public buildings, they attempted, with some success, to capture a part of the expanding market for single-family housing. Although they were joined by reformers like Orson Squire Fowler, the expert on phrenology, who preached the virtue of octagon houses, and writers like Catharine Beecher, who hoped to place housework and childraising on a more professional basis, the architects themselves set the aesthetic standards and provided—admittedly often by borrowing from European sources—the most convincing rationales for particular styles. In the postwar years, in contrast, builders, contractors, and plan-book publishers set forth the most persuasive arguments for revising standards of taste and beauty.[4]

The shift can best be seen by comparing the publications of Henry Hudson Holly, an established architect who had apprenticed with Englishman Gervase Wheeler, with the plan books of the Palliser brothers, two builders from Bridgeport, Connecticut. Holly's first book, *Holly's Country Seats* (1863), was similar to the plan books written by Andrew Jackson Downing and Calvert Vaux. Like these earlier studies, Holly's book was as much a literary effort as it was a book of plans. Holly began with a chapter on the history of architecture, proclaimed the importance of the arts as "a mirror in which we may see reflected the character of a people," and pleaded for an American domestic architecture that "culled" from the structures of all ages and countries "those features which are applicable to our requirements." Like Vaux and Downing, he saw life in the country as an antidote to the evils of the city and as a place where children could grow up more freely and naturally. His homes were "isolated and independent," "free from all intrusions," sited in picturesque scenery, and designed in what he called "the *American Style,* the Hudson River bracketed" (Figure 3.1). These designs mirrored the earlier image of the home as a protected retreat, cut off from the crime and ugliness of urban life.[5]

Little more than a decade later, Holly published a collection of articles, originally written for *Harper's Monthly,* under the title, *Modern Dwellings in Town and Country, Adapted to American Wants and Climate* (1878). These new plans display the continuities with and modifications of the earlier plan-book outlook. Affirming earlier views, Holly asserts that he is furthering the cause of American democracy by leading a crucially important national reform that will provide model homes for the middle class. Like the earlier writers, too, he celebrates the virtues of a rural America. What is new is his case for creating parklike suburban developments within easy commuting distances from the city center. Using arguments drawn from the aesthetic theories of the romantics, Holly presents one of the earliest rationales for suburban neighborhood living.

Holly suggests that a number of families should "club" together and procure "an attractive spot, filled with shady nooks or pleasant streams, which can by mutual agreements, and with some slight restrictions, be laid out in a picturesque manner for building." Such families, he asserts, would have a unique opportunity for creating a parklike neighborhood on the outskirts of the city. Like Central Park in New York, Prospect Park in Brooklyn, and the Fenway in Back Bay Boston, these planned

neighborhood settings could be designed to uplift and inspire the homeowner by reaffirming the romantic ideals of the beautiful, the sublime, and the picturesque.[6]

Holly argues that a properly designed suburban housing development would bring forth particular responses from the homeowner; the beautiful would elicit cerebral appreciation for pure and refined beauty; the sublime, a sense of awe at vistas of great distance and vastness; and the picturesque, an emotional feeling based on the evocative sentiments of home and countryside. Holly is particularly concerned about the relationship between the house and its site. Since most middle-class homes, because of cost limitations, could not be built on a grand or monumental scale, Holly suggests that they should try to evoke picturesqueness. Only a house on a hillside with a grand view of the surroundings could provide a true sense of sublimity. The problem, Holly maintains, is that most developers ignore the topography of the land, subdividing the ground into a rectangular grid and auctioning off the lots. They thereby lose the opportunity to create a sense of the sublime. Thus they should pay more attention to roads and design them carefully to meet the natural curves of the landscape and to take advantage of the significant vistas and distant perspectives.

Similarly, too, whereas Downing and Vaux had borrowed from Englishman John Ruskin's moral theories that related domestic architecture to the character of the family, Holly cribbed his ideas from Charles Locke Eastlake, a member of the Royal Institute of British Architects, who published his *Hints on Household Taste* in 1868. Where Eastlake stressed simplicity of design, particularly in furniture making, and the use of simple, straight-line ornament, Holly used Eastlake's theory to attack Gothic forms and argued for an "American style" following the "Queen Anne" designs currently being used in England. The irony of his argument is that Holly never defines what the "free classic, or Queen Anne" style actually is. Unlike Downing and earlier plan-book writers who insisted that the revival of a historical

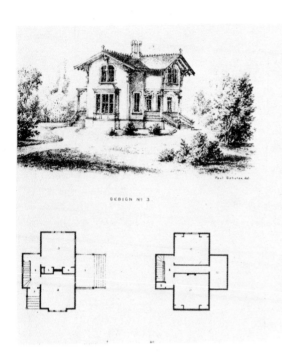

DESIGN No. 3.

FIRST FLOOR PLAN.

1. Veranda.
2. Sitting Room, 15 × 16.
3. Dining Room, 15 × 16.
4. China Closet.
5. Closet (Dumb Waiter).
6. Hall.
7. Porch.

SECOND FLOOR PLAN.

8. Hall.
9. Linen Closet.
10. Bedroom, 13 × 16.
11.   "   15 × 16.
12.   "   8 × 14.

It is often imagined by those who desire to build economically, that beauty is an extravagance in which they cannot indulge, and therefore that a cheap cottage can necessarily have no pretensions to elegance, and barely suffice for the comfort and shelter of its occupants: no higher aim is attempted. This error arises from the false but prevalent idea that beauty and grace are entirely extraneous considerations, rather matters of ornament than proportion and symmetry of parts. For this reason many small houses, whose owners wish to render them objects of taste, are loaded down with unmeaning and expensive decorations, or so frittered away with cheap and ready expedients of boards sawn, cut, planed, and otherwise tortured into utter uselessness and absurdity, that the entire building becomes subordinate to its

Figure 3.1
This house, built at a cost of between $800 and $1,000 near the Morris and Essex Railroad in South Orange, New Jersey, has projecting eaves and large brackets which, the architect suggests, gives it "a pleasant expression of shelter." (Holly, *Holly's Country Seats*)

style must be faithful to tradition, Holly is more eclectic. Other than insisting that it is suitable for "nearly all classes" and that the "picturesque" quality of Queen Anne design is more easily accepted by the public in the country and in "suburban parks" than in the city, he leaves the reader to guess what the main features of the style are[7] (Figure 3.2).

Indeed, Holly's basic eclecticism made his own house designs in some ways the antithesis of what Charles Eastlake had suggested. Whereas Eastlake had reacted against the overly ornate, machine-made woodwork and argued for the inherent worth of particular forms, Holly delighted in "the introduction of irregularities, such as projections of roofs, canopies, verandas, and bay-windows," changes by means of which he hoped to increase the strong contrast between light and shade (Figures 3.3 and 3.4). Variety of colors, diversity of surface treatments, and large decorated chimneys are the hallmarks of his designs. Although Holly cautions his readers not to make colors too bright or to overdecorate the roof with fancy slate, his designs are considerably more elabo-

rate than the simple Italianate or Gothic structures in pre–Civil War plan books.

The other major feature of Holly's plan book is its attention to practical detail. Most of the chapters are devoted not to specific plans—which seem incidentally included as illustrations—but to topics such as specifications, roofing, chimneys, plumbing, heating, and ventilation. He advises on how to test for leaky pipes, how cesspools should be built, what the advantages of steam heating are, and how to interpret the charges and fees of architects. The self-interest in this latter section is apparent. While Holly constantly defends the availability of rural cottages as part of the "economy of country life" and stresses that they may be built even by those of modest means, it is quite clear from the size of the houses pictured and their estimated cost that he is designing primarily for the middle and upper classes.[8]

The trend toward stylistic eclecticism and a looser, more interpretive schema of decoration is even more evident in the best-selling plan books of the Palliser brothers, George and Charles. An English immigrant who arrived in

DESIGN No. 1.

1. Porch ; 2. Main hall ; 3. Kitchen, 10 × 17 ; 4. Living-room, 10 × 12.—*Estimated cost*, $2200.

DESIGN No. 2.
First-floor Plan.

1. Vestibule ; 2. Parlor, 15 × 23 ; 3. Dining-hall, 14 × 18 ; 4. Dining-room closet ; 5. Butler's pantry ; 6. Kitchen, 14 × 16 ; 7. Main stairs ; 8. Back stairs ; 9. Kitchen closet ;
10, 10, 10. Verandas.—*Estimated cost*, $4500.

First-floor Plan of Design No. 2.

the United States in 1868, George Palliser worked as a master carpenter and was a co-owner of a sash-and-door factory before joining with his brother in the 1870s to design residential structures and speculative city blocks. When demand for his designs increased, Palliser published in 1876 his first booklet, *Model Homes for the People, a Complete Guide to the Proper and Economical Erection of Buildings*. Unlike the more lavish and expensive plan books such as A. J. Bicknell's *Village Builder*, which sold for $10 a copy, Palliser's book was printed on cheap paper and cost only twenty-five cents. Its low cost was underwritten by almost twenty-two pages of local advertising (Figure 3.5).

The great success of the book, which sold more than five thousand copies, came from the innovation in selling that Palliser pioneered. The inexpensive booklet suggested a variety of low-cost popular designs to the public. If a prospective client were interested in any of the designs, he could fill out the questions listed on a tear sheet in the back about cost, size of lot, and details. When the sheet was mailed to the Pallisers' office with the appropriate fee, which ranged from fifty cents for lithographed plans of a popular $3,000 house to $40 for a more complex $7,500 home, detailed sketches of the front, side, and rear elevations of the houses pictured in the book and floor plans would be sent out. If the client wished Palliser to custom design a house, the client would have to answer a series of questions about cost, use, and site. Once the answers were received, the finished drawings would be provided for 2 percent of the building's cost, a savings of 1.5 percent over the usual architect's fee of 3.5 percent for plans, specifications, and detailed drawings.

This experiment in mail-order architecture

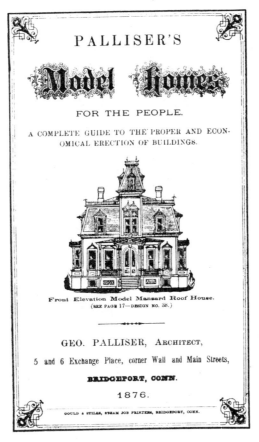

Figure 3.4
This picture shows Holly's fascination with details that give the house a sense of individuality. (Holly, *Modern Dwellings*)

Figure 3.5
Palliser cleverly ties propriety to economy in his title. (Palliser, *Palliser's Model Homes*)

proved remarkably successful. Unlike Henry Hudson Holly, who was interested in educating the middle-class public about his philosophy of design and thus, indirectly, promoting his own talents as an architect, Palliser made it possible for the public to work directly with him, either by purchasing detailed plans of the houses pictured in his books or by having him design a new structure for them at a reduced rate. As a result, thousands of Palliser buildings were constructed throughout the country. By reducing the cost of the expensive client-architect relationship, Palliser's books allowed the rural builder to get expert advice at a minimal price. As Michael Tomlan has suggested, the fact that more than fifty thousand copies of *Palliser's Useful Details* (designs for gates, mantels, bookcases, gables, etc.) and *Palliser's Specifications* were published, meant that most builders and carpenters in the country in the 1870s and

1880s would have heard of the firm. By combining a wide range of house styles with practical advice on building construction, Palliser proved to be far more influential than professional architects. As *Every Man a Complete Builder*, the subtitle of one of his popular books suggested, Palliser democratized the house construction process by arguing that any person with a minimum of professional help could supervise the design and construction of his own house.[9]

To this end, Palliser's books were full of advice and exhortation. If the emphasis in the Holly books was on the talents needed by the architect, the stress in Palliser's writings was on educating the client. The person who contracted to have his own house built had to have "working power," a thorough knowledge of business, energy, tenacity, character, common sense, an eye for detail, and the strength to

Figure 3.6
Palliser stressed the flexibility of his plans and the fact that a house might be redesigned for two families. (Palliser, *Palliser's Model Homes*)

DESIGN NO. 10.

FRONT ELEVATION.

Is a very handsome house as will be seen by cut, arranged for one family or can be used to equal advantage by two families; 1st floor, parlor, dining room, kitchen, pantries and closets, and 2 chambers; 2nd floor, 5 rooms, etc.; cost to erect as plans now are for 2 families, $3,500, and for one family with improvements, $500 additional.

Plans and specifications, $20.

DESIGN NO. 11.

FRONT ELEVATION.

Cheap Cottage, neat and suitable for mechanic of taste; 1st floor, parlor, dining room, kitchen and pantry; 2nd story, 3 chambers, hall room and good closets. Cost, $2,000.

Plans and specifications, $10.

assert his own authority. The point in planning was to design the house the client himself wanted, regardless of what other self-styled neighborhood experts thought. "You may be very inexperienced yourself in building," asserted Palliser, "but if so your architect should know enough for both himself and you, and while your busy neighbor may ply you with his wholesale advice, you need not sacrifice yourself to any whims or suggestions he may make. Never mind how much he don't [*sic*] like your large roof, your gables, or your internal arrangements, if they are what you want; go straight ahead in the path you have marked out." The point was that a house should be an expression of the owner's preference. Palliser's firm could provide the minimal advice and expertise necessary to make this self-expression a reality.

Although Palliser condemns the lack of taste in the "ignorant village carpenter" and local builder and warns the reader about the dangers of shoddy construction, he has almost nothing to say about the stylistic features of his "cottage" designs, except that his plans are simple, flexible, convenient, and comfortable. In a later plan book, he asserts only that "American Homes of today [are] not, however, of any well-defined style of Architecture, except what may be termed our National Style," a reference to the eclectic approach. He does not identify individual plans in his books in terms of a particular historical style. Instead Palliser asserts that the designs preserve the individuality of the true artist. "Simple things become beautiful and attractive by an art inspiration," wrote Palliser about one of his designs. "Interiors and exteriors retain their old forms substantially, but they put on new faces when touched by the real artist, who sees his work completed in his mind when he begins to plan, and so is enabled to produce a harmony throughout."[10] (Figure 3.6).

Here was the secret to Palliser's philosophy of design, an outlook that was to become extremely popular in the late nineteenth century. Neither the floor plans nor the layouts of his houses were unusual. The division of space on the first floor into the formal entrance hall, front and back parlors, and kitchen was essentially the same as that which had been pictured in the pre–Civil War plan books. What was new was the greater emphasis on artistic affect, the heightened sense of the home as personal expression, and the dramatic transformation of roofs and siding to appear both "useful and ornamental." To achieve the desired "artistic" impact, the external and internal features of the home became more exaggerated, the designs more varied, and the ornamentation more profuse. The goal was visual delight (Figure 3.7).

In such an atmosphere, the distinctions between Queen Anne and Eastlake styles were blurred. To some extent, houses became little more than assemblages of intricately machined, factory mass-produced ornament. Whereas some architects referred to Queen Anne in

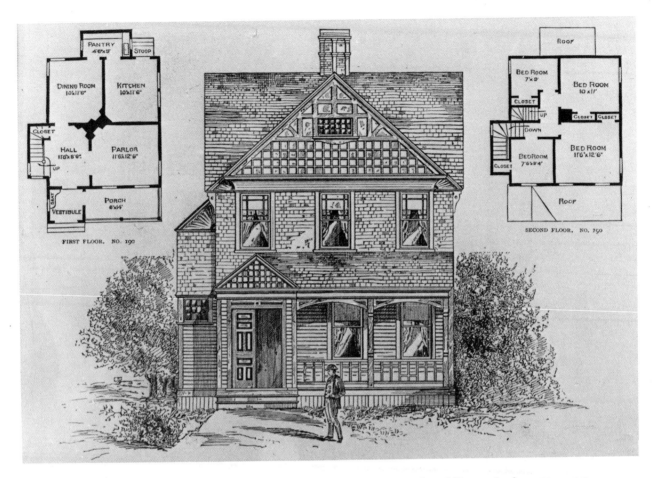

PANTRY 4'6"x9' STOOP

DINING ROOM 10'x11'6"   KITCHEN 10'x11'6"

CLOSET

HALL 11'6"x8'6"   PARLOR 11'6"x12'6"

UP

VESTIBULE SEAT PORCH 6'x14'

FIRST FLOOR. NO. 190

ROOF

BED ROOM 7'x9'   BED ROOM 10'x11'

CLOSET

UP

CLOSET CLOSET

DOWN

BEDROOM 7'6"x11'4'   BED ROOM 11'6"x12'6"

CLOSET

ROOF

SECOND FLOOR. NO. 190

terms of stone and brickwork exteriors, decorative half-timbering, large casement windows, and grouped Tudor chimneys, and others described Eastlake as detailed spindle ornament with tablelike braces and stairway balusters framing doors and windows, the two styles in practice were difficult to tell apart. The complicated and sometimes bizarre combination of detail, the fascination with broken surface and texture, and the assumption of romantic inspiration and symbolic reference made the notion of stylistic purity or integrity of design difficult to support (Figures 3.8 and 3.9).

Not that the professional architects did not try. They did. By the 1880s, when Congress lowered the postage rates for magazines, a number of new journals appeared to support professional practice. Fearful that the mail-order firms would undermine the practices of independent architects and would lower the fee that could be charged, the *American Architect and Building News*, published in Boston, and the *Inland Architect*, published in Chicago, both lashed out against George Palliser, Robert W. Shoppell, and the other "cheap" plan-book authors who purported to be architects even though they lacked formal training. In article after article these magazines lambasted the plan-book writers, using a wide range of arguments to attack the mass-produced designs. One critic, more charitable than some, specifically criticized designs "conceived in what is spoken of by the unprofessional American as the 'Queen Anne style.'" The destructive feature of these plans was that they "depart from the vernacular in that they are emphasized by scroll-work panels, false half-timber work, overhanging gables, marvelously-shaped

Figure 3.7
Shoppell was one of Palliser's major competitors for the mail-order business. This house was designed with expansion space in the attic. (Shoppell, *Modern Houses*)

brackets and piazza posts, and windows of all sorts, shapes and sizes, in ordinary and untoward positions, most of these things wrought in wood and all suggesting of the knowing in such matters of the question of repairs." The comment about repairs is instructive. Some architects, even in this age of extravagant designs, argued for the functionality of their own work. They criticized the multiple roofs that trapped snow and leaked, and they railed against the wasted spaces in plan-book houses. In place of the more common designs, they offered to cut costs, minimize repairs, avoid unnecessary labor, and provide "the greatest amount of display at the least possible expense." The trouble was that the Pallisers and other plan-book writers could easily counter these arguments. They, too, advised their clients on how to deal with the local builder, cut costs, and minimize re-

pairs. And it was usually cheaper for the homeowner to borrow ideas from a plan book and have the local carpenter build the house than it was to hire the services of a professional architect.[11]

Although the architects continually emphasized their mastery of the principles of design and construction, surprisingly few of them in their major journals stressed their knowledge of the plumbing, heating, and lighting technologies. In part, this was because some new technologies like electricity were not completely proven. In the 1880s, one architect even suggested that electric lights should not be used because they caused freckles. As late as 1893, in the *American Architect and Building News*, R. H. Patterson asserted that gas, not electricity, would continue to be the chief means of lighting for years to come because its

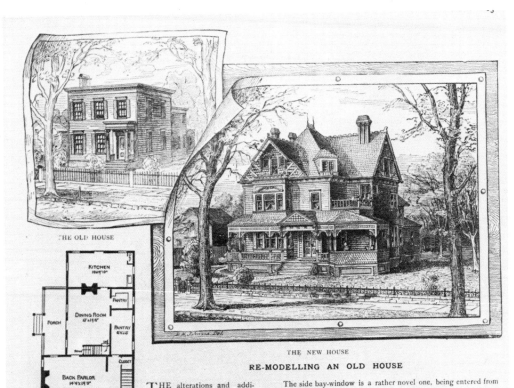

THE OLD HOUSE

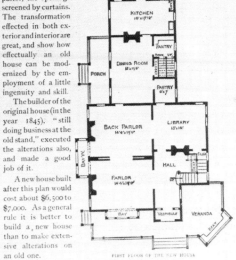

THE NEW HOUSE

FIRST FLOOR OF THE OLD HOUSE

RE-MODELLING AN OLD HOUSE

THE alterations and additions to the old house were as follows: A large portion of the side wall was removed and a wing 8 ft., 8 in.x24 ft. added to the right side; the rear part of the old hall, partitioned off with a part of the new wing, formed a library; the old-fashioned straight staircase was removed and a handsome new one, with landings, erected in that part of the hall formed by the new wing.

A new chimney was built between the library and the hall, serving for each.

In the library and in the front parlor, Jackson's ventilating grates are used, effectually heating the first and second stories, and at the same time giving the cheerful effect of the open fire.

The large front veranda is new, and with its 12 ft. deep secluded bay, formed by the staircase hall, is a feature that is much liked; the side veranda was re-modelled to conform to the style of the other changes.

Large bay-windows were added to front and side.

The servants' staircase was removed from the dining-room and put out of sight, with entrance from the pantry.

The high slated roof that was added in place of the flat tin one gives a fine attic, with four good bed-rooms.

The second story contains five large bed-rooms and bath-room

The first story was re-trimmed throughout, in modern style, with hardwood.

The side bay-window is a rather novel one, being entered from both parlor and back parlor, the openings screened by curtains. The transformation effected in both exterior and interior are great, and show how effectually an old house can be modernized by the employment of a little ingenuity and skill.

The builder of the original house (in the year 1845), "still doing business at the old stand," executed the alterations also, and made a good job of it.

A new house built after this plan would cost about $6,500 to $7,000. As a general rule it is better to build a new house than to make extensive alterations on an old one.

FIRST FLOOR OF THE NEW HOUSE

Figure 3.9
This Greek Revival house was "remodeled" by making the profile and the surface more complex, a change that became popular in the 1880s. (Shoppell, *Modern Houses*)

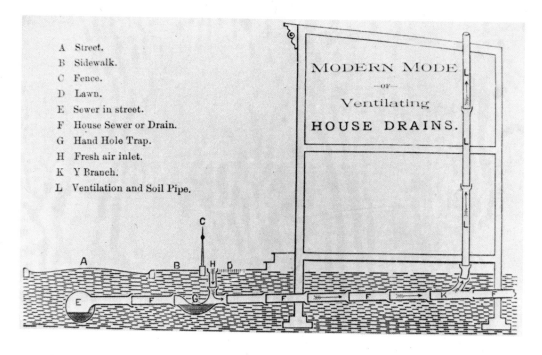

A   Street.
B   Sidewalk.
C   Fence.
D   Lawn.
E   Sewer in street.
F   House Sewer or Drain.
G   Hand Hole Trap.
H   Fresh air inlet.
K   Y Branch.
L   Ventilation and Soil Pipe.

MODERN MODE
—of—
Ventilating
HOUSE DRAINS.

"softer and steadier light" was preferred for sewing and reading. Gas light was not only more similar in color to kerosene and candlelight, but its yellow-orange tint fit in better with the pastel and maroon colors of the house interiors. Perhaps, too, the architects were reluctant to champion new forms of heating or plumbing because of the unusual range of options and the swift pace of technological change.[12] One architect, Frank L. Smith, wrote in his 1887 advice book, *A Cozy Home: How It Was Built*, that the homeowner had a choice of three heating systems—hot air, hot water radiators, or steam radiators. But Smith never stated his own preference. Concerning the plumbing, all he suggested was that the fixtures be "well-trapped" to prevent the entry of sewer gas into the house (Figure 3.10). Yet he insisted that houses designed by architects were better than those put up by the local carpenter. Judging by the numbers of plan-book houses actually built, the public was not convinced by such arguments.[13]

If some architects were neutral about the new building materials and technologies, others were distinctly hostile. Henry Hudson

Holly decried the replacement of the old family fireplace by the modern hot-air furnace as "an abomination grievous to be borne by those who remember fondly the ancient symbol of domestic union and general hospitality." In the 1870s, Russell Sturgis, an architect who had studied at the Academy of Fine Arts and Sciences in Munich, Germany, wrote a detailed article in the *North American Review* protesting against the mass-production techniques that had destroyed the older building trades. "The work of the planing-mill, the jig-saw, the cut-nail machine, the molding mill, the new arts of working iron and cast iron, the introduction of artificial stones and thin metal imitations of stone cornices and dormers" had destroyed the older integrity of design and construction. Instead of stone carvers who chiseled the cornices, there was a machine that stamped out cheap tin imitations. Instead of wood-carvers, a hydraulic press squeezed wood into intricate carved shapes. Knowledge of the crafts was being lost forever, according to Sturgis, and the link between form and function was being eliminated.[14]

To reestablish their authority as the custodi-

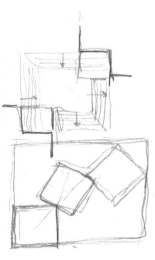

ans of proper design, the architects criticized vernacular and plan-book houses and searched for new artistic standards. A typical target was the vernacular building tradition itself. Vernacular styles such as the continuing Greek Revival designs were criticized as being inflexible and dull. Moreover, the attempt of local carpenters to continue and renew the tradition was shortsighted. The local carpenter's fusion of older square house forms and the new French mansard roof, wrote architecture critic Mariana Griswold van Rensselaer in *Century* magazine in 1886, "was supremely ludicrous and supremely ugly, yet no feature we have ever made our own has been more universally beloved." The roof was not intended to serve as exterior decoration but the public liked to use it that way (Figures 3.11, 3.12, and 3.13). Here was the great paradox. To capture the popular housing market, architects had to adopt the public's interpretation of what was fashionable, but to do so was to accept the ideas of the man on the street as the standard for good taste. "Although we as architects, may think we know a great deal more than our clients," wrote C. Blackall in the *American Architect and Building News*, "and can design much better houses than they can possibly imagine, filling them with what are unknown refinements and niceties, we may very soon find that it is extremely difficult to get very much ahead of the current style." Since architects saw themselves as the experts in design, it was difficult for them to accept popular styles that differed from their own taste. No matter what their own views were, however, the architects had to confront the power of public opinion.[15]

Two alternatives were open to the professional architect: to accept the public taste or to create new architectural standards and educate or indoctrinate the people about them. Both alternatives had their advocates. Some argued that in a democratic society it was natural to trust the general will of the people. Not to do so would run the risk of elitism. The American style, suggested Mrs. van Rensselaer, was to build eclectic structures with large porches and a profusion of wooden ornament. No other

country, she insisted, had the unique combination of temperate climate and abundant resources to create such homes. "Our more freely social, more lavish, more varied and complex ways of living cannot find full and truthful expression in any colonial pattern [derived from Europe], nor our growing love of art full and lawful satisfaction," wrote van Rensselaer. Architects needed to refine and improve the vernacular styles that the public liked. Simplify the design of the small private dwellings, she suggested, and stimulate the public's sense of art.[16]

A few architects tried to do just that. By entering the plan-book world, Henry Hudson Holly, George E. Woodward, and others did in fact support this point of view. George Woodward's first plate in his *Woodward's National Architect* (1869), for example, was simply an improved version of the traditional rectangular-shaped vernacular house with brackets, bay windows, and a wing added at right angles (Figure 3.14).

But the majority of the professional architects, particularly those who built homes for wealthier clients, retained the more elitist view of the architect as the conservator of standards. For them, the general eclecticism of styles remained a distinct problem. The ideal of professional expertise, which so many of them accepted, presupposed that there would be clear, widely accepted standards for evaluating the quality of designs. With so many choices, how could there be any canon of correct judgment? The artistry and inspiration inherent in the older designs was not enough. As William P. Longfellow, editor of the *American Architect and Building News*, commented in 1887, "The only eclecticism which can lead to permanent good is one in which architects shall come to agreement as to what forms they shall select, and set to work in common to shape these selections into an harmonious whole." Richard Morris Hunt, Henry Hobson Richardson, Charles F. McKim, Thomas Hastings, and other eminent architects stressed that such an agreement could come only from scholarly knowledge of the great building traditions. They themselves

Figure 3.11
Bicknell described
this as a "cheap resi-
dence with a French
roof." The mansard
roof, which origi-
nated in Paris, be-
came very popular
in the 1870s. (Bick-
nell, *Bicknell's Vil-
lage Builder*)

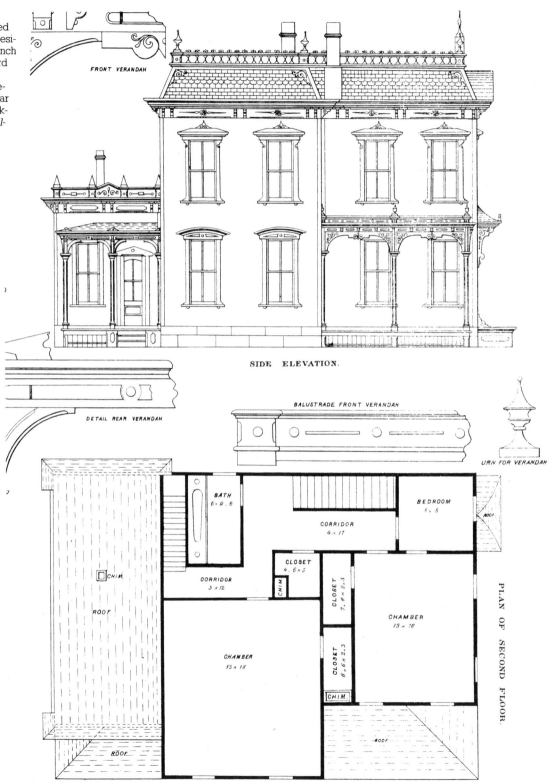

FRONT VERANDAH

SIDE ELEVATION.

DETAIL REAR VERANDAH

BALUSTRADE FRONT VERANDAH

URN FOR VERANDAH

BATH
6 × 9 . 6

CORRIDOR
4 × 17

BEDROOM
8 × 8

ROOF

CLOSET
4 . 6 × 5

CHIM

CORRIDOR
3 × 12

CLOSET
7 . 8 × 2 . 3

CHAMBER
13 × 16

CHIM

ROOF

CHAMBER
13 × 16

CLOSET
8 . 6 × 2 . 3

CHIM

ROOF

ROOF

PLAN OF SECOND FLOOR.

Figure 3.12
Window ornamentation detail for French mansard roofs. (Woodward, *Woodward's National Architect*)

had received this training at the Ecole des Beaux-Arts in Paris. From their study of the great monuments of Greece, Rome, and Renaissance Europe, they had gained a technical knowledge of drawing and a sense of what they thought were the immutable design principles of unity, harmony, balance, and repose. Conceiving of the architect as an artist grounded in both historical tradition and the mechanics of design, these architects gradually gained control of the profession. By 1900, they had required that candidates for membership in the American Institute of Architects must have graduated from an approved school of architecture or passed a special institute examination.[7]

It was a Pyrrhic victory. Although these practitioners who viewed architecture as an elite and scholarly profession had gained control over the graduate schools and licensing requirements, they never succeeded in capturing more than a small proportion of the domestic housing market. The failure was in many ways to be expected. The elitist and paternalistic style, coupled with the vision of the architect as an "artist," was a natural source of friction when working with the middle-class public. Like the Mugwumps, who worked for temperance and civil service reform, the architects sought to base their practice on underlying immutable principles of design. Whereas the Mugwumps, who came from similar, educated, urban backgrounds, hoped to remove corruption from the political parties and base the appointment to government positions on merit only, the professional architects yearned to create buildings based on impartial standards of design. The problem was that both groups, under the guise of impartial expertise, fought to protect their own self-interest by establishing

Figure 3.14
The L-shaped house by George Woodward was simply an improved version of a popular vernacular house type. (Woodward, *Woodward's National Architect*)

norms and controlling standards. Since they, too, controlled the graduate schools of architecture, they never successfully masked their own self-interest in the process. Lower- and middle-class homeowners were not convinced by their arguments or reconciled to the level of their fees, which usually ran to 5 percent of the construction costs.[18]

The history of early savings and loan associations demonstrates how difficult it was for a lower-middle-class family to purchase a house and why additional architectural fees would have been prohibitive. Two examples are instructive. In 1879, a coachman in Roxbury, Massachusetts, who was earning $35 a month, began saving his money. Six years later, he put $200 down on an eleven-room house that cost $1,900. Monthly payments, which were at first $23.80, were afterward reduced to $18.80. Still, they ate up almost half of his monthly income. The same was true of a tailor in St. Paul, Minnesota. He joined a savings and loan association in 1876 and invested $10 a month until 1883 when he bought two lots for $700. Two years later he put up a two-story, eight-room house for $1,860. His monthly payments of $26 continued for eight years. In both cases, a 5 percent architectural fee would have consumed close to three months' income. Both men felt that their houses were entirely satisfactory without spending the extra money. As the St. Paul tailor boasted, "I have as fine a view as any of the nabobs of Summit Avenue [where the wealthy lived], and can see up the river half-way to Minneapolis"[19] (Figure 3.15).

The problem for the professional architects was compounded by the design principles themselves. The purpose of their campaign for professional education in architecture had been to check the dangerous eclecticism of

Figure 3.15
The porch and roof peak of this inexpensive house display its main decorative details. (Linn, "Cooperative Home-Winning")

style and libertarianism of ornament, to handle revival styles with precision, and to design buildings that combined both function and beauty. Because of these standards, the few middle-class houses that they did portray in their professional journals were rather simple and plain. The middle-class public, not surprisingly, was far more attracted to the exaggerated, complex, and often playful forms of the plan books and building contractors.

For all their rhetoric about superior knowledge and ideal beauty, the architects had difficulty translating their artistic ideals into practice. The problem was that the difference between their ideals and the plan books was not that great, nor was their rationale that distinct. Not until the turn of the century did Frank Lloyd Wright, Walter Burley Griffin, William Gray Purcell, George G. Elmslie, and other Prairie School architects in the Chicago area transform the older principles of design into a new aesthetic by revolting against the complexity and eclecticism of the Victorian standards. And even then, curiously enough, the canons of design that emphasized straight forms, integrity of material, avoidance of historical revival styles, interpenetration of interior spaces, and horizontally oriented exteriors were not as innovative or as unusual as the professional architects suggested. By the turn of the century, as we shall see, even the builders and plan-book writers had tired of the profusion of Victorian styles and decoration.

Ultimately the cost of housing and the expense of creating individualized designs kept professional architects from exerting much influence on the domestic housing market. Their self-image as individual artists was too often reinforced by a sense of alienation from contemporary vernacular traditions. Therefore, they had difficulty designing low-cost, mass-produced, middle-class single-family dwellings. Although they continued to express a sense of outrage and disillusionment with popular standards of housing design, they were unable, with few exceptions, to exert their own leadership in the domestic housing market.

The local carpenter had dominated the house construction industry at mid-century, but the builder came into prominence during the Gilded Age. Through a combination of skillful advertising and careful management skills, the builder came to fill the gap between the great demand for housing created by the explosion in population and the need to mass-produce relatively inexpensive dwellings. Some builders were small-scale operators, putting up a single block or two of homes. Others, like Samuel E. Gross in Chicago or Fernando Nelson of San Francisco, planned whole subdivisions and sold thousands of houses.

The building of the suburban neighborhoods began as a haphazard process, an unforeseen by-product of the changing urban landscape. Before the Civil War, merchants lived near their businesses, and residential districts were close to the downtown areas of major cities like Boston, New York, or Philadelphia. Since walking was the main form of transportation, the center city remained the most fashionable place to live and slaughterhouses, tanneries, and other undesirable businesses were relegated to the periphery. By the 1850s, horsecars, ferries, and steam railroads transformed the downtown areas of the older East Coast cities from centers of residence into sites for factories and other commercial enterprises. The explosive growth in population, the increasing noise and filth of the inner city, the expansion of mass-transportation systems, and the popularization of the neighborhood ideal lured people in increasing numbers to what contemporaries called "the suburbs," but which, initially, were simply the lands at the city's periphery.[20]

The expansion of housing in the suburban streets outside the city limits around Boston and New York set a pattern that was duplicated elsewhere around the country. The initial expansion of railroads, streetcar lines, and ferries transformed neighboring towns like Brooklyn near New York and West Roxbury, Roxbury, and Dorchester near Boston into bedroom communities that would eventually be annexed by the cities. In the year 1812, when ferry service began, the Brooklyn Heights area across from Manhattan was largely rural (Figure 3.16). By the 1850s, wealthy residential neighborhoods were being built and New Yorkers had begun to complain that Brooklyn, which was now growing faster than New York itself, was attracting too many of New York's men of wealth. By the 1860s Brooklyn's population had reached 300,000 and by 1898, when it became a borough of New York City, it was an independent city of over a million residents. Roxbury, West Roxbury, and Dorchester followed a similar pattern, becoming suburbs in the 1870s and expanding rapidly from 60,000 to 227,000 inhabitants in the next thirty years. Like Brooklyn, which became part of New York, they were eventually made part of the city of Boston (Figure 3.17).

In the 1820s and 1830s when these Massachusetts towns were still rural crossroads, the neighboring villages had few commuters except for the wealthy who built their summer homes there. After the street railways were constructed, middle-class workers—salesmen, lawyers, small-store owners, teachers, clerks, skilled artisans, contractors—moved to the suburbs and transformed the older, wealthy areas into more homogeneous neighborhoods. Most lower-middle-class families lived in three-story apartment houses or two-family houses relatively close to the city. The majority of dwellings in these areas were built by speculators or small contractors. Yet uniform lot sizes, mass-produced millwork, and fashionable plan-book ideals meant that there was a stylistic uniformity to the homes. Although the type of house varied according to income, the exterior styles remained similar regardless of wealth. Even the apartment houses had their bracketed cornices, bay windows, and complex shingle or rough stone patterns.[21]

Right from the start, the development of suburban residential neighborhoods implicitly segregated housing by income level. Big and

Figure 3.16
As this trade card attests, by the second half of the nineteenth century it was common to see a suburban house in a rural setting at the edge of town. (Courtesy Henry Francis du Pont Winterthur Museum, Joseph Downs Manuscript Collection/Mendsen, vol. 36, p. 35)

Figure 3.17
The towns of Roxbury, West Roxbury, and Dorchester became suburbs of Boston as railroads and streetcar lines proliferated and made commuting to work in the city possible. (Map by Humphrey Costello)

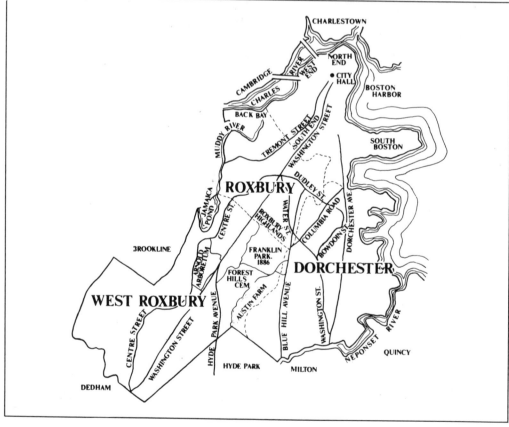

small houses were not mixed together but rather were grouped in certain residential areas. That such a housing hierarchy existed should not have been surprising. The very ideas of evolution and progress, which were central to the Victorian outlook, implied a hierarchy. How else could one move from primitive beginnings to a state of civilization and refinement? The assumption of hierarchy had been present in the plan books of Andrew Jackson Downing and Calvert Vaux in the 1840s, but the limitations of public transportation systems, with few exceptions, kept the wealthy in the center city. With the development of streetcar and steam-railroad networks, towns and cities became far more segregated than they had been in the pre–Civil War era. Given the availability of new transportation, both the middle and the upper classes created new strata of social distinctions that could be seen in the expanding residential neighborhoods where house and lot size became a visible and understood sign of social rank.

At the top of the hierarchy were the wealthy who created their own monumental residences on exclusive urban thoroughfares near the edge of major cities: Fifth Avenue in New York, Commonwealth Avenue in Back Bay Boston, Euclid Avenue in Cleveland, Michigan Avenue in Chicago, and Summit Avenue in St. Paul. A typical example was that of James J. Hill, the president of the Northern Pacific Railroad. When Hill decided to build a family home in 1887, he constructed a thirty-two-room Romanesque house, with thirty-five fireplaces and eighteen bathrooms, costing $280,000, on Summit Avenue in St. Paul[22] (Figure 3.18).

Other rising entrepreneurs quickly followed suit. The houses of the wealthy in St. Paul and other major cities were surrounded on nearby streets by somewhat less affluent structures, creating a continuum from rich to middle class in the outer ring of the city. In Cincinnati, Sidney D. Maxwell wrote in 1870 that

in whichever direction the beholder turns, he sees suburban places. The city is surrounded with hills that are already blossoming like a rose. Beautiful cottages, stately residences, and princely mansions are springing up as by magic. Villages are multiplying along the great thoroughfares. Tasteful suburban homes are each year, in increased number, skirting the waters of the Ohio or peering through the foliage that fringes the summits of the surrounding highlands.[23]

These "princely mansions" were built to preserve the sense of hierarchy and to impress wealthy acquaintances. In a society intensely aware of social differences, the prestigious urban avenue became synonymous with the height of fashion.

Often the wealthy also built a summer house in a more distant suburb. In 1855, a group of well-to-do New York businessmen hired the architectural firm of Alexander Jackson Davis and Ithiel Town to design a rural retreat, Llewellyn Park, near Orange, New Jersey. By planning the whole community, Davis achieved a more private and picturesque effect than was possible on the fashionable city avenues. An imitation English gate lodge marked the entrance to a 400-acre development, complete with curved roads and hidden drives, which contained fifty beautifully landscaped and carefully sited houses.

The emphasis on fashionable summer houses could also be seen in the development of Larchmont Manor, north of New York City on Long Island Sound, in 1872. The Larchmont area was designed by Thompson J. S. Flint, a New York architect, as an exclusive summer playground for the New York rich, complete with a six-acre waterfront park and yacht club, an inland park, and a horse-drawn trolley line that connected the manor to the Chatsworth station of the New York and New Haven Railroad. In these and other exclusive developments, patterns of segregated living arrangements were reinforced by club memberships and participation in the upper-class sports of sailing, polo, golf, and tennis.[24]

The segregation of housing on the basis of wealth was not limited to the New York or

Boston areas. It became the standard practice across the country. During Chicago's dramatic growth from 300,000 in 1870 to more than 1,000,000 in 1890, for example, the city expanded rapidly to the south and north. After the fire of 1871, the city's elite, including meatpacking magnate Philip Armour and department store developer Marshall Field, moved southward to Prairie Avenue around Eighteenth Street, while the city's working population clustered in flats and tenement buildings on the near West Side. The expansion of the cable car and street railway system during the next two decades shifted the more fashionable areas of the city northward. As early as 1855 wealthy Presbyterian families had founded Lake Forest and by 1872, when the number of contiguous suburbs exceeded fifty, North Shore realtors were praising the suburban advantages of "pure air, peacefulness, quietude, and natural scenery." In the 1880s, Potter Palmer and other wealthy socialites moved to Lake Shore Drive, part of the "Gold Coast" on the near North Side, and other wealthy businessmen slowly followed them. The gradual northern exodus of the rich was paralleled by the expansion of the black ghetto on the South Side. The once-fashionable mansions were quickly converted into apartments and filled with newcomers from the South.[25]

By the turn of the century, the march northward of the Chicago rich was accompanied by the movement in the same direction of the major institutions of high culture such as the Chicago Art Institute and the Newberry Library. The network of clubs, libraries, museums, and civic associations tied the merchant and business elite of the city together in a way that gave them great control over public affairs. Because of these connections, the Commercial Club in 1907 was able to hire the services of Daniel H. Burnham, the architect who was the leading designer of the 1893 World's Columbian Exposition, to develop a new plan for Chicago—a plan that created the lakeshore parks and the major avenues that are the hallmark of the city today.

The rich were not the only ones to form their residential clubs and associations. The New York suburb of Mount Vernon, for example, was founded in 1851 by a group of skilled artisans and tailors who were members of Mechanics Mutual Protection No. 11. To avoid the "ruinous rents" and the "rapacity of landlords" in New York City, these mechanics established the Industrial Home Association No. 1, purchased 369 acres from Mount Vernon farmers, subdivided the land into a grid, and began building houses. By October of the following year, three or four hundred houses had been erected and Mount Vernon was functioning as a lower-middle-class suburb.

In Milwaukee, the same pattern of segregated housing existed for all social classes. Settled in the 1830s and 1840s at the confluence of the Milwaukee and Menomonee rivers, Milwaukee initially took advantage of its water power and protected harbor to act as a center for flour processing and the transshipment of grain. The growth of iron mining in the Great Lakes area and the expansion of the railroads during the Civil War period encouraged the development of heavy industry: foundries, machine shops, tool companies, and iron-and-steel mills. By the 1880s, the city was heavily industrialized, with 40 percent of the population foreign-born and most of them coming from Germany. By that same decade the city had clearly defined residential areas: the Poles lived to the south, the Germans to the west, and the more affluent classes located along the lake to the north. Since the city did not have a substantial stock of old housing which upwardly mobile families could sell to newcomers with lower incomes, new housing had to be built for working-class families as well as for the upper-middle classes.

The Germans, who had early dominated the settlement of the city, were generally better off than the Poles, and the contrast could be seen in their housing. Most Poles were located in Ward 14 at the southwest side of the city. Small houses were set on deep and narrow lots, usually with only 30 feet of frontage. Perhaps typical was the 22-by-40-foot, story-and-a-half, Queen Anne cottage of Bartholomew Koperski, a Polish-born railroad car inspector (Figure 3.19). Koperski lived in the house with his wife and six children and rented the basement to George Krzyzaniak, a twenty-nine-year-old Polish carpenter, his wife, and two children. The families in Koperski's ward were working class and as late as 1910 less than half the houses surveyed had indoor plumbing. Although living accommodations were often cramped, the fact that the landlord lived on the premises and rented part of the dwelling meant that the houses were usually kept in good repair.

If Koperski's house represented one of the

Figure 3.19
The house of Bartholomew Koperski, a railroad car inspector, was built in Milwaukee in 1892. It had many of the decorative details of more wealthy residences, including a stained-glass window. (Photograph by author)

poorest working-class wards in the city, the house of Adolph Zebolski, a second-generation German iron molder living in Ward 20 on Milwaukee's northwest side, typified the next step up the social ladder. Zebolski's $2,000 home was one of nine identical houses built for a local real estate promoter (Figure 3.20). The two-story structure had an imposing Neo-Classical Revival front porch and a spacious interior. It was also located in a slightly more affluent neighborhood. Whereas Koperski's neighbors were mostly unskilled Polish workers, all of Zebolski's neighbors were either skilled artisans or small-store owners of German or Swiss extraction.[26]

The increasing availability of housing to middle- and lower-middle-income groups in the 1880s and 1890s, which was evident in the growth of Milwaukee's suburbs, could also be seen in cities as different as Port Townsend, Washington, Kansas City, Missouri, and Savannah, Georgia. Although each city grew for different reasons in this period—Port Townsend in response to the transcontinental railway reaching Tacoma, Kansas City because of the expansion of the stockyards, and Savannah as a

Figure 3.20
Adolph Zebolski's
house in Milwaukee,
built in 1904, was
one of nine identical
houses put up by a
real estate promoter.
It sold for $2,000.
(Photograph by au-
thor)

major southern port—the pattern of residential segregation and small-house construction persisted. Each house in these neighborhoods had a distinctive character. The variety of woodwork and other details achieved because of the economies of mass production meant that even simple cottages like the unidentified house in Bennington, Vermont, or Peter Mutty's home in Port Townsend could have a uniqueness and charm all of their own (Figures 3.21 and 3.22). Although they were not nearly as elaborate as the wealthy residence in Kansas City pictured in *Scientific American*, or the Savannah homes copied from *Shoppell's Modern Houses*, the smaller houses in Bennington and Port Townsend were nevertheless a dramatic statement of the personal aspirations of their owners. They graphically demonstrated the great potential of mass-produced ornament when applied to simple unpretentious houses.[27]

The residential segregation in Milwaukee and other nineteenth-century cities thus followed a consistent pattern. Neighborhoods and new suburban additions developed remarkably similar standards for lot size and house design. By the end of the century people who rode through an expanding city could sense the abrupt shift in wealth from neighborhood to neighborhood as they moved toward the periphery of settlement. To the north, in Milwaukee or Chicago, the more affluent businessmen created spacious estates along the lake shore. Within the expanding limits of the city, two-story apartment houses and small houses served the needs of the lower middle classes while those who could afford it owned larger, single-family dwellings.

Although an 1890 census survey showed that only 38 percent of American families nationwide owned their own houses and that in cities like Chicago the figure was only 23 percent, these statistics must be interpreted in the context of late nineteenth-century urban expansion. In most cities, the population in this period was highly transient, especially because of the arrival of large numbers of immigrants. In Boston, for example, one-half of the city's population would disappear and be replaced every one or two years because of the influx of newcomers and their subsequent movement elsewhere. Thus, for most families, both immigrant and native-born, the early years of married life were spent living with one's parents or renting an apartment. Eventually the young man's job would become more secure, children would be born, and the family would buy a house.

Older people often continued to own their homes until relatively late in life. In 1900, a national sample revealed that 73.4 percent of people ages 65 through 69 were heads of households. While some of these may have been renters, the scattered evidence we have suggests that most people made an effort to purchase a house because it was the surest measure of financial security. Even among the lower classes, multiple incomes of parents and children often made home ownership possible.[28]

Various factors increased the likelihood of home ownership in the second half of the century. One was the growth of the middle class

Figure 3.21
This house in Bennington, Vermont, is a good example of how a small Greek Revival structure could be brought up to date with the addition of a decorative porch and gingerbread detail above the windows. (Photograph by author)

and the general increase of wealth in the population at large. During this period, the middle class was significantly expanded by increased numbers of sales people, clerical workers, factory supervisors, and salaried personnel such as accountants, teachers, and office workers. As historian Gwendolyn Wright has pointed out, annual earnings per working person rose in this period from just under $300 in 1870 to over $425 in 1890. A skilled worker that same year earned from $500 to $800; a clerk in a Chicago insurance company about $1,500; and a lawyer in a small firm about $4,000. With developers building small houses in the 1890s for between $1,000 and $5,000, plus financing charges and land, a family with a yearly income of only $1,000 could buy a house on the suburban periphery of a city.

Fred Winkel, a grocery store owner in a northwest suburb of Milwaukee, was a typical example of a small builder and speculator. Winkel built his store, with an apartment above, in 1890 for $1,600 (Figure 3.23). Nine years

Figure 3.22
Peter Mutty, who managed the local hotel, built this house in Port Townsend, Washington, in 1892. The spindle work on the porch, the stained-glass window edging, and the iron filigree on the roof transformed this house from a simple clapboard building into a distinctive personal residence. (Drawing by Humphrey Costello)

later he built a two-story house next to the store for $3,000 (Figure 3.24). By 1905, Winkel had a mortgage on his home, and in addition to his house and store, he owned three other house lots on the street and several houses. By saving his own funds and borrowing from a local bank, Winkel was able to improve his own economic position substantially.[29]

The growth of building and loan associations also stimulated the expansion of suburban housing in the post–Civil War era. Since banks

Figure 3.23
This store with an apartment above was similar to the one that Fred Winkel built across the street. (Photograph by author)

Figure 3.24
Fred Winkel built this house next to his grocery store in Milwaukee in 1899. (Photograph by author)

often required loans to be paid off on a fixed date with one lump-sum payment, homeowners, as early as the 1830s, looked for alternative methods for purchasing their houses. During the second half of the century, cooperative savings and loan associations were chartered to meet this need. Cities like Reading, Pennsylvania, in 1890 had more than forty such associations where individuals made monthly payments to buy shares of the corporation and, after proper scrutiny of the house and lot, had their funds in turn lent out as mortgages on houses costing between $2,000 and $7,000. Investors were paid between 10 and 12 percent on their savings while borrowers learned thrift, economy, and self-respect. The associations even supplied building plans, complete with personal testimonials such as "the association has kept our boys' money safely invested, and they are $925 better off than two years ago. (These boys had formerly spent all their money for drink)." The associations provided detailed financial sheets for houses actually built, including the cost of the mortgage, insurance, taxes, and the additional "carfare" that was needed to commute to the suburban neighborhood. The results were dramatic proof that tailors, factory workers, and small businessmen could join the ranks of the suburban middle class[30] (Figure 3.25).

Building and loan associations encouraged the movement to the suburban fringe of major cities because they both provided financing and reinforced the moral virtues associated with home ownership. Since the associations were local in scope and democratic in the way in which they were run, they helped transfer the benevolent paternalism that had been the hallmark of village and small-town existence to the new suburban neighborhoods. Emphasis was placed on homogeneity of living arrangements and face-to-face contact. The directors personally inspected the site of the house and the building plans before accepting the mortgage. Those mortgagees who fell behind in their payments were visited and if need be were fined in the presence of the savings and loan association members to encourage them to pay up. Like the temperance associations and the urban Sunday school movements that sought through voluntary cooperation and peer-group pressure to re-create within the city the pattern of social control that had worked so well in small towns, the building and loan associations reinforced middle-class standards of behavior in the new suburban neighborhoods. Discipline was strengthened by personal example. Not only was the failure rate of the associations surprisingly low because of this moral support and peer-group pressure, but the achievement of home ownership was held up as a sign of morality and progress. As the loan associations explained, they were "inspirers of thrift" and "the plain and safe way to fortune." In the new suburban neighborhoods they thus helped re-

Figure 3.25
The owner of this seven-room house, built near Brooklyn, New York, spent $30 a month on his mortgage which was only $11.50 more than he had paid for the rent of his previous apartment. (Linn, "Co-operative Home-Winning")

create the orderly rural ideal of a social environment in which every individual had a clearly defined place—an ideal that was the antithesis of the sprawling and chaotic city.[31]

Building and loan associations were not the only ones to capitalize on the association between home ownership and the Victorian values of sobriety, thrift, order, and security. Samuel Eberly Gross, Chicago's largest developer, skillfully combined a house financing plan beginning as low as $100 down and $10 a month with a vision of the suburban neighborhood home as a haven for the workingman. Publishing his broadsides in German as well as in English and picturing the family house on his brochures as a "heaven" protected by a guardian angel who held a sword marked "justice," Gross provided a personalized design by manipulating the detail on the exterior of his houses (Figure 3.26). Like Fernando Nelson in San Francisco who used a basic floor plan and then "put on a front" to make it appear somewhat different from the houses next to it, Gross put up whatever structures appealed to the popular taste. By the 1890s, he was selling as many as 500 lots a week, running special

Figure 3.26
This advertisement for S. E. Gross and Company of Chicago demonstrated how large builders could price a single-family dwelling within the reach of a lower-middle-class working man. (Advertisement, undated. Courtesy Chicago Historical Society)

horsecars to new suburban subdivisions, and arguing in his advertisements, "*Get a piece of real estate*—not *sometime*, but *now. It will make you independent.*"[32]

Gross's success was extraordinary. By 1892, he had sold more than 40,000 lots and 7,000 houses and had developed over 16 towns and 150 subdivisions near Chicago. Like the building and loan associations, he was careful to combine the promise of financial security and independence with an orderly, controlled environment. For each of his developments, Gross supplied maps showing the major thoroughfares and location of schools, churches, and transportation lines. He built the train depots and put in water and sewage lines. For towns like Gross Park (1882) and Brookdale (1886), he provided a major, gas-lighted boulevard and enforced strict building ordinances. The result was a controlled suburban environment, with clear boundaries between the sections and a strong residential atmosphere, which contrasted dramatically to the business and factory districts of the inner city.[33]

The suburban neighborhood ideal, fostered by Gross and by thousands of other builders and developers, fit well the image of the segmented society that historian Robert Wiebe has described as the central feature of American life in the late nineteenth century. Americans,

Wiebe has argued, assumed that their society was so abundant that the only ingredients necessary for success were determination and hard work. The market was large enough so that all could compete and succeed. People could follow their own lines of work without interfering with anyone else. The goal of personal independence, as Wiebe points out, was thus closely connected with the idea of separation or segmentation. Americans stayed together by staying apart. By moving away from the new German, Italian, and southern European immigrants as well as from problems of crime and disease, middle-class Americans could protect their own self-interests and develop their own talents. The suburban neighborhood thereby became synonymous for many Americans with the ideals of independence and self-determination. The house was a castle, cut off from outside interference where the members of the family could enjoy themselves and express their artistic and recreational desires.[34]

The emphasis on privacy, recreation, affectionate family relationships, and independence that were so central to the suburban ideal of the American family home at the turn of the century were most graphically displayed in the housing illustrations published by plan-book associations and developers. Whether it was a plan-book picture or a painting commissioned for the founder of the United States Building and Loan Association in 1893, the striking feature of the image was the isolation of the house (Figure 3.27). If the viewer did not know that suburban neighborhoods usually contained many such houses closely spaced together, he would, with few exceptions, never guess that that was the case from the pictures. Landscape designer Frank J. Scott unconsciously reflected this sentiment in 1870 when he suggested that the house be considered as "the central interest of a picture" and the suburb as a sequence of separated "pictures" that could be admired while passing along a street. The purpose of planting, for Scott and other suburban developers, was to heighten the sense of the privacy and independence of the home. Landscape design thereby became a system of "picture making and picture framing, by means of the varied forms of vegetable growth."[35]

Paradoxically, the images of independence and self-expression associated with the segmented (segregated) suburban neighborhood were continually compromised in practice. Segregated suburban communities were far more restrictive than their inhabitants acknowledged. The passion for peacefulness, order, and control that lay so close below the surface of the Victorian suburban ideal meant that these neighborhoods and communities rested on the acceptance of rules and regulations. By specifying the sizes of lots and houses, by suggesting which forms of behavior were legitimate and which were not, by reinforcing the image of the family as a protective and affectionate institution, and by tying house financing to building and loan associations or to builders who had a personal stake in the quality of the neighborhood, the suburbs themselves became a mechanism for supervision and social control. If many middle-class Americans associated the suburbs with freedom and independence, they also subconsciously ignored the restrictive features of suburban life. By suggesting standards for both individual behavior and the physical environment, by stressing the crucial importance of appearance, and by combining uniform standards with appropriate levels of income, the builders and plan-book advocates created a suburban ideal that reconciled the central tension in the middle-class outlook between the desire for freedom and the need for control. As one plan-book developer suggested, in a book written for the "thousands of men and women . . . crowded and pinched together in the great cities of this country, waiting, watching, and anxious," "the [suburban] lots have been carefully selected, the houses tastefully and economically built, and all are surrounded by an enterprising, high-minded, sober, industrious, refined Christian people, where health, education, culture, and a generous reward for the expenditure of talent,

Figure 3.27
This plan-book home, which cost $3,000 in 1887, demonstrated the extent to which a bucolic rural environment had captured the popular imagination. (Shoppell, *Modern Houses*)

time, and money are assured." Here indeed was the suburban ideal.[36]

Plan-book writers, architects, builders, and family reformers were united behind the new vision of the suburban American home. They took it for granted that the suburban house should be the antithesis of the urban center—a family retreat that stood in dramatic contrast to the evils of the teeming metropolitan center. If the city's downtown area destroyed vegetation and ignored the beauties of nature, the suburban neighborhood home was nestled in the sheltering embrace of a protected natural landscape, complete with large lawns, trees, shrubs, flowers, and birds. If the city's center, with its immigrants and poorer classes, bred disorder and crime, the suburban neighborhood created a controlled environment with commonly agreed-upon rules and boundaries. If the downtown area permitted licentiousness and debauchery, the suburban neighborhoods were a model of decorum and polite behavior. And if the urban environments ignored individual creativity and artistic development, the suburbs were viewed as the proper supportive and nurturing area for personal growth and artistic achievement.

The gradual transformation of the urban landscape in the last decades of the nineteenth century paradoxically also strengthened the idea of suburban neighborhood life. Since middle-class Americans liked the new cultural amenities of urban life but feared the prevalence of urban crime and disorder, the advocates of suburban living now played upon the theme that life in the suburban neighborhoods was the best of both worlds, urban and rural. In no area was this argument more effective than in the field of public health. The city might have its great libraries and cultural institutions, but problems of illness and disease remained. Family reformers in particular, in contrast to the plan-book writers, architects, and builders who had stressed the artistic and social value of suburban life, concentrated on the advantages to people's health of living in suburban neighborhoods.

They had good reason to do so. Despite the rebuilding of the urban environment at the turn of the century, epidemics of tuberculosis, cholera, smallpox, and typhoid fever were still major urban problems. They were particularly devastating to children. In Chicago in the 1890s, 45 percent of the deaths were those of infants under the age of five. As late as 1906, 1,063 persons in Philadelphia died of typhoid fever. To contemporaries, it was quite clear that suburban neighborhoods were healthier than the downtown areas of cities.[37]

The persuasive power of the healthy suburban ideal was reinforced by the nineteenth-century tendency to view health as a moral as well as a medical issue. The equation of sickness with immorality, debauchery, and lack of self-discipline was understandable. Since medical science was still in a somewhat primitive state and no entirely convincing explanation for illness existed before the discovery of the germ theory of disease in 1883, it was not surprising that most people stressed the link between morality and good health. Henry Ward Beecher and other ministers at mid-century argued that sickness was a form of punishment for man's violations of the laws of medicine that reflected the moderation and balance in the world of nature. Timothy Shay Arthur and the temperance advocates insisted that illness was a by-product of a failure of self-discipline. Even health reformers such as Sylvester Graham, the inventor of the graham cracker, emphasized that disease resulted from an imbalance in diet and an excess in consumption. For all these reformers an indissoluble connection existed between proper behavior, good health, religion, self-discipline, and social control. Since the teeming city centers were notorious for crime, immorality, and debauchery, it seemed logical to Victorian Americans that the incidence of sickness and disease should be higher there. Since the suburban neighborhoods were a model of decorum and self-discipline, it was equally understandable that they should be a more healthful environment in which to live.[38]

During the second half of the century, urban reformers attempted to change the moral environment of the city in order to attack the appalling incidence of disease. John H. Griscom, New York City's principal health official in 1850, made the point most forcefully when he called for a "sanitary regeneration of society." Protesting against the failure of city officials to stem the frequent epidemics, he insisted that the cause of the high incidence of disease was

the sinfulness of human nature. "Cleanliness," he asserted, "is said to be 'next to Godliness,' and if, after admitting this, we reflect that cleanliness cannot exist without ventilation, we must then look upon the latter as not only a *moral but a religious duty.*"[39]

Although Griscom and other urban reformers who struggled to improve urban sanitation and public health made some progress toward the end of the century, they never completely satisfied the middle-class family reformers. For these crusaders the maintenance of good health was too important to be left to the fortunes of city life. During the post–Civil War era, these reformers flooded the periodical press with articles stressing the link between home ownership, suburban life, and good health. At stake was the preservation of the family itself. Nothing was more traumatic than death in the household.

In article after article the family reformers pounded away at the connection between good health, religion, and proper social behavior. One anonymous critic, in a sensationalistic article in *Harper's Monthly* entitled "The American People Starved and Poisoned," identified good ventilation as the central need in the American family home (Figure 3.28). Good ventilation and fresh air alone could prevent the alarming deterioration in the health of middle-class women and children. After a technical and detailed explanation of how fresh air might be introduced continuously into the house, the writer concluded with a brief comment, unrelated to her earlier arguments. "Every family is designed to be a *small* church," she wrote, "in which the young are to be trained to righteousness themselves and then taught how to 'turn many to righteousness'; that thus, in a future life, surrounded and rescued from ignorance and sin, they may shine as stars for ever and ever." It was clear from such comments that religion and good health were indissolubly connected.[40]

Other reformers connected good health and suburban life by stressing the universal need for fresh air, sunlight, and unimpeded views of nature. The leading expositors of this view came from the medical profession. One doctor

of noxious gas. By stressing the inherent problems in the plumbing of the older houses, Waring also implicitly strengthened the arguments for the value of newer construction in the suburbs. Who could read his articles about leaky pipes, defective joints, "large traps, clogged with accumulations of putrefying kitchen waste, soapy compounds, faecal matter, etc.," and not want to be spared such evils by owning a new house with modern plumbing? Under Waring's leadership, sanitation became accepted as a prerequisite for healthy middle-class family life and the campaign to get rid of damp basements, foul sewer gas, and dirty kitchens became a national crusade. By the turn of the century, specialized journals such as the *Sanitary Inspector* and the *Healthy Home* as well as numerous articles in the *Ladies Home Journal*, *Popular Science Monthly*, and the *Chautauquan* made the public far more conscious about the health aspects of house design than it had ever been before.[42]

Thus by the 1870s and 1880s, in response to the exhortations and pleas of sanitary reformers, architects, pattern-book writers, and builders, the vision of the ideal family home began to change. The intense competition for new converts, the growing desire to separate both physically and psychologically suburban neighborhoods from the center of the city, and the reform preoccupation with improving health and controlling excesses of all kinds forced the popularizers to extend even further their claims about what the ideal family and house should be. It was not enough to see the house primarily as a place of refuge, a protected retreat from the evils of the world. The house now had to play a new and more supportive role for family life. It had to be a place that not only retained all the old defensive virtues but also enhanced individual self-expression and creativity. It had to be a supportive and nurturing environment, a place that encouraged and stimulated the growth of each family member's talents, capabilities, and health.

in *Popular Science Monthly* insisted that "the lookout from the living compartments shall be cheerful, lively, and interesting because much of the time of the family must be spent indoors." Another physician in *Appleton's Journal* elevated the need for sunlight into a principle of house design and went on to attack Queen Anne cottages as "dull, red, dark, and gloomy." They might have some artistic merit, he conceded, "but these beetle-browed mansions are not so beautiful as health, and can never be." The suburban neighborhoods, by separating the houses, increased the circulation of fresh air and sunlight, thus reducing the incidence of disease which was a continual threat to the stability of family life.[41]

The reformers' passion for fresh air was matched by great fears about "sewer gas." George E. Waring, Jr., the major nineteenth-century exponent of using U-shaped pipes to trap sewer gas, even designed a new toilet bowl, the Dececo Water Closet, to prevent the spread

Chapter 4

The House as Artistic Expression

Simple things become beautiful and attractive by an art inspiration. Interiors retain their old forms substantially, but they put on new faces when touched by the real artist.

—Palliser, *Palliser's American Architecture* (1888)

A knowledge of architecture is more important to the people of this time than of any preceding age, because the individual counts for more. Who among us builds a home, who would not give it an artistic touch if he could? . . . The spirit of domesticity is a dominant force in our time. The love of home is a sentiment high enough to form the nucleus of great art. . . . Great architecture has always been the expression of high sentiment. . . . It must relate the love of men, women and children, youth and old age. The world has never had a worthier motive for great art.

—Gibson, "Architecture and the People"

The massive social changes in the last third of the nineteenth century had a curious impact on the popular Victorian ideals of women, home, and family. Although the expansion to suburban neighborhoods on the outskirts of cities altered patterns of work, and the vast increase in building created an intense competition between architects, builders, and plan-book authors for control of the national housing market, all those involved denied that they were modifying the older Victorian ideals of domesticity and home. But in fact, by arguing that both men and women should play a more active role in the design and layout of their houses and by suggesting that plan books and promotional literature would provide the necessary technical and artistic advice, they helped to change the popular middle-class image of family life in the 1870s and 1880s. Having once stressed the importance of the household as a protected retreat from urban dangers, they now encouraged the family to be the vehicle for enhancing self-development and creative expression.

The new image of the middle-class family home rested solidly on the expansion of managerial positions and the growth of real wages after 1877. Despite the boom-and-bust economy that produced the depressions of 1873 and 1893, wages for all nonfarm workers increased almost 25 percent and real wages, measured in terms of buying power, rose by more than 20 percent. Although many new immigrants were penniless and almost half of all American families were propertyless, the substantial increases in manufacturing, transportation, and merchandising businesses meant that significantly more people entered the white-collar classes. For these middle-class Americans, salaries replaced wages and their lives reflected a new sense of abundance and security.

As a consequence, the middle-class suburban house, portrayed in the latest Queen Anne, Eastlake, and French Second Empire styles, was now designed with more emphasis on comfort and consumption. The latest styles were thought to express artistic achievement, individual taste, and personal identity. The revised ideal of the American family home was thus a direct extension of the older ideal: it reflected both a weakening of the earlier assumptions about family hierarchy and mutual support, and, at the same time, an enlargement of the concern for aesthetic standards and individual autonomy. Henry Ward Beecher, the most popular preacher in the 1870s and 1880s, put it most succinctly when he suggested that "a house is the shape which a man's thought takes when he imagines how he should like to live. Its interior is the measure of his social and domestic nature. It interprets, in material form, his ideas of home, of friendship, and of comfort."[1]

If the thrust of the mid-century housing reform movements had been to control and stabilize the dramatically changing social system, the focus of the movement in the 1870s and 1880s was more individualistic. From its preoccupation with better stoves, lights, telephones, ventilation, and sanitation to its insistence on artistic achievement and creative expression, the crusade to improve the family and the house was directed toward bettering the quality of life. Central to the new vision was a conviction that each family member should be free to develop his or her artistic and creative talents to the fullest.

From the huge volume of promotional literature published by plan-book writers, architects, builders, and sanitary reformers in the 1870s and 1880s there emerged a revised image of what the ideal family and its house should be. At the center of the image was the belief that the house was the "woman's sphere"—a place where her biological instincts and altruistic desires could best be expressed (Figure 4.1). Nature had created the family that way. As the editor of *Popular Science Monthly* put it, women were as naturally expected to spend their time with the family as birds were fitted to fly or fishes to swim. "Birds often plunge into the watery deep, and fishes sometimes rise into the air," he explained, "but one is nevertheless formed for swimming and the other for flight. So women may make transient diversions from the sphere of activity for which they are constituted, but they are nevertheless formed and designed for maternity, the care of children, and the affairs of domestic life. They are the mothers of human kind, the natural educators of childhood, the guardians of the household, and by the deepest ordinance of things, they are this, in a sense, and to a degree, that man is not"[2] (Figure 4.2).

These comments from the editor of *Popular Science Monthly* aptly reveal the three basic assumptions that lay beneath the modified ideal of the middle-class family in the late nineteenth century. The first axiom was a continuation of the earlier belief that the family was woman's sphere of influence—a part of the world that necessarily should be kept away from the aggressiveness and contentiousness of commercial life. Tied closely to this idea was the faith that such an arrangement had been ordained by nature. Since the Victorians saw the natural world as emblematic of divine truths, to pattern family relationships after nature was, from their perspective, to reinforce society's most basic institution with the underlying laws of the universe. The final assumption tied the special attributes of woman's nature—her concern for children, education, and the household—to her legitimate need for creativity and self-expression. Women were viewed as possessing special gifts, the powers of revelation and creation. They were now expected to utilize these

Figure 4.2
As is evident from this photograph of the James Blaisdell house in Minneapolis, Minnesota, in the early 1890s, this home is literally identified with three generations of women, grandmother (in the picture frame), mother, and daughter. (Courtesy Minnesota Historical Society)

talents for the improvement of civilization. Only they could properly train the children and create the proper artistic home setting.[3]

The notion of separate spheres of appropriate activity for men and women was strengthened by the acceptance of Darwinian ideas in the 1870s and by the movement to suburban neighborhoods, which physically removed many middle-class women from the negative influences of life in the city's center. The idea that women had particular talents intrinsic to their biological makeup was widely accepted as a truism. In addition to being emotional and religious by nature, women were seen as having an aptitude for art and beauty. Women were still expected, as Harriet Beecher Stowe had stressed, to serve the family and to be self-

sacrificing, but increasingly they were also expected to exercise their creative and artistic talents. Middle-class women were taught from an early age to draw and play the piano, crochet and design elaborate "female elegancies" that could be displayed around the house. Earlier in the century, many women had, of course, woven cloth and sewn clothes for their families. Spared these chores because of the availability of ready-made shirts and dresses in the decades after the Civil War, they could now turn their attention to more decorative creations. The new interest in artistic creativity found expression in a wide range of everyday affairs from the decoration of rooms to the preparation of food.

Women's artistic work was expected to be

both creative and useful. Early trade cards, which served as advertisements for Singer sewing machines, pictured women working at their machines in the back parlor, surrounded by their family in the soft light of a kerosene lamp. Sewing, in such a context, was transformed from work into a pleasant form of recreation, a welcome change from the cooking or cleaning that took so much time. Similarly, the trade cards for the parlor organs mostly depicted the organs in a relaxed home setting. One such card pictured a young woman seated at the organ, playing soothing music to inspire her nearby father, mother, and younger sister (Figure 4.3). The church steeple, clearly visible through the window near the organ, reminded the viewer of the moral importance of family hymns. As composer Lowell Mason insisted in his famous hymn book, music was "a sure way of improving the affections, and of ennobling, purifying, and elevating the whole man." Nothing could better express woman's civilizing mission than her command of the piano or organ keyboard (Figure 4.4).

Handiwork, creative stitchery, and other "female elegancies" combined creativity and functionality. Middle-class women spent endless hours crocheting doilies and lace collars (Figure 4.5). These doilies were then used to "drape" furniture, thus helping to preserve the finish on tables and lessen the wear and tear on sofas and chairs. Lace doilies testified to the precision and perseverance as well as the creativity and artistic talents of their makers (Figure 4.6).

The emphasis on women's artistic creativity served as an antidote to the failure of the public at large to acknowledge the importance of cleaning, cooking, and housework. In a society where individual identity was increasingly tied to occupation and men were thought of in terms of the work they did, be it law, carpentry, sales, or medicine, women were caught between the middle-class image that stressed the gentility of being a housewife, a term that is itself revealing, and their desire to be given more credit for the work that they actually did at home. Thus many women deliberately culti-

Figure 4.3
By playing hymns on the parlor organ, a young woman gave testimony both to her religious and artistic nature. (Trade card for *Mason & Hamlin.* Courtesy Henry Francis du Pont Winterthur Museum, Joseph Downs Manuscript Collection/Mendsen, vol. 35, p. 7)

vated the image of being an artist to increase the public stature of their position in the house. Anyone could cook or clean, but only a creative person with keen insight, independence, and appropriate training could be considered an artist.

Nor was this image of artistic creativity limited to women. Middle-class husbands and children were expected to appreciate the virtues of art and music even if they could not become proficient in those areas themselves. Fathers had a responsibility to collect paintings and sculpture, both in the original and in copies, and to build personal libraries which the children could read. Boys and girls, in turn, were subject to music lessons and were instructed about the fine arts.

Thus the emphasis on individual expression and women's artistic creativity remained a central feature of the revised ideal of family life in

Figure 4.4
The Dennis B. Nye
family had this
family portrait taken
in its Minneapolis
apartment in 1888,
creating the ideal-
ized vision of the
family at home in
the parlor listening
to the daughter play-
ing the piano. (Cour-
tesy Minnesota His-
torical Society)

the late nineteenth century. Although the mid-century ideal of the family had stressed the separation of public and private, the protective role of the household, and the importance of order and hierarchy in domestic life, the emphasis in the 1870s and 1880s on creativity and artistic self-expression placed a new stress on individual talents, the display of material possessions, and the equality of household members. When photographers traveled through the states of Minnesota and Wisconsin in the 1870s, taking pictures of both poor and prosperous families, they invariably recorded individuals with their most prized possessions: children with a horse or gun, mothers with a new dress or portrait, fathers with their best crops or with their favorite carriage displayed in front of the house[4] (Figures 4.7 and 4.8).

Before the Civil War children had been viewed with great ambivalence as innocent, mischievous creatures who were prone to get into trouble and therefore needed to be closely supervised, but in the 1870s and 1880s they were seen in a somewhat more permissive light. Children's literature reflected this shift, as historian R. Gordon Kelly suggests, when it changed after 1865 from stressing religious and moral instruction to emphasizing wholesome entertainment. This changed attitude toward children was expressed in John Greenleaf Whittier's nostalgic poem "The Barefoot Boy" and in Winslow Homer's painting, *Snap the Whip* (1872). Both poet and painter idealized childhood as a carefree age that was full of fun. When Harvard president Charles W. Eliot wrote a biography of Maine fisherman John

Figure 4.5
Mrs. Terwilliger was photographed in her parlor in the 1890s while doing the traditional feminine handwork. (Courtesy Minnesota Historical Society)

Gilley in 1899, he described Gilley's children's life on the rugged Maine coast as made up of hard work and simple pleasures. Living amid the "most splendid aspects of nature," according to Eliot, gave the children "a real source of happiness" unavailable to those who lived in the squalid, ugly city. Within such an environment, the children grew up independent and resourceful.[5]

One of the best-known examples of this new attitude toward childhood was Mark Twain's *Huckleberry Finn*. Portraying Huck as an innocent and adventurous adolescent with a natural sense of justice, Twain contrasted him to the rigid widow Watson who personified a straitlaced approach to life. Other genteel children's writers toward the end of the century shared Twain's dislike of the older family hierarchy

Figure 4.6
Even young women were proud enough of the lacework they did to have themselves photographed at work. (Courtesy Minnesota Historical Society)

and were careful to picture the family as an organization of individuals, bound together by love and mutual respect. Such writers urged that patriarchal domination be replaced by gracious manners and thoughtful concern for the welfare of others.

This more egalitarian family ideal also implied that women should be given more independence. A clergyman, J. Max Hark, in the *Andover Review* reflected this view when he insisted that "the true home [is] the one spot on earth where man and woman may meet and each freely, fully exercise the rights of each, and so by fulfilling the law of their own being, fulfill also the will and law of their God." The implicit assumption here was that men and women, though physically and emotionally different by nature, could function in a state of equality within the home. The idea was similar, in some

respects, to the concept of separate but equal handed down by the Supreme Court in 1896 in *Plessy* v. *Ferguson*. Contemporaries saw no contradiction in talking about equality even when both parties differed in fundamental respects. Since Victorians believed in the reality of biological differences, they saw no problem in fusing essentially different groups into one unified whole. The classic moderate statement of this idea was black leader Booker T. Washington's comment about race relations at the 1895 Atlanta Exposition. Speaking of the place of black people, he said "in all things that are purely social we can be as separate as the fingers, yet one as the hand in all things essential to mutual progress." For both women and blacks, the moderate view, as espoused by Washington, was not to deny the ethic of service and sacrifice but rather to urge that both

Figure 4.8
This family in Little Falls, Minnesota, in their Sunday best, is obviously proud of their house, horses, and carriage. (Courtesy Minnesota Historical Society)

blacks and women be given the independence and self-respect that would make them more productive members of society.[6]

Not everyone accepted this emphasis on more egalitarian relations within the middle-class family. More conservative reformers by the 1880s worried that the breakdown of the traditional family hierarchy would threaten the American way of life. John Durand, comparing American to French families in the *Atlantic Monthly*, argued that the Americans had too much freedom. "The moral restraints growing out of this haphazard combination of individuals into a family," he disdainfully commented, "are likewise feeble. Parental cares and duties, the material difficulties of living, prevent both father and mother from carefully superintending the education of their offspring. . . . What is true in relation to associates and amusements in the American family is true of literature and religion: children are free to select their own reading and their own spiritual advisors. It is by no means an uncommon thing to see American families divided on theological questions." Durand clearly distrusted the growing American idealization of freedom and independence among family members. A clearer sense of hierarchy, patterned after the French example, was closer to his own point of view.[7]

Durand also disliked the lack of privacy within the American family. His comments here are telling. "We take delight in the reflection of ourselves in the public mirror," he commented caustically. "Self-exposure seems to us to be a matter of pride. We build our houses so that our neighbors can easily look in at the windows. We lay out our grounds and arrange our flower-beds and shrubbery expressly to be seen from the street. Our sentiment of privacy is symbolized by the open wire fence." Durand's critique of middle-class exhibitionism contained an element of truth. For all the popular concern with privacy, middle-class Victorian Americans seemed obsessed with display and publicity. How else would outsiders know that individual families were trying to live up to the ideals popularized in the advice books and trade periodicals?[8]

Foreign observers also noted the emphasis on individual self-expression and self-development within the middle-class family. Frenchman Thomas Bentzon, a decade after Durand, criticized the lack of unity within American family life. "There is in France a constant exchange of consideration and protection, which has seemed to me scarcely to exist in the American family—where the individuality of each member asserts itself from the cradle, where each one is astonishingly eager to follow an independent career and to assume the responsibility of his own destiny!" Bentzon disliked the apparent coldness of relations between parents and children, the relative lack of parental authority, and the absence of an identification of family with place or religion. Americans moved too often and thus had little sense of having an ancestral seat. What troubled Bentzon most was the American preoccupation with individual self-fulfillment. Comparing American to French girls, he noted that "If girls in France are brought up a little too exclusively with a view to please their future husbands, the Americans are perhaps too much concerned with the purpose of personal development, and both systems have their inconveniences."[9]

The connection between personal self-improvement and the cultivation of artistic talents within the American family ideal became the basis for some of the most telling arguments against it. Indeed, the pervasive emphasis on women's artistic development was used by critics, particularly women, as a basis for their own counter-arguments. Catherine Selden, writing in the *North American Review*, insisted that the tyranny of the kitchen and the chores of running the house had prevented women from fully developing their creative talents (Figures 4.9 and 4.10). What was needed, she argued, were centralized kitchens to make the preparation of food more efficient and less time-consuming. Bertha Monroe Richoff carried the argument one step further by asserting that some experience in that other "sphere"—the world of business—would actually make women more self-sufficient and professional in the governance of the household. If women were to be able to learn from work outside the home, wrote Richoff, "her household will be dominated by the spirit of an enlightened woman, . . . and the home will become, not merely the hotel which best cares for one's physical necessities, but a divine institution where woman's spirit is supreme, a perfect republic where liberty is combined with unity."

By the 1890s Selden and Richoff had joined forces with Ellen Swallow Richards, the first female professsor of chemistry at the Massachusetts Institute of Technology, lecturer Charlotte Perkins Gilman, suffragist Mary Livermore, and a small, articulate group of feminists to advocate a far more radical transformation of traditional women's roles. These feminists advocated what Dolores Hayden has called a "grand domestic revolution," suggesting that the traditional split between domestic life and public life for women be completely overcome. Women, they felt, could play a far more productive role in society if they were relieved of the drudgery and restrictions of home life. They advocated the creation of public laundries, public kitchens, and day nurseries that would give women better control over the domestic sphere and free up the time needed to work for the improvement of society at large. Attacking the single-family dwelling as inefficient and wasteful, feminists such as Mary Kenney even urged that cooperative housekeeping in hotels or apartment houses would be better for most families because it would give them more time and more freedom.

Although Selden, Richoff, and other critics of the American family ideal in the 1890s wanted to encourage women to become more independent, their arguments were in some ways an extension of the traditional ideal that had stressed the importance of artistic achievement and personal self-development. Critical of the restrictions that running a Victorian household placed upon women, they nevertheless insisted that allowing women to engage in work "worthy of their capacity" would actually strengthen the family. So pervasive was the value placed on the traditional family unit that even radical critics often stressed its worth.[10]

For most members of the middle class, this radical vision of a restructured family and society was too threatening to be persuasive. Cooperative kitchens and laundries could lighten the burden of housework, but they seemed more appropriate for the urban center than the suburban neighborhood. They required a degree of centralization, organization, capital, and vision that seemed beyond the reach of many families that were struggling to pay off mortgages and make ends meet. Moreover, the advocates of cooperative housekeeping overlooked the role of the single-family dwelling as a symbol of independence and a sign of middle-class status. Women were even more caught up in this symbol than men since it was so closely tied to their own sense of identity. Raising their children in a stimulating and protective environment and decorating and furnishing their house to reflect their artistic interests and aspirations had become too important to the personal image of middle-class women. Although the radicals' arguments about decreasing the drudgery of housework had great appeal, too often they were combined with ideas about restructuring the family that were usually dismissed by middle-class women committed to the single-family home.

Nevertheless, in an unintended way, the continual stream of feminist magazine articles and speeches helped reinforce the moderate vision of the middle-class family that was built around providing greater independence for individual family members. Balancing their position between the radical critique of domestic life as a straitjacket and the conservative insistence that family life was chaotic and lacked controls, they

Figure 4.9
Wash day at the Grant house in Rush City, Minnesota. (Courtesy Minnesota Historical Society)

Figure 4.10
Washing with friends in Worthington, Minnesota, made the burdensome job somewhat more pleasant. (Courtesy Minnesota Historical Society)

helped create a moderate ideal of the middle-class family life that seemed both ordered and open. Like the popular ideal of middle-class family life in the 1860s and 1870s that traced individual differences back to their roots in nature, stressed the importance of artistic creativity and individual self-development, and praised the protective and nurturing functions of family life, the moderate ideal of the middle-class family home in the 1880s and 1890s insisted that the house fulfill a series of practical and symbolic functions.

One major theme, endlessly repeated in response to the conservative critics, was the belief that the house should be a part of a well-ordered natural system. Toward the end of the century, as Gwendolyn Wright has pointed out, various devices were used to dramatize the connections between the house and the world of nature. One was the elaborate treatment of the house exterior. Surfaces became more complex, and architects used wood, stone, shingles, and stucco to give the house a rugged and textured facade, imitative of nature's diversity. Earth colors—greens, reds, and browns—provided a more natural look. Porches became larger and more elaborate, literally opening the house up to the great outdoors. Even the outline of the house itself, with towers, irregularly shaped roofs, large bay windows, and dramatically overhanging eaves was designed to imitate the natural complexity of the physical world. As plan-book writer A. J. Bicknell suggested, it was important to replace the old "dry goods box" style with a more natural, convenient, and picturesque alternative[11] (Figure 4.11).

Nature was brought into the house in a variety of ways. Plan-book writers suggested that large plants become part of the decorative scheme and noted that complex and ornate wallpapers using floral and leaf motifs could be applied to the walls and the ceilings. Front entrance halls were enlarged so that they could be opened up in the summer, and decorative millwork, with a variety of different woods, was used in great profusion throughout the house interior.

This ideal image of the middle-class house presented by magazine and plan-book writers sometimes suggested that the house itself was an organic system, one that literally, like nature, changed its appearances and functions with the seasons. As architect Bruce Price suggested in 1890, "the heat of summer demands shady porches and wide verandas; the cold of winter snug corners and sunny rooms—two opposite conditions to be reconciled under the same roof. . . . The house must be ample for summer guests and summer hospitality, compact for the family gathering around the winter fireside, and home-like at all times"[12] (Figure 4.12).

If the ideal of the Victorian middle-class home, like the moderate ideal of the middle-class family, rested upon the belief that both should be rooted in the underlying principles of nature, the two ideals also shared an emphasis on self-expression. The ideal house was to be a personal statement—a symbolic representation of what the owner stood for and valued. The ideal Victorian house was thus expected to be an instrument of display. As designer John Brett wrote in the *American Architect and Building News* in 1893, "civilized man has a want which a tent cannot supply, viz., a place for the exhibition of his treasures, especially the treasure of beauty, for which stability, permanence, and good day-light are wanted. He also requires a base of operations for his enterprises, a museum for his archives and trophies, and above all, for the convenient arrangement of his intellectual resources—for his books and his pictures. He may also require means for the entertainment of his neighbors and his children, and for seeing them to the best advantage." The ideal house, in short, was to function as a vehicle for displaying the civilized nature of its inhabitants. Like the urban museums that documented the latest stage in the progress of civilized man by contrasting modern ways of living to the primitive beginnings of ancient empires, the ideal house was supposed to dramatize contemporary achievements and document the march of progress.[13]

Such houses were designed to be read like a book whose symbolic meanings would be almost self-evident to contemporaries. The display area began with the front entrance hall. The hall depicted in plan books and popular magazines was enlarged to accommodate a fireplace and cozy inglenook, symbolic of the protective security of the home environment (Figure 4.13). Although central hot air and hot water heating systems had made the heating function of fireplaces obsolete, their symbolic role became even more apparent. The costlier the house, the more elaborate the fireplace mantel. Often pianos were placed in the entrance hall to increase the sense of the house as a place for entertainment and enjoyment.

One manufacturer of mantels even divided fireplaces into masculine and feminine versions. "The thought that creates a fireplace is first of all ancestral. It means you have a father and a home," the catalog suggested. "[But] when we come to the woman's fireplace, we

Figure 4.11
Implicitly critiquing
the earlier Octagon
houses designed by
Orson Squire Fowler,
Bicknell praised this
$4,000 house in 1880
for its convenience
and picturesqueness.
(Bicknell, *Specimen
Book*)

A PICTURESQUE COUNTRY VILLA.

It is quite possible that propositions which are mathematically accurate may not be true in practice. Thus, while it is true geometrically that a circle encloses the greatest amount of space with the least length of boundary, it is not true architecturally. Led astray by the obvious correctness of the mere geometrical part of the proposition, certain reformers at one time carried the principle to an extreme, and we had a very loud and persistent advocacy, not only of square houses, but of those of which the ground plan was in the form of an octagon, the nearest practical approach to the circle. But practically it was found that mere quantity of cubic contents is not the only thing that is required. Availability is quite as important as quantity, and hence it is found that convenience and utility, as well as appearance, are promoted by a departure from bare rectangular form. The accompanying design illustrates this point very well. By abandoning the old " dry goods box " style, the arrangement of the rooms and their individual comfort and convenience is greatly increased, while to the appearance of the whole there is given such character and picturesqueness as will add greatly to the value and attractiveness of the property. A special and somewhat new feature is the location of a conservatory in front of first landing of stairway in octagon end at the right and dressing room below. The library is in the rear of main hall, and at the right of back hall, which includes the back stairway. The parlor occupies the front of the house at left of hall, with dining-room, butler's pantry, store-room, china closet and dumb waiter in the rear. The plan is arranged for kitchen in the basement, although it can easily be included on principal floor if desired. The second floor contains three bedrooms, bath-room, and five closets. Two or three rooms may also be included in the attic plan. The estimated cost in vicinity of New York is $4,000, although in many sections it may be executed at a cost of $3,000 to $3,500.

Figure 4.12
As Harriet and Catharine Beecher had suggested in their advice book, house plants could provide an inexpensive decoration for a bay window. As this 1876 picture of the Hiram J. Patton home attests, plants could also bring nature into the home, even during the cold Minnesota winter. (Courtesy Minnesota Historical Society)

took place outside the home, provided a window on the larger world.

The plan books and, later on, the furniture manufacturers, suggested that the ideal parlor or dining room be organized around some central theme for which the symbolic associations could be gradually perceived. Like a good mystery story, the meaning of the rooms was to unfold gradually. The visitor was a detective, and part of the enjoyment of visiting someone else's house came from trying to understand the symbolic meanings of the furnishings (Figures 4.15 and 4.16). Robert W. Shoppell, author of the popular 1887 plan book, *Modern Houses, Beautiful Homes*, made these assumptions explicit in his description of a dining room:

> We sum up the hints on the furnishing of a dining-room by a short description of a room we have in our mind. The walls are papered with an olive-toned paper, or rather, the ground is a very dull slaty-blue, over which are tailed the stems and leaves of an orange tree, with rounded fruit in various sizes and stages of maturity from the tender green to the warm orange-yellow. . . . The whole coloring, however, of this paper is so deliciously cool and subdued, that scarcely one thing stands out above another, so it is some time before you grasp the whole of the design. . . . The entire effect is that of a quiet and comfortable, home-like room; ruffled feelings . . . [are] smoothed down in ten minutes.[14]

The overall impact of the downstairs rooms in the middle-class house of the 1880s and 1890s was supposed to be one of soothing repose. Plan-book writers suggested that dark, muted colors—especially russets, violets, and browns—be used to upholster suites of black walnut sofas and chairs to create an atmosphere of coziness and refinement. Rich colors, deeply tufted sofas, machine-carved furniture in Turkish or Queen Anne styles, large pictures with ornate gold moldings, fancy wallpaper with complex borders at the top, and elegant, patterned rugs could also, they suggested, give

find it the symbol of three virtues: illumination, warmth, and purification. . . . A place of fire is also an Altar; that is, an Altar for sacrifice, for refuge, for love" (Figure 4.14). In addition to the fireplace itself, which was emblematic of the parent's virtues, the fireplace opening was framed with elaborate overmantels that displayed curios and other exotica from faraway places and demonstrated the owner's awareness of beauty.

The presentation of family achievements continued on into the front parlor. "Whatnot" shelves (corner shelves designed in ornate patterns), round central tables and easels together with "suits" of upholstered furniture gave the parlor in the 1880s and 1890s an ornate but individual look. The woman of the house could display her artistic skill by exhibiting pictures of weddings and summer outings, symbolic statements of the family's social standing and conviviality. The parlors thus functioned as a treasure house, full of art objects and curios that, by association to events or experiences which

Figure 4.13
The inglenook next to the fireplace was a cozy spot where one could be quiet and secure within the home. (Bicknell, *Specimen Book*)

the parlor a feeling of richness and opulence (Figures 4.17 and 4.18). The juxtaposition of color, texture, and design could become a statement of personal aesthetics and self-expression. Even the spaces themselves could be softened and broken up through the use of room screens and draperies over entrances. The parlor, as described in the plan books, was indeed a "thicket," a contemporary word that expressed both the perception of space and the mélange of objects in the rooms (Figure 4.19).

The ideal middle-class pattern-book house could thus reveal the complex personalities of both wife and husband. Like the stories of Sherlock Holmes and others that catered to the public fascination with disguises, false appearances, different cultures, and exotic lands, the ideal house was to be a mystery to be pondered and figured out. The sophisticated interior was supposed to be, in one sense, a book that would repay several readings, a complex set of ideas about beauty and individual expression that might be explored by friends and visitors. The

Figure 4.14
This 1898 photograph of a mantel for a coal fireplace in a St. Paul home, with its collection of curios and its wolf-skin rug, demonstrates one family's conception of an "artistic mantel." (Courtesy Minnesota Historical Society)

Figure 4.15
This 1890 photograph of the Lucien Warner residence in St. Paul, Minnesota, shows a simple, artistic interior with a decorative parlor stove and the appropriate pictures and statues. (Courtesy Minnesota Historical Society)

Figure 4.16
Even parlor stove makers worked hard to create stoves that might be considered works of art. (Advertisement, undated. Courtesy Smithsonian Institution, Collection of Business Americana)

Figure 4.17
The Uri Lamprey home in St. Paul, Minnesota, followed the decorative motifs of the Robert Shoppell plan book by using tufted furniture, dark muted colors, and appropriate pictures of women and children. (Courtesy Minnesota Historical Society)

Figure 4.18
Even more modest homes like this one owned by a mail carrier were appropriately decorated with patterned wallpaper, whatnot shelves, and velvet-covered furniture. (Courtesy Minnesota Historical Society)

Figure 4.19
This 1895 parlor in the Joseph Brechet house in Glencoe, Minnesota, used elaborate drapes and portieres to show off the owner's artistic tastes and create the sense of drama associated with a stage. (Photograph by Joseph Brechet, Courtesy Minnesota Historical Society)

downstairs with the draped doors, screens, and partially obstructed views was to be a form of maze to be explored and discovered. As plan-book author Robert Shoppell suggested, "many prefer not being able to see all over a drawing room at a glance." Nor was it coincidental that a favorite Victorian way to photograph an interior was to provide a view through several rooms that gave a glimpse of adjoining spaces—just enough to tantalize the viewers into speculation about how those rooms might be arranged.[15]

Thus the image of the ideal house ran parallel to the image of the ideal middle-class family in late nineteenth-century America. Both shared the emphasis on the house as the expression of personality and as an exhibition of personal standards of beauty. As Robert Shoppell proudly proclaimed, with some exag-

geration, "the reproduction of beauty in form and color, in wood and textile fabrics is, happily, so cheap in this country that even poverty is no bar to the possession of a refined and beautiful home." In a society where material possessions were a sign of achievement and social status, the ideal middle-class house had become by the 1880s a prime vehicle for personal display, meriting Thorstein Veblen's caustic comments about "conspicuous consumption" and "pecuniary emulation."

To what extent were these family and house ideals at the end of the nineteenth century a reflection of reality? Did middle-class families accept the injunctions to demonstrate artistic creativity and personal self-expression in their houses? Was there, in short, any connection between the ideals of family and home and the way in which middle-class families actually lived?

Clues to the answers to these questions may be found in recent historical studies of changes in family size and composition as well as in the diaries and personal letters of middle-class families toward the end of the century. From the 1890 U.S. census and from current demographic analyses, we know that family size declined significantly between 1850 and 1899. In 1850 the average family had 5.5 members; by 1890, only 4.93. Fewer children meant more time could be spent with each child.

Not only did women have fewer children but the age at which women married rose slowly in the decades before the turn of the century. Middle-class women were more likely to be educated in high schools and colleges and to marry later in their twenties. In cities like Providence, Rhode Island, by 1900 there was also a 35 percent increase in the numbers of native women aged 30 to 39 who were never married. Better-educated women were more likely to add to family support before marriage and to bear fewer children, and thus middle-class mothers usually had more time to devote to their homes and families. Although most married women stayed home in 1890 and less than 5 percent entered the work force, the real wages of their husbands during the period from 1870 to 1900 increased by about 20 percent; hence middle-class women also had more money to spend on their house and family. Although child-rearing had consumed most of married women's time at mid-century, by 1900 women could expect to spend part of their married life without children.[16]

Not only did most middle-class women spend less time raising their family, but they also tended to spend more time living as widows, either by themselves or with their children. As Howard Chudacoff has pointed out in his studies of Providence, Rhode Island, in the last half of the nineteenth century nearly two-thirds of women in their late sixties and early seventies were widowed. Such women usually moved in with one of their children and spent

their time helping out with their grandchildren or knitted, crocheted, and did other forms of handiwork. As one writer in *Harper's Bazaar* commented in 1907, "within a century we have all noticed the passing of 'grandma' and the continued efflorescence of brilliant ladies who but one generation ago would have been relegated to caps and chimney corners." Even grandmothers now were expected to express their talents and creativity.

If women in their everyday lives, and even in old age, were increasingly expected to be both useful and artistic, men, too, as social historian Daniel Rodgers has pointed out, were subject to similar pressures. Men's work, as portrayed in the popular literature, was expected to be creative, self-expressive, and socially beneficial. But the growth of industry and the expansion of support services meant that many jobs, from assembly-line factory work to accounting and quality control work, were tedious and boring. The constant stress on the centrality of work to living the moral life and the emphasis on artistic creativity helped to obscure for men, as it had for women, the heavy burdens of managing everyday life in Victorian America. Running a large Victorian house, even with help, or providing for the family needs, took a good deal of effort. Yet the expectation was that both men and women should reserve time for individual creativity and self-expression, no matter whether it was through reading, music, painting, or other uplifting arts (Figure 4.20). For most middle-class Victorians, the challenge was to balance off the drudgery of functioning in the everyday world with the pride of aesthetic achievement, to humanize and refine the rigors of an increasingly industrial society by focusing their attention on individual accomplishments and artistic achievements.[17]

Thus a variety of economic and demographic factors helped make it possible for Victorian Americans to place a stronger emphasis on artistic creativity and self-expression. The smaller family size, increased real wealth, and fewer years spent raising children now allowed both men and women to devote themselves to improving the quality of time they

Figure 4.20
Victorian Americans hoped that even young men like William Burkhard, Jr., photographed in 1890 at Gustave Herrmann's home in White Bear Lake, Minnesota, might be inspired by decorations in an artistic parlor. (Courtesy Minnesota Historical Society)

spent with their families. The stress on hard work and productivity, so ingrained in the popular mind at mid-century by the McGuffey readers and other advice books, now was balanced by an attempt to develop creative and artistic lives.

Evidence about individuals, though somewhat fragmentary, confirms both the presence of this artistic ideal and the difficulty in achieving it. The pressure on women to get married and fulfill the domestic ideal, as Carl Degler has pointed out, was intense. Young women often worried about becoming old maids. Mary Waterman Rice in 1874 confided to her father her worries about a close friend remaining a spinster. "I fear Ella is cut out for an old maid," she commented, "and I am very sorry to think so for she would make some young man an excellent good wife." Another young woman, Elizabeth Dwight, who was preparing herself for marriage by taking French and harp lessons, and by visiting widely, was deeply hurt when she had to give up these activities to care for ill relatives. As she explained to her married sister, her aunt had envisioned for her a life that was "literary, musical, social, with time to cultivate my own mind, and enjoy other peoples and it is very hard for her to give it up. . . . I *had* a vision once of such a life, too," she confided, "but I have come to the conclusion that it is not meant for me." Elizabeth Dwight ultimately

married but she remained somewhat frustrated that the burdens of family life prevented her from achieving her potential. She did admit that she did not regret the burdens of marriage because she had learned a good deal about herself "which no books could teach . . . but it costs me an occasional groan to look over the vast seas of ignorance which envelop my mind."[18]

For women such as Mary Waterman Rice and Elizabeth Dwight, the ideal of artistic self-development, though somewhat frustrated in reality, remained a personal goal. For such women, playing a musical instrument, crocheting, and cultivating their minds through reading provided some relief from the endless duties and cares of running the household. The desire for personal autonomy and the pleasure gained from artistic creativity and intellectual self-development provided great satisfaction and helped to counterbalance the endless hours spent at home in the service of others.

Not all women, of course, accepted completely the ideal of artistic self-development. Mary Putnam commented sardonically about her life when she was sixteen years old:

> There is an abstract general idea . . . of a father coming home regularly tired at night (from the plow, I believe the usual legend runs), and being solaced by the brilliant yet touching performance of a sweet only daughter upon the piano. . . . Consequently, to carry out this ideal, although my father is very seldom tired, and certainly never plows, although he is not particularly fond of music and my performance is so far from either brilliant or touching that I suspect he is entirely indifferent to it, I practice, in accordance as I said before, with this ideal.[19]

Mary Putnam's dislike of the ideal but failure to rebel against it was, in some sense, a tacit admission of the ideal's power.

One of the fullest and most complete descriptions of the everyday life of a middle-class Victorian woman comes from Claudia L. Bushman's chronicle of Harriet Hanson Robinson and her New England family. Harriet Robinson's life spanned most of the nineteenth century and she moved from the mid-century vision to the later ideal of family and house in her own lifetime. Harriet Hanson was born in 1825 and grew up in Lowell, Massachusetts. Her father died when she was six, forcing her mother to take in boarders and making it necessary for Harriet to work in the cotton mills. Although she was actively engaged in helping run her mother's household, Harriet gained the rudiments of education by reading in the evenings and eventually attended two years of high school. A strong, ambitious, resilient woman, Harriet was living at home and contributing to her mother's family when she fell in love with William Robinson, a local newspaperman. They were married in 1848.

Because of William Robinson's unsteady work as a newspaper editor for controversial antislavery causes, the family moved from Lowell to Concord to Salem in the 1850s, renting houses, and struggling to make ends meet. All except the last of the four children—two girls and two boys—arrived at two-year intervals starting in 1850. But five-year-old Willie died of typhoid fever in 1859, devastating the family. Not until 1866, after William had secured a steady position as the clerk for the state House of Representatives, did the Robinsons become financially secure enough to buy a house. Even then, their family pattern of uncertain finances persuaded them to purchase an older, less expensive house rather than a more stylish Victorian one.[20]

Nevertheless, Harriet Robinson, as her diaries and letters suggest, accepted both the late Victorian middle-class images of the family and the home. Although she was a woman of remarkable energy and tenacity, she subordinated herself in the years of her marriage to the support of her husband and family. She chastised the writer Lucy Larcom for being "an undeveloped person" because Larcom had not married, and she reveled in her satisfaction with her own world. "I had a good visit but I was *so* glad to get home," she wrote in her diary

after visiting friends. "Truly her home is a woman's world." Mrs. Robinson also believed that cooking was "one of the fine arts" and that housework demanded "a woman of Genius."[21]

Although the Robinsons did not buy a new house, they did make over their older dwelling to bring it up to the acceptable Victorian standards. The house contained the usual first-floor layout of front and back parlors (theirs was called the library), dining room, sitting room, and kitchen. The second floor had three bedrooms and the Robinsons added a fourth in the attic. While they were still renting the house, Mrs. Robinson had the front entrance hall repapered in plain lilac with a crimson and gold border, an upstairs bedroom in green with small figures, and the attic room in a "cunning little red dot." Once they owned the house, they redid the kitchen, built a bay window upstairs, cut an arch between the sitting room and back parlor, making one larger room, rebuilt the fireplace mantels, and eventually modernized the heating and plumbing.

When her husband died in 1876, Harriet Robinson took up being an author, wrote books, and peddled them herself. She thus followed her husband's suggestion, which he had somewhat laughingly made in a letter before he died, that in the hereafter "you shall have a harp for music, or a pencil for painting and or a chisel for sculpture—and I will be your delighted proof reader and critic—and take the money for your golden books. Seriously."[22] Mrs. Robinson was able to support her children as well as her mother who now lived with them by taking in boarders and by writing. She thus fulfilled the Victorian image of the ideal mother, a woman who served as the guardian of the house and who aspired to more noble, artistic achievements.

In her elder years Harriet Robinson's house became her major source of revenue. At eighty-three she could proudly assert in her diary that "my home is very pleasant and I can do just as I like in all things." She had rented out all the rooms except those she meant to "keep and die in." Thus, although Harriet

Robinson never had the money to be mistress of the ideal Victorian house, she did follow that goal, insofar as it was possible.[23]

The testimony of Harriet Hanson Robinson, Mary Putnam, Mary Waterman Rice, and Elizabeth Dwight indicates just how widely held were the late Victorian ideals of home and family. Although these women came from different social classes and geographic areas, each persistently committed herself to the ideals of domesticity, personal self-development, and artistic creativity. The pervasiveness and power of these ideals is also confirmed by three very different kinds of sources—the testimony given in the cases of divorce, the evidence that comes from the expanding world of shopping, and the Victorian preoccupation with cemeteries as homes for the dead.

From historian Elaine May's research on divorces in the 1880s, it is clear that the arguments made in Los Angeles divorce courts appealed to the dominant images of the late Victorian family and home. Wives divorced husbands for not providing adequate food, clothing, and shelter for their families. They also contested the marriage when the husband swore, forced them to enter the work force, drank, gambled, or otherwise polluted the home environment with his moral lapses. Husbands similarly filed for divorce when the wife was immoral, alcoholic, neglectful of the home, or unladylike in her behavior. When Jonathan James sued his wife Sharon for divorce in 1883 claiming that she was "addicted to drinking," she denied the charge and asserted instead that he wrote "lascivious, lecherous, libidinous letters" to another woman. The court decided that Sharon's claims were true and granted her a divorce. In such decisions the courts were upholding the Victorian image of separate social roles for both men and women. Both the defense arguments and the court decisions themselves revealed the extent to which the late Victorian ideals of home and family were taken for granted.[24]

The courts also condoned a double standard for men, allowing men a certain amount of indulgence for their behavior in places of pub-

lic entertainment while expecting women to remain at home. The court's position tacitly recognized the Victorian vision of the public world as dangerous and corrupting. To avoid such temptations, men and women needed a way of legitimizing staying at home and yet being able to enjoy the benefits of the expanding economy. If the wife had to go alone into the city, she needed to spend her time in a proper environment that would protect her feminine virtues and enhance her talents. By the 1880s and 1890s these needs were fulfilled by mail-order firms such as Sears, Roebuck and Montgomery Ward, and by Macy's, Marshall Field, and the other grand department stores (Figures 4.21a and 4.21b, 4.22a and 4.22b).

The Sears, Roebuck and Company catalog not only illustrated the products that could be purchased to beautify the house without the inconveniences of traveling to the cities but also demonstrated indirectly how the middle-class family ideal had become more egalitarian. After an introduction testifying to their honesty and depicting the economical prices for their wares, the Sears, Roebuck catalog displayed all the products that would be needed in the home

from patent medicines to flower stands. The section on parlor furniture in their 1897 catalog was particularly instructive. In the 1870s fashionable parlor "suits" consisted of a sofa, a large gentleman's armchair, a daintier lady's chair, and four straight-backed visitor's chairs. The size and scale of the armchairs mirrored the implicit hierarchical view of the family. The Sears 1897 catalog, by contrast, offered "princely parlor furniture" in "suits" of a sofa, three chairs, and a rocker. Both the "Gents' Easy Chair" and the woman's "Rocker" were now the same size, implying that the family was coming to be seen as a less hierarchical unit. The Sears' advertisement also suggested that the fabrics on all pieces harmonize and urged the reader to "leave it to our designer, as he is an artist in combining colors on Parlor Furniture, so as to harmonize with the colors in any parlor." The most expensive "suits" were "the most beautiful and artistic," built to last a lifetime (Figure 4.23).

Throughout these advertisements the constant emphasis on richness of design and artistic quality reinforced the late Victorian stress on the ideal middle-class family house as a work of art. By combining inflated rhetoric about their artistic achievement in furniture design with the constant pledge that their cheap prices put these parlor "suits" within the easy reach of families with moderate means, the company reinforced the late Victorian ideal

Figures 4.22a and 4.22b
Toward the turn of the century, furniture dealers began to advertise either with humor (a) or with actual pictures of decorated rooms (b). (Advertisements, undated. Courtesy Smithsonian Institution, Collection of Business Americana)

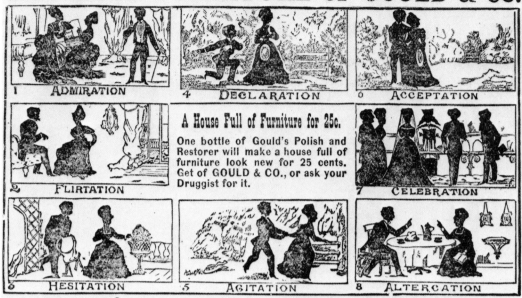

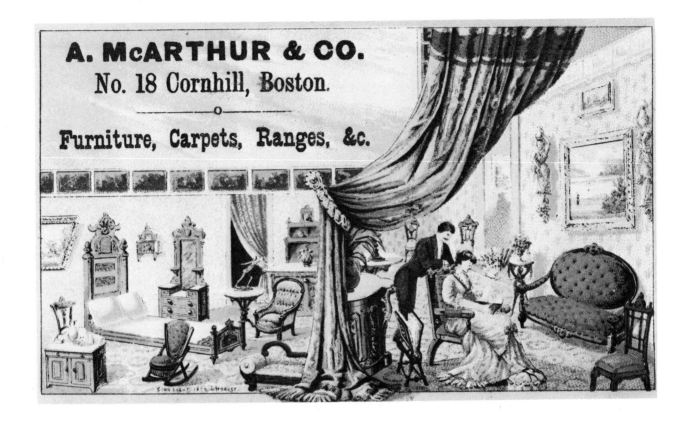

that every individual could enjoy the benefits of a life surrounded with art. Great painting reproductions, the world's classic literature, the finest musical instruments, and the most beautiful furniture were now within the easy access of the common man.[25]

The emphasis on art and beauty in the Sears catalogs was soon challenged by the great department stores built at the turn of the century. Each of these stores was a sumptuous museum filled with rare treasures and designed to stress the artistic and ennobling value of the goods that they sold. When Macy's opened its Fourteenth Street store in 1891, the customers were led into the main section of the shopping area through an "art" room filled with "a carefully selected line of onyx" and bronzes. Marshall Field's 1902 Chicago store, similarly, had an enormous glass dome by Tiffany and a series of rooms filled with rare walnut paneling, Louis XIV furniture, and specially woven English carpets. Shopping in these stores became an adventure in high art. Department stores became museums in which a status hierarchy of objects placed works of art at the top and encouraged the customers continuously to try and raise their standards.[26]

The constant emphasis on artistic achievement that pervaded not only the advice literature about the home but also the merchandising techniques of the mail-order houses, department stores, and the 1893 World's Fair found its ultimate expression in the Victorian cemetery movement. What could be more appropriate than coming to a final rest in a new, parklike cemetery that provided the ideal suburban setting for "homes for the dead." The Victorians had begun transforming cemeteries into rural parks with the building of Mount Auburn Cemetery in Cambridge, Massachusetts, in 1831 and Greenwood Park Cemetery in Brooklyn in 1838. By the 1870s and 1880s,

Figure 4.23
Sears, Roebuck and Company hoped that by creating a hierarchy of value in their catalog they could entice consumers to upgrade their furnishings. (Sears, Roebuck and Company, *Catalog*, 1897)

$23.00 BUYS A $45.00 PARLOR SUIT

OUR SPECIAL OFFER: **SEND US $5.00** as a guarantee of good faith and we will send you the suit by freight. C. O. D., subject to examination; you can examine it at your freight depot, and if found perfectly satisfactory pay the freight agent the balance, $18.00 and freight. Three per cent. discount allowed if cash in full accompanies your order, when $22.31 pays for the suit.

No. 9503 This elegant Turkish parlor suit consists of 1 Tete-a-Tete, 1 Rocker, 1 Gents' Easy Chair, 1 Parlor or Reception Chair. All these pieces are made in extra large size, high backs and large comfortable seats, and are very latest design. The upholstering or cover of this suit is in the latest design and pattern of imported goods; each piece is covered in a different color. We will be pleased to mail you samples of six different colors to select from, or if left to us to make selection in colors our upholsterer will in all cases give you colors on this suit that will please you in every respect. The suit is finely upholstered, with plush band and rolls on top and sides of back and trimmed with a heavy worsted fringe. This suit is made with good steel spring seats and spring edges and every piece is made with spring backs. This is without a doubt one of the best parlor suits ever put on the market at the price we ask for it and will be an ornament in any home. We can furnish this same parlor suit upholstered in good grade of crushed plush, assorted colors, and other styles of covering.

4 piece Parlor Suit, price in cotton tapestry	$23.00
4 piece Parlor Suit, price in crushed plush	25.50
4 piece Parlor Suit, price in silk brocatelle	29.50
4 piece Parlor Suit, price in silk damask	34.00

A $35.00 PARLOR SUIT FOR $24.00.

In offering this Parlor Suit of six pieces for $24.00 we fully believe that no such suit can be secured at less than $35, and if bought at retail at that price you would consider it a great bargain.

Made with a solid oak or a solid birch frame If furnished in solid birch it is finished in imitation mahogany, a most desirable and attractive finish.

No. 9504 The backs of this suit are upholstered in the same quality of material as the seat, and the decorations in the way of hand carving are decidedly unique and attractive Easy spring seat and edges corded with handsome cord with silk plush banded front. The suit is furnished complete with a full set of casters, and weights, when packed for shipment, about 250 lbs. We show in illustrations only pictures of the large sofa, large rocker and large parlor chair. The six piece parlor suit complete consists in addition to the three shown of a divan, same as the sofa only smaller; an extra Parlor Chair and a large Arm Chair of same size as rocker shown. Bear in mind that our C. O. D. terms of shipment are very liberal, also that we allow a discount of 3 per cent when full cash accompanies order. Most of our customers send full cash with order, knowing the goods are guaranteed and may be returned if not satisfactory and money refunded.

Upholstered as follows:
Our special price for 6 piece suit in an excellent grade of cotton tapestry ... $24.00
Our special price for same upholstered in a very excellent quality of imported corduroy ... 26.50
Our special price for same upholstered in a fine grade of brocaline crushed plush or silk tapestry ... 30.00
Our special price for same upholstered in very fine brocatelle or choice silk damask ... 33.00

Be sure to advise us when ordering, what special combinations of colors are desired. We can furnish you with a suit which for harmony of colors as well as durability and elegance will delight you more than you could possibly expect.

A $50.00 PARLOR SUIT FOR $33.00.

No. 9505 It is difficult to imagine a more beautiful and artistic suit than the one which we show in the illustration. Our artist has endeavored to draw the different pieces so that you can get an idea of the handsome design. It is one of the richest and most stylish appearing parlor suits made for the season of 1897. It is after a design executed by expert artists in this line, and the manufacturers are taking particular pains that the suit shall be not only perfect in detail and handsome in outline, but thoroughly substantial and durable in every respect. It is made with a solid oak frame or a frame made of curly birch with imitation mahogany finish. Either wood is decidedly handsome and thoroughly substantial. The frames are beautifully carved after the most stylish pattern, and the suit as a whole has the appearance of one which would retail frequently at from $75.00 to $80.00. It consists of 6 pieces, a large sofa, a large divan, large easy rocker, large arm chair and two parlor chairs. We upholster this suit in five different styles of upholstering. D. E. F. G and H. D is a very fine brocaline crush plush; E is an elegant silk tapestry; F a superb Wilton rug; G a choice grade of silk brocatell and H a very handsome and durable satin damask. You have your choice of upholstering. In all grades the patterns are the very latest designs, and in coloring you will have your choice of all the popular shades. We recommend, however, that you leave the matter of coloring in general to our designer, as we make these parlor suits specially to order and will upholster the various pieces in the latest popular shades, all harmonizing perfectly. The weight of the suit when packed very carefully for shipment is 300 lbs. We pack each of these pieces with the utmost care, covering all parts with burlap so that they will reach you in perfect condition. Casters free.

Our special price for above 6 piece Parlor Suit, upholstered in grade D or E ... $33.00
Same Suit, upholstered in grade F, our special price ... 37.00
Same Suit, upholstered in grade G or H, our special price ... 38.00

the popularity of Sunday outings to these and similarly designed cemeteries encouraged streetcar-line builders to extend their lines out into the countryside.

The cemeteries, like the Queen Anne and Eastlake houses, were designed to be both symbolic and artistic. Like the new housing neighborhoods on the city's periphery, the cemeteries were seen as combining the best of art and nature. Elaborate headstones, with truncated family trees, carved statues of women and babies, and even representations of women greeting men at the house when they came home from work, were set in a nurturing natural environment and were supposed to provide the formality and repose for the final place of rest (Figure 4.24). In such areas, death itself was sentimentalized and controlled, manipulated and transformed into yet another vehicle for uplifting and inspiring the public. Art and nature, even in death, were combined to stimulate the advance of progress.[27]

By the 1890s, therefore, the ideal of the artistic development of the house and family had become pervasive. Beginning originally as an extension of the notion that women possessed an idealistic and self-expressive nature, the artistic ideal had become by the turn of the century an end in itself. Houses, earlier considered a personal statement of the owners' hopes and aspirations, now became individual works of art. In the hope of making a more intensely personal comment about their inhabitants, the structures became even more wildly eclectic. Bizarre houses such as one in Redlands, California, which combined an Italianate tower, a French mansard roof, a Turkish Omar dome, brackets, decorative shingling, and a Chinese railing, became the rule rather than exception (Figures 4.25 and 4.26).

Perhaps the best indication of the pervasiveness of the notion that the woman of the house should display a special sensitivity to art and fashion was the degree to which the ideal became criticized during the 1890s. The preoccupation with money, art, and social status seemed now to be a threat to the family itself. Songs such as "She's Only a Bird in a Gilded

Figure 4.24
Gravestones such as this one in the Grove Street Cemetery in New Haven, Connecticut, which shows a mother entering heaven to rejoin her babies, were enormously reassuring to Victorian Americans. (Photograph by author)

Cage" and "Take Back Your Gold and Make Me Your Wife" warned that the preoccupation with wealth and art could be destructive of family virtues. William Sidney Porter, better known as O. Henry, wrote books of stories critiquing shopgirls who placed fashion and self-display above family relationships. In the story "The Trimmed Lamp" it is the shopgirl, Nancy, who though first dazzled by her wealthy customers, later comes to realize that true happiness cannot be bought. This same sentiment, on a more sophisticated level, was echoed by contemporary economist Thorstein Veblen, who in his book *The Theory of the Leisure Class*, suggested that the woman herself had become an object of conspicuous consumption, a status symbol for the household.[28]

Figure 4.25
By the end of the century, the search for appropriate historical styles had reached a degree of absurdity as seen in this house in Redlands, California, with its French mansard roof, Turkish onion dome, brackets, and Chinese railing. (*Redland Daily Facts*; photograph courtesy of John Maass)

Figure 4.26
This 1890s house in Bennington, Vermont, demonstrates the kind of creative eclecticism that took place when an owner tried to design a house as a work of art. (Photograph by author)

The growing stream of criticism and the testimony from individual families suggests ultimately that a tension remained between the ideal and actual practice in the 1890s. As the testimony of Mary Putnam and others implied, it was difficult to be creative, self-expressive, and artistic and still keep the household functioning smoothly. The individual needs of different family members for personal space and self-expression could easily come into conflict. Family life in the late nineteenth century depended upon compromise and self-denial. It was difficult, as Carl Degler has suggested, not to see self-development "at odds" with the needs of the family itself.[29]

Moreover, there were weaknesses inherent in the stress on the ideal of artistic creativity. So much of what passed for art or "female elegancies" was repetitive, imitative, and unoriginal. The mass production of "art objects," whether they were furniture "suits" or lithograph works of great art, could hardly be part of a highly creative and innovative society. Indeed, critics were soon to see the ideal of the artistic and individualistic house and family to be essentially deceptive—a house with no coherent standard of design cluttered with a collection of miscellaneous debris that obscured rather than expressed individuality. By the 1890s the ideal of the home as a treasure house had begun to pass its prime. New critics were beginning to appear who in less than a decade were to discredit the outlook of Victorian Americans as decadent and dysfunctional and to offer a radically new image of what family life should be like.

Chapter 5

Modernizing the House and Family

When that day dawns in which beauty governs all life, in which conscience is the law of all construction, since truth is part of beauty, and forever orders and directs its works, when Hygeia, the twin of Beauty, walks with her hand in hand, then the microbe will vanish into that limbo from whence he came.

—Helen Campbell, "Household Art and the Microbe"

By 1890 the Victorian commitment to the artistic ideals of home and family had become a popular litany—a publicly ritualized pledge to support the home as sanctuary and work of art and an idealized vision of family life based on mutually fulfilling affectionate relationships. Like motherhood and apple pie, the expression of these ideals had become a stylized formula, a series of verbose phrases and clichés that were endlessly repeated in the newspapers and reform pamphlets of the day. Yet, even as the ritualized formulas were being broadcast from pulpit and press, a growing number of architects, feminists, builders, and homeowners were developing serious misgivings about certain aspects of the older ideals. The chorus of protest was not united. Each group found a different cause for concern and some were more outraged than others. Gradually, common themes emerged from their protests. Social values were changing and certain features of the Victorian house appeared out of date. In particular, they questioned the more formalistic emphasis on decorum and display that underlay the design of front entrance halls and parlors. The Victorian house seemed overly ornate and overly specialized; it had too many rooms crammed with too much clutter. The family ideal, similarly, seemed artificial and awkward. Calling cards, elaborate eight-course meals, and a constant attention to formalities seemed to straitjacket family relationships and take the joy out of life. The family, these dissenters believed, should still be protected as the nation's basic social institution, but its dwelling needed radical modification and its life-style considerable rethinking to bring it into conformity with contemporary needs.

What started in the 1890s as an attempt to revise housing standards and family ideals became after 1900 a full-blown crusade to demolish the older Victorian beliefs. Not content to shift the emphasis within the Victorian vision as the previous generation had done, the turn-of-the-century critics dramatically changed the ideals themselves. In place of the elaborate Victorian dwelling, they substituted the rustic bungalow or the modest colonial home. In place of an aesthetic which valued complexity and richness of design, they advocated a more spartan ethic. Houses should be simple, efficient, neat, and natural. The profile of the residence should be straight and clean. Whether the exterior favored Colonial Revival forms, the low horizontality of Prairie School designs, or the simple outlines of the bungalow, the principles of design were the same: structural simplicity, balanced proportions, and minimal decoration (Figures 5.1, 5.2, and 5.3).

If the exterior styles represented a radical change from late Victorian standards, so, too, did the interior floor plans. In the first major change in floor plans since the 1750s, houses were now organized without the elaborate entrance halls and front and back parlors. In their place was a new multipurpose space—the living room—designed to fit a more informal lifestyle. Whether the home was considered to be a bungalow, a Colonial Revival house, or a Prairie School dwelling, the interior was designed to be more rational and efficient, with built-in buffets for the storage of china, sanitary kitchens for germ-free food preparation, and sleeping porches for fresh air in the summer. In place of the romantic Victorian justification of art and beauty as complex and inspirational was a new theory of aesthetics that stressed practicality and simplicity, efficiency and craftsmanship (Figure 5.4).

Middle-class family ideals similarly changed dramatically at the turn of the century. Instead of a stress on manners and decorum, reformers emphasized informality and spontaneity. In keeping with the popular vogue of a more relaxed and easygoing life-style, advice-book writers urged people to be more open and direct about their feelings and emotions. Mothers were expected to be more active outside the home, although public opinion limited somewhat their options for careers. The "new woman," as contemporaries called her, was more energetic and natural, eager to ride bikes, play tennis, attend college, and receive professional training. Children, too, were viewed as more independent and self-sufficient. They were thought to be passing through developmental stages of growth, learning through experience, and entering, after puberty, a stormy period of "adolescence," a term appropriately first coined in 1910. A more energetic and aggressive ideal replaced the paternalistic, authoritarian, and slightly distant Victorian image of what fathers should be. Fathers were to be, like President Theodore Roosevelt, tough but tender, careless of rules, and supportive of their children. The new middle-class family ideal, as espoused in popular magazines and advice books, placed a premium on naturalness and conviviality, openness and informality.[1]

The popular crusade to replace Victorian aesthetic ideals and family standards reached a crescendo by 1910. Under the constant pounding from architects, social reformers, plan-book writers, and sanitarians, the Victorian system of values crumbled. In less than two decades, Queen Anne and Eastlake houses went from being works of art and monuments of individual achievement to being attacked as "architectural atrocities" and "hideous landmarks of forty years ago" based on "the craze for imitation and deceit." By the start of World War I, the older standards for middle-class housing and family life had virtually disappeared.[2]

Changes of this magnitude in so short a time are difficult to explain. Questions naturally arise. Why were these changes so abrupt? What accounts for the timing of the shift in outlook? Why were the Progressive reformers so much more persuasive than their Victorian predecessors? Why did the public at large so readily

Figure 5.1
This bungalow in Bennington, Vermont, has the simple lines and low profile that stood in marked contrast to its Victorian predecessors. (Photograph by author)

Figure 5.2
After the World's Fair of 1893, Neo-Classical Revival houses, now known as "Colonial," came back into fashion. (Bennett Lumber Co., *Bennett Better-Built, Ready-Cut Homes*)

Figure 5.3
In contrast to the
simple bungalow or
Colonial Revival
house, Victorian
houses seemed awk-
ward and clumsy.
(Shoppell, *Modern
Houses*)

Figure 5.4
The low profile of
this bungalow in
Bennington, Ver-
mont, makes it fit in
more readily on this
hilly site. (Photo-
graph by author)

accept the destruction of the older views? Indeed, were the ideals that replaced the Victorian outlook as innovative or useful as their advocates suggested?

The abrupt and dramatic transformation of the middle-class family home ideal between 1890 and 1910 was part of a more general reorientation of American culture that was taking place at the turn of the century. Although the immediate cause of this change was the loss of confidence in traditional social values precipitated by the depression of 1893 and its aftermath, the search for new standards was strongly, and at times unconsciously, influenced by a more basic transformation of the economy which had been going on for several decades. Beginning in the 1870s and 1880s, underlying structural changes began to take place, unperceived by most people, in the national patterns of production, communication, consumption, and family life. Led by aggressive American business interests, the post–Civil War economy was consolidated into one enormous national unit. Businessmen, aided by the expansion of railroads, the establishment of a national telegraph and telephone network, the systematization of the currency, the growth of newspapers and magazines, and the tremendous influx of immigrants, created national markets for their products and substantially increased factory production. Under energetic and at times unscrupulous business leaders such as Andrew Carnegie and John D. Rockefeller, industrial production expanded tenfold and prices were cut in half. Increasingly, nationally organized companies such as Swift, U.S. Steel, Standard Oil, and General Electric provided products and services for the common man.

The rapid expansion of commerce and industry brought with it a host of technological innovations that simplified everyday life. Laundering, which had once taken as much as one-third of a housewife's time, was made more manageable with the invention of gas hot-water heaters, indoor plumbing, and hand-cranked mechanical washing machines. Home baking, which often took one day a week, could be reduced or eliminated altogether by the purchase of bakery products from urban bakeries or from the National Biscuit Company. Even the production of shirts and dresses was vastly simplified by the invention of the sewing machine. By 1900, the increasing use of products made outside the home had dramatically altered the time and space needed to manage the contemporary household[3] (Figures 5.5, 5.6, and 5.7).

Few individuals initially perceived the subtle and important ways in which the larger changes in the economy were influencing the life of the family itself. In part, these changes were overlooked because they coincided with subtle but important shifts that were taking place in family composition and size. One of these changes was the decline in the birthrate that had begun at the start of the century. The birthrate for white women in 1800 was 7.04; by 1900 it had dropped by almost 50 percent to 3.56. The smaller number of children, the increase in labor-saving equipment, and the tendency to purchase more goods and services from outside the home in the 1880s and 1890s gradually undermined the older Victorian assumptions about women's proper roles. New family magazines such as the *Ladies Home Journal* (1883), *Good Housekeeping* (1885), *House Beautiful* (1896), and *House and Garden* (1905) bombarded the housewife with advice, creating anxiety about what the proper role of the mother should be. Dissatisfied with the obvious restrictions on their choices of careers, middle-class women at the turn of the century began to search for more systematic justifications for their functions within the family.[4]

The position of young adults within the family was also changing in ways that were not initially perceived. In the city of Philadelphia in the 1880s, young men and women commonly entered the work force but continued to live at home and contribute to the family income for an average of seven years. This slow movement toward financial independence was necessitated by the need to support parents whose own livelihood was sometimes threatened by layoffs, accidents, or sickness. As the level of real in-

TIME-SAVERS

(1) A Carafe Which Keeps Beverages Iced Many Hours
(2) Glass Ice-cream Freezer Which Requires No Turning
(3) Speedy Egg-beater Designed on the Turbine Principle
(4) Coffee Pot Permits Making Coffee Hours in Advance
(5) A Quick Toaster for Oil or Gas Fuels
(6) An Egg-Boiler That Boils Eggs Just Right
(7) A Double Pan Which Cooks Two Foods at Once
(8) Measuring Spoon Set Saves Lifting Different Spoons
(9) A Colander and Puree Strainer Which Gives Rapid Results

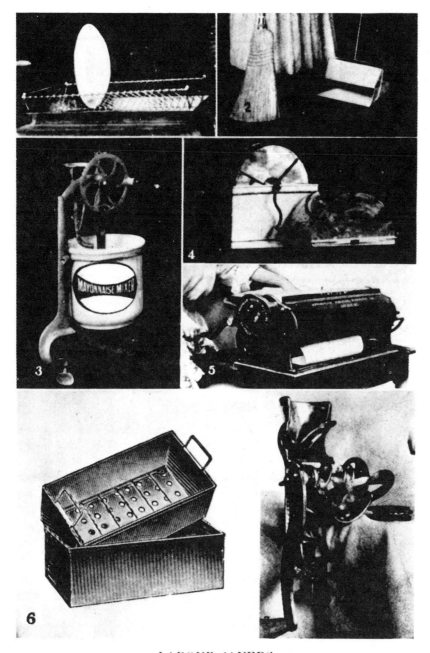

LABOUR-SAVERS

(1) Dish Drainer Allows Dishes to Dry Themselves
(2) Hooded, Long-handled Dust-pan Prevents Stooping
(3) Stationary Egg-beater Prevents Waste Motion
(4) Washboiler with Rotary Wheel Saves Rubbing
(5) Hot Mangle Which Replaces Hand Labour
(6) Silver Clean Pan Which Does Away with Silver Polishing
(7) An Efficient, Easily Cleaned Meat-chopper

Figure 5.7
Christine Frederick's
advice book stressed
the use of gadgets.

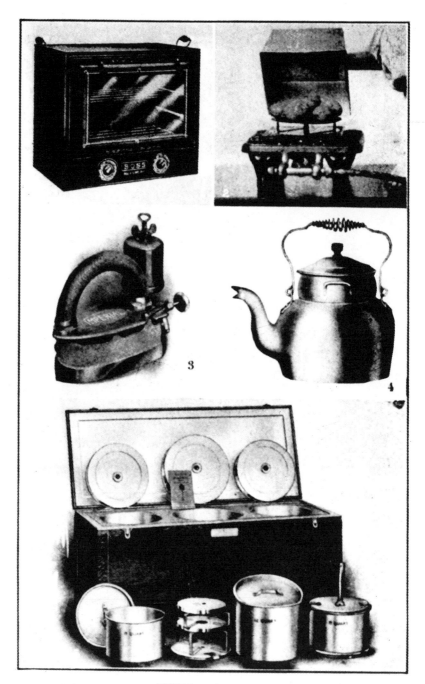

FUEL-SAVERS
(1) Portable Oven with Window Prevents Loss of Heat
(2) Device Utilizing One Burner for Baking
(3) Gasolene Iron with Concentrated Heating Surface
(4) Tea Kettle and Double Boiler Combined
(5) Well-Insulated Fuel-Saving Fireless Cooker

come rose toward the turn of the century and the incidence of epidemic disease began to fall off, young adults were less frequently called on to support their parents and more often used their earnings for their own needs. Contemporaries worried about a new phenomenon—the "fast girl" who spent her extra money on clothes and entertainment.

National economic and communications changes in the late nineteenth century not only subtly modified the traditional roles of women and children within the middle-class family, but they also significantly eroded the sense of small-town regional identity. For most of the nineteenth century, a majority of Americans had lived in small towns and rural areas that had functioned as island communities, autonomous entities cut off to some extent from national concerns by the barriers of poor communications and local customs. As late as 1880, 75 percent of Americans lived in rural areas and produced at home many of the clothing and food products that they themselves consumed.

Although they were never completely isolated, these communities governed their own affairs through the local town fathers and maintained a sense of distinct local identity. Merchants, doctors, and lawyers derived significant status from the recognition they received from being part of the local community. Local autonomy was evident both in the choice of goods available at community dry goods stores and in the political leadership chosen for schools and local government.

By 1900 the predominantly rural character of the country had begun to shift and with it went changes in the quality of life in the local community. In that same year 60 percent of Americans lived outside major cities, but even those who did not move to urban areas felt the influence of urban life. By then the economic and cultural autonomy of these rural communities, already under attack by the growth of large-scale corporate enterprise, had been significantly eroded by the rise of the professions, the transformation of communications, and, most important, by the emergence of a new culture of consumption. Responding to the de-

mand for higher standards and better control of practice, lawyers, doctors, teachers, and other professionals, starting in the 1880s, set up national standards for entry into their occupations. Educated in the new law schools at Stanford, Johns Hopkins, and the University of Chicago, lawyers now often viewed themselves as professionals whose trained expertise would allow them to practice anywhere in the country. No longer did they identify with the town in which they had been born and raised. Instead they saw themselves as educated professionals who combined technical expertise with an allegiance to higher standards; in place of local ties, they identified themselves with national organizations such as the American Medical Association or the American Bar Association.

At the same time that the desire to raise standards and improve professional expertise was influencing the outlook and values of lawyers, doctors, and other small-town leaders, a dramatic shift in the communications industry helped to change substantially the outlook of the man on the street. Part of the change was simply mechanical. The inventions of the typewriter, linotype, photoengraving, and the sextuple printing press led to a revolution in communications at the turn of the century. Before 1880 most American magazines had been limited in circulation and aimed at small, specialized audiences. Before 1882, for example, *Harper's Monthly* refused all advertisements except those of its publisher. Starting in the 1880s, this pattern shifted dramatically. By 1890 thirty-nine new periodicals, including the *Ladies Home Journal, Comfort, Cosmopolitan, Munsey's Magazine,* and *McClure's* had circulations of over 100,000 copies annually and were inundating the public with advertisements for bicycles, pianos, cosmetics, and health care products. Newspaper circulation, similarly, skyrocketed under the aggressive leadership of William Randolph Hearst, Joseph Pulitzer, and James Gordon Bennett. By 1900 two thousand daily papers had a combined readership of more than fifteen million. Huge advertising layouts, Sunday supplements, and technical sections on the latest machines and

[margin note: Emergence of the professional in American society.]

inventions greatly stimulated interest and broke down the preoccupation with local concerns.

Taking advantage of this revolution in communications, the expanding national corporations used aggressive newspaper and magazine advertising to create a new culture of consumption. Although newspaper advertising in 1880 already accounted for 44 percent of American newspaper's receipts, most advertising, like the Reverend Henry Ward Beecher's endorsement of Pears Soap, was a simple testimonial to a product's virtues. The only catchy or humorous sales advertisements circulated in the form of trade cards that were given away by local retailers. During the next decade, newspaper advertising, which now provided over half the newspaper's income, changed dramatically in format. Products were promoted with brand names in major half- and full-page illustrations. Large national corporations such as the National Biscuit Company, Eastman Kodak, and the American Tobacco Company learned that aggressive marketing and advertising campaigns in magazines, department stores, and newspapers resulted in tremendous sales gains. Using these tactics, retail businesses, large and small, began their assault on small-town America. With heavily advertised products that ranged from standardized lumber sizes and standardized cuts of meat to the latest in clothing and home furnishings, the national companies established new norms for home consumption (Figure 5.8).

Implicit in this expanding consumer culture, as historian William Leach has pointed out, was a message that had a transformative effect on women. The vast array of new consumer products, ranging from clothes and cosmetics to foods and appliances, created an imaginative world offering new opportunities and experiences. Brilliantly promoted in the dazzling windows of great urban department stores such as Macy's, Wanamaker's, and Marshall Field's, which had extended their earlier roles as the arbitrator of artistic achievement to include a fantasy world of fashion and service, this dramatically expanding consumer culture implied the possibility of a new individualism founded upon commodity consumption. Because these stores provided a tremendous array of choices of food, clothing, and household furnishings, their existence suggested a life-style that promised to expand the province of rewarding work and of individual expression for middle-class women. Shopping in cities like Boston and Washington, D.C., which had been lighted, cleaned up, and redesigned by urban planners, gave women a new sense of independence which they quickly took advantage of. By 1915, according to the trade journals, women spent more time shopping than men and accounted for between 80 and 85 percent of all consumer purchasing.

The power of this new culture of consumption, dramatized in the colorful displays in department store windows, was perceived as both an opportunity and a threat. Mary Antin, the Jewish immigrant who celebrated her achievements in her patriotic book, *The Promised Land,* could write enthusiastically about shopping with her girlfriends in Boston, pressing "noses and fingers on plate glass windows ablaze with electric lights and alluring with display." For Mary Antin the consumer culture had become a symbol of the opportunities of American life. But not all people shared Antin's enthusiasm. As early as 1881, the *New York Times* warned of "the awful prevalence of the vice of shopping among women," an addiction "every bit as bad as male drinking or smoking." In 1900 newspaperman Lyman Frank Baum penned the classic indictment of glamorized urban life in his book, *The Wizard of Oz.* Baum's heroine, Dorothy, is lured to the magnificent Emerald City in the hopes of getting all her wishes gratified. She is told to follow the "yellow brick road," a rather blatant symbol of money or gold. The Emerald City turns out to be a fraud (Dorothy has to put on green glasses to see it). The remarkable wizard, similarly, is nothing but a well-meaning charlatan. The moral of the story is to trust yourself and beware of the glitter and false promises of urban commercial life. At the conclusion, Dorothy rejoices at being back home again on the Kansas prairie. The lure of consumer life in the

"Standard" GUARANTEED PLUMBING FIXTURES

T HOSE things in your home that are to last a lifetime should be the best you can buy. For the sake of your children—for the tastes you are developing in them, for the clean lives you are training them to live—you need the beauty and perfect sanitation of "Standard" Bathroom Fixtures.

Genuine "Standard" fixtures for the Home and for Schools, Office Buildings, Public Institutions, etc., are identified by the Green and Gold Label, with the exception of one brand of baths bearing the Red and Black Label, which, while of the first quality of manufacture, have a slightly thinner enameling, and thus meet the requirements of those who demand "Standard" quality at less expense. All "Standard" fixtures, with care, will last a lifetime. And no fixture is genuine *unless it bears the guarantee label.* In order to avoid substitution of inferior fixtures, specify "Standard" goods in writing (not verbally) and make sure that you get them.

Standard Sanitary Mfg. Co.   Dept. L   PITTSBURGH, PA.

New York .   35 West 31st Street
Chicago . 900 S. Michigan Ave.
Philadelphia . 1128 Walnut Street
Toronto, Can. 59 Richmond St., E.
Pittsburgh .   106 Federal Street
St. Louis . 100 N. Fourth Street
Cincinnati .   633 Walnut Street

Nashville . 315 Tenth Avenue, So.
NewOrleans,Baronne & St.JosephSts.
Montreal, Can. , 215 Coristine Bldg.
Boston   .   .   John Hancock Bldg.
Louisville . 319-23 W. Main Street
Cleveland . 648 Huron Road, S.E.
Hamilton, Can., 20-28 Jackson St. W.

London .   .   . 57-60 Holborn Viaduct
Houston, Tex. . Preston and Smith Sts.
San Francisco, Cal.
      Merchants National Bank Building
Washington, D.C. . . Southern Bldg.
Toledo, Ohio . . 311-321 Erie Street
Fort Worth, Tex. . Front and Jones Sts.

Figure 5.8
Building material suppliers such as Standard Plumbing worked hard to convince the public that their products would improve the quality of family life. (Standard Plumbing advertisement, *Good Housekeeping*)

city, according to Baum, can never match the self-sufficiency of life on the farm.[5]

Despite the cleverness and power of his imagery, Baum's last-ditch attack on the new culture of consumption was a failure. The exodus from the farm to the city was to continue for most of the twentieth century. Nevertheless, many Americans viewed the endless glitter and variety of consumer goods with suspicion. By the turn of the century, many middle-class Americans were rejecting the glamour and showiness of urban America for a simpler, more self-contained life-style.[6]

The reorientation of social values at the turn of the century implicit in the rejection of the large Victorian house and the acceptance of the bungalow thus rested on the complex and massive changes in communications and economic production that had been underway for more than three decades. For middle-class Americans, the most problematic feature of this change was the new urban-oriented culture of consumption. Enormously attractive and appealing, yet scary and in some ways menacing, the new culture of consumption made the middle class more self-conscious and forced it to reexamine its values and life-style.

These major, underlying shifts in the family and the economy by themselves would have been deeply troubling to a generation that had grown up in the comfortable certainty of the Victorian social ethos. But when the shifts coincided with the depression of 1893, the worst financial setback during the century, the social strain they created was enormous. Coming on top of a series of substantial but dimly perceived changes in national markets, communications, consumer culture, and household structure, the depression of 1893 and the massive social dislocation that followed it provided a major catalyst for rethinking general social ideals. The impact of the depression was particularly devastating because it followed closely a period of spectacular economic growth in which wheat production increased 600 percent and manufacturing rocketed from one to ten billion dollars. The abrupt shift from pros-

perity to depression was a rude shock. Thousands of farmers lost their land, more than two and a half million people were thrown out of work, and violence between capital and labor erupted in the railroad and steel industries. The sheer magnitude of human misery forced most Americans, both urban and rural, to rethink their values. Was capitalism a fair and efficient economic system? Could the vast number of new immigrants be assimilated into American life? Were the country's basic political and social institutions—Congress, the courts, the schools, and the police—powerful enough to deal with these social problems? From Populists to labor leaders, from historians to social reformers, major thinkers from a variety of fields now turned their attention to reevaluating the American way of life.

In the forefront of this investigation were newspaper journalists and magazine writers. Convinced that their role was to discover the underlying causes for the depression and the contemporary crisis in values, men such as Stephen Crane, Jacob Riis, and Hamlin Garland undertook a systematic crusade to investigate the inner workings of large corporate business and grass-roots politics. Uncomfortable with the traditional Victorian ideals of self-help, success, and business enterprise, they sought to cut through the veneer of appearances and find out the reality. What were the real reasons for the drastic decline in farm prices? How did factory workers, street waifs, and the poor actually live? Did they have any chance of improving their economic status? What kind of people ran the national corporations? Only by getting behind the scenes and watching what actually happened could they know, they thought, what really went on.

This drive to know the underlying reality had a profound impact both on the questioners and on their outlook. It was part of a more general reorientation of American culture at the turn of the century. The reformers came to see themselves as iconoclasts, breaking down traditions and establishing new truths. Newspaper correspondents and writers appropriately called themselves "realists." In his book *Crumbling*

Idols (1894) Hamlin Garland sounded the note of rebellion against old traditions. His reference was to literary traditions, but his approach was shared by a variety of other social thinkers. "I do not advocate an exchange of masters," he insisted, "but freedom from masters. Life, Nature,—these should be our teachers. They are masters who do not enslave." Skeptical of conventions and hostile toward the pretensions of those who wrote "romances" about the upper classes, Garland asserted that the most interesting subject for fiction was commonplace, everyday life. Americans needed to reexamine the beliefs and social conventions that governed their everyday lives.[7]

The call for new standards issued by Hamlin Garland, William Dean Howells, and the other literary realists was shared by other social critics at the turn of the century. Muckrakers Ida Tarbell and Lincoln Steffens went behind the scenes to uncover the manipulations of Standard Oil and the corruption of political bosses in St. Paul, Minnesota, and other cities. Philosophers John Dewey and William James contrasted the value of concrete experience to ideas "grown petrified by antiquity." Such an approach, insisted James, "means the open air and possibilities of nature, as against dogma, artificiality and the pretense of finality in truth." Children should learn by doing, seconded Dewey. American education should be transformed from memorizing old truths to learning from experience. The philosopher, taking his social responsibilities seriously, should help create new standards for the nation.[8]

The persistent pressure created by the depression, the transformation of the economy, the revolution in communications, and the emergence of the consumer culture fueled a massive attack on Victorian standards that took place on many fronts. In addition to an iconoclastic search for new standards in politics, journalism, literature, and philosophy, there were parallel onslaughts taken against the late Victorian views of the home and family. Encouraged not simply to modify the old but to place basic social values on a more solid foot-

ing, architects, housing reformers, sanitarians, feminists, and educators turned their attentions to setting new standards for middle-class housing. Building upon changes in aesthetics, medicine, science, and technology, these reformers in the first three decades of the twentieth century created a substantially new ideal for middle-class housing and family life.

The crusade against the 1880 artistic ideal of house and family was initiated by the architects who long had had misgivings about the extravagant decoration and bizarre shapes of many of the plan-book house designs. The architects' critique was amplified by social critics who were troubled by the Victorian preoccupation with social status and display. But the movement's major support came from sanitarians and family reformers who felt that Victorian houses represented nothing less than a menace to the health and happiness of middle-class Americans.

Architects had complained since the 1880s that the worst feature of the eclectic Victorian homes built by plan-book advocates and local contractors was their lack of consistency. Without a supporting aesthetic rationale, such structures seemed overly ornate. "The architect rescues his design from the commonplace by making his window-panes small and his mullions large, by multiplying moldings and tormenting the outlines of his gables with steps, cartouches and finials," wrote one critic in the *American Architect and Building News*, "but why the result pleases his eye he cannot tell." Without a consistent theory of design, house building became too often an exercise of the unchecked imagination[9] (Figure 5.9).

Such houses tended to be overly elaborate; the layout had too many rooms and construction was cheapened to increase the size. In place of the grand Victorian house, critics suggested the need for a smaller dwelling. Writing on the "vanity of Big Houses," social commentator John Burroughs suggested that "a man can fill and warm a cabin, he is not swallowed by it; he can make it a part of himself—he can make it fit him like his old shoes, and be as

Figure 5.9
Because Victorian plan-book houses such as this one were not based upon a clear philosophy of design, they became the target for critics' attacks after the turn of the century. (Shoppell, *Modern Houses*)

expressive of his daily life." But a big house would destroy the man's sense of perspective and humility. Burroughs's ideal house would be simpler, more in tune with nature, informal, and, as his comments about old shoes suggested, comfortable.[10]

In addition to attacking the size of Victorian residences, architects were critical of the restrictive use of the front parlor. "The habit of keeping shut-up parlors for occasional company is so absurd that it is difficult to give people who practice it credit for ordinary common sense," wrote one designer. Elaborate front parlors, like large houses, seemed excessively vain. By the 1890s even those who liked parlors were urging that the decor be redesigned to adapt those rooms to everyday use. As architect Edward Hapgood suggested, the pressure to utilize the parlor frequently and the need to tolerate children and animals in it who might disrupt the furnishings had created a new tolerance for plainer decoration. "The ultra-queer colors have disappeared," Hapgood insisted, "and the carpets and wallpapers no longer suggest perpetual biliousness or chronic nightmare."[11]

Eventually critics suggested that the parlor was superfluous. "Indeed," wrote Edward Hapgood about his design for a $3,500 suburban house for the *Ladies Home Journal*, "if [the homeowner] will do without the time-honored parlor—the sort of room which has no place in

the house we are considering—and if he will consent to make his hall a little smaller than might at first seem wise, it is possible to have one room on the first floor that will offer many advantages over the usual arrangement." A pleasant "living-room," with a cozy fireplace, bookcases, and a cupboard or two would serve the combined functions of library, parlor, and sitting room[12] (Figure 5.10).

By 1900, Victorian homes were being stereotyped as inefficient and gaudy—filled with furniture "made aesthetically repulsive by florid ornamentation." They were stigmatized as part of "that fatuous craze for the crudely ornate," the antithesis of wholesome plainness and simplicity. But what made them most unfit for middle-class families was their lack of national distinctiveness. Simply to copy Eastlake or Renaissance house styles, suggested one architect, was to ignore the possibilities for developing a truly national housing style. Such "servile copying" was a disservice to the American people. Architects, he insisted, needed to launch a campaign for more truly national building designs, ones closer to the simplicity of the vernacular "old clapboard homestead."[13]

The accelerating attack on Victorian designs and aesthetic assumptions during the 1890s gradually evolved into an intense crusade to develop a new philosophy of architectural design. Like the writers and social critics in these same years, architects came to see themselves as iconoclasts, tearing down old standards and erecting new ones. For many of them, the Italian Renaissance provided a model for their efforts. Daniel H. Burnham and the other designers of the World's Fair in 1893 were heartened to hear the sculptor Augustus St. Gaudens exclaim at one of the organizational meetings, "I never expected to see this moment. It has been the greatest meeting of artists since the fifteenth century." Writing in *Harper's Monthly* the following year, architect Thomas Hastings predicted the dawn of a "modern Renaissance" because, he insisted, it will be influenced by the conditions of modern life. "It

THE LIVING ROOM

Published in The Craftsman, December, 1905.

Figure 5.10
Gustav Stickley suggested several variant designs for the new, multipurpose "living-room" in *Craftsman* magazine in 1905. (Stickley, *Craftsman Homes*)

Published in The Craftsman, November, 1905.

BUILT-IN CHINA CLOSETS ON EITHER SIDE OF THE FIREPLACE IN A LIVING ROOM WHICH IS ALSO USED AS A DINING ROOM. BY A SLIGHT DIFFERENCE IN ARRANGEMENT THE CUPBOARDS ABOVE COULD BE MADE TO SERVE AS BOOKCASES AND THOSE BELOW AS STORAGE PLACES FOR PAPERS, MAGAZINES AND THE LIKE.

Published in The Craftsman, December, 1905.

will be the work of the Renaissance architect adapting his art to an honest and rational treatment of new materials."[14]

Hastings's comment held up the architect as the new Renaissance man, an individual who combined vision, expertise, and the drive to get things done. The glorification of Renaissance leaders as men of extraordinary power who might transform the public consciousness was not a unique phenomenon at the turn of the century. In addition to admiring the Renaissance, civic and educational leaders also held up the ideal of Napoleon Bonaparte as a model of how the powerful individual might redirect the course of a nation. Popular magazines such as *McClure's* and *Cosmopolitan* extolled the virtues of Napoleon as an example of how to get things done. Napoleon thus became a popular exemplar for individual success. Writers, politicians, and social reformers used the Napoleonic model to argue that willpower, perseverance, and courage were the crucial determinants for getting ahead. In place of the old virtues of honesty, industry, and thrift, they praised individual determination and energy. Contemporary business and political leaders such as Theodore Roosevelt, Andrew Carnegie, and John D. Rockefeller seemed themselves to embody the Napoleonic ideals of forceful individualism and effective leadership.[15]

Whether one looked at the ambitions of architects such as Thomas Hastings or Louis Sullivan or focused instead on the one-man campaigns of Lincoln Steffens or Theodore Roosevelt, the objective and the means to success were essentially similar. Writers, politicians, and architects sought to dominate and control public opinion by asserting their ability to see through illusions and get below the surface to fundamental realities. Not surprisingly, too, these leaders saw their own work as more "honest" and "rational" than that of their predecessors. As architect John S. Van Bergen admitted, "since the American architect has a great opportunity as a leader of the people toward honesty, simplicity and directness, he

can educate their tastes and control, to a great extent, their morals and happiness."[16]

The architects', writers', and politicians' attempt to create new national standards was both altruistic and egotistical. Shored up by specialized training, technical expertise, and solid experience in the practical, everyday world, architects, like writers and politicians, wanted to improve dramatically their standards as professionals. In so doing, they hoped both to establish a new theory of aesthetics for the popular housing market and to advance their personal power. During the two decades after 1890, their efforts in these areas proved to be remarkably successful. Despite some differences in emphasis from architect to architect and from one region of the country to another, the designers joined with social reformers and sanitarians to establish a broad consensus on basic artistic standards. Although they would continue to disagree somewhat about specific styles, by 1910 they nevertheless generally accepted similar fundamental principles of design.

The foundation of the new theory of aesthetics was a belief in simplicity. Simple, clean lines in a building's exterior and interior were a good in and of themselves. "Simplicity is three-fourths of beauty," wrote Katherine B. Johnson in *Good Housekeeping*. Flat surfaces, straight lines, and sharp angles had a cleanness and precision that was considered to be far more attractive than the complicated curves and intricate detail that had characterized Victorian designs. Simplicity could be achieved in a variety of ways. One was to reduce or remove the ornament. "I have had no difficulty in getting people to allow me to simplify their houses for them," suggested W. L. Price in the *American Architect and Building News*. "The tendency to ornament comes from the architect rather than from the client, almost every time." Another way to simplify was to emphasize the function of the house and cut out superfluous spaces and materials. Gustav Stickley, one of the most forceful advocates of the "craftsman" movement who gained much of his inspiration from

Englishman William Morris's emphasis on naturalistic motifs in design, stressed the need to reduce the dwelling's structure to its essentials in order to simplify the daily life of the homeowner. Fewer objects to be dusted or repaired, more compact and efficient use of space, and a reorganization of the routines of life such as the preparation of meals and the washing of clothes, Stickley thought, would make the house more durable and functional[17] (Figures 5.11 and 5.12).

Although Gustav Stickley represented but one segment of the architectural profession, he was part of a movement toward simplifying living arrangements that was shared by many of his peers. As one architect suggested, many Americans believed that families needed "space to carry on the business of life freely and with pleasure, with furniture made for use; rooms where a drop of water spilled is not fatal, where the life of a child is not made a burden to it by unnecessary restraint; plain, simple and ungarnished if necessary, but honest; and a true artist will find pleasure in serving such clients." The emphasis on freedom, "honesty," and the "true artist" expressed by this architect was constantly reiterated in the popular press.[18]

The link between simplicity and functionality could also be seen in the architects' approach to new building materials such as cement blocks and reinforced concrete. The early articles on cement construction and concrete blocks in the professional journals emphasized the plasticity of the material and its strength, but lamented the lack of "art" in its use. Louis H. Gibson, writing in the *American Architect and Building News*, stressed that concrete blocks were an excellent building material but then complained that he had never seen "an artistically successful" structure built out of them. The growing concern for simplicity and functionality soon reversed this criticism. Simple and functional structures, by the new definition, were obviously beautiful. By 1906 architects had stopped criticizing concrete blocks and were now praising them. Concrete blocks were fireproof, colorful, adaptable, cool in summer and warm in winter, strong, cheap, and earthy, wrote Charles DeKay in the *Architectural Record*. Attractive villas made from concrete, he suggested, might "take us back unconsciously through the labyrinth of long-vanished ancestral days, by the obscure paths of instinct, perhaps, to the ages when the race passed untold centuries as cliff-dwellers, mound-dwellers, [and] inhabitants of wattled mudwalled cabins." The message was clear. The primitive simplicity of concrete structures was the perfect antidote to the sickly complexity and architectural excesses of the older Victorian structures[19] (Figure 5.13).

The ultimate argument for simplicity as the basic element in the new aesthetic theories of design was that it was more American. One of the major criticisms of Victorian buildings was that they too often slavishly copied European historical revival styles. "Are we not all tired of servile copying?" lamented Albert Kelsey in the *American Architect and Building News*. "Do foreign adaptations satisfy either the client or the Architect?" The answer was no. Americans needed their own distinctive housing styles. Guy Kirkham in *Good Housekeeping* echoed Kelsey's views and suggested that the simpler designs were more "modern." Trying to combine historical styles was both false and foolish. "It is a part of that cheap pretentiousness that good taste and good sense alike avoid," he insisted.[20]

This attack on historical styles and the search for a distinctively American architecture reached its fullest expression in the design of the bungalow and Prairie School houses. Although advocates of the bungalow house promoted it as a natural and informal structure that fit the needs of the modern family, Frank Lloyd Wright, Walter Burley Griffin, and others who wrote for the *Western Architect* argued that the clean lines and horizontality of their designs represented nothing less than a new native architectural tradition, born on the prairies near Chicago and thus free from the pretentiousness of East Coast styles.

By using the concept of simplicity to attack

Figure 5.11
In his plan book
Gustav Stickley con-
sistently emphasized
the simplicity of his
designs. (Stickley,
Craftsman Homes)

A SIMPLE, STRAIGHTFORWARD DESIGN

THIS has been one of the most popular of the Craftsman house designs and as shown here it has been modified somewhat from the first plan, the modifications and improvements having been suggested by the different people who have built the house, so that they are all valuable as the outcome of practical experience. Although the illustration shows plastered walls and a foundation of field stone, the design lends itself quite as readily to walls of brick or stone, or even to shingles or clapboards, if a wooden house be desired.

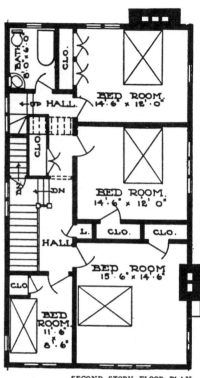

SECOND STORY FLOOR PLAN.

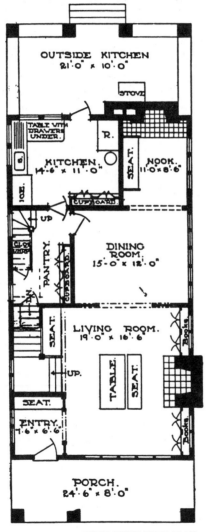

FIRST STORY FLOOR PLAN.

The outside kitchen at the back is recommended only in the event of the house being built in the country, because in town it would hardly be needed. In a farmhouse such an outside kitchen is most convenient as it affords an outdoor place for such work as washing and ironing, canning, preserving and other tasks which are much less wearisome if done in the open air. The position of the chimney at the back of the house makes it possible for a stove to be placed upon this porch for the use mentioned. The house is so designed that this outside kitchen may be added to it or omitted, as desired, without making any difference to the plan as a whole. The plan of the lower story shows the usual open arrangement of the Craftsman house. The entrance door opens into a small entry screened from the living room by heavy portiéres, so that no draught from the front door is felt inside. On the outside wall of the living room is the arrangement of fireplace and bookcases, as shown in the illustration. A large table might be placed in the center, with a settle back to it and facing the fire.

First Floor—Marsden   Second Floor—Marsden

The Marsden $1,355.65

Price, $1,427.00
Cash discount, 5%
Net price, $1,355.65

EACH year the sales of this attractive semi-bungalow far exceed the preceding year, and best of all its rapidly increasing number of owners are invariably delighted with their new home. We wish you could read some of the entertaining letters, without solicitation, received from scores of Marsden owners. They will of course be sent on request. Just study the lines of this bungalow and note how artistically appointed is every part,—the straight line dormer with exposed eaves in exact keeping with the eave of the front porch—the extended bay window with roof and brackets, breaking the gable end—the windows of different sizes and styles and location—these and many other points make the exterior of the Marsden truly artistic. Also note photograph of Marsden on page 14.

In interior planning and arrangement, this modern bungalow presents what might well be said to be the last word in designing. On entering the large living room, 26x16, extending across the entire front, one is attracted by the beautiful bookcase arch separating the living and dining rooms. Beautiful in itself, yet this arch by means of its glass doors and adjustable shelves forms at once a convenient, attractive and useful piece of house furnishings. Notice the abundance of light in living and dining rooms. A well arranged kitchen with stairs leading to grade landing complete the first floor. Ascending to the second floor by the semi-open stairs at end of living room, one enters a central hall from which easy access is gained to each of the three large bedrooms and the bath. Please note the clothes closet with each bedroom—a most appreciated adjunct for every sleeping room. The price includes everything above the foundation to complete the bungalow. Front steps, grade entrance and cellar stairs. Siding can be substituted if desired for wall shingles at no additional cost. See Terms on page 2 and General Specifications on pages 12 and 13.

inherited forms and customs, architects like Wright and Griffin in the Progressive period turned their back on European traditions. Massive numbers of new homes were built with few if any historical details. The two exceptions to this rule, the Colonial Revival and English Tudor homes, had a basic simplicity of form and an association with the early years of settlement that made them appear "American" even though they paralleled European designs. Colonial and Tudor styles, with their cleanness of line and simplicity of shape, were as dra-

matic a rejection of ornate Victorian forms as were the Prairie School homes or the suburban bungalows. By 1915 architect Elkin Wallick could thus confidently assert that "the dominant characteristic of what we may term the American style is simplicity of design."[21]

A second basic principle of design stressed by the architectural reformers was honesty. Great emphasis was placed on allowing the natural features of materials to display their own inherent color and texture. Wood was to look like wood, stone like stone. The inherent

Figure 5.12
This "semi-bungalow" stresses its clean lines and built-in bookcase. (Aladdin Homes, *Catalog 28*)

Figure 5.13
The rustic quality of
this house with its
rough, textured exte-
rior was inherent in
the drawing that this
architect used to pic-
ture his design. (Her-
ing,"Design and
Specifications for an
Inexpensive Brick
Bungalow")

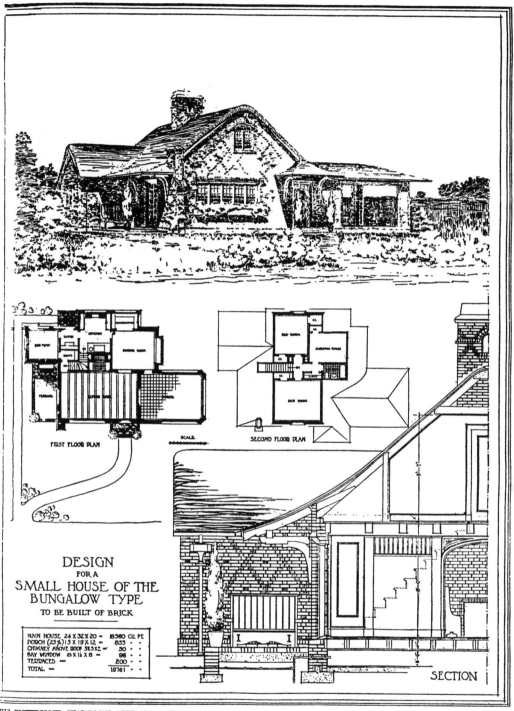

DESIGN
FOR A
SMALL HOUSE OF THE
BUNGALOW TYPE
TO BE BUILT OF BRICK

MAIN HOUSE 24 X 32 X 20 =	18360 CU. FT	
PORCH (25%)15 X 19 X 12 =	855	
CHIMNEY ABOVE ROOF 5½ X 12 =	50	
BAY WINDOW 8 X 1½ X 8 =	96	
TERRACES =	200	
TOTAL =	19761	

THIS PICTURESQUE, YEAR-ROUND COTTAGE OF THE BUNGALOW TYPE, STRONGLY ENGLISH IN ALL ITS DETAILS, CAN BE BUILT OF BRICK AT
AN ESTIMATED COST OF $3,950. GRADING AND PLANTING OF THE GROUNDS ARE NOT INCLUDED

patterns in the material supplied the decorative detail. Instead of applying exterior ornament, architects were more prone to allow the nature of the materials and the outline of the structure to serve as the main forms of ornament. W. L. Price even suggested that the texture of materials be the most important factor in their use. Such an approach to building materials had the further advantage, he noted, of saving money since the cheaper and rougher materials naturally had the better textures.[22]

Two remaining principles of design rounded out the Progressive Theory. Buildings should be "natural" and "organic." Although these terms had also been used to describe Victorian houses, they were now adapted by Progressive architects who changed their meanings. "Natural," as used by Andrew Jackson Downing and his Victorian contemporaries, had referred to the belief that nature would reveal underlying divine laws that once learned could be used to govern building design and family life. One such law held that self-improvement would lead to the progress of civilization. Progressive architects used the term "natural" in a very different way. Instead of conceiving of nature as a divine source of inspiration, they used the term "natural" to indicate the opposite of anything that was contrived or artificial. Like John Muir and Theodore Roosevelt, who rejoiced in the rough and untamed dimension of the western Rockies, architects developed a new appreciation for the natural textures of wood and stone. Whereas nature was emblematic of complexity of form and diversity of color for the Victorians, it symbolized plain truth and hard reality for the Progressives. In place of the elaborately carved and grooved boards and stone capitals, the Progressive architects substituted flat, plain surfaces that displayed the grain of the wood or the texture of the rock. Nature for them was simple, rough, and ordinary.

The emphasis on the "honest" use of natural materials was itself part of the reaction against the sentimentalized vision of the natural world extolled by the Victorians. In place of the beneficent and peaceful Victorian landscape, the Progressives substituted a Darwinian view more in keeping with the economic turmoil of the times. Nature was tough—as Darwin's theory of the survival of the fittest suggested—and the elements were dangerous. Following this line of argument, Progressive architects advised that a good house should be a substantial place of shelter, able to protect its inhabitants. A more forthright way to view the natural world, they asserted, was not to cover up the rough and powerful forces of nature but rather to accept them for what they were. Stone should be rough. That was its natural state. A board was a board. Its grain would show better if the surface was plain and flat (Figure 5.14).

The meaning of the term "organic," like that of the term "natural," was redefined by Progressive architects. Victorians had used the term "organic" in reference to the hierarchy and interconnectedness of the natural world. Using trees and other forms of vegetation as their examples, they stressed the way in which all parts of a plant—roots, limbs, and leaves—contributed to the whole. They also asserted that some parts were more important than others. Trim a branch here and there and the tree would still survive, but cut the trunk and it would die. When architects in the Progressive period described something as "organic," they often used it as a synonym for the word "appropriate." A house should have an organic relationship to its site, they insisted. It should fit in with the surroundings. "As in all logical architecture," wrote Joseph H. Freelander in the *Century* magazine, "the design must be developed from the condition imposed, such as the mode of life of the occupants, the site, and the climate conditions." The term "organic" for Freelander and other architects meant interrelated and fitting in the appropriate context. Gone from his use of the term was the Victorian notion of interdependency and mutual support. Instead the term was redefined to refer to a new reliance on site and context. Buildings had an organic unity if they were stylistically consistent and properly fit on the site.[23]

Although the new principles of architec-

Figure 5.14
Figure 5.14
The more natural way to finish the interior of the bunga-low, according to its promoters, was to use white plaster walls which con-trasted with the sub-stantial, flat, stained-oak woodwork. The result gave rooms a dramatic simplicity that was often softened by stencil-ing. (Stickley, *Crafts-man Homes*)

A PLASTER AND TIMBER HOUSE

darker stone would be very effective with either gray or green cement. As to the woodwork, we would suggest cypress, which is inexpensive, durable and beautiful in color and grain when finished according to the process we describe elsewhere in this book. The color under this treatment is a rich warm brown which, when used for the half-timber con-struction, window framings and balustrades, would look equally well with plaster either left in the natural gray or given a tone of bis-cuit color or of dull green.

Some idea of the interior woodwork is given in the detail drawings. A great deal of wood is used in the form of wainscoting, grilles and

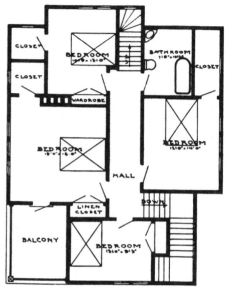

SECOND STORY FLOOR PLAN.

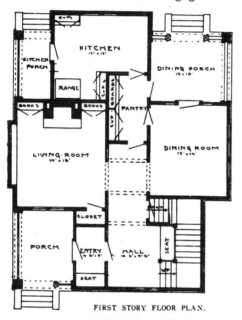

FIRST STORY FLOOR PLAN.

the like, and the whole scheme of decoration and furnishing naturally is founded on this use of wood. It would be best to treat the upper walls and ceilings of the hall, living room and dining room alike, as the object is to give a sense of space, dignity and restfulness to the part of the house that is most lived in and this effect is best obtained by having no change in the background. The rooms open into each other in such a way as to suggest one large room irregularly shaped and full of recesses, and any marked difference in the treatment of the walls is apt to produce an effect of patchiness as well as the restlessness that comes from marked variations in our home surroundings.

DETAIL DRAWING SHOWING CONSTRUCTION AND PLACING OF WAINSCOT, DOOR, STAIRCASE AND LANDING.

tural design, with their emphasis on simplicity, functionality, naturalness, and organicism represented a sharp break with Victorian standards, the Progressive ideal of the home's function held by architects and reformers combined both traditional and new elements. On the traditional side, architects and reformers stressed the role of the home as a place of rest and tranquillity, a refuge from the storms of one's daily occupation. Given the realization at the turn of the century that factory work could often be dull and monotonous, it was even more important to stress the supportive benefits of a properly designed house. The home should be a protective dike against the corrosive forces of modern life, wrote the Reverend S. R. Dennen in the *New England* magazine. "We are rapidly learning to value our own personality and privacy," added Katharine C. Budd in a 1905 article. "We need space around our homes so that we may live free from observation, away from the turmoil of the world, with time to think, to loaf and invite our souls." The pervasive environmentalism of the Victorians with their belief that the individual's outlook could be molded by his surroundings thus continued on past the turn of the century.[24]

The renewed interest in the traditional notion of the shaping power of the home environment was reinforced by psychological theories that stressed the importance of childhood and the subconscious. The theories of Sigmund Freud were beginning to attract the notice of American psychologists such as G. Stanley Hall and Henry Jackson Putnam, who had tried to explain hysteria and other psychiatric problems in terms of physical causes. Although they were somewhat skeptical of Freud's theories of infant sexuality, they eagerly accepted Freud's emphasis on early childhood as the formative period of life and his comments on the importance of the subconscious. Family reformers and advice-book writers had also long stressed the importance of childhood. Freud's theories, particularly after his visit to Clark University in 1909, gave their concerns a new justification and urgency. "We make our houses and they turn upon us the image of our own taste and

permanently fix it in our very nature," wrote Charles Henderson, a professor of sociology at the University of Chicago Business School, echoing the older arguments of Andrew Jackson Downing. "Our works and our surroundings corrupt or refine our souls. The dwelling, the walls, the windows, the roof, the furniture, the pictures, the ornaments, the dress, the fence, the hedge—all act constantly upon the imagination and determine its contents." Now that the house was seen as having a psychological impact on the child, it was more important than ever to design it in an appropriate way.[25]

Architects translated the renewed concern about early childhood into advice about nurseries, playrooms, and household safety. Where the older Victorian homes occasionally had a nursery set off at a distance from the master bedroom, Progressive architects and family reformers now suggested using a room "within eyesight and earshot of mother." Places for exercise and amusement, designed to take spills and messes, were also important. "Every house which shelters children should have, if possible, its children's room," wrote Adelaide L. Rouse in *Good Housekeeping*. "In this room children should be allowed perfect liberty. There should be an opportunity to do anything, from making mud pies to painting in water colors" (Figure 5.15). Other areas of the house, particularly stairs and balconies, also needed to be reviewed by architects to ensure that they were not a threat to the safety of young people.[26]

The concern for early childhood and the emphasis on improvement of home safety hardly marked a significant change from the Victorian image of the ideal home. Nor was the emphasis on the architect as an artist and the house as a work of art a substantial redirection of Victorian views. What was different was the new emphasis on engineering, both in terms of planning the structure and in terms of improving the efficiency of household organization. Inherent in the discussion of engineering was an uneasy attempt to fuse the older ideals into a new outlook. Like much of the writing about architecture and the family, the blend of old

Figure 5.15
Given the importance that Progressives placed on children, it was to be expected that the designs for children's rooms would be presented in popular plan books. (Stickley, *Craftsman Homes*)

THE TREATMENT OF WALL SPACES

Published in The Craftsman, August, 1905.

TREATMENT OF WALLS IN A NURSERY. PLAIN ROUGH PLASTER BELOW AND A SHADOWY SUGGESTION OF A FOREST IN THE FRIEZE. BY THIS ARRANGEMENT THE SURFACE OF THE LOWER WALL IS EASILY KEPT CLEAN AND YET ALL APPEARANCE OF BARRENNESS IS AVOIDED.

Published in The Craftsman, August, 1905.

ANOTHER SUGGESTION FOR THE TREATMENT OF NURSERY WALLS, SHOWING A PICTURE DADO ILLUSTRATING NURSERY TALES AND A BLACKBOARD BUILT INTO THE WAINSCOT WITHIN EASY REACH OF THE LITTLE ONES.

and new ideas was often not consistent. Middle-class Americans tended to give up old beliefs slowly. They seemed to much prefer grafting newer shoots onto older stems in the hopes of revitalizing the plant.

At the turn of the century architects and social reformers faced the question, What was the proper relationship between engineering and art? Initially, reformers voiced some criticism of the excesses in both fields. Architects who tried to be artistic, especially in the nineteenth century, too often lost a proper sense of limits. "The only originality worth having," wrote Herbert Croly in the *Architectural Record*, "is that which issues unconsciously from the frank and well-informed treatment of an artist's special task or material." The best architecture, according to Croly, would be one that went beyond the mere copying of old styles to one that responded to the dictates of local propriety and the needs of the owner. Engineering, too, seemed to some architects at the turn of the century to overrule the canons of good taste. "As to the future of art and architecture in America," wrote Stephen Peet in the 1899 issue of the *American Architect and Building News*, "there is much uncertainty, for architects seem to be inclined nowadays to make their profession subordinate to that of the engineer. . . . The decorating of a steel frame and making a big ornamental box is not architecture."

Other architects were not as convinced that good architecture and engineering were so incompatible. "The architect and the engineer stand back to back," asserted Louis Gibson in 1904. The architect looks to the past, learning from the great monuments of antiquity. The engineer has his face turned the other way. "His inspiration is the future. The past does not cloud his brain." Great buildings needed both perspectives, the impulse of the artistic mind together with the latest technology in the form of practical machines. "Great architecture," he added, "will come out of good engineering, good composition and beautiful ornament."[27]

Like the Victorians, Progressive architects and social reformers ultimately saw no contradiction in the combination of the useful and the beautiful. Beauty was defined far differently in 1910 than it had been in 1880, but it was still seen as utilitarian. Like morality, both beauty and utility helped to improve society. Commenting on the 1904 St. Louis Exposition, John Brisben Walker summed up the new faith that engineering could be combined with art to the advantage of both. "In a day of garish adornment, or vulgar ostentation, where the mere spending of money seems to be regarded as art," he commented, "it is refreshing to find such perfect ideals as those given in house-furnishing in the German section. The most perfect are those of the simplest forms. It is notable that where-ever they get away from simplicity they lose in art." Here was the classic pattern of reconciling two different ideals— art and utility—by combining them. In typical turn-of-the-century pragmatic fashion, the new technology was grafted onto the older faith in utility to form a more effective ideal. As the philosopher William James had candidly remarked in the subtitle to his book *Pragmatism*, such an outlook was "a new name for some old ways of thinking." It was a part of that spirit of "practical idealism" that characterized so much of the Progressive movement[28] (Figure 5.16).

If much of the turn-of-the-century ideal for middle-class housing was either a continuation of earlier beliefs or a refurbishing of them with newer ideas about art and technology, three major areas did reflect substantial changes in outlook: two concerned bringing into the household new theories of sanitation and efficiency, the third extended the rhetoric of domestic life into the outside world. All three changes influenced not only the ideal of what the middle-class house should be, but also added a new and at times inconsistent element to the image of middle-class family life itself. Whatever the American family home had been thought to be in the nineteenth century, it was now clear that the ideal division between the home and the outside world had been eroded.

Feminists, social reformers, philanthropists, architects, journalists, civil engineers, and sani-

Figure 5.16
This bungalow in Pasadena, California, with its cobblestone fireplace and cedar siding, typified the simple, natural look that builders and architects tried to achieve in small houses after 1900. ("Some California Bungalows")

tarians joined forces at the turn of the century to mount a new crusade against germs and disease. Utilizing the revolution in magazine publishing and following closely the latest scientific discoveries about germs and the nature of disease, they undertook a vast campaign to reeducate the nation about the importance of sanitation. Such a crusade fit easily with the universalist mood of the period. Like Woodrow Wilson's later campaign to outlaw war and make the world safe for democracy, Progressive housing reformers argued that all disease should be eradicated. Disease, like war, affected rich and poor alike. No one was immune. Settlement house leader Jane Addams made the point most forcefully in her autobiography *Twenty Years at Hull House*, when she told the story of a widow who lived in an Italian district but refused to associate with her immigrant neighbors and sent her twin daughters to an eastern college. When the 1902 typhoid fever epidemic broke out, one of the woman's daughters died. The moral of the story was clear. No family could effectively isolate itself from community concerns. New standards for sanitation had to be developed if public health were to be improved.[29]

The crusade for public sanitation took a variety of forms. Municipal and state boards of health enacted new standards for sewage, water supplies, and garbage collection. Cities and towns enforced these regulations and set up their own waterworks and dumps. Manufacturers of soaps and household cleansers painted grim pictures of those who failed to clean their premises. Plumbing and heating suppliers held out visions of perfect health if only their products were used. But the most effective pressure came from magazine publishers, the home economics movement, and the National Federation of Women's Clubs.

Magazines such as *Good Housekeeping*, *Outlook*, *Cosmopolitan*, *House Beautiful*, and *Craftsman* were joined by more specialized journals such as *Mother's Friend*, *Today's Housewife*, *Hearth and Home*, *Mother's Home Life*, and *American Kitchen Magazine* in urging that the house be made more healthful. Articles on "The Bacteriology of Household Preserving," "How Any Woman Can Become a Sanitarian," "Science in the Model Kitchen," and "The Bedroom: Health and Economy in an Anti-Microbe Sleeping Room Which May Serve as a Home Hospital" continually reinforced the need to rethink the design and use of kitchens, bedrooms, and bathrooms.

The campaign against dirt and disease was waged in the most graphic manner. Books and magazine articles went into great detail about the harmful nature of dust. Lionel Robertson and T. C. O'Connell in their book, *The Healthful House*, explained that the dangers of dust were not simply a product of scientists' imaginations. "Made up often of the organic filth of the street, of decayed vegetable and animal substances, the waste [dust] blows into the house through open windows and doors and settles on furniture and curtains in thick layers." If not harmful in itself, dust was a powerful medium for producing germs. The public had to be alerted to the dangers of unsanitary homes.[30]

To meet the threats posed by unhealthy living conditions, the popular magazines mounted a systematic crusade to inform the public about the danger of dirt and germs. The continuous emphasis on improving the cleanliness of the home inevitably moved from a discussion of cleaning to an attempt to redesign the interior of a house to make it more healthful. In an 1899 article, "Household Art and the Microbe," for example, Helen Campbell suggested that the elaborate furnishings of Victorian homes provided an ideal refuge for millions of microbes and germs. She then insisted that the lessons of the hospital and the sanitarium—that smooth surfaces easily cleaned were the best way of destroying germs —should be transformed into principles of home design. "Cracks must be impossible," she added, "and machine grooving and carving in woodwork, whether in house or furniture, no less so." New, simpler and more modern room designs were needed to improve the process of cleaning. Only with the extirpation of dust and dirt could the home become a safe and healthy environment.[31]

Kitchens and bathrooms became the special targets for these magazine reformers. The ideal kitchen, according to Katharine C. Budd in *Outlook* magazine, combined the latest in technology with the best in sanitation. Screens were needed to keep out germ-bearing houseflies. Linoleum floors had to be durable, nonabsorbent, soft underfoot, and easily cleaned (Figure 5.17). Electric stoves were the best because they avoided soot and dirty flames. Even the windows and walls had to be easily washed and the walls painted white. "To be perfectly sanitary," she added, "windows and doors should be plain on the kitchen side, and all moldings and other dust-catching projections omitted." Science and technology could thus work hand in hand to ensure purity and comfort in the kitchen[32] (Figure 5.18).

Bathrooms, too, received special attention. The design of toilets and tubs was simplified to facilitate cleaning and the room was reduced in size to waste less space. Enameled fixtures became standard features and manufacturers now stressed the importance of proper installation. Reformers also advised homemakers about the proper soaps to be kept in the bathroom in case visitors dropped in and had to be put up for the night.

When pushed to the extreme, the passion for cleanliness became an end in and of itself. Some magazine writers were so concerned about sanitation that they were willing to see it as the defining principle of decoration in the kitchen and bedrooms. One room in the house, argued E. C. Gardner in *Good Housekeeping*,

should be ready for hospital duties. The space should be utterly spartan.

> [T]he walls should be plastered and painted and made to bear washing with hot water and soap. Not a sign of a picture in the room . . . no paneling, no molding, no carving, nothing to give comfort or seclusion to the invisible germs that live happily in a grain of dust and find right-angled corners desirable building lots. . . . Of course there should be double windows for winter and outside blinds for summer; ventilation goes without saying.[33]

The more they wrote about it, the more the reformers became convinced that improving the public's awareness of dangerous germs and redesigning kitchens and bathrooms was not enough. Mothers needed more sophisticated training in "domestic science." In journal after journal, reformers at the turn of the century argued for a universal program of specialized education for all girls in school. "In domestic life women need two things," wrote Mary Roberts Smith in a typical article. "First, the greatest general culture attainable to enrich the homelife and to retrain the sympathies of children, as well as to store up for themselves resources in hours of difficulty, loneliness, or sorrow; second, they need an education adapted to everyday business, especially to the emergencies of domestic life." In their attempt to improve the role of women within the modern household, Mary Roberts Smith and the other reformers singled out knowledge of psychology, nutrition, hygiene, physiology, manual training, and ethics as important. Like the architect, the homemaker was now expected to be a jack-of-all-trades, a Renaissance woman in her own right.[34]

The difficulty was whose advice to take. Who would provide the necessary training? How were educated women to keep up with the latest developments in the fields of domestic science? And most important, Who should make the decisions and control the individual family? Efforts to answer these questions had begun in the 1870s and 1880s, as historians

A CONVENIENT AND WELL-EQUIPPED KITCHEN

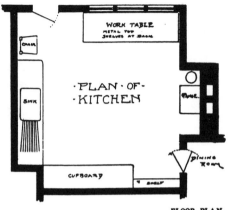

FLOOR PLAN.

planning such a house it should come in for the first thought instead of the last and its use as a dining room as well as a kitchen should be carefully considered. The hooded range should be so devised that all odors of cooking are carried off and the arrangement and ventilation should be such that this is one of the best aired and sunniest of all the rooms in the house.

Where social relations and the demands of a more complex life make it impossible for the house mistress to do her own work and the kitchen is necessarily more separated from the rest of the household, it may easily be planned to meet the requirements of the case without losing any of its comfort, convenience, or suitability for the work that is to be done in it. Modern science has made the task very easy by the provision of electric lights, open plumbing, laundry conveniences, and hot and cold running water, so that the luxuries of the properly arranged modern kitchen would have been almost unbelievable a generation ago. Even if the kitchen is for the servant only, it should be a place in which she may take some personal pride. It is hardly going too far to say that the solution of the problem of the properly arranged kitchen would come near to being the solution also of the domestic problem.

The properly planned kitchen should be as open as possible to prevent the accumulation of dirt. Without the customary "glory holes" that sink and other closets often become, gen-

uine cleanliness is much easier to preserve and the appearance of outside order is not at all lessened. In no part of the house does the good old saying, "a place for everything and everything in its place," apply with more force than in the kitchen. Ample cupboard space for all china should be provided near the sink to do away with unnecessary handling and the same cupboard, which should be an actual structural feature of the kitchen, should contain drawers for table linen, cutlery and smaller utensils, as well as a broad shelf which provides a convenient place for serving. The floor should be of cement and the same material may be used in tiled pattern for a high wainscot, giving a cleanly and pleasant effect.

Published in The Craftsman, September, 1905.

RANGE SET IN A RECESS TO BE OUT OF THE WAY AND WORK TABLE PLACED JUST BELOW A GROUP OF WINDOWS.

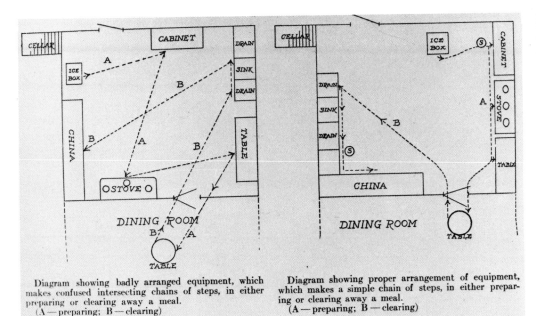

Diagram showing badly arranged equipment, which makes confused intersecting chains of steps, in either preparing or clearing away a meal.
(A — preparing; B — clearing)

Diagram showing proper arrangement of equipment, which makes a simple chain of steps, in either preparing or clearing away a meal.
(A — preparing; B — clearing)

Figure 5.18
Only godliness and cleanliness were more important than efficiency to many house reformers. (Frederick, *The New Housekeeping*)

Sheila Rothman and Gwendolyn Wright have pointed out, with the development of courses in the domestic arts at the land grant universities and with the publication of advice books such as Catharine Beecher's, which had urged women to obtain "appropriate *scientific and practical training* for her distinctive *profession* as housekeeper, nurse of infants and the sick, educator of childhood, trainer of servants and minister of charities." Some organizations such as the Women's Christian Temperance Union had also asserted that women needed to be actively involved with reforms in the public arena. But even the WCTU's campaign for municipal reform and the abolition of saloons, a mission directed toward making "the whole world Homelike," was of little help to housewives who wished to set their own affairs in order. There was too much information, too many conflicting ideas of what was "scientific," and too few clearly recognized authorities to help local women decide what was best. By the 1890s concerned individuals had begun to look elsewhere for help.

Two organizations, the National Home Economics Association and the General Federation of Women's Clubs, moved decisively to aid middle- and upper-class women who were searching for advice and support. The National Home Economics Association, founded at the Chicago World's Columbian Exposition in 1893, enlisted the aid of highly trained experts to create clear models for domestic life. Chemist Ellen Richards of the Massachusetts Institute of Technology, educator Marion Talbott, economist Helen Campbell, and University of Chicago professors Sophonisba Breckinridge and Charles Henderson helped mount a national campaign to develop a better understanding of foods, fuels, and sanitation. By 1900, the year in which the National Home Economics Association changed its name to the American Home Economics Association, more than thirty universities had established home economics departments; by 1916, 195 institutions were offering degrees to 17,778 students who had studied household management (Figure 5.19).

The home economics movement nationally shifted its focus from a concern with training and maintaining servants to mastering new technologies of cleaning and cooking and running a more efficient household. Radical feminists such as Charlotte Perkins Gilman, Ellen

Richards, and Elizabeth Banks had argued in the 1890s that freeing women from the drudgery of household life by providing communal kitchens and child-care services would be a blessing to humanity. "Women as fully developed human creatures, constituting a full half of the people; holding indispensable industrial relations to each other, to men, to society," wrote Gilman, "will be able to make some alterations in the ancient order of things of vast advantage to the world." Although the arguments of radical feminists in the 1890s had drawn little support, the new emphasis on hygiene and nutrition at the turn of the century won them new converts. The common ground between the radical feminists and the moderate home economists was that both believed that the environment of the home had to be changed. Each group was convinced that all women should no longer be left to manage the household without proper advice and training. Women needed careful education by experienced experts who were well versed in the latest theories of nutrition, sanitation, and child care.[35] Lucy Salmon put it most succinctly when she wrote that "these three common mistakes of belief—first, that a knowledge of housekeeping affairs is a matter of inspiration; second, that they concern women alone; and third, that all women have a natural love for such affairs that supplies the place of training—are perhaps sufficient explanation of the present lack of all opportunity for investigation of the household in a professional way." Only the new home economics movement, she thought, would fill this need for expert technical advice.[36]

The General Federation of Women's Clubs, first organized in 1892, followed a similar pattern of development. It began as a mutual improvement society that ran literary discussions and gradually became a national organization with more than ten thousand members whose energies were directed toward retraining the housewife to be a better consumer. Like the home economics movement, the General Federation of Women's Clubs asked the new college-trained women experts to suggest specific improvements of house design and management that would simplify the chores of everyday living. But whereas the home economics movement exhibited a pluralistic perspective, recognizing the variations in life-style that existed at different economic and class levels, some advocates from the General Federation of Women's Clubs preached a more authoritarian gospel.

In 1915 Mrs. Mary Pattison, on behalf of the General Federation of Women's Clubs in New Jersey, published the *Principles of Domestic Engineering* based on work done at the "Experiment Station" in Colonia, New York, and on the results of several thousand questionnaires that had been distributed around New Jersey. Reacting in part to the criticism of the clubs as being dilettante and upper class, Mrs. Pattison promoted the "Scientific Management" princi-

ples of Frederick Winslow Taylor as a means for improving the homes of all social classes. Her goal was to run the household in the most efficient way possible, eliminating the waste of time and energy, increasing sanitation, and standardizing housework by turning it into a new science. Using a stopwatch and chart, Mrs. Pattison timed the operation of cooking, washing, and cleaning. She then explained to homemakers how new inventions such as electric stoves, vacuum cleaners, refrigerators, lazy Susans, and electric washing machines could simplify housework.

Mary Pattison's other objective was to increase the power and independence of the housewife. Her system of "domestic engineering," which dramatized the role of woman as "a cook, nurse, seamstress, house-worker, doctor, minister, teacher, hostess, economist, scientist, artist, [and] business manager," was deliberately designed to raise the social status of the homemaker. By standardizing each of these roles and providing women with new technical expertise, Mrs. Pattison also hoped to make the woman's function in the home less restrictive. As she put it, "the encouragement of personal freedom, or personal independence, and its right use, seems therefore to the writer to be the object of family life." Her system was democratic and progressive, in keeping with the optimistic outlook at the start of the new century. "Our hope is to bring the masculine and feminine mind more closely together in the industry of home-making," she continued, "by raising housework . . . to the plane of Scientific Engineering, . . . to the end that the Home may develop progressively more and more as the efficient unit of the State"[37] (Figure 5.20).

Inherent in the vision of the Progressive household advocated by Mary Pattison and the home economics movement was both a new faith in professional expertise and the notion that the experts should be able to coerce weak families to accept help. In some cases this might mean the subtle disciplining of the husband by the wife. In others, the state itself, in the form of welfare agencies or the juvenile court system, might step in and directly regu-

Figure 5.20
By dressing in white
and wearing a hair-
net, Mrs. Frederick
wanted to convey
the sense of the
kitchen as a clean,
sterile environment,
much like that of a
hospital. (Frederick,
*The New House-
keeping*)

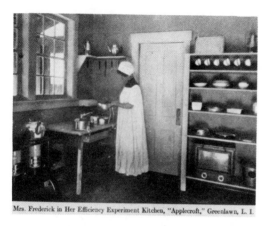

Mrs. Frederick in Her Efficiency Experiment Kitchen, "Applecroft," Greenlawn, L. I.

late family affairs. The way to handle a lazy or wrangling husband, Mary Pattison suggested, was "to make the disgruntled member a committee man; give him something to do and see that he becomes responsible for the doing, working his way into the family management through favors earned and not through demand, or by any act of begging." For cases in which juvenile delinquents or alcoholic husbands were involved, Progressive home reformers used the state, through labor and welfare legislation, to take over the custodial and protective functions of the family.

The willingness to use outside agencies ranging from the federal and state governments to the National Home Economics Association, the General Federation of Women's Clubs, and the National Congress of Mothers to interfere directly in family relationships represented a major shift away from the position held by reformers in the nineteenth century. The difference was that the Victorians had respected the sanctity of families and had hoped to reform them primarily through voluntary advice and moral suasion, but the Progressive reformers were persuaded that the new technical expertise justified actual interference in family affairs. The reformers not only weakened the barriers between home and the outside world, they mobilized national organizations to aid them in their campaigns. As historian Gwendolyn Wright has suggested, "Together they parlayed the traditional ideal of the home's

sanctity into an improved concept of *regulated purity* still based on individual homes, but now overseen by outside agencies. The home would now be the quintessential 'therapeutic environment.'"[38]

By 1915 the separate elements of the Progressive reform vision had coalesced into a powerful crusade that captured the public imagination and replaced the older Victorian ideals of home and family. Combining the new professional expertise about household management with the campaign for improved public sanitation, greater household efficiency, and newer aesthetic standards, Progressive reformers developed a cogent vision of the ideal house, and by extension, of the ideal family. The new ideal for middle-class single-family housing, as Gwendolyn Wright has suggested, represented a dramatic change from the Victorian standard. In place of earlier romantic theories of design, it postulated a powerful minimalist aesthetic, most fully expressed in the new bungalow designs that stressed simplicity of form and compactness of layout. The new ideal for the family, similarly, stressed informality, congeniality, and efficiency. By having to spend less time on the everyday affairs of running the household, the family would be free to devote more time to recreation and to the improvement of relations among its members.[39]

The new Progressive housing ideal combined practical changes necessitated by shifts in building technology with a persuasive ideological justification. The minimalist aesthetic, not surprisingly, fit well with the need to keep costs down. The increased price of building materials, the expense of new plumbing, heating, and wiring technologies that could add as much as 25 to 40 percent to the bill for an average house, and the increase in land values meant that single-family dwellings had to be smaller in size than those of their Victorian predecessors if they were to remain within the price range of the middle-class public. The reductions in space were quite dramatic. A $3,000 house in 1905 was estimated to have between 1,000 and 1,500 square feet of space whereas a comparable house in the 1880s had between 2,000 and 2,500 square feet. However, the substantial reduction of house size, together with the new standardization in house design, counterbalanced the increase in plumbing, heating, and wiring costs. Average house prices thus rose much more slowly than might have been expected, changing from $2,400 in 1891 to only $2,650 in 1910.[40]

The relatively low cost of small bungalows and Colonial Revival houses, which also shared a minimalist aesthetic, was readily accepted by a public that was willing to sacrifice space and complexity for better efficiency and newer technologies. Swayed by the massive educational campaign that had been orchestrated by sanitarians, magazine writers, and home economists, the middle-class public accepted the argument that the Progressive houses represented a decisive aesthetic improvement over their Victorian predecessors. Tangible cost savings and the constant stream of articles and books persuaded them that they were making a tremendous improvement in national housing standards by promoting the new mass-produced bungalows and Colonial Revival homes.

Thus the heart of the vision of the ideal house was simplified design and a standardized layout (Figure 5.21). The first floor usually consisted of a small front porch followed by three rooms—a living room, a dining room, and a kitchen. Instead of assigning specialized functions to individual spaces, the new housing ideal asserted that all first-floor rooms should have multiple purposes. The typical living room now contained bookcases, inglenooks, and a fireplace, which allowed it to combine the functions served earlier by the front and back parlors, the hall, and the library. It could be used as a place for the entertainment of guests or it could function as a space for family recreation. The ideal living room was less a place for display and more a staging ground for family activities. "Our newer conception of the living room," insisted one writer, "is that it is a background in every sense of the word, a curtain against which is enacted the drama of home life. To this end it must be simple, free from elaborate decoration with plain, strong colors against which the family life will appear radiant." By framing the windows and doors with dark oak woodwork, architects, builders, and reformers allowed the living room to retain a degree of formality (Figures 5.22a and 5.22b). But the introduction of pillows, less massive furniture, and simpler window seats made the spaces seem less stuffy and solemn.[41]

In addition to recommending built-in window seats and bookcases, contractors, builders, and magazine writers stressed the notion that fewer pieces of furniture would increase a room's functions. The removal of screens and easels, whatnot shelves, and large cabinets, and the new use of lighter-weight chairs and couches made it easier to rearrange a room for different purposes. Less space was available for the display of curios and works of art, but more area was opened up for entertainment and recreation. The round "turned oak" table so popular in this period could thus function either as a display area for family pictures or as a place for card playing and family games (Figure 5.23). As Hester Poole wrote in *Good Housekeeping* in 1900, the living room "is usually spacious and furnished comfortably, yet with a note of elegance." It was a place "where joy and happiness are contagious."[42]

The dining room, similarly, was portrayed in popular housing magazines as a multipurpose area (Figure 5.24). By widening the connecting passageway to the living room, architects and contractors made the dining room appear to be larger and more spacious. No longer was it considered to be a room only to be used for eating. Built-in buffets replaced the larger and more cumbersome sideboards. Special "dinettes" in the kitchen with built-in tables and chairs allowed the family to eat more quickly and informally. If need be, they could avoid using the dining room for family meals altogether, except for dinner parties or birthday celebrations. The dining room could thus be used for other purposes such as playing the piano, reading, or working on projects like

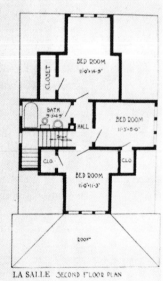

LaSalle

26 ft. x 36 ft. over all
8 Rooms, 2 Baths

Inviting—Distinctive—Practical! This description reveals the secret of the LaSalle's great popularity. Note the artistic overhanging eaves—and the dormers, in front and on either side. These give balance and substantiality. They afford, too, the roominess of a one and one-half story home, with the smart lines of a semi-bungalow design.

See how well-lighted are the bedrooms. Particularly note the ample closet room. And one room upstairs might well be used as a den, sewing room, or nursery.

There is a cosy, sunny bay window in the dining room—there is a window seat there! The roomy, well-protected porch is a splendid feature. The kitchen is ample, but most compact and convenient. And the two bathrooms, one on each floor, give a final touch to an ideal plan.

SPECIFICATIONS

Ceiling height first floor approximately 9 ft.
Ceiling height second floor approximately 8 ft.
Girders 6 in. x 8 in.
First and second floor joists 2 in. x 8 in.
Ceiling joists 2 in. x 4 in.
Rafters 2 in. x 6 in.
Front door—our "Chautauqua," of solid Chestnut, 3 ft. x 6 ft. 8 in. and 1¾ in. thick, glazed with clear glass. *See pages 36–37.*
Prices on oak floors and trim for living room and dining room, maple flooring in kitchen, quoted on application.
Our No. 1 kitchen cupboard and two medicine cabinets included in the selling price. *See pages 36–37.*

See pages 8–9 for general specifications.

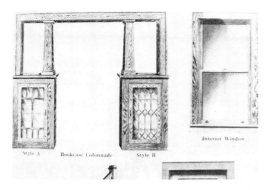

Figures 5.22a and 5.22b
Catalogs for prefabricated bungalows often contained a selection of oak woodwork including this popular "bookcase Colonnade" (a) and a variety of doors (b) that were thought to be both functional and attractive. (Bennett Lumber Co., *Bennett Better-Built, Ready-Cut Homes*)

Figure 5.23
This interior view of the dining room in a house in St. Paul, Minnesota, shows the popular round oak table and dark oak woodwork. (Courtesy Minnesota Historical Society)

Figure 5.24
Creative designers like Gustav Stickley devised a variety of built-in buffets, often with mirrors and stained-glass windows. Local carpenters, relying on the popularity of beveled and stained glass, were able to order prefabricated buffets that, like the colonnades, could be installed in a variety of ways. (Stickley, *Craftsman Homes*)

Published in The Craftsman, November, 1905.

RECESSED WINDOW AND SEAT IN A DINING ROOM. AN UNUSUALLY QUAINT EFFECT IS GIVEN BY THE SMALL LEADED PANES OF GLASS AND THE BROAD WINDOW LEDGE FOR HOLDING PLANTS.

Published in The Craftsman, November, 1905.

WINDOW EXTENDING THE WHOLE WIDTH OF A DINING ROOM AND INTENDED FOR AN EXPOSURE WHERE THERE IS AN ESPECIALLY FINE VIEW.

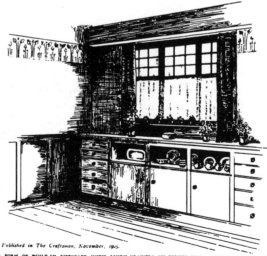

Published in The Craftsman, November, 1905.

ANOTHER FORM OF BUILT-IN SIDEBOARD WITH LINEN DRAWERS ON EITHER SIDE. THIS IS INTENDED TO FILL THE WHOLE SPACE ACROSS THE END OF THE DINING ROOM.

sewing that had to be laid out on a large table. Magazine writers justified these changes in terms of convenience but also insisted that multifunctional rooms allowed for a more "natural" house. "Bring as near together as possible points between which the most traveling is done," wrote E. C. Holtzoper in *Country Life in America*. "Make your plan simple and design the rooms in natural relation to one another; don't compel one to go through a retired room to find a more public one." The well-designed ideal house was thus both easier to use and more pleasurable to be in.[43]

The third room on the first floor, the kitchen, achieved a new importance in the ideal Progressive house. Designed with great attention to efficiency and cleanliness, the kitchen was proof positive that a decrease in size could actually be a benefit to the housewife. A smaller kitchen saved steps and thereby freed up time to do other things. Greater efficiency meant more time for vacations, experimentation with more interesting meals, and better nutrition. Isabel McDougall's comment in *House Beautiful* that the space should be "something on the lines of a Pullman-car kitchen, or a yacht's galley, or a laboratory . . . [or] the scientific cleanliness of a surgery" displayed the idealism and hope implicit in much of the writing about kitchens. Usually compact and square, approximately 11' x 11', the kitchen made the most efficient use of prepared and processed foods now produced outside the household while also freeing space for the rest of the house.[44]

Two other features of the first-floor layout of the ideal house are also worth noting. One was the preservation of a circular pattern for movement on the first floor. Because of the smaller size and the need to use rooms for multiple purposes, the ideal Progressive house often had several alternate ways to enter the house and move within it. Using the front door, a person could walk to the rear of the house either through a hall or door which connected to the kitchen or by moving through both the living room and the dining room. The direct, independent communication between the kitchen and the front door was needed to allow the housewife to answer the door easily during the day while the connection to the dining room was necessary for serving meals there. The alternative routes through the house created a circular pattern of use that delighted young children because they could run endlessly around the first floor. It was also helpful to family members in the living or dining room who were reading or working on a project and did not want to be disturbed. Children and other family members could walk directly to the kitchen without entering other first-floor rooms. Magazines and plan books reinforced the idea that privacy still was available within these multipurpose rooms by stressing the benefits of cozy inglenooks and secluded bay windows.

The kitchen had an outside entrance, too, so that service people could come and go without disturbing the household. The ideal house usually had a direct side entrance to the cellar for the same reasons. In the Midwest it was customary to provide an additional toilet in the cellar for the coal man or other help to use. The ideal Progressive house thus had both fewer rooms and fewer entrances and exits than its Victorian predecessors. Yet flexibility was maintained by retaining alternate circulation routes on the first floor.

The second main difference between Victorian and Progressive middle-class houses was the absence of a back staircase in the homes built after 1910. The back staircase was removed in part because of the precipitous decline in the availability of household servants. In 1870 one out of eight families hired servants to ease the burden of running the household, and one-half of all women wage earners had been domestic servants. Often, they were given a back room upstairs and could come and go from the kitchen without disturbing the family by using the backstairs. But increased costs and better-paying jobs in department stores and factories at the turn of the century made help much less available. By 1930, as David Katzman has pointed out, only one-fifth of all working women were domestics. As a result, the kitchen in the ideal Progressive house was re-designed to be run more efficiently by the housewife herself. The smaller size of the house and the increased use of commercially prepared foods reduced the need for live-in help and consequently made a back staircase unnecessary.[45]

The upstairs of the model Progressive house was appropriately simple. Instead of three or four bedrooms, the ideal house now had two or three, each of which was smaller in size than its Victorian counterpart. Since the family now spent more time outside the home, the bedrooms were used primarily for sleeping. Built-in closets, laundry chutes to the basement, and smaller hallways made the upstairs more compact and functional. Bathrooms, too, were reduced in size to a more standard 5' x 10' area. Porcelain fixtures, built-in medicine cabinets, and improved plumbing made the bathroom, like the kitchen, a model of simplicity and efficiency.

Taken altogether, the radical simplification of the ideal Progressive home represented a dramatic shift in popular attitudes toward the middle-class, single-family house. In place of the Victorian emphasis on the power of art and beauty and the importance of individualistic designs, Progressive reformers stressed coziness, comfort, function, and economy. The Victorians had seen the house as an end in and of itself—a symbolic statement of the outlook and priorities of its owner—but the Progressives valued the house more as a means for enjoying and improving life. The house, in their view, was a staging ground for family activities. It was to be a source of enjoyment rather than a monument to personal success, a place for recreation and relaxation as well as a training ground for self-improvement and moral uplift.

The new ideal for family life presented by the Progressive reformers, like the ideal house, stressed informality and functionalism. Using the latest literature on adolescent development and educational psychology, magazine writers, housing reformers, and architects tied improvements in family life to a better understanding of child development, health, and proper parental expectations. The ideal vision of the family began with a heightened awareness and concern for the upbringing of the children. Much of the advice literature repeated the earlier Victorian concern for shaping the child by controlling the home environment. As Miriam Brozman wrote in *Good Housekeeping*, the child's room should be a "pleasant and inspiring place," one that would tend "to instill morality and refinement."

Like the Victorians, the Progressives tended to sentimentalize childhood, endowing it with the aura of goodness and innocence. "Babyhood is so sweet and so lovingly dependent on a mother's tender care, that it ends too quickly," wrote a woman in *Good Housekeeping*. "I want my little girl to feel that mother is her day and night." Nostalgic memories of rural carefree childhoods made many Progressive reformers insist that children also needed protection from the worries of adulthood and the temptations of urban life. Children appeared to be more complicated and vulnerable than they had seemed earlier. "[O]ur children live too much in the adult world, largely because a child's world is not provided for in the exigencies of modern housekeeping," wrote Katherine Beebe in *Outlook* magazine. Children needed separate spaces in which to grow up so that they would not be contaminated by negative influences. Mother needed the specialized training in child rearing and household management that the home economics movement was insisting upon[46] (Figure 5.25).

To the sentimentalization of childhood and the faith in environmental influences and household management, Progressive reformers added a third concern—natural development. Following a logic that psychologists such as G. Stanley Hall derived from social Darwinism, they insisted that the social development of the child recapitulated the evolution of the race. Children began existence in a primitive brutal state, as witnessed by the tendency of young boys and girls to fight. They gradually learned from experience and became more civilized. The ideal family thus had to provide

Figure 5.25
The new image of the mother as a trained homemaker was reflected in this 1925 photograph. (Courtesy Minnesota Historical Society)

the appropriate separate spaces for natural development and supervised growth. According to psychologists, the home needed to enhance the child's mental and physical powers which could evolve only through a process of exercise and testing. "Today we are studying the child," wrote Helen Campbell, "and [we are] recognizing as new something old as time, yet never acted on before—that in the soul of the child lies the future of the race, and that that future of the race is built upon the homes of the race, homes developed and perfected by every means that science and art can bring to bear." Children needed special germ-free environments, with ample room for play, exercise, and social interaction, where they could enjoy their childhood years to the fullest. The compact but versatile model Progressive house was ideally suited for these needs.[47]

Next to perpetuating the social development and happiness of the children, the ideal Progressive family was supposed to encourage the independence and satisfaction of the housewife. For all the supposed benefits of the Victorian home, it had drained the time and energy of the mother. Cooking, washing, and cleaning, together with managing the household and creating artistic "female elegancies," seemed to the Progressives to have bound and limited the Victorian housewife's world. Much of the twentieth-century reform literature about the family was thus addressed to the question of how to increase her freedom and personal satisfaction.

One option for giving women more time was to have fewer children. Radical feminists such as Ida Husted Harper suggested that women would be far happier and healthier with smaller families. "Where the family is large," she insisted, "it means for parents in moderate circumstances a lifetime of self-denial in the companionship of each other and in the development which comes through means and leisure, as there must be a neverending outlay of time and money in properly clothing, educating, and training the many children." Implicit in Harper's comments was the belief that the wife should be more than a housekeeper. Raising the children was an awesome responsibility to be taken seriously. But women should also have time for romantic "companionship" with their husbands and some leisure to explore their interests in art, culture, or social service outside the home. Marriage was still the ideal held up for middle-class women. The difference was that women were no longer expected to spend the vast majority of their time within the house.[48]

To increase the amount of free time that would be available for other activities outside the house, many women embraced the home economics movement as a source of salvation. The only way an American woman could avoid becoming "too solicitous a housewife, too anxious a housekeeper, . . . too contented a drudge," wrote Elizabeth Banks, was to raise her sights and become more efficient. Christine Frederick, consulting editor to the *Ladies Home Journal*, agreed. Writing about her own personal experience trying to raise two little children, she admitted that "I was constantly struggling to obtain a little 'higher life' for my individuality and independence; and on the other hand I was forced to give up this individuality to my babies and drudgifying housework." Her solution was to develop a more efficient system for household management called "the new housekeeping." By redesigning the kitchen, reorganizing her day, standardizing cooking and cleaning, and improving record keeping, Mrs. Frederick thought that she could significantly improve the happiness of middle-class women.[49]

The flood of books and periodicals designed to improve the ideal of middle-class housekeeping and motherhood could not help but stimulate a revised image of the proper role for women within the family. The constant empha-sis on efficiency and on the economic power of women, both as providers of services and as managers of household finances, modified the image of the ideal family. It reinforced women's sense of value and self-worth by identifying them with a broad public movement to improve family health and happiness. With proper training, they, too, became experts in household management, an indispensable feature in the modern family. By increasing their own importance, women also made themselves less dependent on family life. Christine Frederick stressed again and again that the goal of the efficiency movement was not more work but greater freedom. "Its very purpose," she wrote, "is more liberty, more leisure, a shrewder sense of values, and the elimination of wasted energy."[50]

Frederick and the other magazine writers were careful to point out that the increased freedom of women created by labor-saving devices would not harm the cohesiveness of the family. By reducing housework time, by making house management similar to business management, by saving money through more efficient stoves and appliances, they insisted, men and women would share a similar outlook on the world and have more time for recreation and companionship.

If the ideal Progressive family still retained the image of a nurturing environment for children and a protective retreat for working husbands, it now also was supposed to serve as a starting point for a fuller life for women. "Should woman be educated for the world or for the one career of homemaking?" asked Caroline Hill rhetorically in the 1904 *Journal of Political Economy*. "The solution is easier if the world is looked upon as the home." The ideal family would break down some of the barriers that the Victorians had raised between the home and the outside world. Independence, self-worth derived from expert skills, personal satisfaction, and healthful recreation were now valued as important constituent parts of a normal family life.[51]

Chapter 6

The Bungalow Craze

A house that gives the body all the fresh air that is needed, that provides for the right temperature and that reduces labor to a minimum; a house that will keep the mind tranquil and rested without jarring on one's feeling for beauty—here is the healthful house.

—Lionel Robertson and T. C. O'Donnell,
The Healthful House

Build yourself a bungalow or cottage. Bring nature up to your very threshold—and across it, and learn each day a new lesson in the joy of the world and the freedom of life.

—F. W. Burrows, "Go—Be a Camper"

Progressive housing crusaders, riding on the crest of a wave of national reforms and buoyed up by their vision of the ideal middle-class home and family, fastened onto the bungalow and the suburban development as the great hope for the future. The bungalow represented the antithesis of the Victorian home, simple, informal, and efficient. The suburban development, similarly, symbolized planned community services and expertly managed expansion. Together they demonstrated the practicality and potential of the Progressive vision.

The public fascination with the new bungalow home was reflected in the flood of house design books and articles published after 1905. Substantial coverage of the variations in the new bungalow forms could be found in periodicals as different as the *Architectural Record* and the *Ladies Home Journal*. Women's magazines such as *Good Housekeeping, Country Life in America*, and *Woman's Home Companion* pictured drawings and photographs of bungalows in most of their issues. For those who wanted even more detail about the advantages of bungalow construction, Henry L. Wilson's *Bungalow Book* (1908) (five editions by 1910) and Henry H. Saylor's *Bungalows* (1911) provided hundreds of plans together with an elaborate justification. Saylor even offered plans for an entire housing development. So extensive were these publications and so widespread was the interest in this new form of housing that architect Charles V. Boyd proudly exclaimed in 1919 that "the bungalow is of all American home types that most truly nationalistic" (Figure 6.1).

Architects and magazine writers slowly developed a general consensus on what the ideal bungalow should look like and how it should be

Design No. 5121

Size: Width, 29 feet; Length, 38 feet 6 inches

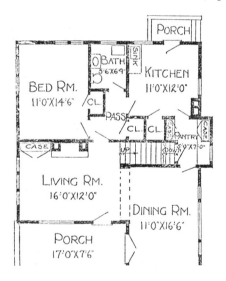

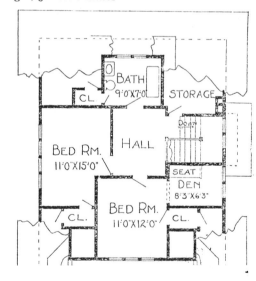

built. The most conspicuous feature of the ideal bungalow was its wide, low-pitched roof. The roof often was connected in one unbroken line to a spacious porch that extended across the entire front of the house. The roof was further broadened by constructing a substantial overhang at the eaves to shade the windows, lower the house's silhouette, and create a feeling of coziness and comfort. As one writer explained in the *National Builder*, such a roof line created a snug appearance and symbolized shelter and safety. Another agreed adding simply that "the design below has the low, sheltering roof lines that always convey an impression of comfort and security."[1]

Normally, the ideal bungalow was a one-story structure. Those that were two-storied were described in the promotional literature as "semi-bungalows." When additional bedrooms were incorporated into the second floor of the bungalow, the roofline was often pierced by a low, flat dormer making the house a story and a half rather than a full two stories high. Such a roof created an overall effect of solidity. The design appeared to have been hewn out of a single block, giving the house a sense of unity and strength.[2]

The front porch was the second most important feature of the ideal bungalow (Figure 6.2). Sometimes called the veranda or piazza, the front porch tied the house directly to the world of nature and was particularly prominent in those dwellings used primarily for camps and summer houses. One architect glowingly called the bungalow the "ideal home for the lover of out-of-doors . . . a house whose atmosphere is, as far as possible, that of the woods and fields." In town, the front porch was the ideal place from which to chat with neighbors as they strolled by on a summer's evening. William T. Comstock, the prominent editor of the *Architect's and Builder's Magazine* which published numerous "how to do it" books on house construction, idealized the veranda as the center of home life. "They should be broadly built," he asserted, "furnished with screens, against the wind or sun, and well supplied with easy chairs, hammocks, and all the paraphernalia of an outdoor summer parlor, for here will be gained the object of the bungalow, the utmost benefit of life in the open air." Other popular writers went even further, suggesting that meals might be taken on the front porch and, if suitable blinds were available, the space might also be used for sleeping[3] (Figure 6.3).

The symbolic use of a spacious front porch and low-pitched roof to create a harmonious relationship to outdoor life was echoed in the materials used to cover the exterior of the house. According to the popular house magazines, the ideal bungalow should be built of a combination of rough, natural materials which would help it blend into its site. Although there was some variation in the materials used from state to state—redwood in California, fieldstone or cobblestone in New England, board-and-batten in Oregon, and adobe in Arizona, the most popular outside sheathing consisted of a combination of stucco and shingles or clapboard (Figure 6.4). In addition to praising the natural qualities of these materials, magazine writers and architects were quick to point out that such exterior sheathing needed little or no maintenance. Shingles weathered beautifully, and stone and stucco needed attention only once every twenty-five years. Naturalness, functionality, and inexpensiveness were thus the hallmarks of exterior bungalow construction.

The design of the interior shared these same qualities. "Inside, the arrangement is a miracle of simplicity and efficiency," wrote one designer in *Good Housekeeping*. "The living-room and dining-room are practically one, so that you may see the cheery fire crackling in the hearth while you are at meals. Again the hall arrangement has been marvelously contrived— a short, straight passage giving entrance to both bedrooms and the bathroom." The simple naturalness of the interior arrangements was extolled time after time. The ideal bungalow was supposed to be a democratic building that defied the conventions and formalities of the Victorian house. As one writer put it, "A room is satisfying only when it completely fulfills the purpose for which it is intended. Its charm and

Montgomery Ward & Co.

"The Vincennes"—Material Supplied Either Ready-Cut or Not Ready-Cut

This Handsome Bungalow Has Four Bedrooms

THIS splendid home follows the true bungalow style, but has as much room as a story-and-a-half house. The outside walls are sided up to the belt course, the gables and dormer being shingled. The most striking feature is the broad porch beam supported by cluster columns. This, together with the wide-open cornice supported by brackets and the sided walls extending clear to the grade line, is typical of genuine bungalow design.

Our "Vincennes" home is one of the most popular, because it combines unusually generous living space with a handsome exterior at a very low cost.

Living room, dining room, kitchen, two bedrooms, bath, hallway, coat closet and linen closet are downstairs. Upstairs are two big bedrooms and a fine light sewing room. Though not spacious in appearance, in living space this is truly a large home. See the fine size of the rooms and the numerous convenient features. Each bedroom has its own big closet. The central hall connecting the bedrooms and bathroom gives space for the stairs and for the linen closet and coat closet. Privacy, so difficult of achievement in the bungalow plan, is amply assured here. While there is an abundance of windows, still there is splendid wall space for furniture in each room. You will find the fine linen closet illustrated on Page 52, and the kitchen case, design No. 863, on Page 53.

The cellar steps lead down inside the house with an entrance into the kitchen and onto the porch. The little inset containing just room enough for the ice box is a great convenience and shows the forethought of the architect. While the ice box is handy, it is in a cool, out-of-the-way place and the ice man does not have to go in and dirty up the kitchen to ice it. The basement is excavated under the entire house. We furnish six sash, which insures its being well lighted and ventilated.

See Prices on Pages 1 to 4
Specifications on Pages 10 and 11

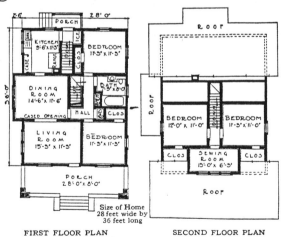

FIRST FLOOR PLAN   SECOND FLOOR PLAN

Size of Home
28 feet wide by
36 feet long

Unless you request otherwise we furnish for this home, cream paint for body, white for trim and bungalow brown stain for wall shingles above the belt course and dormer.

See Page 4 for cost of heating equipment, plumbing, etc., and your option of Radio Asphalt Shingles and oak flooring and finish. Write us for suggestions and estimates on a water supply system and sewage disposal for this home.

Page 14

Figure 6.3
Even the promoters of prefabricated housing stressed the spaciousness of the front porch in their advertisements. (Aladdin Homes, "A $2000 Aladdin House." Courtesy Smithsonian Institution, Collection of Business Americana)

Figure 6.4
Rustic outdoor bungalows, using cobblestones and even logs, were widely promoted for summer homes. (Chapman, "Log Bungalow")

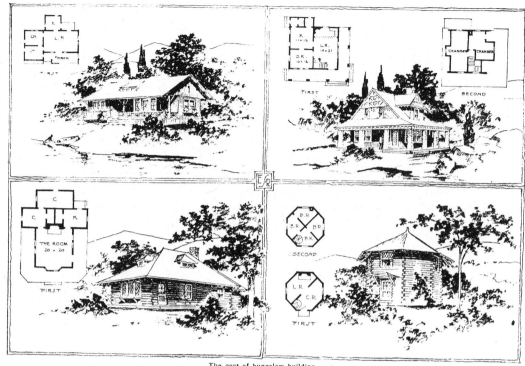

The cost of bungalow building

The upper left-hand plan shows a pole cottage for $645; the lower left-hand plan gives a bungalow for $823, with a large living room; the upper right-hand plan gives the slab cottage, constructed for $1,170; the lower right-hand plan, the octagonal bungalow costing $565. All the sleeping rooms of the octagonal are on the second floor

639

individuality spring from its fitness to meet the needs of the occupants as directly as possible, regardless of custom or convention."[4]

Bungalow interiors, like their exteriors, were supposed to convey a sense of natural unity both through the interpenetration of spaces and the finishing materials in all the rooms. Dark-stained oak or pine woodwork, picture moldings, beamed ceilings, and stenciled borders on the walls were used to create a sense of internal consistency (Figure 6-5). Hence the rooms were more important than the furniture and were supposed to be sparsely decorated. Since they were also provided with built-in seats near the fireplace and a built-in buffet in the dining room, less furniture was necessary (Figures 6.6 and 6.7). Designer Caroline Burrell described one such living room for *Harper's Bazaar*: "As to furniture, there was little needed. In addition to four built-in seats, there were one or two armchairs, made of old-fashioned hickory strips stained brown, and a mission rocker, and these and a large oblong table, bought in the plain white wood and stained, were really all."

When they came to explaining why bungalows were so popular, architects, designers, social reformers, and magazine writers presented a myriad of reasons which not only documented the many-faceted appeal of this small house design but also provided an indirect view of the ways in which middle-class attitudes toward the home and the family were shifting. The promoters endlessly stressed the bungalow's California origins, its openness to nature, its design flexibility, its special convenience and informality, its closeness to apartment living, its suitability for either summer camps or for suburban commuters, its appeal to newlyweds, and, most important, its cheapness. Their arguments implicitly revealed a desire to expand the housing market and to open up

Figure 6.5
In this 1915 photograph of Dr. Robinson's house in St. Paul, Minnesota, the oak floor and the dark oak woodwork match the Mission-style furniture, which was distinctly different from the eclectic furniture popular among middle-class Victorian Americans. (Courtesy Minnesota Historical Society)

Figure 6.6
The Huelster residence, in St. Paul, Minnesota, was furnished sparingly with oak table and rocker almost exactly as designer Caroline Burrell suggested it should be. (Courtesy Minnesota Historical Society)

Figure 6.7
The low cost of pre-fabricated houses appealed to younger families with limited means. (Harris Brothers, *A Plan Book*)

BUILD TO STAY — QUALITY ECONOMY SERVICE — THE HARRIS WAY

$1057

MATERIAL
Sensibly Cut-to-Fit
"The Harris Way"
See pages 4 and 5

Free Plan Offer
See page 3

SPECIFICATIONS

PRICE INCLUDES ALL FRAMING LUMBER, girders, joists, rafters and studding, in No. 1 Yellow Pine Stock, 50 per cent stronger than Hemlock, or Huron Pine; see table of strength, page 4.

WALL PLATES—Foundation wall plates *hydraulic process creosoted*—will not rot.

SHEATHING—Byrkits Patent Lath, sub-floor, and roof sheathing, sound, strong Yellow Pine.

FLOORING—Clear, smooth, well manu-factured Yellow Pine, will take polish and stain perfectly.

OUTSIDE WALLS — Byrkits Patent Sheathing Lath.

OUTSIDE FINISH—Clear, soft Oregon Fir—a thorough weather defying wood.

ROOF—Best quality Extra *A* Washington Red Cedar shingles, including galvanized shingle nails.

INSIDE FINISH—Clear, beautifully fin-ished and grained Yellow or Georgia Pine, style fully detailed on plans.

SASH AND DOORS—Clear, first quality stock sash 1⅜ inches thick, glass puttied in. All glass back puttied. Outside door 1¾ inches thick. Inside doors 1⅜ inches thick.

LATH—We furnish and include in the above price No. 1 Pine Lath.

HARDWARE—Furnished complete, all rough and finishing, everything to the last nail. Many modern designs of locks to select from.

GUTTERING AND SPOUTING—Sheet metal all included in best quality galvanized iron.

BASEMENT—Material consisting of doors, sash, stair material, etc., as shown on plans are included in above price.

SHADES—We will furnish high grade oil opaque cloth shades for this house with best quality spring rollers, for............$18.25

PAINT—We will furnish Harris guaranteed quality painting materials for this house, two-coat work inside and out. Two coats for floors of all porches but no other floor or roof paint, for.....................$27.50

PLUMBING AND HEATING

Complete Plumbing Equipment.....$ 86.95
Complete Warm Air Heating Plant.. 104.59
Complete Steam Heating Plant...... 268.47
Complete Hot Water Heating Plant.. 287.40

Detailed information, delivered prices on above will be furnished upon application.

—and Here's Real Proof

Crivitz, Wisc.

Harris Bros. Co.
Gentlemen:—*I have been living in my house, your Design No. 118A for seven months and wish to state emphatically that all my dealings with your house have been most cordial and you have more than fulfilled all your promises. In the face of strong opposition, I was impelled to investigate and satisfy myself as to your methods of handling lumber and building ma-terial. I found everything exactly as repre-sented in your catalog. All lumber and mill work was fully up to the standard in both quality and grade.* (Signed)
Dr. H. J. Higgs.

MODERN HARRIS HOME DESIGN E-159

The Size
32 ft. x 26 ft.

Ceiling Heights
9 ft. and 8 ft.

7 Rooms
and Bath

A Late Production—Novel Features Everywhere

YOU can build this artistic bungalow in the finest locality with a feeling of pride, for it lacks nothing in exterior elegance or interior arrangement. It is one of those designs that emphasizes all of its attractive features and shows how very charming a home of this kind can be made. Every dollar you invest in this bungalow will show in the beautiful exterior or in comfort and convenience. The sweeping lines of the roof clear over the porch, the wide overhanging eaves and well placed dormer add their charms to the neat effect. Study the picture above and you will find many very pleasing features too numerous to mention.

The entrance is impressive with its latticed front door and harmonious sidelights, giving the needed light to the vestibule. From the central hall the real elegance of the well planned interior is seen. The roominess of the interior is emphasized by the wide cased openings leading to the rear hall, reception room and dining room. To the left we enter the hospitable living room with its fireplace. A pleasing feature is the arrange-ment of well placed high leaded glass windows and the bay window at front. Through a cased opening we enter the den. Note the cozy seat in the bay window. The location of the pantry between the kitchen and dining room is very convenient with its swinging doors. Access from the kitchen to the grade door at the rear, also to the basement and rear porch is facilitated by well placed doors. Note the convenient coat closet in the rear hall and the closet just off the kitchen which may be used as a tin closet or handy coat closet.

The second floor has three good sized bedrooms with an abundance of closet space and a large bath room properly situated for convenient access from any part of the building. Plenty of windows will be found for light and ventilation.

Here is an ideal home built without waste. You'll be sur-prised at the ease and big savings in actual dollars of your money that are yours, if you build of material, sensi-bly Cut-To-Fit—"THE HARRIS WAY"

Our low plumbing and heating estimates should be uncommonly attractive.

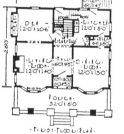

HARRIS BROTHERS COMPANY, 35th and IRON STS., CHICAGO

35

the suburbs to younger, more mobile families. Whereas the Victorian home had been pictured as a place to "settle down" for life, the bungalow was advertised as the starting ground for the young family. The promoters expected that families could switch homes as easily as they bought clothes, choosing those which best fit their life-style at a particular moment in time.

The new bungalow designs were particularly appealing to young women. The simpler construction and plainer decoration meant that the bungalow was far easier to clean and take care of than its Victorian predecessors. The informality of bungalow design also suggested that less time need be devoted to formal visits and entertaining. More important still, the bungalow's promise of a simpler and less formal life-style suggested to women that they would have more time for themselves.

Most of the early magazine articles and plan books dwelt in detail on how the bungalow had first become popular in southern California. Writers described the bungalow as a special building form, derived from the English experience in India, that was especially suitable to the outdoor life-style of Californians. For many Americans at the turn of the century, southern California had become the image of youthfulness and renewal. Because of its mild climate and ever-present sunshine, the area around Pasadena, Los Angeles, and Santa Barbara was equated in the popular mind with the easy-going, slightly sensuous, outdoor life of the Mediterranean. As historian Kevin Starr has suggested, "California-as-Mediterranean challenged Americans to embrace beauty and escape the Puritan past." Southern California, particularly as portrayed by the movie industry that had recently moved there, was viewed as an Edenic land of youth and vigor, a natural garden with fertile possibilities, an ordered and balanced environment that radiated a sense of fresh beginnings and future greatness.[5]

Magazine descriptions of southern California bungalows stressed the particularly fine relationship of these houses to a life-style that combined openness, simplicity, and informality with some degree of order and decorum. "The properly appointed bungalow inside stands for comfort, leisureliness and cheerfulness, comporting with a climate which makes for the same qualities," wrote Charles F. Saunders in *Sunset* magazine. "Bungalow life is informal, but not necessarily bohemian, and at its best is simple, without being sloppy." Here was the classic expression of the new kind of freedom desired by the middle-class public—informal and simple but not without the appropriate and necessary limits.

Saunders gave a homely illustration of what such freedom amounted to in practice by describing the wonderful opportunity presented by having lunch on the veranda of his California bungalow. "The eatables suffered nothing from their outing," he boasted, "while appetite and digestion throve; for we did not allow the meals to degenerate into 'pick-up snacks' but kept them on the plane of serious repasts." Here, again, informality was balanced by order and appropriateness.

Having set the stage with his opening comments, Saunders went on to illustrate the benefits of healthy outdoor California life by describing his meal in great detail. "We were sitting on the porch after a good luncheon, enjoying the warmths of a sunny winter midday," he told his readers. "There was a fragrance of daphne blossoms in the air and the music of humming bees. Beyond the lower end of the garden where the young folks were playing tennis in white flannels, was an orange-grove hanging heavy with its Hesperian fruit, and beyond that, across the green mesa rose the majestic range of the Sierra Madre, its crest white with snow. Now and then the ecstatic note of the meadow-lark floated down the air, and on every side mocking-birds were whistling. Automobiles, filled with pleasure-seekers, whirred by on the street, and occasionally a horse-back party of tanned young men and girls bare of arm and head cantered toward the mountains in gaiety and good health." Given this description of life in the California bungalow, it is not difficult to see how such houses came to symbolize youth, pleasure, fresh air and nature, technology, and the healthy life.[6]

In addition to exemplifying the California life-style, the ideal California bungalow was seen as a way of encouraging individuality and democracy. One architect expressed great satisfaction with the charm of smaller houses which had been totally designed by their owners. "Almost every new bungalow will show some original feature with a gasp of surprise and delight," he chortled, "a window carefully planned to frame a beautiful view, a new solution to the problem of reducing work to a minimum; some cheap material with color added used as curtains or as wainscot paneling." Another writer commented that the unornamented beauty of one southern California bungalow broke down the barriers between social classes, giving to "the man of small means all the necessities and comforts that a mansion house could give." Time and again magazine writers held up the California bungalow as the best inexpensive dwelling available to the common man.[7]

Yet another attestation to the popularity of the California bungalow was its acceptance by professional architects. Initially, commentators in the major architectural journals scornfully criticized the California dwellings as cheap, dull, and unimaginative. They were won over gradually by their simplicity and suitability to the terrain. Architects admitted grudgingly that the "instinctive" creations of the ordinary California country carpenter were "a genuine expression of popular and wholesome habits of country life and habits of country building, and the architects who design more costly and pretentious buildings should do their best to reinforce rather than destroy this tradition and practice." The California bungalow style appealed to the architects, in short, because it fit the new aesthetic ideals of simplicity, functionism, and informality. Architectural theory and popular impulse for once seemed to be working together.[8]

A second reason for the bungalow's popularity with both architects and the public came from its general association with a more informal and outdoor way of life. At first, the bungalow was promoted primarily as an ideal summer house. As more houses were built, the middle-class public began to consider it as particularly appropriate for the suburbs. In California, Herbert Croly, the editor of the *Architectural Record*, predicted that the numbers of bungalows built would increase prodigiously in the next decade. "They are admirably adapted to the California climate," he commented. "They are within the means of all but actually poor and overworked people; and there are an inexhaustible number of charming spots, both on the sea coast, and in the hills and mountains, which are sufficiently accessible from the larger cities to invite their creation." The idea that the bungalow was especially suitable for outdoor living appealed to a generation of Americans who were rediscovering the joys of outdoor life. As Peter Schmitt has suggested, Americans in the Progressive period embraced an "Arcadian" view of nature as a place of simple pleasure and untroubled quiet, an area such as the Adirondack Mountains that was accessible and mildly wild. The universal enthusiasm of Americans for the "back to nature" movement could be seen in the vast expansion of the national park systems under presidents Roosevelt and Taft, the popularity of the outdoor adventures of the Bobbsey Twins and the Rover Boys, the creation of the Boy Scouts (1910) and Campfire Girls (1912), the vogue of "bird-watching" and "sportsman's clubs," and the search for great "scenery" that prompted the opening of Sequoia Park in 1913. Since these organizations valued fresh air and a more active life-style, magazine writers and house builders picked up on the vogue of the "back to nature" movement and developed it in a variety of ways.[9]

Some writers stressed the relationship between the bungalow and good health. One woman described her purchase of a bungalow in a dry western state where she had gone for treatment of asthma as the best decision that she had ever made. Her bungalow was truly a healthy and hygienic environment. Another "business woman" commented that her New England bungalow, built following the California example, was the epitome of simple, economical living, combining the majestic mountain views associated with country life with close access to her work in town. Others praised the seaside settings where their bungalows captured the panorama of the maritime world and the beautiful scenery of natural beaches and tree-clad hills. "Your nature-lover and camper has been a pioneer in a movement that is not without its moral significance," wrote F. W. Burrows. "He has taken counsel of the birds of the air and learned that nature is of itself a home—the most beautiful of all homes, and that man's abode is at its best when it is closest in sympathy and spirit with the great home that our Father has built. And the straining for dollars grows lighter and the struggle for luxury more and more distasteful, as home contentment waxes."

Inherent in the comments about "straining for dollars" and "the struggle for luxury" was the recognition that middle-class Americans were feeling deeply ambivalent about the culture of consumption promoted by national companies and urban department stores in the early twentieth century. Although middle-class Americans had initially embraced the new culture of consumption as a source of opportunity, they slowly began to fear its potentially seductive and corruptive lure. In rejecting the complexities of urban life in favor of a simpler existence, they turned to the bungalow designs as an antidote to commercialism. The bungalow, in short, now had a moral justification as powerful as the cult of true womanhood that had vindicated the large Victorian house. In place of the Victorian rationale that had upheld the moral and spiritual values associated with virtuous females and at the same time justified materialism and ostentatious displays of wealth and possessions, the Progressive bungalow ideal praised the simplicity of a more natural, healthy, and less commercial life-style. The irony was that the promoters of bungalows, despite their insistence that the house was an antidote to the evils of the consumer society,

became themselves participants in the same culture of consumption, albeit in a somewhat different form. As long as the critics of consumerism continued to promote single-family housing for the middle class, they remained trapped within an ethos that stressed the value of possessions.[10]

Although the theme of the bungalow as a natural refuge from the commercial world filled the promotional literature, it was perhaps used most effectively in advertisements by the wave of new companies that produced prefabricated houses. Factory-built homes, manufactured in sections and assembled by the carpenter on the job, had been on the market since the 1880s. They did not become a major force in the housing market, however, until after the turn of the century when they were promoted by Sears, Roebuck, Montgomery Ward, and various lumber companies. The R. L. Kenyon Company of Waukesha, Wisconsin, advertised the utility of their "Take Down House" as a summer vacation home. "It is a three-room bungalow," explained their advertisement in *Colliers*, "with finished hardwood floors, doors, windows, screens, awnings, chimney, ceilings, partitions—a complete house. You can take it with you to the lake, woods or mountains and put it up with your own hands, ready to live in the day you get it." Although the advertisement did not mention how the owner was to get such a house to his mountain retreat, the association with outdoor life was there. Sears, Roebuck went one step further and named their different prefabricated models after scenic vacation areas such as "The Alps" or "Yellowstone." "Wardway Houses" made by Montgomery Ward, "Bennett Better-Built, Ready-Cut Homes" made by the Bennett Lumber Company of North Tonawanda, New York, Aladdin Homes made in Bay City, Michigan, and Harris Homes made in Chicago, Illinois, all carried a variety of prefabricated models in the bungalow style[11] (Figure 6.8).

The surge of interest in prefabricated bungalows after 1910 represented a logical extension of the attitudes toward efficiency and economy that had become part of the

Figure 6.8
Promoters of prefab-
ricated housing
listed appropriate
kitchen and washing
equipment. The
laundry stove was
usually located in
the basement. (Ben-
nett Lumber Co.,
*Bennett Better-Built,
Ready-Cut Homes*)

Puts the Finishing Touch on H

KITCHEN SINK
An attractive sink, massive in construction, cast in one solid piece from best grade of gray iron and heavily white enameled. All corners are rounded to prevent accumulation of grease and dirt. Deep rim hides enter painted bottom of sink. Furnished with drain board either right or left hand side. Length

LAUNDRY STOVE
Combination laundry stove and heater. Heats laundry room and supplies hot water for domestic use. Has flat oval top plate, 16 in. wide, and 25½ in. long. Will accommodate a wash boiler or six flatirons. Has durable grate with draw center. Water jacket surrounds entire firepot. Has capacity for heating 40 gallons of water. *See Home Equipment Book for price.*

new housing ideal. Michigan's International Mill and Timber Company advertised that their prefabricated "Sterling Homes" combined quality, economy, convenience, and speed. They could be put up in only eleven days because standardized materials reduced costs and improved the efficiency of installation. "Every Sterling home," they boasted, "gives the owner the *maximum of useful floor space, proper light* and *ventilation* and is laid out for *economical* heating, lighting and plumbing *installation*." Here was the ultimate expression of the cult of efficiency that was a central part of the Progressive movement.

The initial popularity of the bungalow, therefore, was linked by its promoters to the California life-style, the fascination with outdoor life and summer homes, the ambivalence about the consumer society, and the faith in economy and efficiency. But as more and more people came in contact with the new model home, its proponents broadened their appeal even further by suggesting its appropriateness for apartment dwellers who were moving to the suburbs in increasing numbers and who needed low-cost housing. Sensing this change, one manufacturer of prefabricated bungalows now named his various models after smaller cities with well-known suburbs: "The Evanston," "The Dayton," and "The Canton."[12]

A quick glance at apartment statistics and income levels reveals one reason why the bungalow appealed so strongly to apartment dwellers. Like the inexpensive single-family dwellings put up by S. E. Gross and other developers

in the 1890s, the bungalow pleased renters because it combined a moderate price with an attractive design. More than 75 percent of urban Americans by 1900 lived in rented flats or apartments.[13] Between 1900 and 1917 the average income of these same people more than doubled, increasing from $651 per year to $1,505. By 1910 experts estimated that even a member of the lower middle class earned more than $1,000 a year. Since two-bedroom bungalows in this same period cost between $800 and $3,000, it was now possible for thousands of people who had formerly rented to move to new housing developments on the urban fringe. In the Midwest and on the eastern seaboard, whole districts sprang up in the outer suburbs filled with different bungalow styles.[14]

Recognizing the potential market among the urban apartment dwellers, magazine writers and plan-book authors developed various strategies for moving people out of the city. The classic argument was to stress the special appropriateness of bungalow life for those people "of moderate means." The *Ladies Home Journal* published a series of monthly articles in 1908, showing the variety of bungalow models available in the $1,000, $2,000, and $3,000 price ranges. The magazine also suggested that their designs were especially appropriate "for the bride who does her own work." The comfortable porch, cozy den, and ample windows would fulfill the dream of any young couple who wanted to escape the heat and noise of urban life.[15]

In addition to pressuring newlyweds to move to the suburbs, housing reformers and bungalow promoters focused on the needs of children. Reviving the well-worn theme of how the evils of urban life would corrupt young people, A. F. Weber suggested that "to the Anglo-Saxon race life in the great cities cannot be made to seem a healthy and natural mode of existence. The fresh air and clear sunlight, the green foliage and God's blue sky are dear to the heart of this people, who cannot become reconciled to the idea of bringing up their children in hot, dirty, smoky, germ-producing tenements and streets." Bungalows, he asserted, provided a far better environment for raising children. They were easier to clean and, unlike the Victorian houses which separated young children off into nurseries, their compactness allowed mothers to supervise their children more closely. Other writers suggested that while apartment houses were all right for bachelors and childless families, too often apartment dwellers were nomads and wanderers. Children needed "plenty of room indoors and out for wholesome play." Apartments might be efficient and centrally located, but they were not, in the bungalow promoters' eyes, a good place for families with small children.[16]

Other writers conceded that apartment life might not be that bad. If centrally located, it even had some advantages. But the bungalow's one-floor layout was equally efficient and cheaper in the long run to maintain. "The general interior effect [of a bungalow] is not unlike that of a modern high class apartment," suggested architect Claude Miller. "The difference is that every room is light, and that for two year's rent in the city we can own it in the country." For those whose means were even more limited, another designer suggested that bungalow owners could build double houses and rent out the second section to pay off the mortgage and taxes.[17]

Promoters of bungalow living even anticipated the countercharge that closely packed small houses on narrow suburban lots would be little different from an urban apartment by suggesting that the bungalow design maximized cool breezes and fresh air. As one designer put it, "the extreme ends [of the bungalow] being very narrow, and the roofs low, it would look well even though the ends were very near the lot lines, and its light and air would but plainly be little affected." An entire development of bungalow houses had the further advantage of bringing together people who shared similar values and who thus could create a harmonious neighborhood.

An even stronger argument appealed to those apartment dwellers who wished a country house within commuting distance of the city at a minimal expense. Architects stressed the availability of cheap land within commuting distances of major cities and the lower construction costs that were available further away from the city. These houses would appeal to "the average city man" who usually visited the country for his family vacations. The inexpensiveness of bungalow construction would allow such an individual to build a year-round house in the distant suburbs at a minimal cost.[18]

As the arguments of the bungalow's promoters implied, the greatest advantage of the rustic, simple, efficient dwelling was its tremendous flexibility. One designer even confessed that "the adaptability of the bungalow ... is probably accountable for the bungalow's pronounced popularity." Within the design guidelines suggested by the architects, the bungalow could be modified to fit a wide variety of sites, from mountain retreats to suburban developments. Its exterior design was incredibly adaptable. Colonial, Japanese, Moorish, English, Mission, Swiss, and Dutch Colonial motifs could be added to the outside lines. Architects and magazine writers matched the diversity of bungalow exteriors by offering two or three alternate arrangements of interior space to fit different families' needs. Given the extremely flexible design standards, any exterior style could be considered tasteful and in vogue as long as it was relatively simple. As one architect admitted as early as 1908, "the old-style bungalow was very plain, very low, and with a piazza running all around; the modern one is a law unto itself, and may be in almost any architectural style" (Figure 6.9).

By 1910, therefore, the ideal bungalow had emerged as the all-American family house. Promoted by the popular magazines and plan books, adopted by builders and architects, supported by feminists and writers on home economics, the ideal bungalow made thriftiness and economy respectable. Women, in particular, admired its practicality and efficiency. "The first American bungalow," wrote architect Kate Greenleaf Locke, "was built in California and grew out of my wish for a house, which, being all on one floor, would simplify the problem of housekeeping." Another promoter rhapso-

Figure 6.9
The Milwaukee bungalows on this street display the variety of exterior styles from Tudor to Colonial Revival that could be adapted to the bungalow form. (Photograph by author)

Figure 6.9
The Milwaukee bungalows on this street display the variety of exterior styles from Tudor to Colonial Revival that could be adapted to the bungalow form. (Photograph by author)

dized, "best of all, it combines artistic merit and extreme cheapness." The bungalow ideal was thus seen as a mechanism for expanding the range of middle-class housing to those people of "very moderate incomes" who ordinarily might not have been able to move to the suburbs. It was to be a great boon to the American family because it avoided, in the words of the noted contemporary architectural critic, Montgomery Schuyler, "the vulgarity of crudity on the one hand and the vulgarity of ostentation on the other."[19]

How did the bungalow ideal work out in practice? Was it actually cheaper to build than a standard two-story house? Did it represent a radical shift in the middle-class life-style or a uniquely American design? Was it as cool, functional, and efficient as its promoters suggested? In short, did the bungalow function in all the ways that the housing reformers who so idealized it believed? A look at bungalow construction in Los Angeles, Boise, Salt Lake City, Omaha, and Chicago will help answer these questions. Since the bungalow's popularity spread from the West Coast to the East and not, like all earlier housing fads, from east to west, it is appropriate to begin by examining the subur-

ban expansion of Los Angeles. The popularity of living in southern California grew rapidly after the turn of the century. A land boom began in Los Angeles as early as the 1880s, and its population by 1900 had grown to 102,379, a substantial increase but one that hardly ranked it among the nation's major cities. In the next decade, however, its population more than tripled and between 1904 and 1913 approximately five hundred new subdivisions were opened annually. This phenomenal growth resulted in the annexation in the decade after 1910 of enough of the surrounding countryside to triple the size of the city—making it the fastest-growing suburban area in the nation and producing an unprecedented demand for new housing.[20]

The need for inexpensive single-family dwellings, coupled with the vast expansion of the Pacific Electric Railway's trolley lines, the interest of artists and writers in the Craftsman movement, which stressed comprehensiveness in design and authenticity in materials, and the local fondness for houses in a gardenlike setting, produced a wave of bungalow-style dwellings. Some were elaborate, like the Libby House designed by architects Charles and Henry Greene of Pasadena in 1905. Others were simple, boxlike structures which lined up like dollhouses along many of the city's side streets. But all fulfilled the ideal of California-as-Mediterranean, an easygoing society in which each family could take full advantage of the pleasant outdoor climate. Best of all, these simple structures could be constructed quickly to meet the spectacular demand for new housing within the Los Angeles area.

The massive expansion of bungalow housing within Los Angeles was not without its ironies. The growth of the bungalow ideal in southern California, helped, ironically, to promote the popularity of wood construction in an area with few forests and with the ever-present dangers caused by dry rot and termites. Another irony was that the small size of many of the bungalows, which might have stereotyped them as lower-class housing, now became a source of pride because simple structures had become fashionable. As architect Robert C. Spencer skeptically asserted in the *Architectural Record*, "many so-called bungalows are merely variations or modifications of the universal type of story and a half workingman's cottage, but the name has been a God-send to many who a few years ago would not have dared to build such cheap dwellings in a good middle-class suburban neighborhood." Nor was the one-story house necessarily cheaper to build than its two-story equivalent with the same interior space. As Henry H. Saylor, one of the bungalow's staunchest promoters admitted, a building with all its rooms on the ground floor was actually more expensive to build than a two-story structure because it needed a much larger roof and more land.[21]

The gap between the promotional theories about bungalow design and the reality of bungalow construction in Los Angeles and elsewhere can be seen in two other features of the design: its uniqueness and its Americanness. The California bungalow was constantly extolled in the popular press as a uniquely American design, tailored to meet the needs of the American family. In point of fact, the design was neither as unique nor as American as its promoters insisted. Plan-book writers in the 1880s and 1890s often created one-story cottages which, though not sharing the sloping bungalow roofline or its open interior spaces, provided efficient one-floor living.[22]

The claim that the California bungalow was an original and uniquely American house design can also be questioned because similarly styled dwellings were in vogue in India, England, and Australia during the same period. Although the American popular press sometimes overlooked it, the Craftsman movement with its emphasis on simplicity of design and integrity of materials (wood stained naturally so that it looked like wood) had drawn its inspiration from the Arts and Crafts movement that had begun in England. American magazines such as *House Beautiful* ran feature articles on such topics as "A Derbyshire Bungalow," complete with illustrations. While it is true that the bungalow craze was far more popular in the United States than elsewhere, its popularity was not unique to this country[23] (Figure 6.10).

The appeal of the bungalow in the Los Angeles area was thus more complex than its promoters suggested. Simplicity of design, ease of construction, and comparatively low cost were as important as its evocation of an outdoor life-style and its symbolic image of coziness, comfort, and security. Clearly one of the most important reasons for the bungalow's popularity was its low cost. Since the average California bungalow was smaller than its Victorian predecessors and could be mass-produced easily with common grades of lumber, it represented somewhat of a breakthrough in reducing the cost of housing in middle-class suburban neighborhoods.

A final reason for the popularity of the bungalow in the Los Angeles area was that it also fitted in well with the relatively treeless environment. The bungalow was easily adapted to the low, sculptured hills and flat valley areas, helping to maintain the contour line of the landscape. In such an environment, small single-story houses could be packed relatively closely together without creating a sense of crowding or congestion. When spread out over

Figure 6.10
This English example of a bungalow, built appropriately out of stone, indicates the international popularity of the bungalow form. ("A Derbyshire Bungalow")

A DERBYSHIRE BUNGALOW

THC· PINFOLD · at · FRITCHLEY ♡   J·ALFRED·WOORE ·ARCHITECT·

a large area and surrounded by gardens, bungalow neighborhoods reinforced the sense of openness and spaciousness of the landscape. The Los Angeles bungalow, in short, while not as extraordinary as its promoters suggested, did come close enough in terms of cost and open interior design to justify its praise in the press as an important new house form.

What began in southern California as a local response to a massive housing shortage was soon accepted elsewhere as an inexpensive and artistic innovation. After an initial cautious response, other cities adopted the bungalow form for many of the same reasons that had made it popular in California. The pattern of acceptance in Boise, Idaho, a small western city, was perhaps typical. The first bungalow in Boise was designed in 1904 by J. Flood Walker, a Los Angeles architect who had just moved into the city. The low profile and open interior of the new house were a radical enough departure from contemporary styles to merit comment in the city's newspaper. The local reporter was distinctly pleased by the absence of "the old-fashioned hallway" in the bungalow, and he

admired the way in which the reception and living rooms were separated by only "ledges for potted plants." But the reporter's enthusiasm for the house was not shared by local realtors and bankers. Walker moved out of town in less than two years and the new style did not catch on until the end of the decade.

Two factors influenced the later acceptance of bungalows in Boise. One was the substantial growth of the city from 5,957 to 17,358 inhabitants by 1910. The other was the demise in popularity of the Queen Anne cottage. The tripling of the city's population in one decade made both architects and contractors more interested in inexpensive bungalow designs that could be quickly built and yet had a reputation for solidity and quality. They also encouraged the acceptance of the new bungalow forms by incorporating into them the fireplaces, bay windows, and inglenooks that had been a popular feature of the older Queen Anne designs. Thus, by 1911, the local newspaper could proudly assert that "three or four years ago this style of home architecture was scarcely known in Boise, but now bungalows far outnumber any other sort of home being erected." Citizens now referred to themselves as residents of a "bungalow city."[24]

Although bungalows came to predominate in Boise, they were strongly challenged by Colonial Revival homes which also proved to be very popular. Since both house forms fit the reigning aesthetic theory that emphasized simplicity and functionality, it is important to inquire why individual families chose one design over another. Obviously, various factors were involved. One was the question of social status. The Colonial Revival homes in Boise were favored by wealthy businessmen probably because of their association with the World's Fair of 1893 and the sense of elegance that could be traced back to the nation's early architecture. In Boise, the J. E. Tourtellotte architectural firm that had specialized in Queen Anne designs before 1904 later created the majority of the more pretentious East Coast-influenced designs for local realtors, doctors, and bankers. Although a few prominent business people built large bungalows, which in Boise were set off from the more common designs by their half-timbered and stuccoed gables, the majority of wealthy people in the city favored the more elaborate Colonial Revival styles (Figure 6.11).[25]

The motives that caused individuals to choose one design over another can be seen by looking at the Chicago suburbs and at the Avenues neighborhood in Salt Lake City. In the Chicago area, recent studies of Frank Lloyd Wright's clients are helpful. Wright was a major originator of the Prairie School style that was known for its horizontal shape, overhanging roof, and bands of casement windows. Wright thought of himself as a great innovator, and it is clear that his emphasis on open-house interiors, extended horizontal lines, and the removal of excessive ornament represented a remarkable synthesis of the new aesthetic ideas. But it is also evident that many of Wright's most basic design concepts were similar to those advocated in the general promotional literature about domestic architecture at the turn of the century. Wright himself contributed to that literature by publishing some of his early plans in the *Ladies Home Journal*. Although Wright refused to believe that the *Journal* readers could share his aesthetic vision, his ideas were similar to those of arts and crafts enthusiasts, bungalow designers, magazine authors, and advocates of the home economics movement. The similarities are instructive. Recent studies of Wright's clients by Leonard Eaton demonstrate that they were particularly interested in the functionalism and efficiency of his Prairie School designs. Clearly his clients' concerns were echoed by the purchasers of the popular bungalow designs.[26]

Other reasons for the popularity of bungalows can be seen by examining the process of suburban expansion in Salt Lake City. The systematic study of all the houses in Salt Lake's Avenues neighborhood by Karl Haglund and Philip Notarianni makes it possible to identify the variety of different reasons for settling in that area (Figure 6.12).

The Avenues neighborhood in the rolling hills to the northeast of Temple Square and the state capitol was established in the 1850s by tradesmen who worked in the downtown area. Settlement in the Avenues was slowed somewhat in the 1870s and 1880s because of the lack of water. But the construction of water mains in the 1880s and the opening of electric trolley service in 1889 initiated a new surge of growth there. Lawyers, doctors, realtors, and mining company directors moved into the area and created a pattern of living on the Avenues and working in the downtown business district. Although some of the residents were employed in crafts and trades related to the mining and railroad industries which were the heart of Utah's economy, most of the turn-of-the-century residents on the Avenues were part of the vast expansion of middle- and upper-class "white-collar" workers. Clerks, accountants, salesmen, teachers, doctors, lawyers, bankers, realtors, and even a few teamsters and laborers occupied the Avenues developments by 1900.[27]

One of the major reasons for building in the Avenues neighborhood was for speculation and investment. In 1900 in the city at large the majority of houses were rented rather than

owned by the occupants. Middle- and upper-class families built houses and rented them as income-producing properties. Recognizing the fact that wives frequently outlived their husbands, widows often purchased second houses and rented them as an investment for their old age. Elizabeth Martin, for example, who was a widow of a mining executive, lived at 128 B Street but maintained two other rental houses on the same street. So, too, did Oliver and Georgia Jennings who lived at 353 Sixth Avenue and built two other houses on the same block as investment property. Proximity to the rental houses meant that owners could monitor more carefully the renters' treatment of their property.

In addition to individuals who built one or two houses for retirement income or investment purposes, developers after the turn of the century established residential additions on large tracts of land. Businesses such as the Deseret Savings and Loan, the Heber J. Grant Company, and the Salt Lake Security and Trust Company built numerous homes and advertised widely for clients. They praised the central location and easy access to transportation, the view, and the fact that their houses, which were often taken from the popular magazines and architectural plan books, had "every modern improvement." As the Avenues area expanded, small contractors joined the developers in putting up groups of two or three houses on side streets.[28]

A third reason for building multiple dwellings in the Avenues district was to provide housing for family and kin. The Mormons, in particular, had long emphasized the importance of family relations and home ownership. They constituted over half the residents of the Avenues until 1917 and set the tone for much of the housing constructed in that area. Perhaps the best example of this influence was Heber J. Grant, a wealthy businessman and the president of the Latter-Day Saints church from 1918 to 1945. Grant was the son of Salt Lake City mayor and LDS church apostle Jedediah Grant. In addition to establishing the Utah-Idaho Sugar Company and the State Bank of Utah, he was president of Heber J. Grant Land Company, a real estate and insurance agency heavily involved in the acquisition of land and the construction of houses on the Avenues. In 1915 he also helped organize the Home Benefit Building Society, which encouraged young Mormon families to acquire their own houses.

Grant purchased the south half of the block between A and B streets and Eighth Avenue in 1908, selling lots to others but reserving some of them for his own family. His daughter Mary Grant Judd built a bungalow at 201 Eighth Avenue and another at 420 A Street in 1915, and her father moved his family into the Eighth Avenue house in 1916. In 1909 he deeded land further down the same street to his son-in-law. The bungalow at 219 Eighth Avenue was also built on land purchased from Grant.

It was not surprising that a wealthy business-man like Grant would have lived in a modest bungalow house. The simple lines and plain brick-and-clapboard exterior fit in well with the thrifty life-style that the Mormon church extolled. Grant's house was similar to the bungalow of Orson D. Romney, who was the treasurer of another major real estate company on the Avenues. The prime difference between Grant's and Romney's houses was that the latter's was placed gable end to the street in order to fit on its long, narrow lot. Even architects favored the bungalow style for residences. Lewis Telle Cannon, son of LDS church leader George Q. Cannon, a senior partner in the firm of Cannon and Fetzer, built a bungalow for his mother in 1917 and one for himself at 376 Second Avenue in 1920. Joseph Don Carlos Young, who later became the LDS church architect, built a bungalow in 1908 on U Street for William Cunningham, a Mormon businessman active in railroads, mining, and insurance.[29]

Grant's modest bungalow, like the houses of many of the other Mormon church leaders, contrasted most noticeably with the Colonial Revival mansions built by prominent businessmen. In Salt Lake City, as in Boise, Idaho, and in cities on the East Coast, Colonial Revival houses became associated with upper-class wealth. Although the bungalow itself occasionally was designed in a Colonial Revival style, it lacked the size and stature associated with the larger and more monumental houses of the upper classes. As Joy Wheeler Dow expressed it in *World's Work* magazine, such Colonial Revival homes were "the history of the American people. The history of the Anglo-Saxon house as it has existed in America—which we need in architectural crystallization." On the Avenues in Salt Lake City, Gill S. Peyton, manager of the Mercur Gold Mining and Milling Company, built a large Colonial Revival mansion in 1896. Adrian C. Ellis, Jr., lawyer, businessman, and mine owner, had his own massive Georgian Revival home built on Second Avenue in 1905. Such homes stood out in graphic contrast to those of the church leaders much as the elaborate Italianate houses of the wealthy had over-

Figure 6.13
The small bungalow home of Edwin Felt with its simple lines, large windows, and red-brick exterior represented a very popular house type built in Salt Lake City in the 1920s. (Photograph by author)

looked working-class homes in the cities of Westminster and Kalamazoo in the 1880s.[30]

By 1920, about 25 percent of the houses on the Avenues were bungalows. In some of the developments they comprised a majority of the homes. Contractors after World War I often built whole streets of one-story brick bungalows for speculative purposes. One such house, which was purchased in 1920 by Mr. and Mrs. Edwin Felt shortly after their marriage, provides an excellent example of how far apart the actual motives of house buyers often were from the promotional theory of bungalow design.

The Felt bungalow was a modest one-story, three-bedroom house with a gable-end front porch that faced the street (Figure 6.13). Built of brick by a local contractor who also put up several other houses on the same street, the Felt residence had a garage and a small backyard. The Felts purchased the house in 1920 for $10,000 with some help from the wife's father who owned a company that sold plumbing and heating equipment. They purchased the home, Mrs. Felt relates, not because they had any special interest in bungalows but rather

because they liked the location and bungalows were the houses in vogue at the time. The trolley ran right past the front door to downtown Salt Lake City, the house had a good view of the Salt Lake basin, and it was close to the public schools.

The interior of the house followed the floor plan of a typical plan-book bungalow. Entering the house through the front door, a visitor would step into a large room with the dining area on the right and the living area on the left. The left wall of the living room had a fireplace with built-in bookcases on either side and a long mantel which fit in with the tops of the bookcases and ran the length of the side wall. Behind the dining room and connected by a swinging door was a small kitchen with counters, sink, and refrigerator. A small closet in the kitchen contained a built-in, fold-down ironing board. Behind the living room and separated by curtained French doors was the parents' bedroom. The Felts had four children, two girls and two boys, who shared the other two bedrooms. A bathroom and hallway made up the rear of the house.

The Felt home was small and functional, but Mrs. Felt did not believe that reduced space was more functional than the two-story Victorian home in which she had grown up. In fact, the smaller space, she asserted, made the house more cluttered. Yet the reduced space in the bungalow made the bungalow philosophy to some extent self-fulfilling. With six people in such a small house, space had to be used to the utmost. Because people were very close together, there was also a tendency to use the house as a staging ground for outside activities and to do somewhat less entertainment at home than had been done in the older Victorian houses. The brick exterior and small yard also meant that the house needed far less maintenance than its Victorian predecessors. For the Felts, the house was an efficient, ideal way to raise their family.[31]

The Felt family illustrates the extent to which the bungalow helped to break down the older image of the Victorian family as divided into separate male and female spheres. Although Mrs. Felt had grown up in the large Victorian house of her parents, she felt comfortable in the bungalow because she shared the Progressive interest in a variety of activities outside the home. Where her father's Victorian house had its own pool table and the family was encouraged to spend a good deal of time at home, the compact nature of her own bungalow encouraged the family to engage in a greater variety of outdoor activities. Mrs. Felt got her driver's license in 1916 during her senior year in high school and always enjoyed the freedom to shop and visit friends and relatives that car ownership allowed. A good skater and horseback rider, Mrs. Felt also liked the outdoor life. Each summer the Felts spent time with other relatives at a large family cabin that had been built by her father in the late 1910s in Immigrant Canyon nine miles away. There they could hike, fish, ride horses, and visit with their cousins. The smaller house thus encouraged the Progressive ideals of the companionate marriage, the healthy outdoor life, and a more self-sufficient and independent life-style for women.

The housing experience of the Felts appears similar to that experienced by other middle-class Americans between 1900 and 1920. The substantial expansion of middle-class home ownership followed a pattern that was repeated in city after city in the Progressive period. The best documentation of this pattern is in Howard Chudacoff's study of Omaha, Nebraska. According to Chudacoff, home ownership by Omaha families increased substantially from 27.7 percent in 1900 to 47.2 percent in 1920. The population of Omaha expanded by 87 percent in the same period, but sufficient housing and rental units were built to provide the average middle-class family with a number of housing alternatives. The mass-production of plan-book and builders' houses, often in the bungalow design, meant that it was a buyer's market. Financing of houses—which had once involved annual or semiannual installments— now was often divided into monthly payments. And the initial down payment was reduced, thus placing home ownership within the reach of many Omahans after 1900.[32]

The ready availability of relatively inexpensive housing in Omaha, Salt Lake City, and Los Angeles resulted in a doubling of home ownership between 1880 and 1920. Although fewer than one-fourth of Omaha's families owned houses in 1880, almost half did forty years later. But the substantial increase in home ownership was often matched by frequent changes of residence in the same city. The opening of new suburban developments allowed people to move to better quarters as their families expanded and they needed more space. The same was true for cities as different as Dayton, Toledo, Grand Rapids, St. Paul, Des Moines, and Seattle. The expanding suburbs allowed substantially more families to own their own homes than had ever done so before.

Although the consequences of the combination of increased home ownership and residential mobility can only be speculated about, it is probable that one result was a greater identification with the house and neighborhood than with the families living nearby. The frequent movement from house to house in these expanding cities—in Omaha, there was nearly a complete turnover in a neighborhood in a relatively short time—meant that neighborhood identity had to come more from shared ideas about housing standards and residential services such as police and fire than from contact with one's neighbors. The Felts and Grants, who lived in their Salt Lake City homes for more than sixty years, were the exception. In cities the usual situation of rapid mobility coupled with high home ownership meant that the bungalow craze helped to provide a sense of similarity within diversity. Families could move often but when the neighborhoods contained similar house styles—with the latest refinements and improvements—they could retain a sense of continuity. The people might change, but the expectations about housing and the environment stayed the same.

The immense popularity of the bungalow thus reflected both the reality of a rapidly expanding middle-class housing market and a set of aesthetic and social ideals to which upwardly mobile individuals might aspire. Although individual families such as the Felts or the Grants did not purchase their houses particularly because of the efficiency of the room layouts or the built-in features of the kitchens, they did tacitly accept the assumption that the simple, functional designs represented a practical and attractive home setting in which to live and raise a family.

Although some gap always existed between the elaborate promises of the promoters and actual bungalow living, there was enough truth in the rhetoric of plan-book writers and developers to make the bungalow nationally popular. The house was relatively inexpensive. It did have a rough simplicity and charm in its design, and it did fit in well with a more informal and outdoor life-style. Given these assets, it is not surprising that the house design remained enormously popular into the 1920s and 1930s. The bungalow, as its promoters insisted, turned what might have been the major drawbacks of simplicity and small size into major assets. Here was a house with which middle-class Americans could easily identify.

Chapter 7

Ranch House Modern

Contemporary is usually associated with large glass areas. But it certainly is not a white cube, not a flat roof, not corner windows, but just an unself-conscious attempt to design the best house to live in.

> —Walter Adams, "What America Wants to Build"

Ranch houses are not just a matter of picturesque exteriors with wagon-wheel and Heigh-ho silver decor. What they can offer is a better way of living—not just a fancier facade.

> —Will Mehlhorn, "Ranch Houses Suit Any Climate"

The building boom for single-family housing that began at the turn of the century and, despite a slowdown during World War I, continued on into the 1920s, came to a grinding halt during the Great Depression. For the next decade the housing market remained weak. Middle-class Americans who were fortunate enough to have a job tended to spend their limited funds on small remodeling projects. No sooner had housing prospects begun to brighten in the early 1940s than the outbreak of World War II cut off the supply of building materials. By the war's end, middle-class Americans who had been forced to limit their expectations, now had new hope. The postwar housing market, they believed, would open up vast new opportunities to choose the home of their dreams.

Reacting to the initial postwar euphoria about new housing, Eric Hodgins sounded a note of warning in a satirical story entitled "Mr. Blandings Builds His Castle," published in the April 1946 issue of *Fortune* magazine. The quotation above the article reflected the fears of many Americans who were entering the market for a new home. It was from Samuel Johnson and read, "To build is to be robbed."

The story concerned the attempt of Mr. and Mrs. Blandings to rehabilitate a dilapidated old farmhouse only to find that the structure was beyond repair. They then went to an architect and builder to put up a custom-designed home. The ensuing tale of woe was enough to discourage any prospective home builder. It told of the problems of irresponsible architects, faulty land titles, unforeseen construction delays, wily contractors, material shortages, inflated mortgage money, and lawsuits. Although the final result was touted in *"Home Lovely"* magazine as a "tribute to Taste and Ingenuity with materials old and new," the story was one of inflated expectations and blasted dreams.[1]

Fortune's attack on the construction of single-family dwellings after World War II was a cautious note in what was otherwise an exuberant chorus of optimistic voices. Popular home magazines, interior decorators, architects, appliance makers, and building-material manufacturers joined forces with the federal government in the late 1940s to fuel what became the largest surge of home construction since the 1920s. The legacy of thirty years of depressed hopes and wartime restrictions exploded and was replaced by a new vision of the ideal home—the "Dream House of the Future"—that differed in substantial ways from its bungalow and Neo-Colonial predecessors (Figure 7.1). The editors of *Fortune* were wise to warn their readers about the dangers of forming unrealizable dreams about the new "ranch" and "contemporary modern" homes. As had happened in the past, the vision of the ideal American house and family in the 1950s was overly idealistic and optimistic. But it nevertheless fit well with the strident optimism that characterized the postwar years of the baby boom and the consumer society.

The depression and wartime years had been tough ones for the housing industry, especially since they followed three decades of housing expansion. From 1890 to 1930, new housing starts had increased rapidly, and the proportion of nonfarm Americans owning their own houses had risen dramatically from less than 37 to 46 percent. The 1929 stock market crash abruptly reversed that trend. Together with bank failures and massive unemployment, it knocked the bottom out of the house construction market. Housing starts declined by 90 percent from their peak of 937,000 units in 1925 to their all-time low of 93,000 in 1933. In the same year, more than 1.5 million homes were in default or in the process of foreclosure. This downward slide was only averted by the Federal Home Loan Bank Act of 1932, which stabilized the savings and loan associations, and by the

passage of the Federal Housing Act (FHA) two years later, which represented the first active government support for the housing industry. Initially intended only as a pump-priming process to get house building started, the FHA gave house construction a tremendous boost by issuing twenty-year mortgages with low down payments. Nevertheless, by 1940, even though housing starts had climbed back up to 603,000 a year, a housing shortage continued to exist and only slightly over 41 percent of Americans owned their own dwellings.[2]

The outbreak of war in Europe did little to help the housing shortage. The mobilization of the armament industry begun by President Roosevelt after German troops overran Europe forced many companies to turn from housing materials to wartime construction. Material shortages, government regulations, scarce labor, and reduced incomes compelled many families once again to postpone their hopes for buying a house. Middle-class Americans rationed their consumption of household goods to support the war effort, planted victory gardens, and planned for the day when they could once again buy a house for themselves.

The restrictions on housing during the depression and the war years were not without their benefits for the housing industry. The need to keep costs low during the 1930s helped stimulate the development of new building materials: prefabricated window units, weather-resistant exterior plywood, latex glues and caulking, composition-board products, and improved drywall plasterboard. The war years, which put tremendous pressure on businesses to improve their speed and efficiency, also helped to create technological breakthroughs that were to be of great benefit after 1946[3] (Figure 7.2).

Perhaps typical was the experience of the Andersen Corporation in Bayport, Minnesota. Originally a general lumber company, the firm sold moldings, interior trim, and staircases. In 1903 it incorporated and switched to the production of window and door frames. The windows were sold in pieces and assembled by a carpenter on the job. The company favored

Figure 7.1
A typical one-story
"ranch" house built
in the Rolling Hills
development in Pa-
ramus, New Jersey.
(Andersen Corpora-
tion)

mass production but was hindered by a lack of national standards for window sizes. As late as the 1920s, windows in Boston houses were slightly smaller than those in the Midwest. The Andersen Frame Company, which later changed its name to the Andersen Corporation, helped correct this problem by establishing standardized sizes and then, in 1932, by developing the first prefabricated window unit. The new window unit made it possible to install a finished window in only a few minutes. Caught by a shortage of materials during the war, the factory switched to making war products and turned out nearly five million wooden gun cases and ammunition boxes. To increase production, it developed complex, high-speed machines that allowed it not only to cut the parts more quickly but also to spray-paint and mark them before assembly.

When the war ended, the high-speed machinery and the new production techniques developed for the war effort were transferred back to the manufacture of windows. A new "Pressure Seal" window, which did away with the pulley-and-weight systems, a new picture window with casements on either side, which

was advertised as a "Window Wall," and a new awning window called "Flexivent" were turned out using the mass-production techniques pioneered during the war (Figure 7.3). The company quickly doubled in size and by 1952 was producing more than a million awning windows annually. The lessons of the depression and the war had been put to good use.[4]

Companies like the Andersen Corporation also played on consumer frustration during the war by selling personally embossed scrapbooks for saving ideas for future construction. A dream book for home planners, the scrapbook was divided into sections for the storage of clippings on house plans, kitchens, living rooms, bedrooms, extra rooms, bathrooms, built-ins, porches, outdoor fireplaces, gardens, and, to promote their own product, a section on "Window Beauty Ideas." Before the war ended, the Andersen Window Company had stimulated the hopes of future home buyers by distributing nationally more than 350,000 copies of their scrapbook (Figure 7.4).

Although both consumers and building-material manufacturers in the early 1940s had begun to plan for postwar housing expansion,

Same slab foundation served prefab and masonry houses.

Roof trusses came precut, were assembled at each house.

Prefab wall panels came by truck from Milwaukee Expandable Homes, Inc.

Erecting trusses was a matter of only a few minutes and roof sheathing was done just as fast.

Small field crew rapidly set up panels. The inside walls were also prefabbed.

peace was declared before either business or the public was fully prepared. Housing starts had slipped to a low of 141,800 by 1944. By the end of 1945 there were 3,600,000 families lacking homes. The return of thirteen million servicemen and women thus created a massive housing shortage overnight. Housing was so limited that North Dakota surplus grain bins were turned into shelters and Benny Goodman gave a benefit concert in Cleveland at which the audience pledged to rent rooms to the war veterans instead of making cash donations.

Top
Speed of getting house enclosed was greatest advantage in use of prefabs.
Bottom
Finished house with three bedrooms and garage was popular.

Congress, building upon its experience with the Federal Housing Administration in the 1930s, responded by passing the Serviceman's Readjustment Act (the GI Bill) that provided Veterans Administration loans to returning soldiers to purchase, build, or improve their houses. With new government support, the mad scramble to increase all forms of housing had begun and architects, home-magazine writers, and social reformers rushed into print in an attempt to influence the growing housing market. The stakes were high. Never before had so great a public demand won the financial support of the federal government.[5]

As usual, the architects were the first ones to crusade for new housing standards. Writing in the *Architectural Record*, Joseph Hudnut, the dean of Harvard's Graduate School of Design, complained that the "cloudburst of new houses" lacked "that *idea* which is the essential substance of a house." Most people appeared to want to combine the latest in technology, planning, building materials, and labor-saving de-

Figure 7.4
The Andersen Corporation helped encourage middle-class Americans during World War II to think about building their own dream house at the war's conclusion by offering this inexpensive scrapbook for saving house design ideas. (Andersen Corporation)

work on new fashions in artificial light we ought to suspect not new efficiencies merely or new economies merely, but new radiances in living."

Hudnut's aim was to harness the new technology to aid human needs and to exploit its aesthetic potential. Decrying the "arid materialism" and the social scientist's mechanistic measurements which sought to discover, for example, how much living room space 3.8 children needed in which to play, the Harvard dean asserted that the family home, despite its origins in the machine processes, ought to be a refuge against modern society. The architect's role in the postwar rush to create new housing, he asserted, was to use the new technology to bring out true and beautiful feelings about the family home.[6]

Despite Hudnut's plea for new aesthetic standards, most architects in their professional journals concentrated on more practical questions of size, efficiency, and cost. Royal Barry Wills struck the common note when he acknowledged that despite the unprecedented demand and the expanding availability of mortgage funds, the construction cost of an average house had almost doubled in the decade of the 1940s. The challenge for architects and builders, therefore, was not to create a new aesthetic for the houses that were being built. For Wills as well as for most house planners in the popular magazines of the period, the question of exterior styles—modern or traditional—was of secondary importance. Modern houses, by which term he meant one-story ranch houses— had the advantage of flexibility of interior space. Often, however, that advantage was overwhelmed by too many built-ins. Wills's approach was to transform the nature of the living and dining rooms by combining them, or by combining the dining room with the kitchen (Figure 7.5). Most rooms in the modern house, he asserted, would have to have multiple functions. Study-guest room, kitchen-laundry room-sewing room-playroom for toddlers, and terraces that could serve as extensions of the living room, dining room, or bedroom (Figure 7.6). Use became the defining element of Wills's designs. Questions of decoration took a

vices with the outer shell of the older Cape Cod cottage. Architects as well seemed to believe that new building materials and technology would, by themselves, define beauty. Rebelling against the notion that function and efficiency alone would provide a new aesthetic for home construction, Hudnut suggested that "of all the inventions of modern architecture the new space is . . . the most likely to attain a deep eloquence." New, stronger building materials gave the architect greater freedom to model and define space, directing its flow and relationships, and giving it "an ethereal elegance unknown to the historic architectures." Modern space could be bent or curved; it could flow through glass walls or splinter apart around alcoves or galleries. Similarly, the new technologies had in effect invented a new kind of light. "We can direct light," Hudnut explained, "control its intensity and its colorations; diffuse it over space, throw it in bright splashes against a wall, dissolve it and gather it up in quiet pools; and from those scientists who are at

1. All-Purpose Living Room

As often happens in middle class homes as well as in minimum housing—the living room must serve for study and library, music room, play and hobby space, and even guest room. Therefore extreme flexibility of furniture groupings must be planned for and space carefully provided to store the equipment and supplies for many activities. If the area allowed for living room is large enough to equal two decently sized rooms, there could be an adjustable partition separating quiet-private and noisy-public activities. Otherwise the solution must just be "areas of activity" with furnishings grouped accordingly.

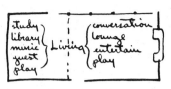

Figure 7.5
Architect Royal Barry Wills sketched some of the multiple functions possible for a combination "living room–dining room." (Wills, "Space." Reprinted from *Architectural Record* [May 1945] copyright McGraw-Hill, Inc.)

2. Living Room—Dining Room

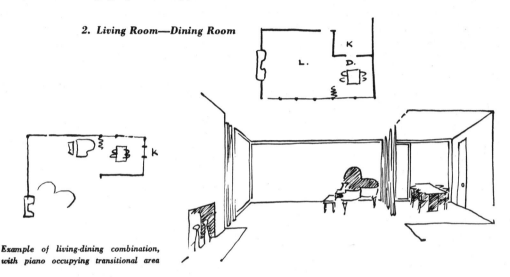

Example of living-dining combination, with piano occupying transitional area

back seat to the needs created by function and utility.[7]

The editors of *Architectural Forum* agreed with Wills. Challenging the idea "that a Cape Cod cottage remains the snappiest idea in a home," they published a new guide to house construction, appropriately entitled *Tomorrow's House*. In place of the popular "Colonial"-style house—"pathetic little white boxes with dressed-up street fronts, each striving for individuality through meaningless changes in detail or color"—the editors suggested a more modern design that would recognize the changed needs of contemporary family life. Because many wives now worked outside the home and had less time to cook and clean, because more entertainment now took place at movies, churches, nightclubs, and other outside agencies, because children moved out of the family more quickly than they had hitherto, the tradi-

tional form of the house had to be changed. But the new designs could still be traditional in the sense that they were "unself-conscious and honest" solutions to building problems. "This book," they asserted, "is an argument for the traditional approach to house design, for an expression in homes of modern life as we live it. It is also a plea for individuality against regimentation." Individuality, honesty, functionality—these were the watchwords of the new architectural canon of good taste.[8]

Instead of asserting the validity of any particular style or design, the editors of *Architectural Forum* suggested that the criterion for judging excellence in domestic architecture should come from a specific feature of the design process itself. Rejecting Hudnut's plea for new aesthetic standards based upon a more imaginative conceptualization of light and space, they insisted on the central importance

Figure 7.6
Given the small size
of postwar houses in
the early 1950s, it
was important to ex-
plain to the middle
class how it might
maximize the use
of space. (Wills,
"Space." Reprinted
from *Architectural
Record* [May 1945]
copyright McGraw-
Hill, Inc.)

1. Sick-isolation Room.

Screen around patient's bed; couch bed at right for nurse. Flap table for medicines, supplies. Radio by nurse's bed or near the fireplace

2. Play-Hobby Room.

Games, tea parties, or study at folding table. Other bed moved near the fireplace, screen stored in closet, rug under bed. Displays on wall

3. Guest Room.

Furniture much as in sick room. Flap table should now have standing mirror for dressing use. Stand by day bed replaced with luggage rack

4. Office or Study

Without much change, room becomes study or office. Good lighting for painting at window (sketch above). Desk instead of flap table.

of function. According to their view, the latest in building technology had to be paired with the needs of the modern family. "It is a simple idea, but it has interesting possibilities," they asserted. "If one were to take the best planning ideas, the best structural schemes, and the best equipment that have gone into the best modern houses, and combine them appropriately in a single house, the result would look like something out of the day after tomorrow." The new style, in other words, would emerge in an innovative and nonideological way from the design process itself. Like the new canons of objectivity and professional expertise that were beginning to dominate the fields of social science and medicine, the architects stressed an unself-conscious and almost intuitive functionalism. "Tomorrow's house as we see it is not a potpourri," they insisted, "but an integrated, highly individual expression of how a twentieth-century family lives."9

Inherent in the arguments of the editors of *Architectural Forum* was a curious paradox. The attack on past architectural standards and the insistence on a more radical functionalism represented a new stylistic position. Yet the architects denied that their views reflected any new stylistic criteria and insisted instead that they were being neutral and objective. In this respect, their curiously unself-critical perception of themselves was similar to that of other intellectuals in the 1950s whom historian Robert Fowler has described as "believing skeptics." Such a position could be seen in sociologist Daniel Bell's best-seller, *The End of Ideology*, which asserted that old ideologies were dead and implied that the position of the United States in the Cold War was motivated less by a distinctive ideology than by technical decisions about defense. Similarly, Will Herberg's *Protestant, Catholic, Jew* asserted that the distinctiveness of religious faiths had disappeared. A realistic assessment of American religion, Herberg asserted, would view Protestantism, Catholicism, and Judaism as becoming increasingly similar; all three were essentially related to the inner and more secular evolution of American society. The intellectuals' attack on ideology paralleled the architects' attack on

style. Both groups felt that the focus on ideology or style tended to distort people's understanding of the fields of inquiry. They insisted that their own position was only based on common sense. In their confident assertion of their own objectivity, however, both groups failed to recognize the assumptions that lay behind their own points of view. Thus the architects' preoccupation with escaping from the past and their assertion that an emphasis on efficiency and function was simply objective was itself a reflection of the naive single-mindedness that Americans felt at the end of World War II.10

The architects' problem was how to bridge the gap between their expertise and the client's dreams. The first step was to get a more accurate assessment of a house buyer's concerns. *McCall's*, the *Ladies Home Journal, House and Garden, Better Homes and Gardens, Good Housekeeping*, and *Parents' Magazine* initiated this process by using social science surveys of public opinion to understand more systematically the views of their readership. Between 1936 and 1950, more than forty-one surveys were taken. Perhaps typical was the survey done by Walter Adams for *Better Homes and Gardens* in 1946, based on a questionnaire answered by 11,428 families. According to the response, the typical American looking for a new house who had already consulted a builder or architect was still attracted to the "Cape Cod." But the house buyer wanted more space and therefore also favored "the low, rambling style called Ranch House which has come out of the Southwest" (Figure 7.7). In order to get a larger lot, most people planned to build in the suburbs or countryside where they would have more space for children's play areas and gardens.

Although almost half of those surveyed were living in two-story houses, only a fourth wanted to build them. Most also wanted a basement where they might locate the laundry (a cheaper alternative than putting it into a utility room on the first floor) and a multipurpose hobby or recreation room (Figure 7.8). "We want to combine our recreation and living room," wrote one respondent, "but yet have it warm and cozy looking. One end will be carpeted, and there we'll have our soft sofa and a couple of com-

Figure 7.7
The typical housing development, such as this one in Paramus, New Jersey, changed the front roofline and fenestration from house to house to give each home a more individual look. (Andersen Corporation)

Figure 7.8
Royal Barry Wills, in his design for a combination study-playroom, included a variety of built-in counters and cupboards for storage in this multipurpose hobby room. (Wills, "Space." Reprinted from *Architectural Record* [May 1945] copyright McGraw-Hill, Inc.)

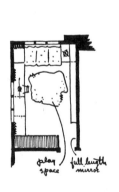

fortable chairs. The rest of the room will be given over to recreational purposes. There will be occasional chairs spaced about invitingly. And there'll be a pool table which can be used for table tennis by attaching a top to it. And a card table, and a piano. And a large fireplace with a grate for broiling frankfurters, and a small refrigerator concealed in a built-in cabinet for soft-drinks." Such a view reflected the more informal life-style of younger families. Room design and furnishings had to be tougher to absorb the wear and tear of active family life.

On the first floor, most families hoped for a living room, kitchen, bath, and three bedrooms. Although these families preferred eating breakfast and lunch in the kitchen, most of those surveyed, even among those who were planning to build for under $5,000, wanted a dining area (Figure 7.9). The other major request was for built-in wardrobes and for whole storage walls of cupboards and closets. Each family had some special wish: attics with easy access, a private sun porch for tanning, a special outside basement door for cellar storage of baby carriages and sleds, a removable soapdish in the bathroom that would be easy to clean, and a trapdoor in the kitchen floor to catch the sweepings. One family claimed that it had no unusual demands: "The only special features we would like—that is, if the cost is not prohibitive—are a domed ceiling [and] a circular staircase." In other words, what came through in these responses was the high level of expectation. Most people surveyed had no idea how expensive their dream home might be.

Walter Adams placed the impractical idealism of those surveyed in perspective by asking seven "top-notch" architects to comment on the most often wished-for features. The architects pointed out that large spaces, built-in wardrobes, and large areas of glass were expensive. "They'll compromise," suggested one New York designer, "[When] cost [goes] up, space [must come] down." But what was also clear was that other than recognizing the problems of expense, the architects themselves were not in agreement. Some liked basements, others did not. Some saw combination living-

dining rooms as the wave of the future, others feared a negative reaction when a child spilled milk and jam all over the living-room rug. The overriding problem that the architects faced, then, was how to reconcile the inflated expectations and limited budgets of new house buyers with the practical considerations of cost and convenience that were the province of the architect. The problem for middle-class families, conversely, was how to get the most for their money.[11]

The architect's problem was particularly difficult because lengthy conferences with clients were expensive. One solution was suggested by architect Frederick Gutheim. The designer had to find a means of quickly scaling down the client's wishes. Because the architect had superior knowledge both of family needs and of how they might find architectural expression, it was his responsibility to sell the final solution to the client. The way to persuade the client, Gutheim suggested, was to make use of public opinion polls and to stress planning about "livability problems." Home buyers might compromise their ideas more quickly if they knew that thousands of other Americans had modified their house plans in a similar fashion.

Take the question about where the family should eat. Most families surveyed did not want to eat in the living room. It was too far away, risked messing up the room, and was inconvenient if guests dropped in unexpectedly. But they also did not want to eat all their meals in the kitchen. The solution was to separate visually the dining area from the living room, either with a folding partition or with an L-shaped plan. Such a combination would be both convenient and private. Even more important, it would give a greater flexibility to eating arrangements as the children grew up.

Other architects agreed. The professional journals now featured more and more articles that attempted to fuse technical knowledge about building materials and the aesthetics of design with a professional expertise about family life. One architect suggested room dividers or folding partitions "so that the parents need not be engulfed or the children driven

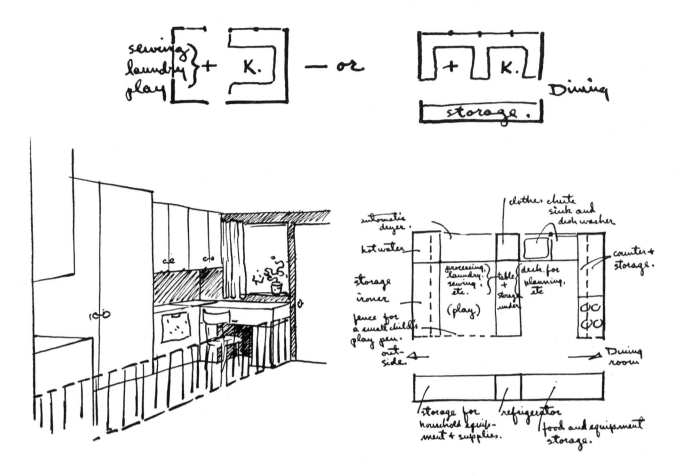

Figure 7.9
One advantage of a
separate dining area
was that the laundry
room, sewing room,
and play areas for
young children
could be incorpo-
rated into the
kitchen. (Wills,
"Space." Reprinted
from *Architectural
Record* [May 1945]
copyright McGraw-
Hill, Inc.)

to out-of-the-home social life" (Figure 7.10).
Partitions would combine easy supervision with
the need for some quiet and privacy. They
could be used only when needed, thus giving
family life a new flexibility. Another architect,
Arthur Stires, suggested that only the skillful
designer could respond sensitively to the needs
of a particular family. Sleeping porches, for
example, had been a fad twenty years earlier,
he asserted, but now they had virtually disappeared. The kitchen, moreover, which had
been separated off into a sterile laboratory
for food preparation, now could become more
centrally important. "Since we do our own
cooking now, and guests are a commonplace in
the kitchen," he continued, "why not bring the
kitchen out of its ancient obscurity and make it
a room—or part of a room—with social standing equal to other rooms?" The architect, in

other words, could use design to improve
family life itself and thereby increase personal
happiness[12] (Figure 7.11).

Despite their attempts to make the architect
an expert in both house design and family life,
professional architects were waging a losing
battle to get a bigger share of the vast expansion
in single-family housing that began after World
War II. The stress in the architectural journals
on combining planning and functionalism with
a new understanding of family life was a deliberate attempt to get into a housing market that
was being eroded by the escalating costs of
building materials. As architect Frederick Gutheim publicly admitted, even a 12 percent
fee on an expensive $15,000 house would not
cover the office costs of lengthy consultations
with a client, let alone the expenses of drawing up the plans and checking on construc-

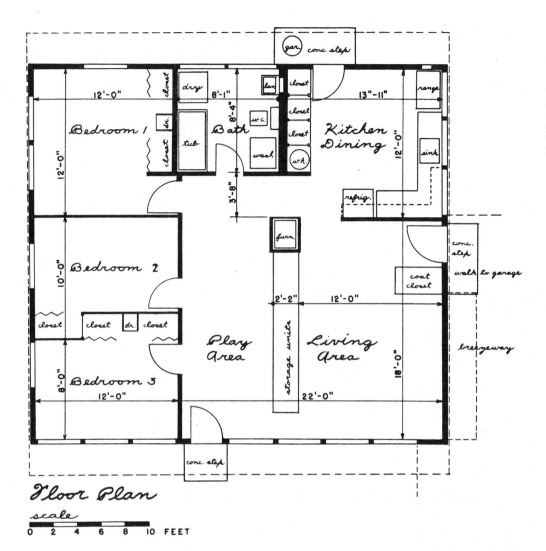

Figure 7.10
The floor plan for this government-sponsored ranch house was designed with a specific play area for children. (Harrell and Lendrum, "A Demonstration of New Techniques")

tion. Factory prefabricated or developer mass-produced houses would always be less expensive than those designed by an architect. So the architect's chief selling point had to be planning, convenience, and a new expertise about family life. Getting a larger share of the middle-class housing market was a losing battle, but professional architects were not willing to admit defeat.

Architects were not the only ones who asserted their expertise about family life in the 1940s and 1950s. Doctors, social workers, sociologists, psychologists, appliance manufac-turers, and even the writers of television serials suggested, with varying degrees of authority, new images of what the ideal American family should be like. The rush to create a new model of middle-class family life was in part a response to the extraordinary baby boom of the postwar period. Despite the cautious predictions of census demographers during the war, the returning GIs and the recovery of the economy encouraged more and more families to have children: the result was a phenomenal increase in the birthrate, rising from 2.2 births per woman in the 1930s to 3.51 by the end of the 1950s. The population grew by nineteen

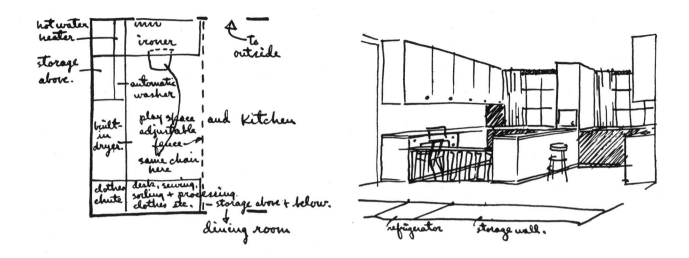

Figure 7.11
Architect Royal
Barry Wills designed
a kitchen so that a
fence might be put
up to keep toddlers
from wandering off
into the rest of
the house. (Wills,
"Space," Reprinted
from *Architectural
Record* [May 1945]
copyright McGraw-
Hill, Inc.)

million in the 1940s, doubling the growth rate of the depression decade, and surged to twenty-nine million in the 1950s. In these same two decades, the overall population increase reached 33 percent. As one foreign visitor commented in 1958, "It seems to me that every other young housewife is pregnant."[13]

This phenomenal growth dramatically changed the overall characteristics of the population at large. The number of marriages increased significantly, reaching a peak of 4.3 million in 1957. Not only were 94 percent of women between the ages of thirty-five and thirty-nine married, but they had been married at younger ages and had a far lower rate of divorce than any earlier decade in the century. High employment and great optimism about the expansion of the economy encouraged people to have more children and to upgrade their style of living through the purchase of new consumer products. Women who had worked in the defense industries during the war continued to hold part-time jobs adding to the increase in real earnings in this decade. With 35 percent of American women fourteen years and older employed by 1960 (up from 29 percent in 1950 and 25 percent in 1940), and with the expanding economy opening up new business opportunities at a rapid rate, it is not surprising that the membership in the middle class grew proportionally larger. In terms of

standard 1959 dollars, median family income jumped from $3,800 in 1949 to $5,700, an increase of about 50 percent. With such a large number of young families with growing incomes, the market for advice books and advertising seemed immense.[14]

Pediatrician Benjamin Spock was one of the first and most successful people to speak to this need. Spock's *The Common Sense Book of Baby and Child Care* went through more than two hundred printings and had sales of over twenty million copies. Reacting against the child-raising literature of the Progressive period and the 1920s that stressed the importance of fixed feeding schedules, a "system" of early toilet training, and the dangers of indulging the child, Spock asserted in his classic opening passage that mothers should "Trust themselves. . . . What good mothers and fathers instinctively feel like doing for their babies is usually best." Positing a positive image of children as naturally inquisitive and wanting to please their parents, Spock encouraged an easy indulgence of parental impulse. At the base of his advice book, as historian Michael Zuckerman has suggested, was a faith in making the home a congenial environment, free of friction and animosity. Childhood was portrayed as a happy time.[15]

Spock's book fit in well with the contemporary fear of "parental inadequacies." Sociologists such as Margaret P. Redfield and Evelyn M. Duvall insisted that the "traditional" parent was far too concerned with the child's discipline and habits. "An emphasis on the duties rather than the joys of parenthood," wrote Redfield, "often makes an already difficult task still more so." Spock agreed. Instead of bullying the child into eating vegetables, he suggested that mothers should "enjoy" their children and remember that "feeding is learning." Let children alone and they would consume a balanced diet. Surveying midwestern women in 1946, Duvall concurred, suggesting that "upper-class" women who were concerned about the "emotional well-being" of their children were more likely to raise a happy, contented, well-adjusted child.[16]

The emphasis on "fun morality" also pervaded the literature of the Children's Bureau of the U.S. Department of Labor. Children's play, earlier considered disruptive or potentially harmful, now was encouraged as healthy and productive. Whereas the mother's role in the Progressive period was seen as a model of strong moral devotion entailing "self-control," "strength," "persistence," and "unlimited patience," mothers in the 1940s and 1950s were exhorted to enjoy their children, follow their instincts, and change duties into opportunities. Giving the baby a bath, for instance, should be scheduled when there is plenty of time, suggested the 1951 *Infant Care* bulletin. "If you feel hurried, bath time won't be the fun for either of you that it should be."[17]

When examined closely, the easygoing, permissive approach to child rearing espoused by the *Infant Care* bulletin and by Dr. Spock appears somewhat deceptive and contradictory. Although Spock continually refers to "how smoothly Nature works things out" and praises the "instinctive predilections" of mothers, he is always standing in the background as the professional expert who might help should something go wrong. Like the architects and sociologists of the 1950s who often held up their own positions as the "natural" responses of neutral, disinterested experts, Spock gave mothers contradictory advice. Try things, use

trial and error, trust yourself. But if you have any questions whatsoever, consult an expert. As Michael Zuckerman points out, "to just the degree that Spock directs mothers and fathers to medical specialists who then preempt responsibilities he promised they could manage, he obstructs the path he wants to clear for such parents—and their children—to enjoy a ready run of impulse."[18]

Spock's philosophy of child rearing, with its optimistic support of parental impulse backed by generous doses of professional expertise, reflected the contradictory outlook that underlay much of the 1950s housing expansion. Optimistic and positive, this generation of Americans abandoned the more cautious psychological stance of those who had lived through the Great Depression. Jobs were plentiful, personal incomes were rising, and peace seemed attainable. But behind it all, there was always the lurking suspicion that something might go wrong. Middle-class Americans were convinced that it was time to take advantage of new opportunities and enjoy the present. Yet they were careful to protect themselves with the professional expertise of specialists such as Spock who could quiet anxieties about mistakes or possible failures. No one wanted to follow the example of the Blandings and, because of inappropriate advice, turn the construction of their dream house into a nightmare.

Since Dr. Spock and the other advisers of child-rearing practices set forth an ideal of personal behavior without talking about the physical environment in which such activities would take place, they created a magnificent opportunity for American business. The idea that "fun" and "happiness" should be central goals of family life became a real boon to the advertising industry because both ideals were essentially subjective. Who could say exactly what sorts of things would provide enjoyment? Dr. Spock's suggestion, for example, that essential tasks such as feeding and toileting the baby might become a source of parental satisfaction appealed to the promoters of the

new cooking and cleaning technologies (Figure 7.12). Cooking and cleaning could now be transformed from work into play, from being a burden to being "fun." In following up this opportunity, advertising agencies added a new degree of sophistication to promotional techniques that stretched back to the 1920s. They also reinforced the psychological and sociological ideals of family life now being praised by home economists and medical experts.[19]

Before the turn of the century few businesses had advertised directly to the consumer. Instead they had worked through local merchants to distribute their wares. The exceptions were Sears, Roebuck and Montgomery Ward—the two major mail-order catalog companies which sold a vast range of furniture and household appliances. The closest the catalogs came to encouraging the consumer to identify with the product purchased was to name different sewing machine models and other large appliances after states—the Minnesota, the Wisconsin, the Indiana.[20]

During the 1920s, some advertisers had suggested that the consumption of goods and services could itself be a major source of happiness and self-fulfillment. Christine Frederick, the Progressive advocate of engineering efficiency in the household, put it succinctly when

she asserted that "it is admitted today to be the greatest idea that America has to give to the world; the idea that workmen and masses be looked upon not simply as workers and producers, but as *consumers.* . . . Pay them more, sell them more, prosper more is the equation." Playing upon people's interest in beauty, prestige, and self-advancement, advertisers in the 1920s worked to create new products that would enhance the individual's self-image. Using Freudian psychology, they also sought to undermine confidence in old ways of doing things and to create a desire for change. In their efforts to increase sales, the manufacturers of soap, beauty products, and cleansers deliberately made consumers self-conscious about their own limitations. As one nail polish company declared in the *Ladies Home Journal,* "You will be amazed to find how many times in one day people glance at your nails. At each glance a judgment is made." Advertisements thus played upon guilt and envy as well as on the desire to improve oneself.[21]

Until the 1940s home products and building-material companies used a somewhat different advertising strategy. In addition to the usual stress on the high quality and durability of their materials, manufacturers praised the healthful and efficient features of their products (Figure 7.13). Plumbing, lighting, and heating companies in the 1920s promoted their products as useful and aesthetically pleasing. Sinks and lights were objects of both beauty and efficiency. By the late 1930s kitchen-cabinet manufacturers were also suggesting that their cabinets cut down waste and saved energy. "Time wasted in a kitchen is gone forever and with it goes the opportunity to do many things that make life more complete," counseled the Elgin Stove Company. "Every woman is entitled to her share of social life, companionship and recreation, and she should not be robbed of time and energy by the drudgery of kitchen duties." Household technology was not a good in and of itself. It was rather a means that would free up the housewife to explore other opportunities.[22]

The vast housing expansion and baby boom

of the 1950s encouraged even appliance makers and building-materials manufacturers to shift their arguments. In 1945 Westinghouse advertised a line of refrigerators, stoves, and washing machines as being a "friend in need to harassed housewives." Eight years later, Regina electric broom advertisements proclaimed, "New! Have a '*Company-Clean*' home every day . . . in minutes," suggesting implicitly that a major reason for cleaning was not sanitation but rather the desire to make a good impression on visitors. In a major issue devoted to "the neat America," *House Beautiful* in 1953 suggested that there would be no limits on the house of the future where toil would be turned into fun. "Comfort" and "convenience" were the new watchwords. In place of traditional designs, one could have a rambling ranch house with "comfort *and* performance *and* beauty" in which "nearly everyone will cook like a connoisseur." To get away from the idea that the kitchen was associated with drudgery, one writer suggested that it be done away with and replaced by a "living kitchen," a part of the living room. The housewife would appropriately be returned "from exile" to "cook leisurely and at the same time talk with her guests and/or watch her children." The new kitchen range would be designed in decorator colors to make it a more pleasant part of the house. The virtues of new cleaners and appliances were further pushed by the popular home magazines. *House and Garden* featured a regular column, "The Notes of a Happy Housekeeper," which described the joy of finding a new oven-cleaning product.[23]

The advertisements of appliance makers and building-materials manufacturers in popular magazines such as *Life* and *Better Homes and Gardens* presented a new model of middle-class family life. At the center of the model was the image of the family as the focus of fun and recreation. Happiness came from raising healthy, independent kids, decorating the home to one's own tastes, and sitting back in the evening with other family members and relaxing in front of the new television set. Television, together with the ever-present radio, brought

Figure 7.13
This advertisement for a coal furnace was typical of the 1920s. By the 1950s, the introduction of oil burners had the advantage of taking less space and of being cleaner. (Bennett Lumber Co., *Bennett Better-Built, Ready-Cut Homes*)

entertainment directly to the home and thereby reduced the necessity of getting out of the house as often. Happiness came also from working together to improve the home, taking family vacations together, and enjoying the outdoor "patio" and backyard barbecue. Even the child-rearing advice columns in the magazines were designed to make marriages happier by reducing the anxiety involved in taking care of the children.[24]

The second basic premise underlying the 1950s model of the ideal American family was the belief that family life was not static. Instead of the nineteenth-century view of the family with its acceptance of large numbers of children and a relatively short life expectancy, social commentators and magazine advertisers pictured a conjugal unit that went through several stages. *Life* magazine explained to its readers that during the average forty-year marriage the family would first expand and then contract. The first two or three years would be childless and would be spent in a small apartment. Then would come the "crowded" phase when the family bought a house and the average 2.17 children were born. During the "peak" years, defined as the period when the youngest child would reach the age of seven, heavy demands would be placed on the parents and on their living quarters. But the last fifteen years of marriage would be spent together in a childless household. Even the classic sociological textbook on the family during this period—Clifford Kirkpatrick's *The Family as Process and Institution*—recognized the stages of family life in its title.[25]

The emphasis on happiness and the "stage theory" of family life put contradictory pressures on women in the 1950s that were reflected most clearly in the way women were depicted in magazine advertisements and on television. Single women were usually presented in beverage and cigarette advertisements as attractive, independent, and carefree—what Marshall McLuhan has called the "frisky Coke-ad girl." Married women in the house-magazine advertisements, similarly, were often depicted as being creative and having fun. In contrast, married women in television family serials such as "I Love Lucy," "Ozzie and Harriet," and "The Honeymooners" often faced difficult and trying problems. Situation comedies made fun of the inept father whose hairbrained ideas would have wrecked the family were it not for the common sense and hard work of the wife. Keeping the family together was a constant struggle.[26]

The common ideal that was supported by both the television series and the house magazines was the image of the efficient, hardworking wife who, whether she held a job outside the house or stayed at home, stabilized family life. But even this ideal was never consistently supported. Magazine advertisements, in particular, also occasionally depicted her, in the words of the National Advertising Review Board, as "stupid—too dumb to cope with familiar everyday chores, unless instructed by children, or by a man, or assisted by a man, or assisted by a supernatural male symbol" as with the advertisement of "Mr. Clean."[27]

This tension between self-sufficiency and ineptitude, which we saw earlier expressed in Dr. Spock's contradictory emphasis on both self-reliance and professional expertise, placed women in an ambivalent position. As the decade of the 1950s wore on, the contradictory advertising images together with the increasing number of women who were working outside the home began to erode the image of the contented housewife. The contrast could be seen in *Life* magazine. When *Life* ran a special issue in 1956 entitled "The American Woman," Catherine Marshall insisted that her great achievements were not her job but her first date, her marriage, and her children. A scant five years later, the magazine's position had changed. In "Love and Marriage," the editors insisted that the old-fashioned wife and mother who was totally dedicated to her home and husband—the "companion type" of wife being glorified in the movies and television serials—was being replaced by the new "career" woman who would now be a full partner in marriage because her earnings would insure "full and equal treatment."[28]

This shifting image of the ideal woman and the family in the 1950s was bound to influence the conception of the ideal home environment projected in the popular press. The household magazines, ignoring the drawbacks to family life pictured in the television comedies, retained their perfectionist ideal. Not only did they suggest that with the right lawn tools and the latest cooking ranges the husband and wife could do a more professional job—special lawn mowers and never-fail cake mixes would take all chance of failure out of lawn work and cooking—but they also insisted that a properly designed modern ranch house would solve the family's needs for work and recreation. Such specially designed homes could match the fun-loving compassionate family's needs for a home environment that would be useful, convenient, and enjoyable.

From their earliest beginnings in the 1930s to their enthusiastic promotion by home magazines in the 1940s and 1950s, ranch houses were identified in the popular housing litera-ture with the new ideal of the family. The basic features of the ranch house—its simple, infor-mal, one-story structure, its low-pitched eaves, its large expanse of glass which included "pic-ture" windows or "window walls"—were fused in the public mind with the easygoing life-style that was identified with the Southwest and the West Coast. When *Sunset* magazine reviewed a history of architect Cliff May's western ranch houses, it went out of its way to praise May's approach. "What made Cliff May exciting to anyone interested in those early days," wrote the editors, "was this drive to perpetuate ideas in livability rather than form and facade. His passion was not so much architecture as the way people wanted to live." May's houses were described as relaxed, comfortable, and casual. They were designed around a generous, open patio—the perfect complement to the informal family that loved the out-of-doors.[29]

Sunset magazine went even further to suggest that the ranch house was not so much a style as an "approach to living." One major feature of the ranch house was its low silhouette. The editors of *House and Garden* praised the low profile of one Oregon ranch house for the way in which it blended into the natural landscape. The house was both very "personal and yet a thoroughly adaptable background for good liv-ing." Another magazine explained that the uni-versal appeal of the ranch house was its simple, efficient look and its "long, low silhouette with a gently sloping and overhanging roof shelter-ing the house against sun and rain" (Figure 7.14). These popular house magazines invari-ably pictured the ranch house in a country landscape, overlooking a valley or nestled into the brow of a hill.[30]

A few designers saw the new ranch home as a healthy rebellion against the older com-pressed, boxlike bungalow house that had dominated house construction from the turn of the century until the 1930s. The shift from the Victorian house to the bungalow had been based upon a wholesale rejection of previous popular designs, but most advocates of the ranch house concentrated their attention pri-marily on the interior plan. As long as the house was handsome and had relatively little decorative detail, a variety of external features were acceptable. As the authors of *Tomorrow's House* admitted in 1946, "even a poor architect has a hard time making a spreading, one-story house unattractive."[31]

In addition to having a low silhouette and rambling plan that made it fit well with the western landscape, the ranch house was also designed to allow Americans to re-create the California life-style elsewhere. Given the fasci-nation with the West Coast and the Southwest that was reflected in the startling increase in the population of the Pacific states between 1940 and 1960, it was not surprising that Americans tried to duplicate the West Coast life-style in other parts of the country. By 1963 California had replaced New York as the num-ber one state in population. Many magazines not only praised the sunny openness of the California ranch house with its inviting picture windows and large areas of glass, but they also explained how the new heating and cool-ing technologies would allow California ranch houses to be built anywhere. Radiant heat with zone controls, porches with jalousie-type win-dows, and home air-conditioning systems now allowed any American to enjoy a mild, temper-ate climate equivalent to that of the West Coast. Excessive heat and freezing cold could quickly be transformed by modern technology into a uniform zone of comfort. As the editors of *American Home* explained about a Detroit ranch house, "Mr. Rush said Mrs. Rush was the inspiration behind the interior planning—she, being a California gal whose dreams of a truly western ranch house with lots of refreshing color, was not deterred by the Michigan tradi-tions of a somber house." Given the existence of cheap energy and the potential of the new technology, the ranch house could re-create a California environment anywhere.[32]

As a part of the attempt to sell the ranch house as a perfect place for duplicating the California life-style, magazine designers and interior decorators insisted that the ranch house established a new relationship be-

Figure 7.14
The low-pitched roof, attached carport, and protective fence of this Illinois ranch house gave it a sheltered look. (Harrell and Lendrum, "A Demonstration of New Techniques")

tween the house and nature. Reflecting on the changes that had taken place in domestic architecture in the past thirty years, William Scheick in *Parents' Magazine* suggested that the ranch house created an indoor-outdoor unity that reflected the modern style of living. Large, insulated plate-glass windows and the new "sliding glass walls" (called, by the 1960s, sliding glass doors) made the seasons into an ever-changing wall decoration—a design feature that architect Philip Johnson extended to its logical conclusion when he built his all glass-walled house in New Canaan, Connecticut, in 1949. The interior walls of the house literally changed color with the seasons and made nature a direct part of the home decor. Not satisfied with the changing scenery of the picture window, some interior decorators designed photo-mural wallpapers that re-created the Rockies or a seashore scene across an entire wall. These photo murals were often used in those doctors' offices that lacked any windows.[33]

Given the high cost of house construction and the related reduction of interior space, architects and magazine designers used patios, breezeways, and, on the expensive houses in the Southwest, interior courtyards, to enhance the feeling of ranch house spaciousness. By building both house and patio on the ground

level so that family members could come and go without stepping up or down, the ranch house designer helped create a sense of continuity between the indoors and the outdoors. By removing the customary thresholds and moldings that traditionally marked the boundaries of rooms, designers made patios appear to be outdoor extensions of indoor living space. Where glass was the main component of the wall, ceiling beams or walls were continued out into the yard to extend the sense of enclosure and destroy the feeling of barriers in the home. As one designer put it, such devices make "the structure fraternize with nature" and create a sense of interior and exterior unity[34] (Figure 7.15).

In the more expensive "Hallmark houses" in *House and Garden* and in the "Better Homes for all America" series in *Better Homes and Gardens*, various devices were used to mediate between the house and nature. In addition to focusing on the ever-present patio, the magazines used pierced roof beams over a recessed door to create a garden area at the house entrance and a glassed-off interior atrium to bring a sense of nature inside the house. Most often what resulted was a highly stylized version of nature. As one magazine put it, the entrance area plantings were "simple, smart, just right for the setting." Since the typical ranch houses had low

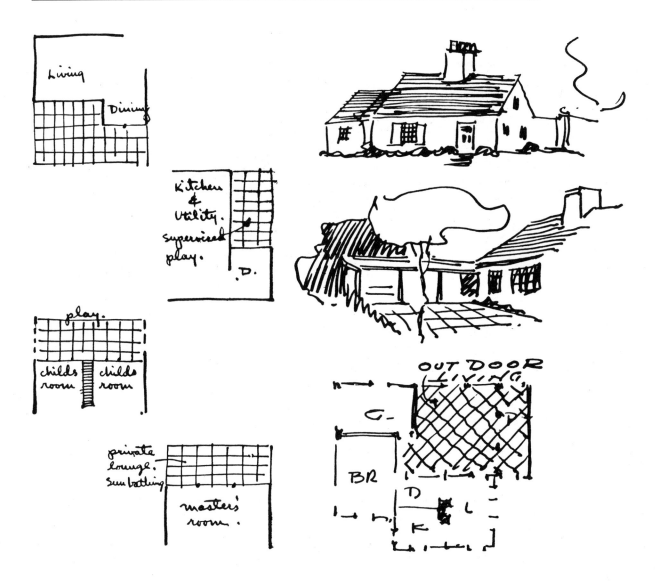

profiles, architects and decorators scaled down the natural world to fit them by using clumps of miniature birch trees, Russian olive bushes, and low-spreading yews. The ranch house, like both its Victorian and bungalow predecessors, was thus seen as creating a unity with nature, but it was a unity that pictured nature as a tamed and open environment. Like the technological re-creation of the temperate California climate, the 1950s design standards conceived of the natural world in a simplified and controlled way that eliminated anything that was wild or irregular. Photographs of the suburban ranch house invariably showed a broad expanse of perfect lawn without weeds or dandelions.[35]

In addition to the access to nature and the long, rambling plan, another feature common to most ranch house designs was the separation of the interior into three different "zones": the housework center, the area of living activities, and the private area (Figure 7.16). Most architects urged builders of ranch houses to create a "utility core" of kitchen, bathrooms, and laundry at the center of the house for reasons of efficiency and convenience. The typical ranch house changed the kitchen from its earlier po-

Figure 7.15
In these sketches, architect Royal Barry Wills demonstrated how "a living terrace" might be attached to various rooms of the house, creating a sense of continuity with the outdoors. (Wills, "Space." Reprinted from *Architectural Record* [May 1945] copyright McGraw-Hill, Inc.)

Figure 7.16
House designers in the 1950s were careful to suggest alternate plans, built around a kitchen-bathroom core, to meet the needs of families at different stages in their development. (Harrell and Lendrum, "A Demonstration of New Techniques")

PLAN VARIATIONS

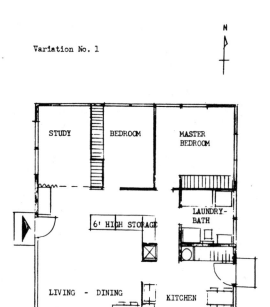

Variation No. 1

Variation No. 2 (A)

FIGURE 69.

Variation No. 1 is similar to the original plan, but provides for two bedrooms and a separate study or hobby room istead of three bedrooms and a play area. The kitchen has been enlarged to provide a more generous dining area and play space for small children, and a more spacious living area is provided. This scheme might be used as a guide if the original plan must be varied in orientation or fenestration. The interior plumbing and heating layouts remain the same as in the original plan, but the circulation area is somewhat increased.

FIGURE 70.

Variation No. 2 may be provided either with two large bedrooms and a dining alcove, or with two smaller bedrooms, a study, and dining room separated from the living area by tall storage cabinets. The kitchen becomes a workspace only, having no provision for eating. Variation 2A provides eating space in a small alcove which may be concealed from the living area by a curtain or folding door, while 2B permits a more formally enclosed dining area.

sition as a hygienic service area into a living space for the whole family. Kitchens were no longer relegated to the back of the house but were now placed to the front, often at the end of the house where they could be entered directly from the garage. Kitchens were built in a U-shape, separated from other rooms only by a low counter. Because they were now open to the view of guests as well as of family members, kitchens also became the focus of decorators' attention. New tile and linoleum designs, pastel colors for stoves and refrigerators, and the use of brick walls and natural-wood cabinets all helped to soften the austere lines inherited from the turn-of-the-century room. As the editors of *House and Garden* suggested, "instead of looking like a clinic, the kitchen is now a friendly, congenial common room."[36]

Convenience, efficiency, flexibility, and excellence were the terms most often applied to kitchen designs by magazine writers. The latest in cooking, refrigeration, and washing technologies were all used in sales pitches that suggested how women might become better mothers. Not only could a woman now cook the perfect meal and wash the whitest clothes, but she could get her housework done more quickly than her own mother had been able to do, thus allowing her to spend more time with the children. In extolling the benefits of the newly designed kitchen, some magazine writers likened it to a military command post. By opening up the kitchen directly to the living room, the woman could run the house without ever leaving the kitchen. She could cook a gourmet meal for guests and still talk with them as she prepared the food. Or she could do the laundry and still keep an eye on the children.

This new idea of the multipurpose kitchen was in keeping with the popular image of the multiple roles that needed to be played by women. Mothers, in the advice-book literature, were supposed to be jacks-of-all-trades: child psychologist, homemaker, cook, cleaner, and consultant on consumer products. For the increasing numbers of women who had outside jobs as well, the ranch house kitchen, full of electric appliances, was absolutely necessary

for accomplishing the many tasks that were expected of her.

The kitchen usually opened out into the second major "zone" of the house—the living-room and family-room spaces. *Parents' Magazine* defended the need of "family" or "play" rooms as "don't-say-no" places for children and teenagers. Given the more permissive attitude toward child rearing encouraged by Dr. Spock and others, families felt that they needed a room where the children could play without disturbing the adults or threatening the furniture. In *House and Garden*'s "House of Ideas," a model home built outside New York City in 1951 to exhibit the very latest in comfort, children were given a large space, divided by a partition, in which to play with their trains and Hopalong Cassidy cowboy clothes. Other designers insisted that the playroom be made of durable materials so that free play without rules would not be inhibited.[37]

Another reason for having a family room or playroom in addition to the living room was to separate the world of the television from that of the adults who might want to read or have some peace and quiet to themselves. The 1950s improvement in television and record-playing technologies—together with the surge in rock-and-roll music and the emergence of a distinctive teen culture—made parents wish to separate off different household functions. A separate family room or playroom allowed the children to play their music or to engage in more active games with their friends without disturbing the other members of the house.

The remaining zone of the house consisted of the bedrooms and baths. As the home-building magazines made abundantly evident, the "private" areas of the house were to be just that—private. One mechanism for increasing the privacy of the suburban ranch house was to add more bathrooms. Even economy homes usually boasted of a second lavatory or half-bathroom for guests. Whereas the bungalow predecessors in the Midwest had placed a toilet in the basement for delivery men to use, the new ranch houses put a half-bath on the first floor and added a sink. In so doing, they made it easier to keep nonfamily members away from their own bathrooms and bedrooms. More expensive homes went one step further, adding a separate bathroom directly onto the master bedroom. "Parents and children can have as much privacy as they like to concentrate on their separate interests," wrote one designer for *House and Garden*, implying that for all the rhetoric about families being together, there was also the need to be alone.

Another magazine designer was even more candid about the need for private bedroom spaces. "Much as you may enjoy the friendliness of a house with a minimum of walls and a maximum of glass," he suggested, "there comes a time when everyone longs for privacy." The very openness of the ranch house plan, with its emphasis on increasing the sense of spaciousness, meant that privacy was more difficult to achieve. Additional bathrooms and master bedroom suites helped redress the balance between public and private.[38]

The other feature of the private area of the house—the bath and bedrooms—that was stressed in the magazine designs for ranch houses was the availability of additional storage space. The increasing number of consumer goods, which ranged from board games such as Monopoly to a proliferation of clothes, created storage problems for many families in the 1950s. This problem was sometimes alleviated by using storage areas in the cellar or in the two-car garage that was connected directly to the house. But most homeowners demanded more built-ins, including wardrobes with sliding doors, in the private bedroom areas of their homes.

What is clear from the flood of magazines promoting the suburban "ranch house" in the 1950s, with their endless pictures of built-in closets and "exciting" kitchens, was that the plans pictured did not aim simply to satisfy minimal housing needs. The plans were designed, as their predecessors had been, to create a new image of family life. In place of the more austere and antiseptic vision of the Progressive period, the ranch house was designed to facilitate a more comfortable existence. For the families who had grown up with the ever-present legacy of depression frugality, the new home stressed the pleasures of consumption—the emphasis on relaxation, children, and enjoyment. As the television commercials suggested, now the family could have fun together, cooking hamburgers at its barbecue and playing catch in the backyard.

The constant emphasis on family rooms and master-bedroom suites in the magazine literature also implied the decreasing force of the older ideals of separate male and female spheres. In place of the nineteenth-century view of specialized spaces for each member of the family, a new vision of a more companionate marriage and a more interactive family had emerged. While the ideal was not fully realized and the father sometimes still had his workbench in the basement and occasionally a den, the nineteenth-century ideal of distinct male and female areas of the house had been significantly eroded. The space restraints of the ranch house together with the emphasis on family interaction created a positive vision of harmonious family life.

What was new about the image of the ranch house as the focus for family fun and relaxation was not that the ideal home would be a retreat from the hardships of the working world, which had been the view of the mid-nineteenth century. What was new was the glorification of self-indulgence. Convenience rather than style, comfort rather than some formal notion of beauty became the hallmarks of the new designs. In 1956 one commentator on the changes in housing put it this way: "To the Average Family—that indescribable but extraordinarily powerful influence—the changes in housing over the last three decades would add up to something like this: thirty years ago they somehow had to fit themselves into the house, now the house is planned to fit them." Theoretically, then, the consumer was king. The housing industry, together with the appliance manufacturers and the house-design magazines, were now trying to assure the public that, for the first time in history, house designs reflected the desires of the people. Consumers would get exactly what they wanted.[39]

Chapter 8

The Suburban Complex

Little boxes on the hillside,
Little boxes made of ticky tacky
Little boxes on the hillside,
Little boxes all the same;

   —Melvina Reynolds, *Little Boxes*
      and Other Handmade Songs

"For literally nothing down . . . *you too can find*
a box of your own in one of the fresh-air slums
we're building around the edges of American cities
. . . inhabited by people whose age, income, number
of children, problems, habits, conversation, dress,
possessions and perhaps even blood-type are pre-
cisely like yours. . . . [They are] developments con-
ceived in error, nurtured by greed, corroding every-
thing they touch, they . . . actually drive mad
pyramids of housewives shut up in them."

   —John Keats, *The Crack in*
      the Picture Window

Architects, housing magazine writers, pediatricians, and family counselors in the 1950s helped popularize the new image of the informal companionate family with its more relaxed life-style. Despite the promoters' exuberant commitment to giving the consumers what they wanted, however, the developers and the builders were the ones who had to face reality and come to terms with the trade-offs between cost and convenience in the actual construction of the house. It was one thing for architects and planners to create a rosy image of the bucolic, middle-class suburban utopia. It was quite another to put such ideals into practice. Pressured by the popular press and the incredible demand which led to more than a million housing starts in 1950, large and small builders alike turned to national trade associations and the federal government for advice. The homes that they built were neither entirely pleasing to the popular press nor to the people who bought them. Some social critics, especially sociologists who wrote about suburbia, gleefully lambasted ranch house developments as the tasteless hallmark of a homogenized society. Yet most Americans were reasonably content with the homes that they bought. Although not without its drawbacks, ownership of the single-family home remained the defining mark of middle-class status.

More than most people realized, the determining factor in 1950s middle-class suburban house construction was cost, measured both in time and money. Since the price of the average house almost doubled in the 1940s, rising from $3,825 to $7,525, both developers and builders were forced to search for ways to increase quality while holding down expense. At the 1948 Family Life Conference held in Washing-

Figure 8.1
This was a typical
prefabricated house
built in the 1950s by
U.S. Steel. ("Bride's
House")

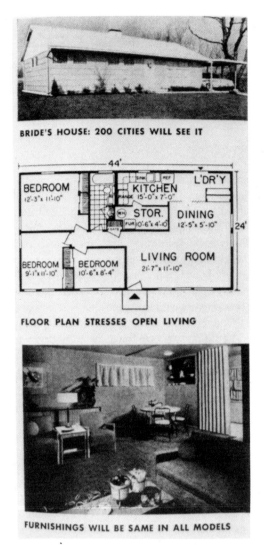

BRIDE'S HOUSE: 200 CITIES WILL SEE IT

FLOOR PLAN STRESSES OPEN LIVING

FURNISHINGS WILL BE SAME IN ALL MODELS

Figure 8.1
This was a typical
prefabricated house
built in the 1950s by
U.S. Steel. ("Bride's
House")

overwhelming priority. Two examples, extremely different in character, serve to illustrate this need. One was a small construction company started in 1946 by John La Pan in Hoosick Falls, New York. La Pan was typical of the small builders who put up two-thirds of the houses built in the 1950s. The other example is that of William Levitt who built 17,000 homes in Hempstead, Long Island, in the late 1940s and who went on to build another 22,000 homes in Pennsylvania and New Jersey in the following decade. In 1949, when only nine hundred contractors, or less than 1 percent of all builders, constructed a hundred or more houses annually, William Levitt stood out as a pioneer in large-scale mass production.

Both La Pan and Levitt had to start from scratch after World War II. Having served in a construction battalion in Europe, John La Pan returned to upstate New York in 1946 and formed a partnership with his brother Murray. Because construction materials were in short supply, the brothers initially concentrated on remodeling older homes and enlarging local manufacturing plants. As business picked up, they purchased a farm on the edge of town, subdivided it into lots, and began to put up single-family homes. But the cost of materials and labor threatened to price their homes out of the market. They responded by switching to prefabricated houses made by the Aladdin Company of Bay City, Michigan. Business prospered and within two years their construction crew had increased to thirty men (Figure 8.1).

Even with a larger crew, putting up the houses proved to be a labor-consuming process. Short of the heavy equipment needed to dig the foundations, they built each house on a concrete slab and used an old horse scoop pulled by a truck to excavate a small cellar hole for the furnace and hot water heater. Precut materials facilitated their work considerably. The walls could be assembled in a matter of hours and the precut roof rafters put in place in a day. The prefabricated house could be finished within two weeks.[2]

Given the high demand for his construction

ton, D.C., and attended by President Truman, the keynote speaker criticized the low housing standards and bad bargains found in the contemporary housing market. "Families seeking a place to live find homes too small and too expensive," he insisted. "We need a larger proportion of houses of three or more bedrooms to serve the needs of optimum families." Faced with a critical public and with an incessant demand for new housing, builders turned to new technologies, mass production, and improved design features to keep the costs down.[1]

Whether one was a small builder or a large developer, the need to contain costs was an

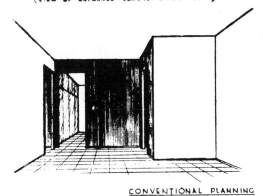

INFLUENCE OF OPEN PLANNING TECHNIQUE
ON INTERIOR SPATIAL EFFECTS
(VIEW OF ENTRANCE - DEMONSTRATION HOUSE)

CONVENTIONAL PLANNING

OPEN PLANNING

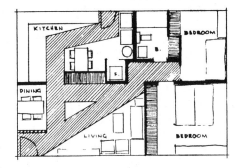

INFLUENCE OF DOOR LOCATIONS
ON CIRCULATION PATTERNS

CIRCULATION PATH AREA = 20.5 % OF FLOOR AREA

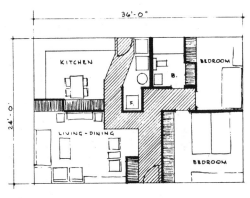

CIRCULATION PATH AREA = 14.4 % OF FLOOR AREA

crew, La Pan was constantly concerned about how to increase its efficiency. Using resin-bonded plywood that had been developed during the war as well as prefabricated subassemblies that ranged from complete window units to closets and kitchen cabinets, he was able to cut construction time significantly. Still, he was not satisfied. So he went to Washington, D.C., in the early 1950s to get help from the National Association of Home Builders and the Federal Housing and Home Finance Agency. In Washington, La Pan found that both the federal government and the newly formed National Association of Home Builders Research Institute were ready to supply housing plans and suggest new methods of construction that would cut costs. Reacting to the popular demand for more appliances—washing machines, dryers, mechanical refrigerators, toasters, and food mixers—and responding to the concern that houses be designed so that mothers could supervise small children more directly from the kitchen, both the federal government and the Research Institute came up with designs that were meant to save money and provide a greater sense of openness (Figure 8.2). The latter feature was particularly important because houses in the late 1940s decreased in size until the middle 1950s when the Federal Housing Administration's liberalization of loans and reduction in down payments made it possible to purchase a $12,000 house with the same mortgage payments that had been required for a $10,000 house a decade earlier.[3]

The most important construction features—modular designs in four-by-eight-foot sections

Figure 8.2
In addition to designing houses in terms of activity zones, architects of small houses, as seen in this example, carefully analyzed traffic patterns to save space. (Harrell and Lendrum, "A Demonstration of New Techniques")

Figure 8.3
Another way to save space and money was to combine different functions in the same room as in this laundry-bathroom both of which use the same plumbing. (Harrell and Lendrum, "A Demonstration of New Techniques")

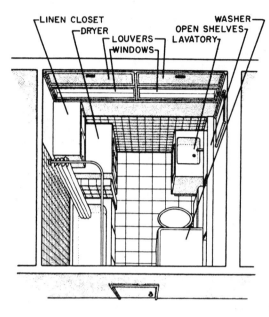

and the use of preassembled cabinets and window units—were themselves a response to problems created by high costs of construction and shrinking amounts of space. Since many of the new houses were built on concrete slabs with low-pitched roofs, they lacked the traditional storage spaces in the basement and attic. To compensate, builders had to include more cabinets and storage areas within the house. Often this was done by extending the functions of an already existing room by placing built-in storage cabinets within it. A good example was the popularity of the bathroom-laundry room (Figure 8.3). If the bathroom were made a little bit larger, a washing machine and a dryer could be placed in it. Often louvered doors were used to hide the machines while they were not in use. By keeping the plumbing in one room, the cost of the house was thus reduced.

The open plan and large window areas, which were devices to increase the sense of spaciousness within the small house, themselves created problems that needed to be solved. To control excess sun during the summer, federal and industry consultants suggested orienting the house to the south and using larger roof overhangs. To prevent the drafts created by traditional corner windows in small bedrooms, they urged that a standard window on one wall be balanced by a transom casement window on the other (Figure 8.4). The casement window had the further advantage of allowing a bed or a couch to be placed under it without obstructing the view. When the windows were used in conjunction with the modular four-by-eight-foot system, construction costs were significantly reduced. The key was the standardization of design based on modular construction.

If the house were carefully planned in multiples of four-foot sections, the need to cut standardized drywall plasterboard and two-by-fours would be reduced to a minimum. Ceilings could be set at an eight-foot height. Drywall seams, which had to be taped and spackled with plaster, could be reduced. Cabinets and counters could all come in predetermined sizes. Window openings, closets, and the general interior layout could thus be simplified. Cutting materials on site could thus be drastically reduced, and tremendous amounts of labor could be saved.

The consultants to the federal government who suggested these plans recognized that the use of modular units was restrictive. "The repetition of modular units gives the house a structural regularity and affects the plan to some extent," they admitted. If extra inches were needed anywhere in the house, an additional module would have to be added. But the cost of adding it would be more than counterbalanced by the savings realized by having reduced the cutting and fitting of materials. Industry spokesmen agreed. By the 1950s the National Door Manufacturers Association had adopted the four-foot increment as the standard for all their products.[4]

By using an open plan with multifunctional rooms and a centrally located circulation path, the main areas of the house—living room, dining room, and bedrooms—could be reduced to a minimum functional size. Since beds, for example, came in standardized lengths and widths, bedrooms could be planned with minimum clearances. "In a single bedroom," suggested one federal government researcher, "where the bed is pushed against one wall, there should be a clear area at least 4′-0″ wide for moving about and dressing. A 3′-0″ clearance should be observed between a bed and the face of a dresser to allow easy access to the chair. This also permits passage behind when the desk is being used."[5]

In his visit to Washington, John La Pan found that the design-and-assembly ideas supplied by the Home Builders Research Institute and the Federal Housing Administration, when added to low-roof lines and an open plan, gave his small houses a "bigger" look and a greater sense of spaciousness while keeping costs down. Horizontal window lines, outdoor living areas such as patios and open courts, and careful planning for built-in appliances were also incorporated into the houses that he and others built. By 1953, three-bedroom ranch houses, constructed with prefabricated techniques such as he used, were being touted as the wave of the future in glowing articles that appeared in *Life* magazine.[6]

Although William Levitt built on a far greater scale than did John La Pan, putting up entire subdivisions and towns, he, too, spent much of his energy on developing ways to use prefabrication and planning to keep costs down. An aggressive and outspoken entrepreneur—he described his company as "the General Motors of the housing industry"—William Levitt entered the construction business with his brother Alfred in the 1930s. In 1934 he built his first development, "Strathmore at Manhasset," on Long Island for the upper middle class. The houses sold for from $9,100 to $18,500, and the development included two country clubs. After building for the Navy during the war and a stint with the Seabees, William Levitt returned in 1946 and began putting up mass-produced houses for the returning GIs (Figure 8.5).

Levittown, the housing development that he planned with his brother, was started on Long Island potato fields in 1946. The town was a fully designed community that included large

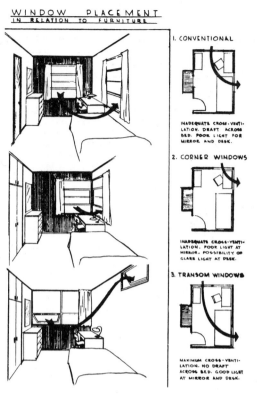

Figure 8.4
This government-sponsored study explained the advantages of using transom windows in small bedrooms. (Harrell and Lendrum, "A Demonstration of New Techniques")

recreational and shopping areas, baseball diamonds, handball courts, six 75-by-125-foot swimming pools, and meeting places for fraternal clubs and veterans' organizations. The houses, which sold for the uniform price of $7,900, came in either ranch or Cape Cod styles (Figure 8.6). Each had a picture window, radiant-floor heating (no basement), a twelve-by-sixteen-foot living room with a built-in twelve-and-a-half-inch television set, a tiled bath, a kitchen, and two bedrooms on the first floor (Figure 8.7). The house also included an "expansion attic" that could be finished off to include two more bedrooms. Levitt advertised that the walls of the house were "abrasion resista ″ and offered to supply color-coordinated furnishings for the entire living room for an additional $1,261. Using federally insured loans from the Federal Housing Administration, Levitt was able to offer thirty-year

Figure 8.5
Levittown was perhaps the best known of the many large housing developments in the early 1950s that used mass-production techniques. (Emil Reynolds, *Time*, July 3, 1950)

mortgages with no down payments for returning veterans. A veteran could buy a Levitt house for only $56 a month, which was a real bargain since the average monthly rental for an apartment in many cities was $93. At these low prices, Levitt sold more than 10,600 houses by 1950. When the latest-model Levitt home was put on display that same year, more than forty thousand people saw it during the first week that it was shown.

Levitt's enormous success was built on careful use of standardization and economies of scale. Unlike a small builder like John La Pan, William Levitt achieved a great advantage by buying large quantities of appliances directly from the manufacturer. When lumber, lighting switches, and nails were expensive and in short supply, he set up his own subsidiary companies to produce them. The actual construction of the homes took place on an assembly-line basis

and was broken down into twenty-six steps. At a central warehouse, lumber was precut to size, plumbing fixtures were preassembled, staircases were prefabricated, and kitchen cabinets were built. At the site, after the concrete foundation slabs were poured, teams of workers went from house to house and worked on preassigned tasks. Some put up the walls. Others put in the kitchens. Still others tiled the bathrooms in the special decorator colors that Levitt praised in his ads. Thus, at the building site itself, only 20 percent of the construction work was done by skilled labor. Using these methods, Levitt was able to complete a new house every fifteen minutes at a cost that lower-middle-class Americans could afford. As an article in *Life* magazine glowingly reported, "While More Houses Go Up, Costs at Last Stay Put."[7]

Although Levitt's homes contained only

Figure 8.6
The Levittown development, with its Cape Cod and ranch houses, was designed with schools and even a community pool. (Ben Martin, *Time*)

eight hundred square feet of living space, the houses included a fireplace and kitchen appliances, both of which appealed to families who listened to advertisements about comfort, convenience, and efficiency. The open plan and the picture windows gave a sense of spaciousness to the house, especially for those who had just moved from small apartments. As veteran Wilbur Schaetzl put it, his old apartment "was so awful I'd rather not talk about it. Getting into this house was like being emancipated."[8]

Levitt's construction methods for "ranch houses," a term the building trades generally used to refer to any house whose rooms were concentrated on the first floor, were quickly copied by other major developers. Near Lexington, Massachusetts, Boston contractor Joseph F. Kelly, who had been building about 1,000 Cape Cod houses a year, started 400 Levitt-type homes in a new development. So,

too, did a Portland, Oregon, builder. Outside Los Angeles, Aetna Construction and Biltmore Homes put up 17,150 one-story houses on a former beet farm. And in Park Forest, near Chicago, 1,300 of a planned 5,000 homes were built in 1952 (Figure 8.8). Through the use of mass production and assembly-line techniques, large developers such as Levitt and Aetna built close to one-third of the almost a million and a half homes that were put up in 1950[9] (Figure 8.9).

In the decade of the 1950s, the new construction techniques pioneered by Levitt and others, together with the liberal loan policy that increased the Federal Housing Administration's mortgage insurance commitments and lowered the down payments on FHA loans, resulted in an explosive surge in new construction. The volume of housing starts reached a record 1.65 million in 1955 and leveled off at

Figure 8.7
The living room in the Levittown homes came with a built-in television. (Emil Reynolds, *Time*, July 3, 1950)

over 1.5 million for the rest of the decade. By the early 1960s, housing construction in the United States averaged $14 billion a year. Two-thirds of the construction consisted of private one-family dwellings. The typical house had increased in size from near 800 to 1,240 square feet, sold for $14,585, and was a detached one-story home with three bedrooms, one and a half baths, and a garage or carport. With the significantly increased availability of single-family housing, even working-class Americans were able to move to the suburbs in large numbers. Some families like the Bernard Leveys on

Long Island changed homes the way they bought cars, purchasing a new model every year to take advantage of the latest changes in appliances and new features.[10]

To promote the thousands of new houses under construction, builders like Levitt made lavish claims about the efficiency and convenience of the homes they built. The question was, Did the buyers like what they purchased? To what extent did the new suburban communities live up to the extravagant assertions of their designers and builders?

Right from the start, some critics saw the

Figure 8.8
The Park Forest development, thirty miles south of Chicago, was planned with schools, churches, single houses, and apartments. ("Park Forest Moves into '52")

new Levittowns and the Park Forest, Illinois, developments as potential disasters (Figure 8.10). A few planners argued that in the process of easing the housing shortage, the sheer volume of new homes put unacceptable pressures on schools, hospitals, and sewage facilities, creating a potential "slum of the future." "Nonsense," said Bill Levitt, and he blunted such criticisms in his subsequent development in New Jersey by providing schools, roads, water mains, and sewage plants so that the taxes of the homeowners would be reduced and kept within manageable proportions. Because his firm used a comprehensive general plan, Levitt felt that his new communities were prototypes for the residential suburbs of the future.[11]

But the critics remained skeptical. Sociologists, in particular, often saw the new housing developments as part of a creeping consumer conformity. Critical of the deluge of advertising that was appearing in the popular press, sociologist David Riesman's best-selling book *The Lonely Crowd* depicted the "other-directed" American as an individual whose social radar was always focused on what others were doing.

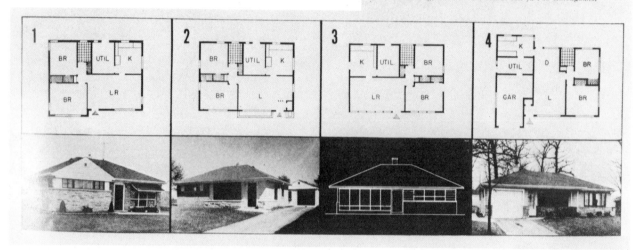

1. This is standard masonry house, selling for $13,025 to $13,575 depending on amount of exterior stone and brick. 2. Another of the same type, to which buyer has added a garage at his own expense. 3. This is the new, "stripped-down" version about to go on sale for $11,995, with slightly less equipment than earlier models. 4. This is the new $15,000 house with garage. It has approximately 950 sq. ft. plus garage. Old design, bad planning notwithstanding. Park Forest homes sell fast to Chicagoans.

Figure 8.9
In Park Forest the houses were sold, as in the automobile industry, in a range of models and prices. ("Park Forest Moves into '52")

Figure 8.10
Park Forest was unusual in that the developers kept the older trees. In Levittown and other mass-produced housing developments, the treeless landscape and the similar house models became the target for critics who feared the homogenization of society. ("Park Forest Moves into '52")

Although Riesman was careful to warn that no single individual was completely "other-directed," many readers did not see the distinction. To them, most middle-class Americans seemed to be blindly following the herd instinct. Vance Packard's *The Hidden Persuaders*, a biting critique of the advertising profession, and William H. Whyte's *The Organization Man*, an analysis of the conformist forces within the expanding corporate world of big business, also made Americans wary of excessive uniformity. Not surprisingly, then, other social critics were quick to add the suburban housing developments to the long list of coercive and conformist institutions in modern society.[12]

The critique of suburbia pictured rows of

identical houses run by domineering wives, who were driven by spoiled children and absent husbands to the verge of mental breakdowns. In place of the house magazines' image of relaxed, informal, efficient home life, the social critics pictured loneliness, boredom, and despair. Commentators on contemporary architecture such as Lewis Mumford and Ada Louise Huxtable concurred. Mumford castigated the suburbs as "a multitude of uniform, unidentifiable houses, lined up inflexibly, at uniform distances, on uniform roads, in a treeless communal waste, inhabited by people of the same class, the same income, the same age group, witnessing the same television programs, eating the same tasteless pre-fabricated foods, from the same freezers, conforming in every outward and inward respect to a common mold." Huxtable agreed, adding that aesthetic disasters also produced social, cultural, and emotional problems for the people who lived there.[13]

So shrill and devastating were the attacks that even promoters like William Levitt were forced on the defensive. Writing in *Good Housekeeping*, Levitt admitted that mass-produced houses attracted younger families, exhibited some degree of uniformity, and encouraged a somewhat conformist behavior. His early housing developments had clear rules about when wash could be put out on the line (not on Sunday) and how often the grass should be cut (once a week). But he denied that there was any lack of privacy and asserted that the people who lived in housing developments were neither dull nor conformist. "Houses are for people, not critics," he asserted somewhat defensively. "We who produce lots of houses do what is possible—no more—and the people for whom we do it think that it's pretty good."[14]

A closer examination of the suburban housing developments by other sociologists, survey teams for house magazines, and the federal government showed that neither the defenders nor the critics were entirely accurate in their assertions about suburbia. The suburban ranch houses were neither the disasters the critics predicted nor the utopias that the promoters

hoped for. In fact, careful surveys of new home buyers done by the federal government's Housing and Home Finance Agency in 1950 and by *Better Homes and Gardens* in 1955 reveal that the reasons for the purchase of a single-family dwelling were more complex than either the promoters or the detractors had anticipated.

According to these surveys, two different kinds of families bought houses in the years 1949 and 1950. Nearly half of the home buyers were veterans of World War II. They were a younger group, with a median age of thirty-five, who had young children and had run out of space in their apartments. Dissatisfaction with the rental market, the desire for more independence and privacy, the ease of obtaining loans, and the belief that home ownership was a good investment prompted this younger group to buy its first house. Buoyed up by the expanding economy and confident that their future income prospects were good, these families decided to buy, usually in a new suburban development. When asked why they had moved, the "need for more space," "comfort and roominess for family members in a new house," and "privacy and freedom of action in owned home" were the reasons most often given. Contrary to the utopian visions put forth by architects and home magazines, the inadequacies of their previous housing were more important precipitants of the decision to buy than the emphasis on convenience or the lure of the new designs. As one interviewer confirmed, the increased space of the new house was the primary reason for its purchase.[15]

The other largest group of buyers in the 1949–50 housing market was made up of older families whose median age was forty-five. Many of these families moved from a previously owned house because the space was inadequate and their family needs had changed. Others preferred the quiet of being further from the central city or moved because of a change in job. This group had higher incomes which allowed them to purchase more expensive homes on larger lots. Together with the younger families of the veterans, these home buyers helped fuel a massive exodus from the cities that was to increase suburban growth by more than 50 percent during the decade.[16]

When asked why they bought the particular house that they did, most buyers made a startling admission. They were forced to compromise their goals because of price and location. Most buyers wanted a larger lot for more privacy than the 11,100-square-foot one that was the median that year. Most also wanted a house with more than 983 square feet that was the average of those being built and which represented a 12 percent *decrease* from the average size in 1940. Given this desire for more space, four buyers out of ten in 1950 were dissatisfied with the number of rooms in their new home. Most wanted three bedrooms and were forced to compromise with two.

Although architects and developers had stressed the convenience of a combined living room–dining room, 60 percent of the respondents to the surveys preferred a separate dining room. Most also wanted a breakfast nook or an equivalent kitchen eating space. They explained that a combination of the two would allow more convenient meals in the kitchen but also would permit a change of scene and a more formal meal without disrupting the living room. Since 56 percent of the houses built that year had dining rooms, a relatively small number of families had to turn to older homes for larger, more formal dining rooms.

Another concern was the number of bathrooms. Most families wanted two bathrooms, one with a toilet, a sink, and a tub-and-shower, the other with only a toilet and a sink. Yet only 17 percent of the homes built in 1949–50 had more than one bathroom. The cost of additional plumbing was thus another frustration to the new homeowner.[17]

Porches were another desired home feature that were sacrificed in 1949–50 because of cost. Earlier generations during the Progressive period had always had a front porch. The front of the house was well set back from the street, facing the neighbors across a broad stretch of lawn. Such porches facilitated entertaining and talking to friends as they strolled by during the summer evenings. Post–World War II families,

in contrast, wanted the porch in the back, overlooking an expanded backyard or garden. The front yard could thereby be correspondingly reduced, shortening the driveway to the garage. Such an arrangement recognized that automobiles had now become the almost universal form of transportation in the suburbs. Because the increased car traffic was noisy and because fewer neighbors went walking in the evening, most suburbanites still wanted a porch, but now they wanted it at the side or back of the house.

Despite the almost universal desire for porches, however, less than half the houses built in 1949–50 included them. Although more expensive "custom-built" homes often incorporated porches and sun rooms, the average mass-produced tract house offered only the alternative of the potential backyard patio. Family rooms, too, although strongly desired, were only rarely added. Again, problems of cost kept such extra features to a minimum.[18]

But not all deletions from earlier standards were missed. Although many people longed for the extra storage space and porches that had been common fifty years earlier, few lamented the passing of the separate stair hall, enclosed inside vestibule, or the so-called coffin niches that once were built into the stairwell so that a six-foot casket could be maneuvered around a four-foot stair landing. Weatherstripping, concrete walks, relatively cheap furnaces, and thermostatic temperature control cut heat losses to a point where the front vestibule was no longer necessary. The space once allocated to large stair halls, stair landings, and coffin niches could now be better used elsewhere. For custom-built, two-story houses, the Federal Housing Administration recommended that the stairway be moved from the traditional central hall (where it connected directly to the front hall) to a position between the kitchen and the living room. "Unnecessary traffic through the living room to reach the stairs thus is avoided," the Federal Housing authorities suggested. "Travel up and down stairs is given privacy from the living room, and vice versa." Certain areas of the ranch house—particularly the bedrooms—were to remain less accessible to outsiders and were usually located at the side opposite from the more heavily trafficked part of the home.[19]

Despite the claims of the critics, therefore, that there was no consideration for privacy in the new rambler houses and that the big picture window served only to display the latest items for consumption, the 1950s ranch house retained the traditional nineteenth-century distinction between public and private spaces. The major difference was that kitchens, once considered private spaces, were redefined as public areas (Figure 8.11). As such, they now needed to be integrated into the decorative schema of the house. For those who really desired privacy, the bedrooms and the bathroom, especially the separate bathroom attached to a master-bedroom suite, remained the most secluded areas (Figure 8.12).

From the federal government surveys done in the 1950s, therefore, it is evident that a major gap existed between the home buyers' expectations and what they were able to afford—just as it had since the nineteenth century. Larger rooms and more of them, larger lot sizes, porches, and more storage space were high on most buyers' lists. But builders were unable to supply these features at a cost that the average middle-class home buyer could afford. Nevertheless, most home purchasers were initially more than satisfied with their new houses. And why shouldn't they have been? Small though the houses were, they were still a good deal larger than the apartments in which most people had been living.

This initial satisfaction with the new suburban ranch houses came through most clearly when sociologists moved directly into the mass-produced middle-class suburbs and lived there, talking to the people and participating in community life. Although the development houses appeared to some outsiders as monotonous, treeless wastes, those who lived there thought otherwise. "We're not peas in a pod," a mother with two children in a midwestern suburb told one interviewer. "I thought it would be like that, especially because incomes are nearly the same. But it's amazing how different and varied people are. . . . I never really knew what people were like until I came here."[20]

People in the new suburbs tried to retain their distinctive identity in several ways. They often customized the house by adding a porch, garage, or new room. Sometimes they sited the house on the lot differently. When the DeLong family built a new house in Bennington, Vermont, in 1956, for example, they took the plans directly from an issue of *House and Garden*, but reversed the house so that the main picture window looked out over the mountain valley in the distance instead of facing the road (Figure 8.13). Other families individualized their houses through planting, exterior paint colors, and interior decoration.

Although the furniture that the family purchased was often modeled after what they had seen in the popular housing magazines, the large number of choices meant that the interior could be adapted to an enormous array of tastes. As one interviewer admitted, "In hundreds of houses I never saw two interiors that matched—and I saw my first tiger-striped wallpaper." In fact, most homeowners believed that choosing the correct color and decorative scheme was one of the most important decisions that they would have to make. When the editors of *House and Garden* did a survey in 1955 entitled "The New House Next Door," they found that families ranked choosing the appropriate color scheme from the sparkling array of new colored appliances, furnishings, and household accessories as the most frustrating problem in home decoration. Hours could be consumed in looking for wallpaper and trying to match colors.[21]

A second reason why people so easily accepted the mass-produced houses was that they considered their purchase as merely their "first" house. Given the young age of many of the families in 1955—men averaged thirty-one years, women about twenty-six—most looked forward to increased buying power in later years. In the middle-class suburbs where 50 percent of the men were college graduates, business transfers and increasing incomes

made housing turnovers high. As one man told an interviewer, "After all, this is only the first wife, first car, first house, first kids—wait til we get going."[22]

A third reason for the widespread middle-class acceptance of mass-produced housing was that 70 percent of the new home buyers had held back enough money to make improvements as soon as they moved in. Some added a porch or an extra room. Others modified a bathroom or rearranged a kitchen. Still others added to the heating and cooling or the piping and wiring. Physically changing the house helped ease their discontent and retain their hope that if this house was not all they wanted, they would be able to make further modifications in the future that would make it more acceptable.

Despite the obvious physical limitations of the houses, the optimism of the 1950s home buyers was justified. By 1955, when *Better Homes and Gardens* did another national survey, the number of homes being built with six or more rooms had increased by 6 percent and more than half of all new houses had three bedrooms. Substantial numbers of families were now willing to trade off a separate dining room for a combination living-dining room *and* kitchen eating area. The number of porches built had increased slightly, and most significantly, the floor area for houses costing under $10,000 had increased from 983 square feet to 1,100.

How had the space in these houses been increased despite the inflation in building-material costs? The startling answer was that

Figure 8.12
This fashionable master bedroom in the Harold J. Sauick home in Lakeland Shores, Minnesota, was published in a 1950 St. Paul newspaper. (Photograph by *St. Paul Dispatch-Pioneer Press.* Courtesy Minnesota Historical Society)

62 percent of all home buyers now did some of the construction work themselves. A surprising 23 percent did all or almost all of the work themselves. The do-it-yourself movement had reached the stage where it had a substantial impact on middle-class housing.

The other feature of the new suburban housing developments that made them attractive to middle-class home buyers despite the limitations of the houses was their obvious separation from the congestion of nearby cities. Suburban homeowners clearly wanted to leave the noise and insecurity of the urban metropolis. In this desire they were substantially aided by the tremendous increase in highway development that was spurred on by the $100 billion Interstate Highway Act of 1956. The rapid construction of new roads together with a mas-

sive increase in automobile ownership helped reinforce the image of the suburbs as a haven of peace and safety. The middle-class image of the suburbs as a peaceful refuge was further reinforced by the use of restricted covenants to exclude blacks and other minorities who were identified, through newspaper coverage, with urban crime and disorder. But perhaps the most important factor "pushing people to the suburbs," wrote the editors of *House and Garden*, "is the desire of families for elbowroom— the desire to get away from it all, where life is more informal, where there is plenty of yard room for the children, and where they can enjoy a maximum of outdoor living."[23]

Related to the popular image of the suburb as a protective retreat where the homeowner

Figure 8.13
The James DeLong family built this house in Bennington, Vermont, in 1956 from plans copied directly from *Good Housekeeping*, but they reversed the plan so that the living room would look out over the nearby mountain range. (Photograph by author)

could enjoy life without the fears of living in a city was an implicit ideal of community. Central to the ideal was a belief in security. "Here, for the first time in my life," a suburban salesman told one interviewer, "I don't worry about my family when on the road. Here at least a dozen families are constantly in touch with them and ready to help if anything goes wrong, whether it's the car, the oil heater, or one of the kids getting sick." Another commented, "We're a pioneer family. We've helped to organize our church, the car pools, and the first nursery." Because a concern for family security was one of the factors that prompted them to move to the suburbs and to buy a house, many family heads accepted leadership roles that would help them shape the community's political and

educational institutions. The newness of the suburbs created a need for civic involvement. Many responded to that need.[24]

In the working-class suburbs, there was an even greater feeling of belonging to a distinct community. Although most blue-collar families shared a life-style that was somewhat different from that of the middle class, they identified strongly with their suburban neighbors. Unlike the traditional upper-class suburb of Westchester, New York, where community cohesion was reinforced by elegant churches, private schools, and country clubs, and unlike middle-class suburbs such as Park Forest, Illinois, where managing the children and preserving upward mobility were the major preoccupations, blue-collar suburbanites in Detroit,

Michigan, or Milpitas, California, felt that they had invested their life savings in the community and worked to preserve it against the forces of change. Forming a closely knit society whose members felt that they had little or no chance for upward mobility, blue-collar suburbanites developed a strong sense of neighborhood. Segregated by income, working-class suburbanites held attitudes toward consumption and success that were different from those of the middle class, but they found a similar security in associating with people who shared their own outlook and values.[25]

The negative side of this association by income and outlook was the way in which other individuals who were not exactly like the inhabitants were excluded. The complex suburban mosaic that emerged in the 1950s and 1960s, which allowed middle- and upper-class Americans to seek residence among others who shared their own values, also trapped blacks in the older urban centers. With the exodus of whites to the suburbs in the 1950s, blacks, who were excluded from developments such as Levittown, entered the cities in large numbers. Although the nation's twelve largest cities lost 3.6 million whites between 1950 and 1960, they gained 4.5 million nonwhites. Faced by a wide variety of discriminatory housing practices, blacks, in the 1960 census, made up under 5 percent of all suburban residents.[26]

Nor did the homogeneity of the middle-class suburbs by income necessarily lead to harmony. Herbert Gans, the Columbia University sociologist who lived in Levittown, New Jersey, for two years, found that segregation by income and by stage in life cycle produced their own problems. So many young families were having children that some community members jokingly referred to themselves as living in the nursery suburbs. Pregnancy was called "the Levittown look." In Park Forest, they amusingly referred to their community as "Fertile Acres." The unusually large numbers of children in the community—at the peak of the postwar baby boom in the 1950s, 4.3 million babies were born in the United States compared with 2.4 million in 1937—created special problems of

supervision and control as well as enormously straining the school systems. In a town where everyone simultaneously had small children, the kids were often the cause of tension and irritation. Walking through gardens and flowerbeds, taking over new play equipment in a neighbor's yard, or simply trapping the mothers in the home, the children created resentments.[27]

The schools in particular, Gans found, created tension because of the strain that they placed on community tax structures. Historically, even in Puritan times, maintaining the schools was a community's largest expense. The baby boom in the 1950s turned this problem into a crisis. In the Long Island Levittown, the school population went from three thousand to nine thousand students in just two years, overflowing the original buildings put up by the developer and forcing the community to run split sessions during the day. In the New Jersey Levittown, growing classroom sizes together with disagreements over curriculum embroiled the community in a debate over educational philosophy and the schools. Educational changes during the next decade forced up taxes rapidly—they accounted for three-quarters of the total tax bill—and the debate over the school budget became extremely bitter. Behind the debate, Gans reported, was a difference in class aspirations. The lower-middle-class parents objected to the taxes not only because they strained their budgets, but also because the schools appeared to teach "the culture of their more affluent and higher status neighbors."[28]

Adolescents were also discontent in the new suburban developments. The winding street patterns and lack of neighborhood stores were seen as a major drawback. The teenagers wanted more recreational facilities and less supervision. Levittown had been planned for families with very young children. The houses had been designed with the little children in mind. Bedrooms were just large enough to serve as playrooms as well as sleeping quarters, and kitchens were positioned so that mothers could keep an eye on their children playing outside. But these same rooms were perceived as inadequate by the teenagers. The bedrooms were too small to use for anything but study or sleep. Teenagers found that they could not invite friends over because of the lack of privacy and soundproofing. And the community had few soda shops or restaurants where the teenagers could get together.[29]

More intense than the malaise of the teenagers was the plight of the young housewife. Some young mothers, particularly with little children and without a car, felt "stuck." As one former Philadelphian commented to Gans, "It's too quiet here, nothing to do. In the city you can go downtown shopping, see all the people, or go visit mother." In Levittown, with two small children, she felt trapped. For those women whose children were older and who worked outside of the home, boredom and loneliness were sometimes less of a problem.

In fact, Herbert Gans's thorough study of Levittown reported that the problems of dealing with babies, teenagers, school growth, and loneliness were not nearly as disturbing to the suburbanites as outsiders thought. Responding to the critics, Gans admitted that there was a large degree of homogeneity in the new suburbs, but he also asserted that the negative consequences that had been predicted by social critics did not appear. Most people seemed to have chosen the suburban housing developments precisely because they wanted a familiar environment. "Compatibility," Gans suggested, might be a better term than conformity to describe the quality that these suburbanites sought. One Levittowner described her next-door neighbor by saying simply that "we see eye to eye on things, about raising kids, doing things together with your husband, living the same way; we have practically the same identical background." As Gans argued, by bringing together people of relatively similar age, educational background, and income, the new suburbs created sufficient homogeneity to allow people to get along together well. "In the communities I have studied," he commented, "many people say that they have never had such friendly neighbors."[30]

In addition to liking one's neighbors, the suburbanites received a great deal of satisfaction from their house. Most people felt that the increased space, despite its limitations, had a major impact on family life. Although their general daily routines did not change much— one Levittowner admitted that "you have a pattern you go by, and that stays the same no matter where you live"—they felt that the additional space made child rearing easier, offered more room for family activities, increased the privacy for individual family members, and thereby reduced family friction.

The impact of the cleaning and cooking technologies was more problematic. Improved cooking and cleaning appliances gave housewives a bit more time to spend with the kids, but they also raised their standards. Although appliance makers advertised that women who used their products would have more time for themselves and for their own interests, that did not turn out to be the case. Instead, housewives spent more time cleaning their houses, cooking more elaborate meals, and in general keeping the home environment under greater control. Families also devoted considerable effort to "fixing up" the house. After all, the house was still a symbol for middle-class achievement. "As one Levittowner put it, his home provided "something to show for all your years of living."[31]

Yet in the new suburbs homeowners felt that they had more time for recreation. Whether it was taking the kids to the pool, playing in the community softball league, or simply cooking dinner outside on the backyard patio, suburbanites believed that their leisure time could be spent at home more enjoyably than in the crowded city.

Underlying this satisfaction with the suburban ranch house was a heightened sense that the environment was more controlled and safer than it had been in the city. Not only was the air cleaner, the traffic less heavy, and the children's play areas safer, but also standards of behavior were more regulated both by informal customs and by specific rules. People had similar aspirations. Neighbors joined local organizations and daily saw evidence that their homes existed in an environment where people cared about standards.

Implicit in the suburban housing developments, therefore, was an underlying conservatism. People wanted their lives as controlled and protected as possible. Once the initial phase of construction was finished, the general pace of social change slowed down dramatically. As Gans put it, "Levittowners came not to build a new community but to move into a new house in which they could carry on old ways of family life, neighbor relations and civic activity." The public consensus was that conflict, whether in community or family, was bad and should be minimized. Like the consensus philosophy that historians in the 1950s found in the pattern of American history, community homogeneity was seen as an achievement to be valued.[32]

The overwhelming evidence thus points to the fact that suburban homeowners in the 1950s substantially accepted the theories about family life and domestic architecture that were being promoted by the house magazines and family experts. Despite the major criticisms voiced initially by sociologists and made more pointed in the 1960s by Betty Friedan and other feminists, most middle-class suburban homeowners remained generally satisfied with their lives. To a greater extent than had been the case in 1880 or 1910, the new ideal of a relaxed, informal family life-style, with its emphasis on outdoor activities and its stress on enjoyment and personal satisfaction, was incorporated into the personal ideals of middle-class suburbanites. To the older ideal of house as refuge they fused the new vision of the home as a center for recreation. Even when commuting to work for a half an hour or more, which was the case in most of the larger suburban developments, meant that husbands actually had *less* time to spend with their children than they had had before, people in the suburbs argued that living in the new community improved their family life.

Yet the great preoccupation with family life —which some social critics have seen as a form of self-indulgence and narrowness, a forerunner of the "me" decade of the 1960s, and a movement away from a commitment to community—appeared not to have the destructive effect that the critics had feared. Generally, families expressed great satisfaction with their suburban existence. Still, life in the suburbs was not as bucolic as the suburbanites desired. Although Gans argues that if anything the pace of life was more relaxed in the ranch house suburbs than in the cities, the evidence does not support his claim. The greater amount of time spent commuting, the increased time taken by participation in organizations such as the PTA, the Girl Scouts, and church groups, not to mention the time spent constantly driving the children to their music lessons and athletic events, and the hours taken by decorating, painting, and "improving" the house meant that there was little time spent "relaxing" in most suburban communities. With the men rising early and coming home late and the women maintaining the house, chasing the kids, and, in 25 percent of the cases holding down a part-time job, life in the ranch house suburbs was anything but relaxed. As one suburbanite put it, "we never get time to see each other—we merely pass coming and going." When one interviewer suggested that life in the new suburbs was more promiscuous, the respondent commented, "Tell me, with my schedule, how would I fit it in?"[33]

The growth of suburban single-family housing since the 1950s testifies to the continuing popularity of the ranch house and its more recent successor, the split-level, and the concomitant ideal of the relaxed and informal family life-style. In many ways the preoccupation with controlling the environment and creating a protective family enclave in the home became even stronger in the twentieth century than it had been in the nineteenth. Bombarded incessantly by the newspapers and television networks with reports of crime, rape, and murder, suburban homeowners have tightened the locks on their doors and windows and have rejoiced that suburban life remains more peaceful than life in the city.

Although this image of the house as a protected oasis in a conflict-ridden society is a legacy from the nineteenth-century housing reformers, it is clear from interviews with inhabitants of suburban neighborhoods that their views have been strongly reinforced by the advertisements in home magazines and on television. When asked what most influenced the planning of their new houses in the 1950s, suburban home builders singled out magazine articles as most helpful, followed by the advice of the contractor and advertisements. Television advertisements also reinforced the image of the happy family in the protective home environment. Many families conceded that the television, by bringing entertainment into the home, strengthened a sense of family cohesiveness and self-interest. Stimulated by consumer advertisements, the protective instincts of the homeowner intensified. Almost without thinking, middle-class suburbanites took the protected-home vision of the nineteenth-century reformers and turned it into their central preoccupation. The reform vision had finally become the national standard.[34]

Such a response has not been without its problems. Zane Miller, in his study of Forest Park, Ohio, has pointed out that as American society has become more segmented into homogeneous suburban neighborhoods and has become more preoccupied with protecting family life and its middle-class standards of consumption, there has been a corresponding loss of civic consciousness. The earlier civic leaders in Levittown or Park Forest in the 1950s earned a certain status among their neighbors by speaking for the whole community, but now many suburban neighborhood leaders are primarily interested in protecting their part of town from change. Local political leaders have become increasingly the advocates of special interests. Working through petitions and litigation, they show an increased inability to understand the needs of the community at large. As ownership of the single-family home has become more expensive and has placed families with two working adults in a more precarious financial position, commitment to the broader community in the middle-class suburbs has eroded. Protecting the suburban family ideal has become a vehicle for resisting change.[35]

Chapter 9

The American Family Home and the American Dream

If you don't relish the idea of living in a goldfish bowl: plan your house to be a retreat, indoors and out. Separate sleeping wing from the comings and goings of the living wing. Give your children a terrace and playground outside their bedrooms.

—"House of Ideas, Upper Brookville, Long Island"

By the 1960s it was clear that the nineteenth-century housing promoters' and reformers' vision of an America filled with communities of mass-produced single-family dwellings had been realized. From California to New York, from Maine to Texas, millions of mass-produced houses had been built. Standardized construction materials, simplified building methods, long-term federally backed mortgages together with generous tax credits and massive highway construction had helped make the single-family home a reality for millions of middle-class Americans.

The tremendous housing boom in the twentieth century, particularly in the two decades after World War II, was a response to pressures created by a rapidly increasing population and rising material expectations. To what extent, therefore, should the promotional activities of the architects, housing reformers, developers, builders, magazine advocates, and advice-book writers, stretching back for more than a century, be credited with encouraging this massive housing expansion? What were the components of their ideal of the American single-family home and to what extent was their dream realized?

Looking at the history of advice manuals, plan books, and housing magazines, it is evident that their basic aim was to give domestic architecture a symbolic and moral meaning. In this endeavor they were highly successful. Once the reform and promotional campaigns had gathered speed in the middle decades of the nineteenth century, houses were no longer simply the physical structures in which families lived. The design, layout, and style of the house were invested with a moral purpose. Single-family houses were designed not only to strengthen the family but also to fulfill a symbolic function. The house became a special environment, a protected retreat designed to nurture and support the family and to symbolize its values. Thereafter, domestic architecture was to be judged in moral terms; it was good or bad, honest or dishonest, truthful or deceitful.

Inherent in this powerful promotional and reform vision of the middle-class house was the idea that the family home, as a retreat protected from the instability of a transient society and the competitiveness of the business world, could serve as the central, stabilizing force for American democratic society. In magazine after magazine, plan book after plan book, the same theme was repeated over and over again. A properly designed single-family house would protect and strengthen the family, shoring up the foundations of society and instilling the proper virtues needed to preserve the republic.

This ideal reflected a society-wide need that gave it an ongoing vitality for more than a century. From the 1840s on, the tremendous mobility of the population lent credence to the reformers' vision of the single-family house as an island of stability in the midst of an unstable social system. Fueled by a high birthrate and the influx of millions of immigrants, the American population expanded rapidly and swept across the continent. As historians have recently pointed out, the transiency of this population was phenomenal. The number of inhabitants of eastern cities increased between 40 and 60 percent every ten years in the latter part of the century. During the same decades, six to twelve times the number of people present at the start of each decade moved in and out of the same cities. Given the tremendous mobility of the American people—today Americans continue to move on an average of once every five years—it is not surprising that the assertion of architectural promoters and family reformers that ownership of a single-family home was a mark of stability and security should have been so easily accepted.[1]

The image of the single-family house as a protected retreat was further reinforced by the middle class which, because of its persistent antiurban bias, deliberately reshaped the landscape to strengthen the power of the family. From the middle of the nineteenth century on, middle-class housing promoters sited their dwellings in controlled suburban environments, natural settings outside of and protected from, yet accessible to, city centers. The suburban landscape was itself redesigned to reinforce a feeling of protectiveness by using trees, lawns, and parks to create a pastoral-like setting. With its green lawns, special plantings, flowering shrubs, and shade trees, nature itself was tamed and controlled in the suburbs.

In addition to the emphasis on soothing the discomforts created by a highly mobile population and providing an alternate environment to that of the dangerous cities, the suburban, middle-class house was held up by developers and family reformers as an instrument for calming the insecurities created by the instability of American capitalism. Despite the growth of personal income in terms of real dollars in the past century, the American economy had gone through an unsettling pattern of expansion and recession every twenty or thirty years. Given the real possibility that individuals might lose their jobs during an economic downturn, home ownership came to be seen as a short-term form of economic insurance. Although home ownership could never compensate for the permanent loss of a job, it might provide collateral for a short-term loan that would tide the family over until the economy recovered.

The promoters' and reformers' vision of the house as a stabilizing force in an otherwise chaotic society has also been reinforced by the competitive nature of capitalism. Built on an aggressive search for new products and markets, the American economy has idealized competition as a healthy factor in the struggle for self-improvement. Faced by an unstable market system that puts a premium on a principled conflict for goods and services, it is understandable that middle-class Americans, particularly those with salaried jobs, would want to picture their homes as a peaceful antidote to the hectic scramble for success in the outside world. To a great degree, therefore, the strong and persistent popularity of the reformers' ideal of the single-family home as a peaceful retreat can be understood as a reaction to basic features of the American social system. Ownership of the single-family home not only provided a useful way to separate the private from the public dimensions of one's life, but it also represented a financial asset of considerable value that could testify to the individual's position in society itself.

Indeed, ownership of the single-family dwelling has persisted as one of the major symbols of middle-class social status. Although there has been considerable regional variation in the numbers of people who have owned their own homes in the past century, usually less than half the population has been able to purchase a single-family house. Even when these figures are adjusted to account for younger middle-class families who have had to save for a number of years before purchasing a dwelling, they indicate that home ownership has been the basic sign of having achieved financial stability. Thus, the one satisfaction that the middle class could always treasure was the knowledge that in a society perennially short of single-family homes, a homeowner could at least consider himself or herself better off than the renters in the lower class. In a democratic society where class differences have been frowned upon, ownership of a single-family dwelling has remained a noninvidious way of indicating the attainment of higher social status.

This fact also helps explain why in the 1980s, despite the forceful critiques of Gwendolyn Wright, Dolores Hayden, and other observers who point out that the detached, single-family dwelling wastes time, space, and resources, middle-class Americans seem to have little inclination to abandon the dream of owning their own home. Reinforced by an aggressive campaign of promotion and support that stretches back for more than a century, the ideal of owning a single-family dwelling has proved to be remarkably strong and persistent. Home ownership has been too closely associated not only with social status but also with freedom of choice and personal independence, ideals that seem even more valuable in the modern, mass society of the present day, to be easily given up. Middle-class Americans remain remarkably tenacious about their commitment to home ownership.[2]

Yet this promotional and reform vision of the house as a sign of financial independence and as an agent of stability has been inherently flawed from the start. Home ownership has guaranteed neither independence nor permanence. In fact, given the constant middle-class emphasis on progress and self-improvement, the paradox is that, in a society in which promoters were constantly changing the standards for what constitutes quality housing, home ownership was itself subject to unsettling pressures. To move, either from one house to another—the perennially favorite activity of small-town America—or from one city to another, suggested the possibility of improving one's social status. Therefore, the constant cries of architectural promoters and family reformers for new and better housing designs, instead of ensuring the stability that they so much desired, often had just the opposite effect. For middle-class Americans, moving, building, or remodeling became the norm.

What the plan-book writers and family reformers did do was to moderate and tone down the impact of middle-class mobility and transiency by helping establish the criteria by which house designs might be judged. Their efforts to create a common stylistic vocabulary, whether for the Victorian, bungalow, or ranch houses, together with the mass production and standardization of millwork and building materials, created a variety of recognizable house types that could be found in small towns and on the periphery of cities from coast to coast. Whether one drives through Springfield, Massachusetts, St. Paul, Minnesota, or Salt Lake City, Utah, one can find the section of bungalow homes built between 1900 and 1929. Similarly, a family who moved across the country in that period would be certain to find a new neighborhood with houses that were very similar to the ones they had just left. Thus, although the plan-book writers and family reformers did not actually stabilize the transiency of the middle class, they did create the impression, through the promotion of common house types, that middle-class Americans could have the best of both worlds: they could move frequently but still be assured that the disruption in housing standards in going from region to region would be minimized.

A second basic feature of the reformers' moralistic vision of the middle-class home, which has persisted for more than a century, is the identification of the house with family growth and improvement. Although the arguments about the influence of the home on family life have shifted substantially over time, plan-book promoters and family reformers have consistently asserted that the home environment can shape and mold each individual family member for the better. When the argument was first introduced during the middle years of the nineteenth century, reformers insisted that the middle-class house be thought of as a protected retreat which could serve as an instrument for sustenance and revitalization. Toward the end of the century, the argument had shifted to emphasize creativity. The house, they asserted, should be the locus of artistic and creative activity, a place where women especially could show off their stitchery and decorative talents. After 1900, magazine writers and architects again modified the middle-class housing ideal by stressing the home's role in the promotion of improved health and physical hardiness. A physical environment of unsurpassed cleanliness, the new bungalow was pictured not so much an agent for maintaining the status quo as a stimulus to improved health and physical hardiness. Outdoor sleeping porches, sanitary kitchens and plumbing, and open interior spaces became devices for promoting a more natural life-style. The home came to be seen increasingly as a staging ground for recreational activities that would take place elsewhere.

In the two decades after World War II, the image of the ideal family home was further expanded to include an emphasis on psychological well-being. Since the nineteenth century, the home had been a major indicator of status and material consumption, but by the middle of the twentieth century, with the ever-expanding range of consumer choices, it became even more important as a reflection of personal accomplishment. People took immense satisfaction in the fact that their new home, like their new car and new appliances, reflected their ongoing achievements and measured their climb up the ladder of success. The image of the ideal American family home now included the prediction that home ownership would bring with it psychological satisfaction and personal enjoyment. The terms most often used in the advertising—"comfort through convenience," "livability," "charm," "character," and "fun,"—reflected the promoters' and reformers' belief that the middle-class family home was now a bulwark of the family's psychological health.[3]

Although this vision of the protective and supportive functions of the middle-class home has been a popular litany for the past century, it has never been fully realized by the experience of the middle class. For one thing, arguments for imaginative designs and creative styles have often masked self-serving purposes. During the nineteenth century, architects hoped to gain new clients, developers to expand their sales, and reformers to protect their role as arbitrators of moral standards. By the middle decades of the twentieth century, the promotion of the new house types, furnishings, and fixtures had become a major national business of substantial proportions. Popular magazines, supported by building-materials manufacturers, architects, interior decorators, and family counselors, directed their energies on a full-time basis to encouraging the latest fads and fashions. Selling homeowners on what was best for their houses and their families had become a national industry.

It is now apparent that design changes that were promoted as stylistically fresh and efficient have often been necessary simply to reduce costs. Especially in the postwar decades, but in the Progressive period as well, simplification of design, opening up interior spaces by reducing the number of walls, and using built-ins for storage have often been reactions to the escalating costs that have reduced house size. New lighting and window technologies were creatively used in the post–World War II period, as anyone who has lived in both a Victorian and a ranch house will attest, to give the more cramped quarters of the ranch house a new sense of spaciousness. More than either the reformers or the promoters have been willing to admit, the need to reduce costs has had a major impact on style and design.

Nor has the family home always been the center of stability. In their attempt to escape the insecurities in the public world, middle-class Americans have not always found their own private lives to be peaceful and free of conflict. In fact, it can be argued that the ideals of peaceful family life have been set so high that for most people the reality has been a source of some frustration. Given the large expenditures necessary for the house, it was practically inevitable that some disagreements would develop within the family over the allocation of the scarce resources that remained. Should families spend their money on clothes and entertainment, or save it to improve the furnishings of the house? Should they try to expand their living quarters or use what little money they had left for vacations? Such questions arose almost inevitably and created family strife.

Moreover, given the ever-present costs of purchasing and maintaining the single-family dwelling, it has almost always been necessary to compromise the family's expectations about space and convenience. Although the available

evidence indicates that middle-class Americans commonly modified their interior spaces by tearing down walls or building small additions, the continuous advertising of the reformers, promoters, and magazine writers has encouraged a constant escalation of expectations. Given the ever-present pressure for upgrading and improving one's home, it was not surprising that complete satisfaction was rarely attainable. Keeping up with the current fashions was difficult, but it was even more frustrating if one happened to build at a time when the larger standards shifted, as they did between the Victorian homes and the bungalows, or between the bungalows and the ranch houses. In such cases, the owners of the older homes were constantly faced with the knowledge that they possessed an outmoded dwelling.

A further problem with the image of the family home as a restful retreat has been the inescapable fact that the house and grounds demand constant maintenance. Painting the exterior and interior, repairing broken plumbing and windows, putting up and taking down screens and storm windows, fixing or replacing worn-out doors and flooring, all take an immense amount of time. For many middle-class Americans, the cost of having painters or plumbers come in to make repairs is prohibitive. So they have been forced to take on these activities themselves. The result is that the vaunted ideal of home life as restful and restorative is often belied by the facts.

For women, especially, the ideal of a peaceful and sedate family life has been a myth. As feminists such as Betty Friedan began to point out in the early 1960s, the role of middle-class women in the home during the past century has restricted their opportunities in the public world. Even for those who remained within the home and accepted the idea that taking care of children and "keeping house" was their primary responsibility, the increase in appliances and household technology has failed to lighten their burden. A report done by Bryn Mawr College after World War II noted that women still spent more than eighty hours a week cleaning the house, cooking meals, and taking care of the children. Given the enormous amount of work necessary to run the home, middle-class women who were raising a family had little time to consider other career opportunities. In the 1940s and 1950s, this problem was exacerbated by the decentralized nature of suburban development. Any free time that had been gained from new cooking or cleaning technologies was spent in learning how to meet higher standards and in taking on new responsibilities. Chauffeuring children to music lessons and other activities reduced even further the time that women could use to pursue their own interests and careers.[4]

If the promoters, plan-book writers, and family reformers did not establish standards for house construction and family behavior as independently as they have insisted, it is still important to note that their reform vision has often been a yardstick against which middle-class Americans have judged the quality of their own personal and family life. The constant promotion of the American family home ideal by countless advice manuals, plan books, and housing magazines has served to set a standard for middle-class aspirations and expectations. Insecure about their behavior and eager to act in ways that would ensure personal and economic success, middle-class Americans have looked to the advice manuals and plan books for reassurance that their preoccupation with security and consensus is justified.

In each period, plan books and housing magazines have helped to define and sanction the boundaries of personal and family behavior. Starting with the late Victorian houses, the boundaries between public and private life were physically laid out in the designs of the entrances, front halls, and staircase landings. Upstairs bedrooms and the kitchen as well as the back parlor were seen as the private areas of the family. Over time, as the interior spaces have been opened up and the kitchen has become a legitimate arena for the entertainment of friends, the areas of the house considered to be truly private have decreased. While children's bedrooms were considered appropriate

places to entertain their friends, particularly when they were on the lower level in the split-level homes being put up in the late 1950s, the parents' bedroom, often part of a master bedroom–bathroom suite, has remained private. Similarly, the changing layout of the living room and dining room has encouraged the replacement of dinner parties with other less formal kinds of entertainment.

Thus, the continuing flood of plan books and advice magazines has contributed to maintaining the creative tension, so central to the outlook of the middle class, between the concern for security and social control and the desire for enhancing individual creativity and self-expression. From the nineteenth century on, middle-class Americans have tried to create a safe environment in which to live and bring up their children. To avoid excesses and dangers associated with urban life, they have purchased houses in uniform suburban neighborhoods which conform to widely accepted design and stylistic standards. Whether one looks at nineteenth-century plan-book houses or twentieth-century tract developments, it is clear that the choices created by mass-production techniques have resulted in a relatively narrow range of housing options within these suburbs. Yet this relatively narrow range of choices has been just what most people seemed to want. Middle-class Americans have always desired the reassurance that comes from shared standards for behavior. The limitations and boundaries inherent in suburban living have helped perpetuate the middle class's sense of security. Be it humble or pretentious, the single-family home has remained a symbol of that security. Protecting the middle-class family has continued to be a national concern.

At the same time, within these narrowly defined stylistic and design boundaries, the plan books and house magazines have also encouraged diversity and individual expression. Although social critics from the nineteenth century on have worried about the conformity that would be generated by the advent of mass production, middle-class Americans have looked upon the vast number of choices created by machine-tool technology as a way of making their own individual statements. Within the framework of a broadly accepted canon of design, they have interpreted the dazzling array of color and decorative choices as making possible a new world of personal choice. Notwithstanding the limitations inherent in suburban life, middle-class Americans have persisted in believing that theirs is the best of all possible worlds—one that combines both independence and social control.

Even now, two and a half decades after the postwar housing boom, the ideal of the middle-class family home persists with amazing tenacity. Despite the increasing number of single-parent households and the ongoing frustration with rising housing costs and home maintenance problems, middle-class families continue to find their house to be a major source of pride and personal satisfaction. With all its problems, the American family home retains its position as the central element within the middle-class dream of security, self-determination, and independence.[5]

Notes

This book was written for a general as well as a scholarly audience. Accordingly, the documentation is presented as simply as possible. To keep the text uncluttered, the sources for quotations and other references are summarized in notes at the end of one or several paragraphs. Sources in each note are given in the order in which the information appears in the text. The bibliography, which presents a full citation for each book, article, or other item, allows a shortened form of the title in the notes. By matching text and notes, and by finding the full title in the bibliography, the reader will be able to identify all the sources readily. Scholars will have the further advantage of having a separate bibliographic listing, divided into primary and secondary sources, of all the plan books and magazine articles cited in the text.

INTRODUCTION

1. Tocqueville, *Democracy in America*, 1:315.

2. On the definition of the middle class, see Katz and Stern, "Fertility," pp. 72–74, 84–85, and Blumin, "The Hypothesis of Middle-Class Formation," pp. 299–338.

3. See Hareven, ed., *Themes and Transitions*; on family history see Vinovskis, "American Families in the Past," pp. 115–38.

4. Dolores Hayden, in her perceptive studies, *Seven American Utopias*, *The Grand Domestic Revolution*, and *Redesigning the American Dream*, strongly argues in favor of the superiority of some of the nineteenth-century reform visions to the traditional single-family dwelling ideal. Gwendolyn Wright, in two excellent books, *Moralism and the Model Home* and *Building the Dream*, is also candid about the limitations of the single-family dwelling for the future.

5. For an excellent survey of the current work in the fields of vernacular architecture and material culture see Upton's "The Power of Things" and Ames's "American Decorative Arts/Household Furnishings"; for recent pioneering overviews of middle-class housing see Handlin, *The American Home*, and Cohn, *The Palace or the Poorhouse*.

CHAPTER I

1. Cleaveland and Backus, *Village and Farm Cottages*, p. 4; Judah, "Home," p. 94.

2. Cleaveland and Backus, *Village and Farm Cottages*, p. 3; Gardner, *Home Interiors*, p. 177; Atwood, *Atwood's Country and Suburban Houses*, p. 143.

3. "Architecture," p. 433; Wheeler, *Homes for the People*, p. 21.

4. Glassie, *Pattern in the Material Folk Culture*, p. 49; see also Clark, "Domestic Architecture," pp. 33–56; Wright, *Building the Dream*; and Handlin, *The American Home*.

5. Carson et al., "Impermanent Architecture," pp. 135–96; Upton, "Vernacular Domestic Architecture," pp. 95–120; Cummings, *Framed Houses*; on the family in seventeenth-century Chesapeake see Walsh, " 'Till Death Us Do Part,' " and Rutman and Rutman, " 'Now-Wives and Sons-In-Law,' " pp. 126–52, 153–82.

6. Benjamin, *The American Builder's Companion*, pp. 33–35; Upton, "Pattern Books," pp. 107–50.

7. The literature on the family is vast. Most helpful is Demos, *A Little Commonwealth*, and Myerhoff and Tufte, "Images of the American Family," pp. 43–61; see also Shammas, "The Domestic Environment," pp. 3–24; on the problems of family survival see Old Sturbridge Village, "Reform Poverty" and "Making a Living"; Zwelling, "Working in Rural New England."

8. Kerber, *Women of the Republic*, pp. 11, 283–88; on the importance of business and political connections see Bailyn, *The New England Merchants* and *The Origins of American Politics*.

9. Greven, *The Protestant Temperament*, chap. 4; Ryan, *Cradle of the Middle Class*, pp. 230ff.

10. Upton, "Vernacular Domestic Architecture," pp. 102–3, 114–19; Mayhew and Myers, *A Documentary History*, pp. 20–21, 31–33, 56. The infor-

mation on genre paintings is from Cary Carson, personal correspondence, September 26, 1983.

11. Thomas Jefferson to James Madison, September 20, 1785, in Jefferson, *Papers*, 8:534–35; see also Wills, *Inventing America*, epilogue.

12. For a discussion of the transformation of work see Brown, "Modernization and the Modern Personality," pp. 201–28; on the pervasive sense of social dislocation see Berthoff, *An Unsettled People*; Beecher, "A Plea for the West," p. 59.

13. On the emerging middle-class consciousness see Ryan, *Cradle of the Middle Class*, pp. 230–42, Halttunen, *Confidence Men and Painted Women*, pp. 35–40, and Blumin, "The Hypothesis of Middle-Class Formation," pp. 299–338.

14. These totals, which were drawn from Hitchcock, *American Architectural Books*, were tabulated by counting both the original edition and the subsequent reprintings. A good estimate of the popularity of the different revival styles, as published in *Godey's Lady's Book*, can be found in Hersey, "Godey's Choice," p. 110. Interestingly, most of the "house pattern books" between 1840 and 1870 were written by architects who hoped thereby both to give their profession more status and to stir up more business for themselves. For an example of the way in which architects tried to increase their business see Riddell, *Architectural Designs*, preface.

15. Shaw, "Architecture in the United States," p. 476; "Architecture," p. 421.

16. Vaux, "Hints for Country House Builders," p. 763.

17. Wheeler, *Rural Homes*, p. 32; see also Douglas, *The Feminization of American Culture*.

18. Todd, *Todd's Country Homes*, p. 33.

19. Downing, *The Architecture of Country Houses*, pp. 109–10; Wheeler, *Homes for the People*, p. 44. Although the "bracketed mode," as it was called by contemporaries, was a label that was often applied to the first two revival types (i.e., "Gothic cottages in the bracketed mode" and "Italian villas in the bracketed mode"), from an eclectic sampling of its use at mid-century, I would argue that it achieved a status of its own as a style. For a contemporary view supporting my own, see the *Architectural Review and American Builders' Journal* as quoted in Peat, *Indiana Houses*, p. 96.

20. Downing, *Cottage Residences*, p. 99. It is difficult to judge the number of houses actually built in each style.

21. For the aesthetic theory of the romantic revival see Early, *Romanticism*, pp. 34–35; Hipple, *The Beautiful, the Sublime, and the Picturesque*; Cleaveland, "American Architecture," p. 380.

22. President Timothy Dwight, as quoted in Cleaveland and Backus, *Village and Farm Cottages*, p. 47.

23. Young, *The Washington Community*, chap. 1.

24. Atwood, *Atwood's Country and Suburban Houses*, p. 143; Downing, *The Architecture of Country Houses*; Halttunen, *Confidence Men and Painted Ladies*, pp. 96–98; on Downing's aesthetic theories see Handlin, *The American Home*, pp. 30–46.

25. Atwood, *Atwood's Country and Suburban Houses*, p. 143; Cleaveland and Backus, *Village and Farm Cottages*, p. 43; on the technological innovations in building see Fitch, *American Building*, chap. 4. Most of the technological innovations were adopted first by the wealthy and were only later picked up by the middle class. Indoor plumbing did not become widespread in small towns and cities until the 1890s. See Strasser, *Never Done*, pp. 95–103.

26. Higham, "From Boundlessness to Consolidation," pp. 1–28; "The Houses We Live in," p. 740; Hammond, *The Farmer's and Mechanic's Practical Architect*, p. 27; Sloan, *City Homes*, pp. 746–47.

27. Jeffrey, "The Family as Utopian Retreat," pp. 21–41; Olmsted, Vaux & Co., "Preliminary Report," pp. 7, 26–27; see also Lang, *Views*.

28. Miller, *The Life of the Mind*, pp. 3–98; McLoughlin, *Modern Revivalism*, pp. 1–23, 98–140.

29. Bushnell, *Christian Nurture*, pp. 106–7. The other forces behind the shift from revivalism to liberal Protestantism are too complex to go into here. See McLoughlin, *The Meaning of Henry Ward Beecher*; Ahlstrom, *A Religious History*, chaps. 36 and 46.

30. "Architecture," p. 432; Ranlett, *The Architect*, p. 3. There is a growing literature on children and the family. See Wishy, *The Child and the Republic*; Saveth, "The Problem of American Family History," pp. 311–29; see also Shorter, *The Making of the Modern Family*.

31. Walter and Smith, *Two Hundred Designs*, p. 33; for furniture see Maass, *The Gingerbread Age*, p. 88; for stained glass see Sloan, *City Homes*, p. 57; on the symbolism in Gothic architecture see Donnell, "A. J. Davis," p. 187.

32. Beecher, "The Nation's Duty," p. 220; Kraditor, *Means and Ends*, chaps. 5 and 6; Gusfield, *Symbolic Crusade*, chap. 2; Lincoln, *Works*, as quoted in Foner, *Free Soil*, p. 20.

33. Smith, *The Domestic Architect*, p. iii; Eggleston, "Domestic Architecture," p. 61; Cleaveland and Backus, *Village and Farm Cottages*, p. 4.

34. On the nature of American Victorian culture see McLoughlin, *The Meaning of Henry Ward Beecher*, and Howe, "American Victorianism," pp. 507–32; on the connection between art and nature see Novak, *Nature and Culture*.

35. Jeffrey, "The Family as Utopian Retreat," pp. 21–41; Todd, *Todd's Country Homes*, p. 33; Rawls, *The Great Book of Currier and Ives*, pp. 137, 184, 254, 265–67. For a study of the importance of a "middle landscape" to Americans' self-image see Marx, *The Machine in the Garden*, and Faoretti and Faoretti, *Landscapes and Gardens*.

36. *The Illustrated Family Christian Almanac*, p. 18.

37. "The Social Condition of Woman," p. 489.

38. Olmsted, Vaux & Co., "Preliminary Report," p. 7; *Descriptive and Pictorial Catalogue*, p. 1; Handlin, *The American Home*, p. 101.

39. Riley, "Home," p. 38.

40. *The American Builder*, p. 33.

41. "The Social Condition of Woman," p. 489; Hale, "Domestic Economy," p. 42; for the cult of domesticity see particularly Jeffrey, "The Family as Utopian Retreat," pp. 21–41; Hill, *Hill's Manual*, p. 161.

42. Hale, "Domestic Economy," p. 42.

43. Cott, *The Bonds of Womanhood*, chap. 1.

44. On the literature of self-help see Clark, "The Changing Nature of Protestantism," pp. 832–46; *A Woman's Thoughts about Women*, p. 121; "Domestic Management," p. 314; Dresser, "The Family Constitution," p. 17.

45. Beecher and Stowe, *American Woman's Home*, pp. 19, 23, 42; Sklar, *Catharine Beecher*, p. 264.

46. Handlin, *The American Home*, pp. 407–8, 419, 453. Handlin sees a pervasive tension between the traditional and the new in American housing as an indication of an ambivalence about progress. My own argument would be that most Americans do not feel uncomfortable about blending the old with the new. Hayden's position is most forcefully expressed in her "Catharine Beecher and the Politics of Housework," pp. 40–49.

47. Bakewell, *The Mother's Practical Guide*, p. 15; Beecher and Stowe, *American Woman's Home*, p. 277.

48. Durand, "French Domestic Life," p. 175; Kett, *Rites of Passage*, pp. 137 ff.; *Uncle Sam's Almanac*, p. 11.

49. Robinson, *Facts for Farmers*, pp. 275–76; Wheeler, *Rural Homes*, pp. 116, 277; Fowler, *A Home for All*, p. 63; "House Building," p. 428.

50. Palliser and Palliser, *Palliser's New Cottage Homes*, dedication.

CHAPTER 2

1. Editorial, "The Uses of Home," p. 308.

2. Wheeler, *Homes for the People*, p. 192.

3. Fowler, *A Home for All*, p. 63. Merchants in the larger cities usually came home by 3:00 P.M. when they had their dinner. They stayed home for the rest of the afternoon, often working on their accounts in the library. Bunting, *Houses of Boston's Back Bay*, p. 129.

4. Vaux, *Villas and Cottages*, p. 44; Cross, *The Educated Woman*, pp. 1–13.

5. Hervey, *The Principles of Courtesy*, p. 213; Hartley, *The Ladies' Book*, pp. 66–75; Arnot, *Gothic Architecture*, p. 32.

6. Ames, "Meaning in Artifacts," pp. 19–46.

7. Duffey, *What Women Should Know*, p. 111.

8. See, for example, Kennedy, *Minnesota Houses*; Peat, *Indiana Houses*; Bunting, *Houses of Boston's Back Bay*; Lockwood, *Bricks and Brownstone*; Frary, *Early Homes of Ohio*; Downing and Scully, *The Architectural Heritage of Newport*; Dutchess County Planning Board, *Landmarks of Dutchess County*; Foerster, *Architecture Worth Saving*; New York State Council on the Arts, *Architecture Worth Saving*; Lyle and Simpson, *The Architecture of Lexington*; McArdle and Hamilton, *Carpenter Gothic*; Johnson, *The Building of Galena*; Weeks, *The Building of Westminster*; Schmitt and Karab, *Kalamazoo*; Sommer, *The Heritage of Dubuque*; Lancaster, *Old Brooklyn Heights*; Sanchis, *American Architecture*; Bach, *A Guide to Chicago's Historic Suburbs*.

9. Webster Groves Historical Society, "Hawken House"; Guter, "Acorn Hall," p. 119. Acorn Hall is the residence of the Morris County Historical Society.

10. Junior League of Mobile, *Historic Mobile*, p. 11; "Moongate House" brochure.

11. Bishir, "Jacob W. Holt," pp. 1–31.

12. Weeks, *The Building of Westminster*, pp. 74–76.

13. Schmitt and Karab, *Kalamazoo*, pp. 23, 110, 144.

14. Johnson, *The Building of Galena*, pp. 25, 41, 97, 149.

15. McNee, "Dundas"; on the dynamics of mill owner–mill worker relationships see Wallace, *Rockdale*.

16. "The Uses of Home," p. 308.

17. Sloan, *City Homes*, p. 542.

18. Downing, *The Architecture of Country Houses*, pp. 300–301; McArdle and Hamilton, *Carpenter Gothic*, pp. 111–13; Hammond, *The Farmer's and Mechanic's Practical Architect*, p. 27.

19. Wheeler, *Homes for the People*, p. 189.

20. Uhlenberg, "Changing Configurations," p. 74; Vinovskis, "Angels' Heads," p. 38; and Chudacoff, "New Branches," p. 58.

21. Chudacoff, "New Branches," p. 58; Dublin, *Women at Work*, pp. 5ff.

22. Strasser, *Never Done*, pp. 24–42.

23. Sommer, *The Heritage of Dubuque*, p. 70; Rawls, *The Great Book of Currier and Ives*, pp. 184, 246, 251, 253–54. Despite Rawls's comment that most Currier and Ives' illustrations depict houses that have been modified, those republished in his book are frequently standard plan-book houses.

24. Degler, *At Odds*, p. 83; Hareven, ed., *Transitions*, p. 266.

25. Boyer, *Urban Masses*, p. 61.

26. H. B. Stowe to C. Stowe, June 16, 1845, as quoted in Wilson, *Patriotic Gore*, p. 17.

27. H. B. Stowe to C. Stowe, January 1, 1847, as quoted in Degler, *At Odds*, p. 63; H. B. Stowe to C. Stowe, July and [May] 1844, as quoted in Kelley, "At War with Herself," p. 27.

28. See also Kelley, *Private Woman, Public Stage*, pp. 250–84.

29. H. B. Stowe to C. Stowe, August 1844, as quoted in Degler, *At Odds*, p. 43.

30. H. B. Stowe to C. Stowe, January 1, 1847, and Stowe, *Pink and White Tyranny*, p. 366, as quoted in Kelley, "At War with Herself," p. 36.

31. Van Why, "Harriet Beecher Stowe's House."

32. H. B. Stowe to C. Stowe, November 6, 1850, and April 4, 1860, as quoted in Kelley, "At War with Herself," p. 29.

CHAPTER 3

1. I am indebted to Gwendolyn Wright's excellent study, *Moralism and the Model Home*, for its insights into the power struggle between architects, builders, plan-book writers, and reformers.

2. Modell, "Suburbanization and Change," pp. 621–46; Posadas, "A Home in the Country," pp. 134–49; for pre–Civil War suburban development see Binford, *The First Suburbs*; for twentieth-century suburban change see Edel, Sclar, and Luria, *Shaky Palaces*.

3. Boyer, *Urban Masses*, pp. 67, 123.

4. "Architectural Reform," p. 439.

5. Holly, *Holly's Country Seats*, pp. 7, 18, 23.

6. Holly, *Modern Dwellings*, pp. 22–23.

7. For an attempt at the definition of architectural styles as well as a comparison of the standard architectural "guides" of Marcus Whiffen and Stuart Blumenson, see Bach, *A Guide to Chicago's Historic Suburbs*, pp. 38–39; for San Francisco Victorian architecture see Baer et al., *Painted Ladies*, p. 11. The best discussion of this question of high Victorian styles is to be found in Wright's *Moralism*, pp. 55–68.

8. Holly, *Modern Dwellings*, pp. 21–25.

9. Tomlan, "The Palliser Brothers"; see also Goeldner's introduction to *Bicknell's Village Builder* and Garvin, "Mail-Order House Plans," pp. 309–34.

10. Palliser and Palliser, *Palliser's American Architecture*, preface, plates 7, 18. Other plan-book companies quickly followed the Pallisers' example and published cheap plan books. The *Scientific American*, to take but one example, circulated 40,000 copies weekly of their *Architect's and Builder's* edition! See Mitchell et al., *American Victoriana*, pp. v–vi; *Gordon, Vantine, and Company's Book of Plans*; Shoppell, *Modern Houses*.

11. Review of J. H. Kirby, *The Portfolio of Cottages*, p. 104; "Concerning the American Style," p. 53; Garvin, "Mail-Order Plans," pp. 321–26.

12. "Effect of the Electric Light," p. 250, and "Artificial Illumination," p. 110.

13. Smith, *A Cozy Home*, pp. 16, 63.

14. Holly, "Modern Dwellings," p. 859; Sturgis, "Modern Architecture," pp. 174, 386–89.

15. "American Vernacular Architecture," p. 280; Blackall, "The Wholesale Architect," p. 44; Cohn, *The Palace or the Poorhouse*, pp. 96–97.

16. van Rensselaer, "American Country Dwellings," p. 19.

17. Longfellow, "The Course of American Architecture," p. 129; Draper, "The École des Beaux-Arts," pp. 209–35; on the tensions inherent in the concept of professionalism see Haskell, *The Authority of Experts*, pp. ix–83.

18. Wright, *Moralism*, pp. 46–54, 77–78; on architects' fees see Vaux's list in his *Villas and Cottages*, p. 319.

19. Linn, "Co-operative Home-Winning," pp. 573, 582.

20. Jackson, "The Crabgrass Frontier," pp. 198–200.

21. Warner, *Streetcar Suburbs*, pp. 9, 44, 52–58.

22. Sandeen, *St. Paul's Historic Summit Avenue*.

23. Jackson, "Crabgrass Frontier," p. 199.

24. Newton, *Town and Davis*, p. 108; Wright, *Building the Dream*, pp. 96–101; Sanchis, *American Architecture*, pp. 88–89.

25. Mayer and Wade, *Chicago*, pp. 145–46, 250–54; Jackson, "Crabgrass Frontier," p. 198; Wright, *Building the Dream*; Spear, *Black Chicago*; Horowitz, *Culture and the City*.

26. Simon, "The City-Building Process," pp. 12, 17–18, 35–36.

27. Denison and Huntington, *Victorian Architecture*, p. 153; Mitchell et al., *American Victoriana*, p. 11; Reiter, "Restoration," p. 167; Ehrlich, *Kansas City*, pp. 24 ff.

28. Knights, *The Plain People*, pp. 59 ff.; Bushman, "Family Security," p. 250; Thernstrom, *Progress and Poverty*, pp. 135–37, and *The Other Bostonians*, p. 99; Katz and Stern, "Fertility," p. 84.

29. Long, *Wages and Earnings*, pp. 72, 109; Wright, *Moralism*, p. 83; Simon, "The City-Building Process," p. 27.

30. Barnard, "A Hundred Thousand Homes," p. 484; Linn, "Co-operative Home-Winning," p. 584; Handlin, *The American Home*, pp. 238–43. Savings banks even published booklets containing designs and estimates. See *New York Mutual Improvement Company*.

31. For the role of Sunday school societies see Boyer, *Urban Masses*, pp. 36 ff.

32. Mayer and Wade, *Chicago*, pp. 165, 263, 267.

33. Wright, *Moralism*, pp. 40–45.

34. Wiebe, *The Segmented Society*. Although Wiebe's general argument is persuasive, he neglects to point out how the ideal of independence and segmentation were so often compromised in practice.

35. Scott, *The Art of Beautifying Suburban Home Grounds*, p. 19.

36. Hussey, *Home Building*, p. iii.

37. Wright, *Moralism*, p. 118; Warner, *The Private City*, p. 109; Bremner, ed., *Children and Youth*, vol. 2, pt. 7, pp. 811–15.

38. Clark, *Henry Ward Beecher*, pp. 93–94.

39. John S. Griscom, "The Uses and Abuses of Air," as quoted in Rosenberg, *No Other Gods*, p. 113.

40. "The American People," p. 772.

41. Hayward, "Health and Comfort," p. 73; Richardson, "Health at Home," pp. 311–12; Stone, "The Plumbing Paradox," pp. 283–310.

42. Waring, "Sanitary Drainage," pp. 62–67; Wingate, "Sanitary Needs," pp. 607–9; Stillman, "The Unhealthfulness of Basements," pp. 114–16; Health Primers, *The House*.

CHAPTER 4

1. U.S. Bureau of the Census, *Historical Statistics*, vol. 1, bk. 2, p. 166; Trachtenberg, *The Incorporation of America*, p. 99; Nugent, *From Centennial to World War*, pp. 80–81; Beecher, "Building a House," pp. 285–92.

2. Youmans, "The Higher Education of Women," p. 748.

3. McLoughlin, *The Meaning of Henry Ward Beecher*, pp. 134–40; Novak, *Nature and Culture*, pp. 3–9.

4. Talbot, *At Home*, p. 43.

5. Eliot, *John Gilley*, pp. 22–23; Kelly, *Mother Was a Lady*, pp. 4–5, 166–67.

6. Hark, "The Evolution of the Home," p. 522; Ames, "Material Culture," pp. 619–41; Washington, *Up from Slavery*, pp. 221–22.

7. Durand, "French Domestic Life," p. 175.

8. Ibid., pp. 165–66.

9. Bentzon, "Family Life," pp. 3, 5, 16.

10. Starrett, "Housekeeping," p. 114; Selden, "The Women of To-day," pp. 434, 440; Rickoff, "The Women of To-day," p. 454; Hayden, *The Grand Domestic Revolution*, pp. 1–21, 150–70.

11. Wright, *Moralism*, pp. 26–29; Bicknell, *Specimen Book*, p. 14.

12. B. Price, "The Suburban House," pp. 6–7.

13. Brett, "Daylight," p. 21.

14. Robinson, *Artistic Mantels*, p. 2. Comstock, in his *Interiors and Interior Details*, wrote that "the design [of a room should] have a dominating or central feature, or main idea or theme" (p. 1); Shoppell, *Modern Houses*, p. 317.

15. Wright, *Moralism*, pp. 32–40; Handlin, *The American Home*, pp. 343–56; Shoppell, *Modern Houses*, p. 317; Conrad, *Victorian Treasure-House*.

16. U.S. Bureau of the Census, *Report on the Population, 1890, Part 1*, p. clxxxviii; Chudacoff, "The Life Course of Women," p. 284; Hayden, *The Grand Domestic Revolution*, p. 13; Long, *Wages and Earnings*, p. 61.

17. *Harper's Bazaar*, as quoted in Chudacoff, "The Life Course of Women," p. 286; Rodgers, *The Work Ethic*, pp. 13–14.

18. M. W. Rice to R. W. Waterman, March 1, 1874; Diary of E. Dwight, February 24, 1853; E. Dwight to E. Twistleton, February 24, 1854; all quoted in Degler, *At Odds*, pp. 153–54.

19. Kreuter, "The Role of the Piano," p. 47.

20. Bushman, *"A Good Poor Man's Wife,"* pp. 33, 83, 95.

21. Diary of H. H. Robinson, as quoted in Bushman, *A Good Poor Man's Wife*, p. 104.

22. W. Robinson to H. H. Robinson, 1868, as quoted in Bushman, *A Good Poor Man's Wife*, pp. 115–17, 137.

23. Diary of H. H. Robinson, November 7, 1904, as quoted in Bushman, *A Good Poor Man's Wife*, p. 208.

24. May, *Great Expectations*, pp. 30–31.

25. Darling, *Chicago Furniture*, pp. 74–77; Sears, Roebuck & Co., *1897 Consumer's Guide*.

26. Harris, "Museums, Merchandising, and Popular Taste," pp. 151–53.

27. Farrell, *Inventing the American Way of Death*, pp. 7, 34, 71, 93; Gillon, *Victorian Cemetery Art*.

28. O. Henry, "The Trimmed Lamp"; Veblen, *The Theory of the Leisure Class*.

29. Degler, *At Odds*.

CHAPTER 5

1. The best study to date of the shift in architectural and social ideals at the turn of the century is Wright's *Moralism*. Robert Winter's *The California Bungalow* is helpful for understanding the early popularity of the bungalow style.

2. Wallick, *The Small House*, p. 12.

3. The best general surveys of economic changes in this period are Hays, *The Response to Industrialism*; Wiebe, *The Search for Order*; and Rothman, *Woman's Proper Place*. The best analyses of the reorientation of American culture are Commager, *The American Mind*; White, *Social Thought*; Lears, *No Place of Grace*; and Higham, *Writing American History*, pp. 73–104.

4. Wandersee, *Women's Work*, p. 56; Degler, *At Odds*, pp. 384–85; Hershberg, *Philadelphia*, p. 335.

5. Pope, *The Making of Modern Advertising*, pp. 30, 40–56; Leach, "Transformations in a Culture of Consumption," pp. 320–23, 332–36; Littlefield,

"The Wizard of Oz"; Harris, *The Land of Contrasts*, pp. 10ff.; Greene, *America's Heroes*, pp. 57ff.

6. Norris, "The 'Fast' Girl," p. 5.

7. Garland, *Crumbling Idols*, introduction.

8. James, *Pragmatism*, pp. 31, 37; Dewey, *The School and Society* and *The Child and the Curriculum*.

9. "House Architecture," p. 15.

10. Burroughs, "The Vanity of Big Houses," p. 89.

11. Grant, "The Art of Living," pp. 307–8.

12. Hapgood, "A $3500 Shingle House," p. 19.

13. Buckham, "The Parade of Cheapness," pp. 452–53; Kelsey, "The Advancement of American Architecture," p. 14.

14. Horowitz, *Culture and the City*, p. 87; Hastings, "The Relations of Life," p. 962.

15. Greene, *America's Heroes*, chap. 4.

16. Van Bergen, "A Plea for Americanism," pp. 27–28.

17. Johnson, "Lighting the Home," p. 59; Price, "A Philadelphia Architect's Views," p. 28; Stickley, *Craftsman Homes*, pp. 3–9; for a discussion of the Craftsman movement see Jordy, *American Buildings*, 3:217–20.

18. "The Sentiment of Domestic Architecture," p. 83.

19. Gibson, "Cement Block Architecture," p. 72; Price, "The Possibilities of Concrete," p. 119; Hoyt, "Design," pp. 83–84; DeKay, "Villas All Concrete," p. 88; and DeKay, "Concrete in Its Modern Form," pp. 761–65.

20. Kelsey, "The Advancement of American Architecture," p. 14.

21. Wallick, *The Small House*, p. 15.

22. Price, "A Philadelphia Architect's Views," p. 27.

23. Freelander and Stillman, "Sketch Plans," p. 624.

24. Dennen, "The Great Dike," pp. 338–41; Budd, "The American Country House," p. 335.

25. Hale, *Freud and the Americans*, pp. 77, 266; Charles Henderson as quoted in Block, *Hyde Park Houses*, p. 74.

26. Briggs, "The Child Brought Up at Home," p. 230; "An Ideal Nursery," pp. 10–12; Rouse, "The Children's Room," p. 166; Gilman, "Housing for Children," pp. 434–38.

27. Croly, "A New Use of Old Forms," pp. 271–79; Peet, "Architecture in America," pp. 22–23; Gibson, "Art and Engineering," pp. 71–72.

28. Walker, "New Household Methods,"

pp. 567–68; James, *Pragmatism.*

29. Addams, *Twenty Years at Hull House*, p. 210; Wright, *Moralism*, chaps. 4 and 5; Johnson, "The Civil Engineer," p. 46; Gerhard, "A Half-Century of Sanitation," pp. 61–63, 67–69, 75–76.

30. Robertson and O'Donnell, *The Healthful House*, p. 155.

31. Campbell, "Household Art," pp. 220–21; Wright, "Sweet and Clean," pp. 38ff.; Handlin, "Efficiency," pp. 50–54.

32. Budd, "Model Kitchens," p. 956.

33. Gardner, "The Bedroom," pp. 102–3.

34. Smith, "Education for Domestic Life," pp. 521–25; Handlin, *The American Home*, pp. 409–25; Wright, *Moralism*, chap. 5; Rothman, *Woman's Proper Place*, pp. 21ff.; Beecher, "On the Needs and Claims of Women Teachers" (1873), as quoted in Rothman, *Woman's Proper Place*, p. 22.

35. Smith, "Education for Domestic Life," pp. 521–25; Stetson, "Women's Economic Place," p. 313; Banks, "The Educated American Drudge," pp. 433–38; "Martyrdom of the Housewife," p. 317; Wright, *Moralism*, pp. 156–70.

36. Salmon, "Education in the Household," p. 188.

37. Pattison, *Principles of Domestic Engineering*, pp. 1, 174, 194.

38. Ibid., p. 178; Wright, "Sweet and Clean," pp. 38ff.; Ryerson, *The Best-Laid Plans*; Rothman, "The State as Parent."

39. Wright, *Moralism*, pt. 3.

40. Ibid., pp. 237–39.

41. Robertson and O'Donnell, *The Healthful House*, p. 120.

42. Ibid., p. 119; Poole, "The Best Way," p. 265.

43. Holtzoper, "The Planning of a House," p. 621.

44. McDougall, "An Ideal Kitchen," p. 27; Keith, "The Modern Pantry"; Leach, "Science in the Model Kitchen," p. 104.

45. Sutherland, *Americans and Their Servants*, pp. 9–10; Strasser, *Never Done*, p. 163; Katzman, *Seven Days a Week*, pp. 52–55; Abbott, "How to Solve the Housekeeping Problem," p. 778; Speed, "Servants in the Country," p. 235; Wells, "The Servant Girl," p. 717.

46. Brozman, "A Child's Play Room," p. 445; "An Ideal Nursery," p. 11; Beebe, "The Child's Place," pp. 429–30; Rothman, *Woman's Proper Place*, chap. 3.

47. Campbell, "Is American Domesticity De-creasing?," p. 96; Taylor, "American Childhood," pp. 723–27; Gilman, "Housing for Children," pp. 434–38; Briggs, "The Child Brought Up at Home," pp. 228–33.

48. Harper, "Small vs. Large Families," p. 3058.

49. Banks, "The Educated American Drudge," p. 437; Frederick, *The New Housekeeping*, p. viii.

50. Frederick, *The New Housekeeping*, p. 195.

51. Hill, "The Economic Value of the Home," p. 418.

CHAPTER 6

1. Boyd, "An American Bungalow," p. 54; Winter, *The California Bungalow*, pp. 13–41; for a critical view of the fad see Thomson, "The Rampant Craze," pp. 20–21. The *Ladies Home Journal* advertised a book in 1917 called *Journal Bungalows* for fifty cents.

2. For contemporary definitions of the bungalow see Massarene, "A Bungalow," p. 9; Spencer, "Building a House," pp. 37–45; Riley, "What Is a Bungalow?," pp. 11–12; Locke, "Four California Bungalows," pp. 446–49; on the importance of the roofline see "Bungalows," p. 35, and "Under Your Own Vine," p. 25.

3. Darrach, "Why Not a Bungalow?," p. 637; Comstock, *Bungalows*, p. 7.

4. "Under Your Own Vine," p. 25; "The Living Room," p. 59.

5. Burrell, "How to Build a Bungalow," p. 1006; Starr, *Americans and the California Dream*, p. 370; Lancaster, "The American Bungalow," pp. 239–53; Kirker, *California's Architectural Frontier*, pp. 127–29; Mumford, *Roots of Contemporary American Architecture*, pp. 14–15; May, *Screening Out the Past*, pp. 97ff.

6. Saunders, "Bungalow Life," pp. 33, 35, 38; Locke, "Four California Bungalows," pp. 446–49.

7. Lazear, "The Evolution of the Bungalow," pp. 2–4; Williams, "Southern California Bungalow," pp. 2–4.

8. Grey, "Architecture in California," pp. 4–5; "Some California Bungalows," pp. 217–23; "Notes and Comments," pp. 395–96; Arthur, "An Architect of Bungalows," pp. 306–15.

9. Croly, "The Country House," pp. 494–96; Schmitt, *Back to Nature*, pp. xvii–xxiii, 106–14, 160–66; Kett, *Rites of Passage*, pp. 246 ff.

10. Swayne, "Venture in Bungalow-Building,"

p. xxxix; DeLuce, "How We Built Our Bungalow," pp. 53–54; Shrimpton, "Bunga-Lee," p. 498; Burrows, "Go Be a Camper," p. 416.

11. Portable House and Manufacturing Company, Advertisement in *American Architect and Building News*, p. 215; Aladdin Garage Company, Advertisement in *Colliers*, May 20, 1916; Sears, Roebuck & Co., *Simplex Sectional Garages*, pp. 4–6; Bennett Lumber Co., *Bennett Better-Built Homes*; Aladdin Homes, *Catalog 28*; Harris Brothers, *A Plan Book*, p. 35.

12. International Mill and Timber Company, *Sterling Homes*, p. 8.

13. Mayhew and Myers, *A Documentary History*, p. 200.

14. King, *Wealth and Income*, pp. 224–35; U.S. Bureau of the Census, *Historical Statistics*, 1:320–22.

15. "Three Thousand Dollar Bungalow," pp. 29, 23, 33; "For the Bride," p. 37; Hopkins, "The Young Folks," p. 39.

16. Weber, "Suburban Annexations," pp. 612–17; Architects Small House Service Bureau, *100 Bungalows*, p. 18.

17. Byers, "Apartment for Business Women," p. 163; Elwood, "A 'Different' Bungalow," p. 54; Miller, "A Bungalow for $2000," pp. iii–iv.

18. Howe, "A Country Home," p. 64; Israels, "Busy Man's Bungalow," pp. 486–88.

19. Boyd, "The Popular Low-Cost Bungalow," p. 35; "Here You Have a Choice," p. 68; Dally, "A Few Bungalow Building Hints"; Byers, "Colonial Influence," pp. 445–47; Holman, "Colonial Style," p. xxii; Locke, "Four California Bungalows," p. 446; Swayne, "Venture in Bungalow-Building," p. xxxix; Burrell, "How to Build a Bungalow," p. 1006; Schuyler, "Round About Los Angeles," pp. 431, 437–40.

20. Foster, "The Model T," pp. 463, 473; McKelvey, *American Urbanization*, p. 73.

21. Gebhard and Winter, *A Guide to Architecture*, pp. 18–19; Spencer, "Building a House," p. 38; Saylor, *Bungalows*, pp. 7–9.

22. Richter, *Saint Paul Omnibus*, pp. 92–93; Haglund and Notarianni, *The Avenues of Salt Lake City*, p. 62.

23. "A Derbyshire Bungalow," pp. 45–46.

24. Hubbard, "Domestic Architecture," pp. 2–18.

25. Ibid., p. 4.

26. Wright, *Moralism*, pp. 137–38; Eaton, *Two Chicago Architects*, pp. 31–42, 126–31.

27. Haglund and Notarianni, *The Avenues of Salt Lake City*, pp. 8, 14.

28. Ibid., pp. 14, 16–17.

29. Ibid., pp. 11, 16–17; Hinckley, *Heber J. Grant*, pp. 54–71, 77–93.

30. Dow, "The Best House," p. 4306; Haglund and Notarianni, *The Avenues of Salt Lake City*, p. 88.

31. Interviews with Edna Felt, July 31, 1981, July 23, 1982, and October 20, 1984, Salt Lake City, Utah.

32. Chudacoff, *Mobile Americans*, pp. 122, 129.

CHAPTER 7

1. Hodgins, "Mr. Blandings Builds His Castle," pp. 138–89. See also Colean, *American Housing*.

2. Mason, *History of Housing*, pp. 6–7, 134; Yearns, "Government Housing Programs," pp. 83–85; U.S. Federal Housing Administration, *The FHA Story*, pp. 4–6; U.S. Bureau of the Census, *U.S. Census of Housing: 1950*, 1:xxx–xxxii; Kirk and Kirk, "The Impact of the City," pp. 471–98.

3. Mason, *History of Housing*, p. 27.

4. Ruble, *The Magic Circle*, pp. 32, 74, 110, 135.

5. Davis, *Housing Reform*, pp. 18–22; Mason, *History of Housing*, pp. 44–46.

6. Hudnut, "The Post-modern House," pp. 70, 75.

7. Wills, "Space," pp. 76–84; Wills, *Living on the Level*.

8. Nelson and Wright, *Tomorrow's House*, foreword, pp. 1–7.

9. Ibid., pp. 8–9.

10. In *Believing Skeptics* Fowler states, in terms that would be equally applicable to many architects in this period, that "the mood of political intellectuals was more complex than it often appeared. It was skeptical but it was also believing; it was anti-ideological but it was also ideological; it was detached but it was also committed; it was liberal but it was also conservative" (p. 4); Bell, *The End of Ideology*, pp. 90–92; Herberg, *Protestant, Catholic, Jew*, p. 3.

11. Adams, "What America Wants to Build," pp. 23–26.

12. Gutheim, "Planning for Family Living," pp. 118–21; Brigham, "Residence," p. 113; Stires, "Home Life," pp. 103–08; see also "Houses Are for Humans," pp. 118–22.

13. Eberlin, *Marriage, Divorce, Remarriage*, pp. 6–26; Leuchtenburg, *The Unfinished Century*, p. 714.

14. Leuchtenburg, *The Unfinished Century*, pp. 722–23; U.S. Bureau of the Census, *U.S. Census of Population: 1960*, 1:liv, lxv, lxxi.

15. Spock, *Baby and Child Care*, pp. 3–4; Zuckerman, "Dr. Spock," pp. 204–5; Weiss, "Mother," pp. 519–46.

16. Redfield, "The American Family," p. 182; Spock, *Baby and Child Care*, p. 281; Duvall, "Conceptions of Parenthood," pp. 195, 202–3; Humes, *Enjoy Your Child*.

17. Children's Bureau, *Infant Care*, as quoted in Wolfenstein, "Fun Morality," pp. 173–76.

18. Spock, *Dr. Spock Talks*, passim; Zuckerman, "Dr. Spock," p. 190.

19. In fact, Spock was embarrassed by the number of baby products whose advertisements filled his book, *Baby and Child Care*.

20. Schlereth, *Artifacts*, pp. 48–65.

21. Frederick, *Selling Mrs. Consumer* and *Cutex Hand Preparations*, as quoted in Ewen, *Captains of Consciousness*, pp. 22, 38.

22. Brass Association, *Wiring and Re-wiring*, p. 8; Elgin Stove Company, *Freedom from Kitchen Worries*, pp. 6–7; Strasser, *Never Done*, chap. 13.

23. Westinghouse, Advertisement in *House Beautiful*, p. 43; Regina Brooms, Advertisement in *House Beautiful*, p. 17; Bryson, "The Next America," pp. 116–45; Falter, "Notes," p. 24; Brown, *Images of Family Life*.

24. Coughlan, "How to Survive Parenthood," pp. 113–26.

25. "Statistics of Average U.S. Marriage and Family," p. 43; Kirkpatrick, *The Family as Process*.

26. Wahlstrom, "Images of the Family," pp. 193–227.

27. Brown, "Images of Family Life," pp. 69–77; Wahlstrom, "Images of the Family," p. 26.

28. "The American Woman," p. 2; "Today's Dilemmas of Love and Marriage," p. 114.

29. "The Story of the Western Ranch House," p. 74; "Eastward Ho," pp. 131–32.

30. "What's Been Happening to That Easy-going Western Favorite?," pp. 54–59; "From the Rancho," pp. 58–59; "This Oregon Ranch House," pp. 104–11; "The Oregon Ranch House on the Cover," pp. 56–57.

31. Mehlhorn, "Ranch Houses," p. 66; "A Clean and Handsome Example," pp. 74–75; Nelson and Wright, *Tomorrow's House*, p. 195.

32. Mehlhorn, "Ranch Houses," p. 66; "From the Rancho," p. 58; "It's Roomy, Ranchy and Buildable," p. 147.

33. Scheick, "What's Happened to Housing?," p. 67.

34. "What's Been Happening to That Easy-going Western Favorite?," pp. 56–58; Gordon, "Exploding the Box," pp. 256–58.

35. "How to Choose," pp. 115–16; "Total Environment," pp. 64–75; "Ranch House," p. 83.

36. "House of Ideas," pp. 51–52; Brenneman, "Modern Simplicity," p. 96.

37. Scheick, "What's Happened to Housing?," p. 93; "House of Ideas," pp. 48–49.

38. Bloodgood, "Better Homes," pp. 40–43; "Total Environment," pp. 64–75; "House of Ideas," p. 45.

39. Scheick, "What's Happened to Housing?," p. 63.

CHAPTER 8

1. Fish, *The Story of Housing*, pp. 244–45; "Housing Gets No. 1 Spot," p. 125; on suburban growth in general see Muller, "Everyday Life," pp. 262–77; Modell, "Suburbanization and Change," pp. 621–46.

2. Interview with John La Pan, July 24, 1983, Bennington, Vermont.

3. Fish, *The Story of Housing*, p. 472; Mason, *History of Housing*, pp. 64–66, 70.

4. Andersen Corporation, *Modular Framing Catalog*, p. 1.

5. Harrell and Lendrum, *A Demonstration of New Techniques*, pp. 85–89; Wagner, "Design for Livability," pp. 1–10; "Greater Livability."

6. "$15,000 Trade Secrets," pp. 8–15.

7. "Up from the Potato Fields," pp. 67–72; "U.S. Building Boom," p. 31.

8. "Up from the Potato Fields," p. 69.

9. "Structure of the Residential Building Industry, 1949," pp. 454–56; Mason, *History of Housing*, p. 61.

10. "Labor and Material Requirements for Private One-Family Construction," pp. 1–6; Mason, *History of Housing*, p. 61; "Levitt Adds 1950 Model to His Line," pp. 141–47.

11. "Up from the Potato Fields," p. 69; Gans, *The Levittowners*, pp. 16–17.

12. Riesman, *The Lonely Crowd*, pp. 19–23.

13. Mumford, *The City in History*, p. 486; Huxtable, " 'Clusters,' " pp. 10, 37; Donaldson, *The Suburban Myth*, pp. 60–77; Gans, *The Levittowners*, p. xvi.

14. Levitt, "What! *Live* in a Levittown?," pp. 47, 175–76.

15. Housing and Home Finance Agency, "What People Want," pp. 5–7; Gans, *The Levittowners*, pp. 31–41; Polenberg, *One Nation Divisible*, pp. 128–29.

16. Polenberg, *One Nation Divisible*, p. 128.

17. Housing and Home Finance Agency, "What People Want," pp. 23–25, 35–36, 46.

18. Ibid., pp. 50–52.

19. Ibid., p. 54.

20. Henderson, "The Mass-Produced Suburbs," p. 26.

21. Ibid., p. 26; Better Homes and Gardens, *The New House*, p. 10.

22. Henderson, "Mass-Produced Suburbs," pp. 27–29, 31.

23. Better Homes and Gardens, *The New House*, pp. 8, 12, 16, 23.

24. Henderson, "Mass-Produced Suburbs," p. 32; Henderson, "Rugged American Collectivism," p. 83.

25. Berger, *Working-Class Suburb*, pp. 12–13, 82–90, 97–98; Muller, "Everyday Life," pp. 268–72.

26. Polenberg, *One Nation Divisible*, p. 150; Muller, "Everyday Life," p. 272; Lake, *The New Suburbanites*.

27. Henderson, "Mass-Produced Suburbs," p. 29; Modell, "Suburbanization and Change," pp. 645–46; Eberlin, *Marriage, Divorce, Remarriage*, p. 6; Gans, *The Levittowners*, p. 226.

28. Gans, *The Levittowners*, pp. 92–102.

29. Ibid., pp. 206–12.

30. Ibid., pp. 153–55; Gans, "Planning and Social Life," pp. 163–65.

31. Gans, *The Levittowners*, pp. 277–78. For the impact of technology on women's lives see Cowan, "The 'Industrial Revolution' in the Home," pp. 1–23, and *More Work For Mother*; Vanek, "Time Spent in Housework," pp. 116–20; Strasser, *Never Done*; and Lopata, *Occupation: Housewife*.

32. Gans, *The Levittowners*, pp. 148–49.

33. Ibid., p. 212; Henderson, "Mass-Produced Suburbs," p. 28; Henderson, "Rugged American Collectivism," p. 84. Gans argues that "a historical analysis of the media would show that they follow taste rather than lead it" (p. 286). Although it is difficult to prove the argument one way or the other, the evidence from the housing literature suggests that the advice from the house magazines and family experts did have a strong influence on people's perceptions and family ideals.

34. Better Homes and Gardens, *The New House*, p. 9.

35. Miller, *Suburb*, pp. 230–33; see also Sennett, *The Fall of Public Man*.

CHAPTER 9

1. Hershberg, *Philadelphia*, p. 14.

2. Hayden, *The Grand Domestic Revolution*, pp. 270–305; Wright, *Building the Dream*, pp. 262–81.

3. Mehlhorn, "Ranch Houses," p. 61; "House for Family Living," pp. 40–43.

4. Goldwater, "Women's Place," pp. 578–85; Vanek, "Time Spent in Housework," pp. 116–20; Strasser, *Never Done*, pp. 263–81.

5. On the role of architects in the design of new single-family housing in the 1980s see Langdon, "The American House," pp. 45–73; on the changing nature of housing in the 1980s see Louv, *America II*, pp. 83–126.

Bibliography

PRIMARY SOURCES

Abbott, Francis M. "How to Solve the Housekeeping Problem." *Forum* 44 (February 1893): 778.

Adams, Walter. "What America Wants to Build: With Comments by Architects." *Better Homes and Gardens* 24 (June 1946): 23–26.

Addams, Jane. *Twenty Years at Hull House*. New York: Macmillan, 1910.

Aladdin Garage Company. Advertisement. *Colliers*, May 20, 1916.

Aladdin Homes. "A $2000 Aladdin House." *Associated Sunday Magazines*, January 25, 1914.

———. *Catalog 28*. Bay City, Mich.: Aladdin Homes, 1916.

The American Builder and Journal of Art. New York: Charles Lakey, 1873.

"The American People Starved and Poisoned." *Harper's Monthly* 32 (May 1866): 762–72.

"American Vernacular Architecture." *American Architect and Building News* 2 (September 1877): 280.

"American Vernacular Architecture IV." *American Architecture and Building News* 4 (July 1878): 5.

"The American Woman: An Introduction by Mrs. Peter Marshall." *Life* 41 (December 24, 1956): 2–3.

Andersen Corporation. *Modular Framing Catalog No. 10-A*. Clinton, Iowa: Pinney Printing, April 1950.

Architects Small House Service Bureau. *100 Bungalows of Architectural Distinction*. Minneapolis: Architects Small House Service Bureau, 1927.

"Architectural Reform." *Nation* 2 (April 1866): 438–39.

"Architecture." *New Englander* 8 (August 1850): 418–34.

Arnot, David H. *Gothic Architecture Applied to Modern Residences*. New York: D. Appleton, 1850.

Arthur, David C. "An Architect of Bungalows in California." *Architectural Record* 19–20 (October 1906): 305–15.

"Artificial Illumination." *American Architect and Building News* 42 (December 1893): 109–10.

Atwood, Daniel T. *Atwood's Country and Suburban Houses*. New York: Orange, Judd & Co., 1871.

Bakewell, Mrs. J. *The Mother's Practical Guide in the Physical, Intellectual, and Moral Training of Her Children*. New York: Lane & Tippett, 1846.

"Balloon Frames." *Illustrated Annual Register of Rural Affairs for 1862*. Boston: A. William & Co., 1862.

Banks, Elizabeth. "The Educated American Drudge." *North American Review* 179 (September 1904): 433–38.

Barnard, Charles. "A Hundred Thousand Homes: How They Were Paid For." *Scribner's Monthly* 11 (February 1876): 477–87.

Beebe, Katherine. "The Child's Place in the Home." *Outlook* 58 (February 1898): 429–30.

Beecher, Catharine E., and Harriet Beecher Stowe. *The American Woman's Home*. 1869. Reprint. Introduction by Joseph Van Why. Hartford: Stowe-Day Foundation, 1975.

Beecher, Henry Ward. "Building a House." In *Star Papers*, pp. 285–92. New York: Derby & Jackson, 1859.

———. "The Nation's Duty to Slavery." In *Patriotic Addresses in America and England*, edited by John R. Howard, pp. 203–23. New York: Howard & Hulbert, 1891.

Beecher, Lyman. "A Plea for the West." Cincinnati: Truman & Smith, 1835.

Benjamin, Asher. *The American Builder's Companion*. 7th ed. Boston: Benjamin B. Mussey, 1826.

Bennett, Ray H., Lumber Co. *Bennett Better-Built, Ready-Cut Homes*. North Tonawanda, N.Y.: Bennett Lumber Co., 1924.

Bentzon, Thomas. "Family Life in America." *Forum* 21 (March 1896): 1–20.

Better Homes and Gardens. *The New House Next Door 1955*. Des Moines, Iowa: Meredith Publishing Co., 1955.

Bicknell, A. J. *Specimen Book of One Hundred Architectural Designs*. New York: Bicknell & Comstock, 1880.

Blackall, C. "The Wholesale Architect as Educator." *American Architect and Building News* 46 (November 1894): 44–45.

Bloodgood, J. D. "Better Homes for All America—Plan no. 3309-A." *Better Homes and Gardens* 42 (March 1964): 40–43.

Boyd, Charles V. "An American Bungalow." *Woman's Home Companion* 46 (October 1919): 54.

_____. "The Popular Low-Cost Bungalow." *Ladies Home Journal* 24 (October 1907): 35.

Brass Association. *Wiring and Re-wiring to Modernize the Home.* New York: Copper and Brass Association, 1926.

Brenneman, J. "Modern Simplicity." *Ladies Home Journal* 76 (August 1959): 96.

Brett, John. "Daylight in the Dwelling House." *American Architect and Building News* 39 (January 1893): 21.

"Bride's House." *House and Home* 7 (April 1955): 57.

Briggs, Flora Z. "The Child Brought Up at Home." *Cosmopolitan* 28 (December 1899): 228–33.

Brigham, George B. "Residence for Mr. and Mrs. Harris D. Dean." *Architectural Record* 102 (November 1947): 113.

Brozman, Miriam E. "A Child's Play Room." *Good Housekeeping* 30 (March 1900): 145.

Bryson, Lyman. "The Next America." *House Beautiful* 95 (April 1953): 116–45.

Buckham, James. "The Parade of Cheapness." *Good Housekeeping* 32 (June 1901): 452–53.

Budd, Katharine C. "The American Country House." *Outlook* 79 (February 1905): 327–35.

_____. "Model Kitchens." *Outlook* 83 (August 1906): 956.

"Bungalows." *National Builder* 55:7 (July 1913): 35.

Burrell, C. B. "How to Build a Bungalow." *Harper's Bazaar* 41 (October 1907): 1006–8.

Burroughs, John. "The Vanity of Big Houses." *Cosmopolitan* 41 (May 1906): 89.

Burrows, F. W. "Go—Be a Camper." *New England Magazine* 38 (June 1908): 411.

Bushnell, Horace. *Christian Nurture.* 1847. Reprint. New York: Charles Scribner, 1900.

Byers, Charles A. "Apartment for Business Women." *Ladies Home Journal* 36 (April 1919): 163.

_____. "Colonial Influence Brings the Bungalow to Greater Perfection." *Art World* 3 (February 1918): 445–47.

Campbell, Helen. "Household Art and the Microbe." *House Beautiful* 6 (October 1895): 18–21.

_____. "Is American Domesticity Decreasing, and If So, Why?" *Arena* 19 (January 1898): 86–96.

Chapman, Elmer R. B. "Log Bungalow." *Country Life in America* 8 (October 1905): 639.

Chavasse, Pye Henry. *Woman as a Wife and Mother.* Philadelphia: William B. Evans, 1871.

"A Clean and Handsome Example of the West's Ranch House." *Sunset* 10 (April 1853): 74–75.

Cleaveland, Henry W. "American Architecture." *North American Review* 18 (1836): 380.

Cleaveland, Henry W., and William S. Backus. *Village and Farm Cottages.* New York: Appleton, 1856.

Colean, Miles L. *American Housing: Problems and Prospects.* New York: The Twentieth Century Fund, 1944.

Colgate Palmolive Company. "Swing Through Spring with Ajax." *Good Housekeeping* 160 (April 1965): 74–75.

Comstock, William T. *Bungalows, Camps, and Mountain Houses.* New York: William T. Comstock, 1908.

_____. *Interiors and Interior Details.* New York: William T. Comstock, 1882.

"Concerning the American Style." *American Architect and Building News* 41 (July 1893): 53–54.

Coughlan, Robert. "How to Survive Parenthood: Theories on how to Raise Children Have Come Full-Circle as Parents Get 'Neurosis-Neurosis' Wondering What to do with and to the Kids." *Life* 28 (June 26, 1950): 113–26.

Croly, Herbert D. "The Country House in California." *Architectural Record* 33–34 (December 1913): 482–519.

_____. "A New Use of Old Forms: Two Houses by Mr. John Russell Pope." *Architectural Record* 17 (April 1905): 271–93.

Darrach, Jas. M. A. "Why Not a Bungalow?" *Country Life in America* 14 (October 1906): 637.

DeKay, Charles. "Concrete in Its Modern Form and Uses." *Craftsman* 8 (1905): 761–65.

_____. "Villas All Concrete." *Architectural Record* 17 (February 1905): 85–100.

DeLuce, F. J. "How We Built Our Bungalow for $450." *Country Life in America* 21 (February 1912): 53–54.

Dennen, S. R. "The Great Dike: An Old Fashioned Homily on Home." *New England Magazine* 5 (November 1891): 338–41.

"A Derbyshire Bungalow." *House Beautiful* 26 (July 1909): 45–46.

Descriptive and Pictorial Catalogue of . . . Eden Park Property. Cincinnati: Hallum and Surguy, 1872.

Dewey, John. *The Child and the Curriculum.* Chicago: University of Chicago Press, 1902.

_____. *The School and Society*. Chicago: University of Chicago Press, 1900.

"Domestic Management." *Godey's Lady's Book* 62 (1861): 314.

Dow, Joy Wheeler. "The Best House to Live In." *World's Work* 7 (1904): 4306.

Downing, Andrew Jackson. *The Architecture of Country Houses*. 1850. Reprint. New York: Dover Publications, 1969.

_____. *Cottage Residences; or, A Series of Designs for Rural Cottages and Cottage Villas*. New York: Wiley & Putnam, 1842.

Dresser, Horace. "The Family Constitution." In *The Family Circle and Parlor Annual*, p. 17. New York: James G. Reed, 1852.

Duffey, E. B. *What Women Should Know: A Woman's Book about Women*. Chicago: J. S. Goodman, 1873.

Durand, John. "French Domestic Life and Its Lessons." *Atlantic Monthly* 48 (August 1881): 164–78.

Duvall, Evelyn M. "Conceptions of Parenthood." *American Journal of Sociology* 52:3 (November 1946): 194, 202–3.

"Eastward Ho: California Home Styles Invade the Rest of the U.S." *Life* 32 (March 17, 1952): 131–32.

"Effect of the Electric Light on the Skin." *American Architect and Building News* 9 (May 1881): 250.

Eggleston, N. H. "Domestic Architecture." *New Englander* 9 (February 1851): 57–70.

Elgin Stove Company. *Freedom from Kitchen Worries*. Elgin, Ill.: Elgin Stove Company, 1938.

Eliot, Charles W. *John Gilley*. Boston: American Unitarian Society, 1904. Republished as *John Gilley of Baker's Island*. Acadia, Maine: National Park Service, 1978.

Elwood, Charles S. "A 'Different' Bungalow." *Woman's Home Companion* 45 (April 1918): 54.

Falter, Mary E. "The Notes of a Happy Housekeeper." *House and Garden* 104 (May 1965): 24.

"$15,000 'Trade Secrets' House." *Life* 34 (January 5, 1953): 8–15.

"For the Bride Who Does Her Own Work." *Ladies Home Journal* 27 (October 1910): 37.

Fowler, Orson Squire. *A Home for All; or, The Gravel Wall and Octagon Mode of Building. . . .* New York: Fowler & Wells, 1856.

Frederick, Christine. *The New Housekeeping: Efficiency Studies in Home Management*. Garden City, N.Y.: Doubleday, Page & Co., 1913.

Freelander, Joseph H., and Michael Stillman.

"Sketch Plans for Outing Cottages." *Century* 72 (August 1906): 618–24.

"From the Rancho, a Contemporary Style." *Life* 40 (January 16, 1956): 58–59.

Gardner, E. C. "The Bedroom: Health and Economy in an Anti-Microbe Sleeping Room Which May Serve as a Home Hospital." *Good Housekeeping* 33 (August 1901): 102–3.

_____. *Home Interiors*. Boston: Houghton, Osgood & Co., 1878.

Garland, Hamlin. *Crumbling Idols*. New York: Harper & Brothers, 1894.

Gerhard, William Paul. "A Half-Century of Sanitation." *American Architect* 63 (February–March 1899): 61–63, 67–79, 75–76.

Gibson, Louis H. "Architecture and the People." *New England Magazine* 18 (March 1898): 21–25.

_____. "Art and Engineering." *American Architect and Building News* 84 (May 1904): 71–72.

_____. "Cement Block Architecture." *American Architect and Building News* 89 (February 1906): 71–72.

Gilman, Charlotte Perkins. "Housing for Children." *Independent* 57 (August 1904): 434–38.

Gladding-McBean & Co. *Catalog No. 18*. N.p., 1890.

Goldwater, Ethel. "Woman's Place." *Commentary* 4 (December 1947): 578–85.

Gordon, Elizabeth. "Exploding the Box to Gain Spaciousness." *House Beautiful* 101 (October 1959): 256–58.

Gordon, Vantine, and Company's Book of Plans for Everybody. Davenport, Iowa: National Building Plan Association, 1907.

Grant, Robert. "The Art of Living, House Furnishing, and the Commissariat." *Scribner's Magazine* 17 (March 1895): 305–15.

"Greater Livability at Small Additional Cost." Washington, D.C.: Housing and Home Finance Agency, 1951.

Grey, Elmer. "Architecture in California." *Architectural Record* 17-18 (January 1905): 1–17.

Gutheim, Frederick. "Planning for Family Living." *Architectural Record* 103 (May 1948): 118–21.

Hale, Sarah Josepha. "Domestic Economy." *Godey's Lady's Book* 20 (n.d.): 42.

Hammond, J. H. *The Farmer's and Mechanic's Practical Architect. . . .* Boston: J. P. Jewett, 1858.

Hapgood, Edward. "A $3500 Shingle House." *Ladies Home Journal* 13 (March 1896): 19.

Hark, J. Max. "The Evolution of the Home." *Andover Review* 10 (November 1888): 509–22.

Harper, Ida Husted. "Small vs. Large Families." *Independent* 53 (December 1901): 3055–59.

Harrell, Raymond H., and James T. Lendrum. *A Demonstration of New Techniques for Low-cost Small Home Construction, Housing Research Paper, no. 24.* Washington, D.C.: U.S. Government Printing Office, April, 1954.

Harris Brothers. *A Plan Book of Harris Homes.* Chicago: Harris Brothers, 1916.

Hartley, Florence. *The Ladies' Book of Etiquette.* Boston: G. W. Cottrell, 1860.

Hastings, Thomas. "The Relations of Life to Style in Architecture." *Harper's Monthly* 88 (May 1894): 957–62.

Hayward, Dr. John W. "Health and Comfort in House-Building." *Popular Science Monthly* 4 (November 1873): 69–75.

Health Primers. *The House and Its Surroundings.* New York: D. C. Appleton & Co., 1879.

Henderson, Harry. "The Mass-Produced Suburbs: I. How People Live in America's Newest Towns." *Harper's Magazine* 207 (November 1953): 25–32; "Rugged American Collectivism: II. The Mass-Produced Suburbs." *Harper's Magazine* 207 (December 1953): 80–86.

"Here You Have a Choice of Floor Plans." *Sunset* 45 (July 1920): 68.

Hering, O. C. "Design and Specification for an Inexpensive Brick Bungalow." *Country Life in America* 22 (July 1912): 19.

Hervey, George W. *The Principles of Courtesy.* New York: Harper & Brothers, 1852.

Hill, Caroline M. "The Economic Value of the Home." *Journal of Political Economy* 12 (June 1904): 408–19.

Hill, Thomas E. *Hill's Manual of Social and Business Forms.* Chicago: Hill's Standard Book Co., 1882.

Hodgins, Eric. "Mr. Blandings Builds His Castle." *Fortune Magazine* 33 (April 1946): 138–89.

Holly, Henry Hudson. *Holly's Country Seats.* New York: D. Appleton & Co., 1863.

————. "Modern Dwellings." *Harper's Monthly* 52 (May 1876): 855–67.

————. *Modern Dwellings in Town and Country, Adapted to American Wants and Climate. . . .* New York: Harper & Brothers, 1878.

Holman, E. E. "Colonial Style in Bungalows." *International Studio* 35 (July 1908): xxii.

Holtzoper, E. C. "The Planning of a House." *Country Life in America* 8 (October 1905): 619–24.

Hopkins, Una N. "The Young Folks' First Bungalow." *Ladies Home Journal* 30 (May 1913): 39.

"House Architecture." *American Architect and Building News* 8 (July 1880): 15.

"House Building." *Atlantic Monthly* 10 (October 1862): 423–31.

"House for Family Living." *Life* 29 (July 10, 1950): 40–43.

"House of Ideas, Upper Brookville, Long Island." *House and Garden* 100 (July 1951): 31–63.

"Houses Are for Humans." *Architectural Record* 101 (May 1947): 118–22.

"The Houses We Live In." *Harper's Monthly* 30 (1865): 735–40.

Housing and Home Finance Agency. "What People Want When They Buy a House: A Guide for Architects and Builders." Washington, D.C.: U.S. Department of Commerce, 1955.

"Housing Gets No. 1 Spot at Family Life Conference." *Journal of Housing* 5 (May 1948): 125.

Howe, Francis B. L. "A Country Home within Commuting Distance for Less than $1000." *Country Life in America* 21 (March 1912): 64.

"How to Choose a Good One-Level House." *Better Homes and Gardens* 41 (May 1963): 115–16.

Hoyt, Francis W. "Design and the Choice of Materials." *American Architect* 90 (September 1906): 83–84.

Hudnut, Joseph. "The Post-Modern House." *Architectural Record* 97 (May 1945): 70–75.

Humes, James L., Jr. *Enjoy Your Child—Ages 1, 2, and 3.* New York: Public Affairs Committee, 1948.

Hussey, Elisha Charles. *Home Building.* New York: Leader & Van Hoesen, 1875.

Huxtable, Ada Louise. "'Clusters' Instead of 'Slurbs'." *New York Times Magazine* (February 9, 1964): 10, 37.

"An Ideal Nursery and Its Teachings." *Good Housekeeping* 34 (January 1902): 10–12.

Illustrated Family Christian Almanac for the United States. New York: American Tract Society, 1850.

Illustrated Register of Rural Affairs and Cultivator Almanac for the Year 1858. Albany: J. J. Thomas, 1858.

International Mill and Timber Company. *Sterling Homes.* Bay City, Mich.: International Mill and Timber Co., 1920.

Israels, Charles H. "Busy Man's Bungalow." *Good Housekeeping* 48 (April 1909): 486–88.

"It's Roomy, Ranchy and Buildable on a 54-foot Lot: J. L. Rush House, Detroit." *American Home* 44 (November 1950): 147.

James, William. *Pragmatism*. New York: Longman's, Green & Co., 1897.

Jefferson, Thomas. *The Papers of Thomas Jefferson*. Edited by Julian Boyd. Vol. 8. Princeton: Princeton University Press, 1953.

Johnson, J. B. "The Civil Engineer as a Guardian of the Public Health." *American Architect and Building News* 63 (February 1899): 46.

Johnson, Katherine B. "Lighting the Home." *Good Housekeeping* 30 (February 1900): 58–60.

Judah, Uriah H. "Home." In *The Family Circle and Parlor Annual*, p. 94. New York: James G. Reed, 1851–52.

Keats, John. *The Crack in the Picture Window*. New York: Ballantine Books, 1957.

Keith, Katharine A. "The Modern Pantry." *Good Housekeeping* 31 (December 1900): 358–59.

Kelsey, Albert. "The Advancement of American Architecture." *American Architect and Building News* 65 (July 1899): 13–14.

King, Wilford I. *The Wealth and Income of the People of the United States*. New York: Macmillan, 1919.

Kirkpatrick, Clifford. *The Family as Process and Institution*. New York: The Ronald Press, 1955.

Lake, Robert W. *The New Suburbanites: Race and Housing in the Suburbs*. New Brunswick, N.J.: Rutgers University Center for Urban Policy Research, 1981.

Lang, William B. *Views, with Ground Plans of the Highland Cottages at Roxbury. . . .* Boston: L. H. Bridgham & H. E. Felch, 1845.

Langdon, Philip. "The American House: What We're Building and Buying in the Eighties." *Atlantic Monthly* 254 (September 1984): 45–73.

Lazear, M. H. "The Evolution of the Bungalow." *House Beautiful* 36 (June 1914): 2–4.

Leach, Anna. "Science in the Model Kitchen." *Cosmopolitan* 27 (May 1899): 104.

Levitt, William J. "What! *Live* in a Levittown?" *Good Housekeeping* 147 (July 1958): 47, 175–76.

"Levitt Adds 1950 Model to His Line." *Life* 28 (May 22, 1950): 141–47.

Linn, W. A. "Co-operative Home-Winning." *Scribner's Magazine* 7 (May 1890): 569–86.

"The Living Room, Its Many Uses and Its Possibilities for Comfort and Beauty." *Craftsman* 9 (October 1905): 59.

Locke, Kate. "Four California Bungalows." *American Homes and Gardens* 6 (November 1909): 446–49.

Longfellow, W. P. "The Course of American Architecture." *American Architect and Building News* 21

(March 1887): 129.

McDougall, Isabel. "An Ideal Kitchen." *House Beautiful* 13 (December 1902): 27.

"Martyrdom of the Housewife." *Nation* 77 (October 22, 1903): 317.

Massarene, William G. "A Bungalow That Can Be Built for $600." *Woman's Home Companion* 33 (June 1905): 9.

Mehlhorn, Will. "Ranch Houses Suit Any Climate." *House Beautiful* 89 (January 1947): 60–69.

Miller, Claude H. "A Bungalow for $2000." *Country Life in America* 11 (November 1906): iii–iv.

Miller, Zane. *Suburb: Neighborhood and Community in Forest Park, Ohio, 1935–1976*. Knoxville: University of Tennessee Press, 1981.

Mother's Magazine and Family Circle. New York: E. T. Farr, 1878.

Mumford, Lewis. *The City in History*. New York: Harcourt, Brace, and World, 1961.

Nelson, George, and Henry Wright. *Tomorrow's House: A Complete Guide for the Home Builder*. New York: Simon and Schuster, 1946.

New York Mutual Improvement Company. New York: J. D. Butler, 1881.

Norris, Frank. "The 'Fast' Girl." *San Francisco Wave* 15 (May 9, 1896): 5.

"Notes and Comments: The California Bungalow." *Architectural Record* 19–20 (May 1906): 395–96.

O. Henry. *The Trimmed Lamp and Other Stories of the Four Million*. Garden City, N.Y.: Doubleday, 1912.

Olmsted, Vaux, & Co. *Preliminary Report upon the Proposed Suburban Village at Riverside, near Chicago*. New York: Sutton, Brown & Co., 1868.

"The Oregon Ranch House On the Cover, Sheltering Roofs, a Low Silhouette, and a Sprawling Plan. . . ." *Sunset* 111 (September 1954): 56–59.

Palliser, Charles, and George Palliser. *Palliser's American Architecture*. New York: J. S. Ogilvie, 1888.

_____. *Palliser's New Cottage Homes and Details*. New York: Palliser, Palliser & Co., 1887.

"Park Forest Moves into '52." *House and Home* 1 (March 1952): 114–21.

Pattison, Mary. *Principles of Domestic Engineering: or the What, Why and How of a House*. New York: Trow Press, 1915.

Peet, Stephen. "Architecture in America." *American Architect* 66 (October 1899): 22–23.

Poole, Hester M. "The Best Way." *Good Housekeeping* 30 (June 1900): 265.

Portable House and Manufacturing Company. Advertisement in *American Architect and Building News* 11 (May 1882): 215.

Price, Bruce. "The Suburban House." *Scribner's Magazine* 8 (July 1890): 3–19.

Price, W. L. "A Philadelphia Architect's Views on Architecture." *American Architect* 82 (October 1903): 27–28.

Price, William T. "The Possibilities of Concrete Construction from the Standpoint of Utility and Art." *American Architect* 89 (April 1906): 119–20.

"Ranch House with One Open Wall. . . ." *Sunset* 113 (September 1954): 83.

Ranlett, William H. *The Architect, a Series of Original Designs for Domestic and Ornamental Villas. . . .* New York: William H. Graham, 1847.

Redfield, Margaret P. "The American Family: Consensus and Freedom." *American Journal of Sociology* 52:3 (November 1946): 182.

Regina Brooms. Advertisement in *House Beautiful* 95 (May 1953): 17.

Review of *The Portfolio of Cottages* by J. H. Kirby. *American Architect and Building News* 18 (August 1885): 104.

Reynolds, Melvina. *Little Boxes and Other Handmade Songs.* New York: Oak Publishing, 1964.

Richardson, Dr. B. W. "Health at Home." *Appleton's Journal* 8 (1880): 311–12.

Rickoff, Bertha Monroe. "The Women of To-day. IV. Women and the World." *North American Review* 157 (October 1893): 451–55.

Riddell, John. *Architectural Designs for Model Country Residences.* Philadelphia: Lindsay & Blakiston, 1861.

Riesman, David. *The Lonely Crowd.* New Haven: Yale University Press, 1950.

Riley, Mrs. C. A. "Home." In *The Family Circle and Parlor Annual,* p. 38. New York: James D. Reed, 1851–52.

Riley, Phil M. "A Few Bungalow Building Hints." *Country Life in America* 19 (February 1911): 338.

———. "What Is a Bungalow?" *Country Life in America* 22 (July 1912): 11–12.

Robertson, Lionel, and T. C. O'Connell. *The Healthful House.* Battle Creek, Mich.: Good Health Publishing Co., 1917.

Robinson, Mary Y. *Artistic Mantels.* Wholesale Catalog #46. Chicago: Charles F. Lorenzen Co., ca. 1900.

Robinson, Solon. *Facts for Farmers: Also for the Family Circle, I.* New York: A. J. Johnson, 1867.

Rouse, Adelaide L. "The Children's Room." *Good Housekeeping* 31 (October 1900): 166.

"St. Paul View on Summit Avenue of James J. Hill's New Residence." *Northwest Magazine* (July 1890): 27.

Salmon, Lucy M. "Education in the Household." *New England Magazine* 10 (April 1894): 185–88.

Saunders, Charles F. "Bungalow Life: The Cost of Living It." *Sunset* 30 (January 1913): 33, 35, 38.

Saylor, Henry H. *Bungalows.* New York: McBride, Winston & Co., 1911.

Scheick, William H. "What's Happened to Housing in the Last 30 Years?" *Parents' Magazine* 31 (October 1956): 67.

Schuyler, Montgomery. "Round about Los Angeles." *Architectural Record* 24 (1908): 431, 437–40.

Scott, Frank J. *The Art of Beautifying Suburban Home Grounds of Small Extent.* New York: D. Appleton & Co., 1870.

Sears, Roebuck & Co. *1897 Consumer's Guide.* New York: Chelsea House Publishers, 1976.

———. *Simplex Sectional Garages and Summer Cottages.* Chicago: Sears, Roebuck & Co., 1922.

Selden, Catherine. "The Women of To-day. II. The Tyranny of the Kitchen." *North American Review* 157 (October 1893): 431–40.

"The Sentiment of Domestic Architecture." *American Architect and Building News* 74 (December 1901): 83.

Shaw, Edward. "Architecture in the United States." *North American Review* 58 (April 1844): 436–80.

Shoppell, Robert W. *Modern Houses; Beautiful Homes. . . .* New York: Cooperative Building Plan Association, 1887.

Shrimpton, Louise. "Bunga-Lee." *Country Life in America* 14 (October 1906): 478.

Sloan, Samuel. *City Homes, Country Houses, and Church Architecture. . . .* Philadelphia: Claxton, Remsen, & Haffelfinger, 1871.

Smith, Frank L. *A Cozy Home: How It Was Built.* Arlington Heights, Mass.: T. O. Metcalf, 1887.

Smith, John J., and Thomas U. Walter. *Two Hundred Designs for Cottages and Villas. . . .* Philadelphia: Carey & Hart, 1846.

Smith, Mary Roberts. "Education for Domestic Life." *Popular Science Monthly* 53 (August 1898): 521–25.

Smith, Oliver P. *The Domestic Architect.* Buffalo: Derby & Co., 1852.

"The Social Condition of Woman." *North American Review* 42 (April 1836): 489–513.

"Some California Bungalows." *Architectural Record* 17–18 (September 1905): 217–23.

Speed, Jno. Gilmer. "Servants in the Country."

Harper's Weekly 36 (March 1892): 235.

Spencer, Robert C. "Building a House of Moderate Cost." *Architectural Record* 31–32 (July 1912): 37–45.

Spock, Benjamin. *Baby and Child Care.* New York: Pocket Books, 1946.

———. *Dr. Spock Talks with Mothers: Growth and Guidance.* Boston: Houghton Mifflin Co., 1961.

Standard Plumbing. Advertisement in *Good Housekeeping* 55 (December 1912): 73.

Starrett, Helen Ekin. "The Housekeeping of the Future." *Forum* 8 (September 1889): 108–15.

"Statistics of Average U.S. Marriage and Family." *Life* 29 (July 10, 1950): 43.

Stetson, Charlotte Perkins [Gilman]. "Woman's Economic Place." *Cosmopolitan* 27 (July 1899): 309–13.

Stickley, Gustav. *Craftsman Homes.* New York: Craftsman Publishing Co., 1909.

Stillman, Dr. W. O. "The Unhealthfulness of Basements." *Popular Science* 32 (November 1887): 114–16.

Stires, Arthur McK. "Home Life and House Architecture." *Architectural Record* 105 (April 1949): 103–8.

"The Story of the Western Ranch House." *Sunset* 121 (September 1958): 74.

"Structure of the Residential Building Industry, 1949." *Monthly Labor Review* 73:4 (October 1951): 454–56.

Sturgis, Russell, Jr. "Modern Architecture." *North American Review* 112 (January 1871): 160–77 and (April 1871): 370–91.

Swayne, Josephine L. "Venture in Bungalow-Building." *House Beautiful* 39 (March 1916): xxxix.

Taylor, Henry Ling. "American Childhood from a Medical Standpoint." *Popular Science* 41 (October 1892): 721–32.

"This Oregon Ranch House Lives as Well as It Looks: P. L. Menafee House near Yamhill." *House and Garden* 95 (March 1949): 104–11.

Thomson, L. D. "The Rampant Craze for the Bungle-oh." *Country Life in America* 22 (July 1912): 20–21.

"Three Thousand Dollar Bungalow." *Ladies Home Journal* 25 (March-April-May 1908): 23, 29, 33.

Tocqueville, Alexis de. *Democracy in America.* 2 vols. Edited by Philips Bradley. New York: Vintage Books, 1946.

"Today's Dilemmas of Love and Marriage." *Life* 51 (September 8, 1961): 99–119.

Todd, Sereno E. *Todd's Country Homes and How to Save Money.* . . . New York: J. D. Denison, 1870.

"Total Environment That Fosters a New Pattern of Living." *House and Garden* 119 (January 1961): 64–75.

Uncle Sam's Almanac. Flemington, N.J.: J. B. Alpaugh, 1867.

"Under Your Own Vine." *Good Housekeeping* 66 (April 1920): 24–25.

"U.S. Building Boom Hits New Peak." *Life* 28 (March 20, 1950): 27–33.

U.S. Bureau of the Census. *Report on the Population of the United States at the Eleventh Census: 1890, Part 1.* Washington, D.C.: U.S. Government Printing Office, 1895.

"Up from the Potato Fields." *Time* 55 (July 3, 1950): 67–72.

"The Uses of Home." *Manufacturer and Builder* 1 (January 1869): 308.

Van Bergen, John S. "A Plea for Americanism in our Architecture." *Western Architect* (April 1915): 27–28.

van Rensselaer, Mariana Griswold. "American Country Dwellings." *Century* 32:1 (May 1886): 3–20, 32:2 (June 1886): 206–20, 32:3 (July 1886): 421–34.

Vaux, Calvert. "Hints for Country House Builders." *Harper's Monthly* 11 (November 1855): 763–68.

———. *Villas and Cottages.* . . . New York: Harper & Brothers, 1857.

Veblen, Thorstein. *The Theory of the Leisure Class.* New York: Macmillan Co., 1899.

Wagner, Bernard. "Design for Livability: A Discussion of Livability Problems Arising from Proper Orientation in Regard to Sunlight." Washington, D.C.: Housing and Home Finance Agency, 1951.

Walker, John Brisben. "New Household Methods and Art as Exhibited at the Exposition." *Cosmopolitan* 37 (May 1904): 567–74.

Wallick, Elkin. *The Small House for a Moderate Income.* New York: Hearst's International Library Co., 1915.

Waring, George E., Jr. "Sanitary Drainage." *North American Review* 137 (July 1883): 57–67.

Washington, Booker T. *Up from Slavery: An Autobiography.* New York: Doubleday, Doran & Co., 1936.

Weber, A. F. "Suburban Annexations." *North American Review* 166 (May 1898): 612–17.

Wells, Kate Gannett. "The Servant Girl of the Future." *North American Review* 157 (December 1893): 716–21.

Westinghouse. Advertisement in *House Beautiful* 87 (June 1945): 43.

"What's Been Happening to That Easy-going Western Favorite . . . the 'Ranch House'?" *Sunset* 112 (February 1955): 54–59.

Wheeler, Gervase. *Homes for the People in Suburb and Country.* . . . New York: Charles Scribner, 1855.

————. *Rural Homes: or, Sketches of Houses Suited to American Country Life, with Original Plans, Designs, &c.* . . . New York: Charles Scribner, 1851.

Williams, F. "Southern California Bungalow." *International Studio* 30 (January 1907): 2–4.

Wills, Royal Barry. *Living on the Level.* Boston: Houghton Mifflin Co., 1955.

————. "Space: Flexibility for the Small House." *Architectural Record* 97 (May 1945): 76–84.

Wingate, Charles F. "Sanitary Needs of Town Houses." *Chautauquan* 7 (July 1887): 607–9.

A Woman's Thoughts about Women. Columbus: Follett, Foster, and Co., 1858.

Woodward, George E. "Balloon Frames." In *The Illustrated Annual Register for Rural Affairs for 1862*, pp. 186–87. Boston: A. Williams, 1862.

Youmans, George. "The Higher Education of Women." *Popular Science Monthly* 4 (April 1874): 748.

SECONDARY SOURCES

Ahlstrom, Sydney. *A Religious History of the American People.* New Haven: Yale University Press, 1972.

Ames, Kenneth L. "American Decorative Arts/Household Furnishings." *American Quarterly* 35:3 (Bibliography 1983): 280–303.

————. "Material Culture as Non-Verbal Communication: A Historical Case Study." *Journal of American Studies* (1981): 619–41.

————. "Meaning in Artifacts: Hall Furnishings in Victorian America." *Journal of Interdisciplinary History* 9:1 (Summer 1978): 19–46.

Bach, Ira J. *A Guide to Chicago's Historic Suburbs on Wheels and on Foot.* Athens, Ohio: Swallow Press, 1981.

Baer, Morley; Michael Larsen; and Elizabeth Pomada. *Painted Ladies: San Francisco's Resplendent Victorians.* New York: E. P. Dutton, 1977.

Bailyn, Bernard. *The New England Merchants in the Seventeenth Century.* New York: Harper and Row, 1955.

————. *The Origins of American Politics.* New York:

Vintage Books, 1967.

Bell, Daniel. *The End of Ideology.* New York: Free Press, 1960.

Berger, Bennett M. *Working-Class Suburbs.* Berkeley: University of California Press, 1960.

Berthoff, Rowland. *An Unsettled People: Social Order and Disorder in American History.* New York: Harper and Row, 1971.

Binford, Henry C. *The First Suburbs: Residential Communities on the Boston Periphery, 1815–1860.* Chicago: University of Chicago Press, 1985.

Bishir, Catherine W. "Jacob W. Holt: An American Builder." *Winterthur Portfolio* 16:1 (Spring 1981): 1–31.

Block, Jean F. *Hyde Park Houses: An Informal History, 1856–1910.* Chicago: University of Chicago Press, 1978.

Blumenson, John J.-G. *Identifying American Architecture.* Nashville: American Association for State and Local History, 1977.

Blumin, Stuart M. "The Hypothesis of Middle-Class Formation in Nineteenth Century America: A Critique and Some Proposals." *American Historical Review* 90:2 (April 1985): 299–338.

Boyer, Paul. *Urban Masses and Moral Order in America, 1820–1920.* Cambridge, Mass.: Harvard University Press, 1978.

Bremner, Robert H., ed. *Children and Youth in America.* Vol. 2. Cambridge, Mass.: Harvard University Press, 1971.

Brown, Bruce W. "Images of Family Life in Magazine Advertising." Ph.D. diss., University of New Hampshire, 1979.

Brown, Richard D. "Modernization and the Modern Personality in Early America, 1600–1865: A Sketch of a Synthesis." *Journal of Interdisciplinary History* 2 (1972): 201–28.

Bunting, Bainbridge. *Houses of Boston's Back Bay.* Cambridge, Mass.: Harvard University Press, Belknap Press, 1967.

Bushman, Claudia L. *A Good Poor Man's Wife.* Hanover, N.H.: University Press of New England, 1981.

Bushman, Richard L. "Family Security in the Transition from Farm to City, 1750–1850." *Journal of Family History* 6:3 (Fall 1981): 250.

Carson, Cary; Norman F. Barka; William Kelso; Garry Wheeler Stone; and Dell Upton. "Impermanent Architecture in the Southern American Colonies." *Winterthur Portfolio* 16:2/3 (Summer 1981): 135–96.

Chudacoff, Howard P. "The Life Course of Women: Age and Age Consciousness, 1816–1915." *Journal of Family History* 5:3 (Fall 1980): 274–92.

———. *Mobile Americans*. New York: Oxford University Press, 1972.

———. "New Branches on the Tree: Household Structure in the Early Stages of the Family Cycle in Worcester, Massachusetts, 1860–1880." In *Themes in the History of the Family*, edited by Tamara K. Hareven, pp. 55–72. Worcester, Mass.: American Antiquarian Society, 1978.

Clark, Clifford E., Jr. "The Changing Nature of Protestantism in Mid-Nineteenth-Century America: Henry Ward Beecher's *Seven Lectures to Young Men*." *Journal of American History* 57:4 (March 1971): 832–46.

———. "Domestic Architecture and the Cult of Domesticity in America, 1840–1870." *Journal of Interdisciplinary History* 7:1 (Summer 1976): 33–56.

———. *Henry Ward Beecher: Spokesman for a Middle-class America*. Urbana: University of Illinois Press, 1978.

Cohn, Jan. *The Palace or the Poorhouse: The American Home as a Cultural Symbol*. East Lansing: Michigan State University Press, 1979.

Commager, Henry S. *The American Mind*. New Haven: Yale University Press, 1952.

Conrad, Peter. *Victorian Treasure-House*. London: Collins, 1973.

Cott, Nancy F. *The Bonds of Womanhood*. New Haven: Yale University Press, 1977.

Cowan, Ruth Schwartz. "The 'Industrial Revolution' in the Home: Technology and Social Change in the 20th Century." *Technology and Culture* 17:1 (January 1976): 1–23.

———. *More Work for Mother*. New York: Basic Books, 1983.

Cross, Barbara, ed. *The Educated Woman in America*. New York: Teachers College Press, 1965.

Cummings, Abbott Lowell. *The Framed Houses of Massachusetts Bay, 1625–1725*. Cambridge, Mass.: Harvard University Press, Belknap Press, 1979.

Darling, Sharon. *Chicago Furniture*. New York: W. W. Norton and Co., 1984.

Davis, Richard O. *Housing Reform during the Truman Administration*. Columbia: University of Missouri Press, 1966.

Degler, Carl. *At Odds: Women and the Family in America from the Revolution to the Present*. New York: Oxford University Press, 1980.

Demos, John. *A Little Commonwealth*. New York: Oxford University Press, 1970.

Denison, Allen T., and Wallace K. Huntington. *Victorian Architecture of Port Townsend, Washington*. Seattle: Hancock House Publishers, 1978.

Donaldson, Scott. *The Suburban Myth*. New York: Columbia University Press, 1969.

Donnell, Edna. "A. J. Davis and the Gothic Revival." *Metropolitan Museum Studies* 5:2 (1936): 183–233.

Douglas, Ann. *The Feminization of American Culture*. New York: Alfred A. Knopf, 1977.

Downing, Antoinette F., and Vincent J. Scully, Jr. *The Architectural Heritage of Newport, Rhode Island, 1640–1915*. New York: C. N. Potter, 1967.

Draper, Joan. "The École des Beaux-Arts and the Architectural Profession in the United States: The Case of John Galen Howard." In *The Architect*, edited by Spiro Kostoff, pp. 209–35. New York: Oxford University Press, 1977.

Dublin, Thomas. *Women at Work: The Transformation of Work and Community in Lowell, Massachusetts, 1826–1860*. New York: Columbia University Press, 1979.

Dutchess County Planning Board. *Landmarks of Dutchess County, 1653–1867*. New York: New York State Council on the Arts, 1969.

Early, James. *Romanticism and American Architecture*. New York: A. S. Barnes, 1965.

Eaton, Leonard K. *Two Chicago Architects and Their Clients*. Cambridge, Mass.: M.I.T. Press, 1969.

Eberlin, Andrew J. *Marriage, Divorce, Remarriage*. Cambridge, Mass.: Harvard University Press, 1981.

Edel, Matthew; Elliott Sclar; and Daniel Luria. *Shaky Palaces: Homeownership and Social Mobility in Boston's Suburbanization*. New York: Columbia University Press, 1984.

Ehrlich, George. *Kansas City, Missouri: An Architectural History, 1826–1976*. Kansas City: Historic Kansas City Foundation, 1979.

Ewen, Stuart. *Captains of Consciousness*. New York: McGraw-Hill, 1976.

Faoretti, Jay P., and Rudy J. Faoretti. *Landscapes and Gardens for Historic Buildings*. Nashville: American Association for State and Local History, 1978.

Farrell, James J. *Inventing the American Way of Death, 1830–1920*. Philadelphia: Temple University Press, 1980.

Fish, Gertrude S. *The Story of Housing*. New York:

Macmillan, 1979.

Fitch, James M. *American Building*. 2d ed. New York: Schocken Books, 1973.

Foerster, Bernard. *Architecture Worth Saving in Rensselaer County, New York*. Troy, N.Y.: Rensselaer Polytechnic Institute, 1965.

Foner, Eric. *Free Soil, Free Labor, Free Men*. New York: Oxford University Press, 1970.

Foster, Mark S. "The Model T, the Hard Sell, and Los Angeles's Urban Growth: The Decentralization of Los Angeles during the 1920s." *Pacific Historic Review* 44:4 (November 1975): 463, 473.

Fowler, Robert B. *Believing Skeptics: American Political Intellectuals, 1945–1964*. Westport, Conn.: Greenwood Press, 1978.

Frary, Ihna T. *Early Homes of Ohio*. New York: Dover Publications, 1970.

Gans, Herbert J. *The Levittowners: The Ways of Life and Politics in a New Suburban Community*. New York: Pantheon, 1967.

_____. "Planning and Social Life." In *Human Needs in Housing: An Ecological Approach*, edited by Karen Nattrass and Bonnie Morrison, pp. 156–62. Milburn, N.J.: R. F. Publishing, 1975.

Garvin, James L. "Mail-Order House Plans and American Victorian Architecture." *Winterthur Portfolio* 16:4 (Winter 1981): 309–34.

Gebhard, David, and Robert Winter. *A Guide to Architecture in Los Angeles and Southern California*. Santa Barbara: Peregrine Smith, 1977.

Gillon, Edmund. *Victorian Cemetery Art*. New York: Dover Publications, 1972.

Glassie, Henry. *Pattern in the Material Folk Culture of the Eastern United States*. Philadelphia: University of Pennsylvania Press, 1968.

Goeldner, Paul. "Introduction." In *Bicknell's Village Builder and Supplement*, pp. i–vii. Watkins Glen, N.Y.: American Life Foundation, 1976.

Greene, Theodore P. *America's Heroes: The Changing Models of Success in American Magazines*. New York: Oxford University Press, 1970.

Greven, Philip. *The Protestant Temperament*. New York: New American Library, 1977.

Gusfield, Joseph R. *Symbolic Crusade*. Urbana: University of Illinois Press, 1963.

Guter, Robert. "Acorn Hall." *New Jersey History* 96:34 (1978): 118–22.

Haglund, Karl T., and Philip F. Notarianni. *The Avenues of Salt Lake City*. Salt Lake: Utah State Historical Society, 1980.

Hale, Nathan G., Jr. *Freud and the Americans: The Beginnings of Psychoanalysis in the United States, 1876–1917*. New York: Oxford University Press, 1971.

Halttunen, Karen. *Confidence Men and Painted Women: A Study of Middle-Class Culture in America, 1830–1870*. New Haven: Yale University Press, 1982.

Handlin, David F. *The American Home: Architecture and Society, 1815–1915*. Boston: Little, Brown and Co., 1979.

_____. "Efficiency and the American Home." *Architectural Association Quarterly* 5 (Winter 1973): 50–54.

Hareven, Tamara K., ed. *Themes in the History of the Family*. Worcester, Mass.: American Antiquarian Society, 1978.

_____. *Transitions: The Family and Life Course in Historical Perspective*. New York: Academic Press, 1978.

Harris, Neil. "Museums, Merchandising, and Popular Taste: The Struggle for Influence." In *Material Culture and the Study of American Life*, edited by Ian Quimby, pp. 140–74. New York: W. W. Norton and Co., 1978.

_____, ed. *The Land of Contrasts, 1880–1901*. New York: George Braziller, 1970.

Haskell, Thomas L. *The Authority of Experts*. Bloomington: Indiana University Press, 1984.

Hayden, Dolores. "Catharine Beecher and the Politics of Housework." In *Women in American Architecture: A Historic and Contemporary Perspective*, edited by Susana Torre, pp. 39–49. New York: Whitney Library of Design, 1977.

_____. *The Grand Domestic Revolution: A History of Feminist Designs for American Homes, Neighborhoods, and Cities*. Cambridge, Mass.: M.I.T. Press, 1981.

_____. *Redesigning the American Dream*. New York: W. W. Norton and Co., 1984.

_____. *Seven American Utopias: The Architecture of Communitarian Socialism, 1790–1975*. Cambridge, Mass.: M.I.T. Press, 1976.

Hays, Samuel P. *The Response to Industrialism 1885–1914*. Chicago: University of Chicago Press, 1957.

Herberg, Will. *Protestant, Catholic, Jew*. 1955. Revised ed. New York: Doubleday and Co., 1960.

Hersey, George L. "Godey's Choice." *Journal of the Society of Architectural Historians* 18 (October 1959): 104–11.

Hershberg, Theodore, ed. *Philadelphia: Work, Space, Family, and Group Experience in the*

Nineteenth-Century City. New York: Oxford University Press, 1981.

Higham, John. "From Boundlessness to Consolidation: The Transformation of American Culture, 1848–1860." Ann Arbor, Mich.: The Clements Library, 1969.

———. *Writing American History*. Bloomington: Indiana University Press, 1970.

Hinckley, Bryant S. *Heber J. Grant*. Salt Lake City: Deseret Book Co., 1954.

Hipple, Walter J., Jr. *The Beautiful, the Sublime, and the Picturesque in Eighteenth-Century British Aesthetic Theory*. Carbondale: Southern Illinois University Press, 1957.

Horowitz, Helen. *Culture and the City: Cultural Philanthropy in Chicago from the 1880s to 1917*. Lexington: University Press of Kentucky, 1976.

Howe, Daniel Walker. "American Victorianism as Culture." *American Quarterly* 82:5 (December 1975): 507–32.

Hubbard, Don J. "Domestic Architecture in Boise, 1904–1912: A Study in Styles." *Idaho Yesterdays* 22:3 (1978): 2–18.

Jackson, Kenneth T. "The Crabgrass Frontier: 150 Years of Suburban Growth in America." In *The Urban Experience*, edited by Raymond A. Mohl and James F. Richardson, pp. 198–200. Belmont, Calif.: Wadsworth Publishing Co., 1973.

———. *Crabgrass Frontier: The Suburbanization of the United States*. New York: Oxford University Press, 1985.

Jeffrey, Kirk. "The Family as Utopian Retreat from the City: The Nineteenth-Century Contribution." *Soundings* 55 (1972): 21–41.

Johnson, Carl H., Jr. *The Building of Galena: An Architectural Legacy*. Stevens Point, Wisc.: Worzella Publishing Co., 1977.

Jordy, William H. *American Buildings and Their Architects*. Vol. 3, *Progressive and Academic Ideals at the Turn of the Twentieth Century*. Garden City, N.Y.: Doubleday and Co., 1972.

Junior League of Mobile. *Historic Mobile: An Illustrated Guide*. Mobile: Junior League of Mobile, 1974.

Katz, Michael B., and Mark J. Stern. "Fertility, Class, and Industrial Capitalism: Erie County, New York, 1855–1915." *American Quarterly* 33:1 (Spring 1981): 63–92.

Katzman, David M. *Seven Days a Week: Women and Domestic Service in Industrializing America*. New York: Oxford University Press, 1978.

Kelley, Mary. "At War with Herself: Harriet Beecher Stowe as Woman in Conflict within the Home." *American Studies* 19:2 (Fall 1978): 23–40.

———. *Private Woman, Public Stage*. New York: Oxford University Press, 1984.

Kelly, R. Gordon. *Mother Was a Lady: Self and Society in Selected American Children's Periodicals, 1865–1890*. Westport, Conn.: Greenwood Press, 1974.

Kennedy, Roger. *Minnesota Houses*. Minneapolis: Dillon Press, 1976.

Kerber, Linda K. *Women of the Republic: Intellect and Ideology in Revolutionary America*. Chapel Hill: University of North Carolina Press, 1980.

Kett, Joseph F. *Rites of Passage: Adolescence in America, 1790 to the Present*. New York: Basic Books, 1977.

Kirk, Carolyn T., and Gordon K. Kirk. "The Impact of the City on Home Ownership." *Journal of Urban History* 7:4 (August 1981): 471–98.

Kirker, Harold. *California's Architectural Frontier*. New York: Russell and Russell, 1960.

Knights, Peter R. *The Plain People of Boston, 1830–1860*. New York: Oxford University Press, 1971.

Kraditor, Aileen S. *Means and Ends in American Abolitionism*. New York: Pantheon, 1969.

Kreuter, Gretchen. "The Role of the Piano in the Lives of American Women in the Nineteenth and Early Twentieth Centuries." In *The Piano, Mirror of American Life*, edited by Bruce Carlson, pp. 41–49. St. Paul: Schubert Club, 1981.

Lake, Robert W. *The New Suburbanites: Race and Housing in the Suburbs*. New Brunswick, N.J.: Rutgers University Center for Urban Policy Research, 1981.

Lancaster, Clay. "The American Bungalow." *Art Bulletin* 40:3 (September 1958): 239–53.

———. *Old Brooklyn Heights: New York's First Suburb*. New York: Dover Publications, 1979.

Langdon, Philip. "The American House: What We're Building and Buying in the Eighties." *Atlantic Monthly* 254 (September 1984): 45–73.

Leach, William. "Transformations in a Culture of Consumption: Women and Department Stores, 1890–1925." *Journal of American History* 71:2 (September 1984): 319–42.

Lears, T. Jackson. *No Place of Grace*. New York: Pantheon, 1981.

Leuchtenburg, William E., ed. *The Unfinished Century: America since 1900*. Boston: Little, Brown and Co., 1973.

Littlefield, Henry M. "The Wizard of Oz: Parable on Populism." *American Quarterly* 15:4 (Winter 1963): 47–58.

Lockwood, Charles. *Bricks and Brownstone: The New York Row House, 1783–1929.* New York: McGraw-Hill, 1972.

Long, Clarence D. *Wages and Earnings in the United States, 1860–1890.* Princeton: Princeton University Press, 1960.

Lopata, Helena. *Occupation: Housewife.* New York: Oxford University Press, 1971.

Louv, Richard. *America II.* New York: Viking Penguin, 1983.

Lyle, Royster, Jr., and Pamela H. Simpson. *The Architecture of Historic Lexington.* Charlottesville: Historic Lexington Foundation, 1977.

Maass, John. *The Gingerbread Age.* New York: Rinehart, 1957.

McArdle, Alma deC., and Frederick Hamilton. *Carpenter Gothic: Nineteenth-Century Ornamental Houses of New England.* New York: Watson-Guptill, 1978.

McKelvey, Blake. *American Urbanization: A Comparative History.* Glenview, Ill.: Scott Foresman and Co., 1973.

McLoughlin, William G. *The Meaning of Henry Ward Beecher.* New York: Alfred A. Knopf, 1970.
_____. *Modern Revivalism.* New York: Ronald Press, 1959.

McNee, Karla. "Dundas: History through Architecture." Unpublished essay, Carleton College, 1979.

Marx, Leo. *The Machine in the Garden: Technology and the Pastoral Ideal in American Life.* New York: Oxford University Press, 1964.

Mason, Joseph B. *History of Housing in the U.S., 1930–1980.* Houston: Gulf Publishing Co., 1982.

May, Elaine Tyler. *Great Expectations: Marriage and Divorce in Post-Victorian America.* Chicago: University of Chicago Press, 1981.

May, Lary. *Screening Out the Past.* New York: Oxford University Press, 1980.

Mayer, Harold M., and Richard C. Wade. *Chicago: Growth of a Metropolis.* Chicago: University of Chicago Press, 1969.

Mayhew, Edgar de N., and Minor Myers, Jr. *A Documentary History of American Interiors from the Colonial Era to 1915.* New York: Charles Scribner's Sons, 1980.

Miller, Perry. *The Life of the Mind in America.* New York: Harcourt, Brace and World, 1965.

Miller, Zane. *Suburb: Neighborhood and Community in Forest Park, Ohio, 1935–1976.* Knoxville: University of Tennessee Press, 1981.

Mitchell, Eugene; William J. Murtagh; and Judith Lynch Waldhorn. *American Victoriana.* San Francisco: Chronicle Books, 1979.

Modell, John. "Suburbanization and Change in the American Family." *Journal of Interdisciplinary History* 9:4 (Spring 1979): 621–46.

"Moongate House." Brochure. Mobile, Ala., n.d.

Muller, Peter O. "Everyday Life in Suburbia." *American Quarterly* 34:3 (Bibliography 1982): 262–77.

Mumford, Lewis, ed. *Roots of Contemporary American Architecture.* New York: Reinhold Publishing, 1952.

Myerhoff, Barbara, and Virginia Tufte. "Images of the American Family, Then and Now." In *Changing Images of the American Family*, edited by Barbara Myerhoff and Virginia Tufte, pp. 43–61. New Haven: Yale University Press, 1979.

Newton, Roger H. *Town and Davis, Architects.* New York: Columbia University Press, 1942.

New York State Council on the Arts. *Architecture Worth Saving in Onondaga County.* Syracuse: New York State Council on the Arts, 1964.

Novak, Barbara. *Nature and Culture: American Landscape Painting, 1825–1875.* New York: Oxford University Press, 1980.

Nugent, Walter T. K. *From Centennial to World War: American Society, 1876–1917.* Indianapolis: Bobbs-Merrill, 1977.

Old Sturbridge Village Resource Packet. "Making a Living: Factory." Sturbridge, Mass.: Old Sturbridge Village Museum Education Department, 1977.
_____. "Reform Poverty." Sturbridge Mass.: Old Sturbridge Village Museum Education Department, 1979.

Peat, Wilbur D. *Indiana Houses of the Nineteenth Century.* Indianapolis: Indiana Historical Society, 1962.

Polenberg, Richard. *One Nation Divisible.* Middlesex, England: Penguin Books, 1980.

Pope, Daniel. *The Making of Modern Advertising.* New York: Basic Books, 1983.

Posadas, Barbara M. "A Home in the Country: Suburbanization in Jefferson Township, 1870–1889." *Chicago History* 7 (Fall 1978): 134–49.

Rawls, Walton. *The Great Book of Currier and Ives.* New York: Abbeville Press, 1979.

Reiter, Beth Lattimore. "Restoration of Savannah's

Victorian District." *Georgia Historical Quarterly* 63:1 (1979): 164–72.

Richter, Bonnie, ed. *Saint Paul Omnibus: Images of a Changing City.* St. Paul: Old Town Restorations, 1979.

Rodgers, Daniel T. *The Work Ethic in Industrial America, 1850–1920.* Chicago: University of Chicago Press, 1978.

Rosenberg, Charles E. *No Other Gods: On Science and American Social Thought.* Baltimore: Johns Hopkins University Press, 1961.

Rothman, David J. "The State as Parent: Social Policy in the Progressive Era." In *Doing Good: The Limits of Benevolence,* edited by Willard Gaylin, pp. 67–96. New York: Pantheon, 1978.

Rothman, Sheila. *Woman's Proper Place.* New York: Basic Books, 1978.

Ruble, Kenneth D. *The Magic Circle.* Minneapolis: North Central Publishing Co., 1978.

Rutman, Anita, and Darrett Rutman. " 'Now-Wives and Sons-In-Law': Parental Death in a Seventeenth-Century Virginia County." In *The Chesapeake in the Seventeenth Century: Essays on Anglo-American Society,* edited by Thad W. Tate and David L. Ammerman, pp. 153–82. Chapel Hill: University of North Carolina Press, 1979.

Ryan, Mary P. *Cradle of the Middle Class: The Family in Oneida County, N.Y., 1790–1865.* Cambridge, England: Cambridge University Press, 1981.

Ryerson, Ellen. *The Best-Laid Plans: America's Juvenile Court Experiment.* New York: Oxford University Press, 1978.

Sanchis, Frank E. *American Architecture: Westchester County, New York.* Westchester, N.Y.: North River Press, 1979.

Sandeen, Ernest R. *St. Paul's Historic Summit Avenue.* St. Paul: Living Historical Museum, 1978.

Saveth, Edward N. "The Problem of American Family History." *American Quarterly* 21 (Summer 1969): 311–29.

Schlereth, Thomas. *Artifacts and the American Past.* Nashville: American Association for State and Local History, 1980.

Schmitt, Peter J. *Back to Nature: The Arcadian Myth in Urban America.* New York: Oxford University Press, 1969.

Schmitt, Peter J., and Balthazar Karab. *Kalamazoo: Nineteenth-Century Homes in a Midwestern Village.* Kalamazoo: Kalamazoo Historical Commission, 1976.

Sennett, Richard. *The Fall of Public Man.* New York: Alfred A. Knopf, 1977.

Shammas, Carole. "The Domestic Environment in Early Modern England and America." *Journal of Social History* 14 (Fall 1980): 3–24.

Shorter, Edward. *The Making of the Modern Family.* New York: Basic Books, 1975.

Simon, Roger D. "The City-Building Process: Housing and Services in New Milwaukee Neighborhoods, 1880–1910." *Transactions of the American Philosophical Society* 68:5 (July 1978): 3–64.

Sklar, Kathryn K. *Catharine Beecher: A Study in American Domesticity.* New Haven: Yale University Press, 1973.

Sommer, Lawrence J. *The Heritage of Dubuque: An Architectural View.* Dubuque, Iowa: First National Bank, 1975.

Spear, Alan. *Black Chicago: The Making of a Negro Ghetto.* Chicago: University of Chicago Press, 1967.

Starr, Kevin. *Americans and the California Dream.* New York: Oxford University Press, 1973.

Stone, May N. "The Plumbing Paradox." *Winterthur Portfolio* 14:3 (Autumn 1979): 283–310.

Strasser, Susan. *Never Done: A History of American Housework.* New York: Pantheon, 1982.

Sutherland, Daniel E. *Americans and Their Servants.* Baton Rouge: Louisiana State University Press, 1981.

Talbot, George, ed. *At Home: Domestic Life in the Post-Centennial Era, 1876–1920.* Madison: State Historical Society of Wisconsin, 1976.

Thernstrom, Stephen. *The Other Bostonians.* Cambridge, Mass.: Harvard University Press, 1974.

———. *Progress and Poverty.* Cambridge, Mass.: Harvard University Press, 1964.

Tomlan, Michael A. "The Palliser Brothers and Their Publications." In *The Palliser Late Victorian Architecture,* pp. i–v. Watkins Glen, N.Y.: American Life Foundation, 1978.

Trachtenberg, Alan. *The Incorporation of America.* New York: Hill and Wang, 1982.

Uhlenberg, Peter. "Changing Configurations in the Life Course." In *Transitions: The Family and Life Course in Historical Perspective,* edited by Tamara Hareven, pp. 65–97. New York: Academic Press, 1978.

U.S. Bureau of Labor Statistics. "Labor and Material Requirements for Private One-Family Construction." *Bureau of Labor Statistics Bulletin,* no. 4 (June 1964).

U.S. Bureau of the Census. *Historical Statistics of the United States: Colonial Times to 1970.* Vol. 1.

Washington, D.C.: U.S. Government Printing Office, 1975.

———. *U.S. Census of Housing: 1950. Vol. 1, General Characteristics, Part 1: United States Summary*. Washington, D.C.: U.S. Government Printing Office, 1953.

———. *U.S. Census of Population: 1960. Vol. 1, Characteristics of the Population*. Washington, D.C.: U.S. Government Printing Office, 1964.

———. *U.S. Census of Population: 1970. Vol. 1, Characteristics of the Population*. Washington, D.C.: U.S. Government Printing Office, 1973.

U.S. Federal Housing Administration. *The FHA Story in Summary*. Washington, D.C.: U.S. Government Printing Office, 1959.

Upton, Dell. "Pattern Books and Professionalism: Aspects of the Transformation of Domestic Architecture in America, 1800–1860." *Winterthur Portfolio* 19:2/3 (Summer/Autumn 1984): 107–50.

———. "The Power of Things: Recent Studies in American Vernacular Architecture." *American Quarterly* 35:3 (Bibliography 1983): 262–79.

———. "Vernacular Domestic Architecture in Eighteenth-Century Virginia." *Winterthur Portfolio* 17:2/3 (Summer/Autumn 1982): 95–120.

Vanek, Joan. "Time Spent in Housework." *Scientific American* 231 (November 1974): 116–20.

Van Why, Joseph. "Harriet Beecher Stowe's House in Nook Farm, Hartford." Hartford, Conn.: Stowe-Day Foundation, 1970.

Vinovskis, Maris A. "American Families in the Past." In *Ordinary People and Everyday Life*, edited by James B. Gardner and George Rollie Adams, pp. 115–38. Nashville: American Association for State and Local History, 1983.

———. "Angels' Heads and Weeping Willows: Death in Early America." In *Themes in the History of the Family*, edited by Tamara Hareven, pp. 25–54. Worcester, Mass.: American Antiquarian Society, 1978.

Wahlstrom, Billie Joyce. "Images of the Family in the Mass Media." In *Changing Images of the Family*, edited by Virginia Tufte and Barbara Myerhoff, pp. 193–227. New Haven: Yale University Press, 1979.

Wallace, Anthony F. C. *Rockdale: The Growth of an American Village in the Early Industrial Revolution*. New York: Alfred A. Knopf, 1978.

Walsh, Lorena S. "'Till Death Us Do Part': Marriage and Family in Seventeenth-Century Maryland." In *The Chesapeake in the Seventeenth Century: Essays on Anglo-American Society*, edited by Thad W. Tate and David L. Ammerman, pp. 126–52. Chapel Hill: University of North Carolina Press, 1979.

Wandersee, Winifred D. *Women's Work and Family Values, 1920–1940*. Cambridge, Mass.: Harvard University Press, 1981.

Warner, Sam Bass, Jr. *The Private City*. Philadelphia: University of Philadelphia Press, 1968.

———. *Streetcar Suburbs: The Process of Growth in Boston, 1870–1900*. Cambridge, Mass.: Harvard University Press, 1969.

Webster Groves Historical Society. "Hawken House." Brochure. Webster Groves, Missouri, n.d.

Weeks, Christopher. *The Building of Westminster in Maryland*. Annapolis: Fishergate Publishing Co., 1978.

Weiss, Nancy P. "Mother, the Invention of Necessity: Dr. Benjamin Spock's *Baby and Child Care*." *American Quarterly* 29:5 (Winter 1977): 519–46.

Whiffen, Marcus. *American Architecture since 1780: A Guide to Styles*. Cambridge, Mass.: M.I.T. Press, 1969.

White, Morton. *Social Thought in America*. Boston: Beacon Press, 1947.

Wiebe, Robert. *The Search for Order, 1870–1920*. New York: Hill and Wang, 1967.

———. *The Segmented Society*. New York: Oxford University Press, 1975.

Wills, Garry. *Inventing America*. New York: Random House, 1978.

Wilson, Edmund. *Patriotic Gore*. New York: Oxford University Press, 1966.

Winter, Robert. *The California Bungalow*. Los Angeles: Hennessey and Ingalls, 1980.

Wishy, Bernard W. *The Child and the Republic*. Philadelphia: University of Pennsylvania Press, 1967.

Wolfenstein, Martha. "Fun Morality: An Analysis of Recent American Child-Raising Literature." In *Childhood in Contemporary Cultures*, edited by Margaret Mead and Martha Wolfenstein, pp. 173–76. Chicago: University of Chicago Press, 1955.

Wright, Gwendolyn. *Building the Dream: A Social History of Housing in America*. New York: Pantheon, 1981.

———. *Moralism and the Model Home: Domestic Architecture and Cultural Conflict in Chicago, 1873–1913*. Chicago: University of Chicago Press, 1980.

———. "Sweet and Clean: The Domestic Landscape in the Progressive Era." *Landscape* 20:1 (October 1975): 38–43.

Yearns, Mary H. "Government Housing Programs: A Brief Review." In *Housing Perspectives*, edited by Carol Wedin and L. Gertrude Nygren, pp. 83–85. Minneapolis: Burgess Publishing Co., 1979.

Young, James S. *The Washington Community, 1800–1826*. New York: Harcourt, Brace and World, 1966.

Zuckerman, Michael. "Dr. Spock: The Confidence Man." In *The Family in History*, edited by Charles E. Rosenberg, pp. 204–5. Philadelphia: University of Pennsylvania Press, 1975.

Zwelling, Shomer. "Working in Rural New England, 1790–1840." Sturbridge, Mass.: Old Sturbridge Village Museum Education Department, 1977.

INTERVIEWS AND CORRESPONDENCE

Carson, Cary, Director of Research, Colonial Williamsburg Foundation, Williamsburg, Virginia. Personal correspondence, September 26, 1983.

Felt, Edna, Salt Lake City, Utah. Interviews, July 31, 1981, July 23, 1982, and October 20, 1984.

La Pan, John. Bennington, Vermont. Interview, July 24, 1983.

Index